LONDON, NEW YORK,
MELBOURNE, MUNICH, AND DELHI

Senior editor Julie Ferris
Project editors Francesca Baines, Niki Foreman
Senior designer Smiljka Surla
Art editors Jim Green, Marilou Prokopiou
Editors Ashwin Khurana, Spencer Holbrook, Philip Letsu,
Designers Dave Ball, Sheila Collins, Spencer Holbrook, Philip Letsu,
Hoa Luc, Johnny Pau, Owen Peyton Jones, Jacqui Swan

US editor Margaret Parrish
Managing editor Linda Esposito
Managing art editor Diane Thistlethwaite

Commissioned illustrations Maltings Partnership
Picture researcher Nic Dean
Publishing manager Andrew Macintyre
Category publisher Laura Buller
DK picture researchers Lucy Claxton, Rose Horridge,
Emma Shepherd, Romaine Werblow
Production editor Andy Hilliard
Senior production controller Angela Graef
Design development Martin Wilson
Jacket designer Junkichi Tatsuki
Jacket editor Mariza O'Keeffe
Jacket manager Sophia M. Tampakopoulos Turner

First published in the United States in 2009
by DK Publishing
375 Hudson Street
New York, New York 10014

09 10 11 12 13 10 9 8 7 6 5 4 3 2
LD098 – 04/09

Copyright © 2009 Dorling Kindersley Limited

DK books are available at special discounts when purchased in bulk for
sales promotions, premiums, fundraising, or educational use. For details, contact:
DK Publishing Special Markets, 375 Hudson Street, New York, New York 10014
SpecialSales@dk.com

A catalog record for this book is
available from the Library of Congress.

ISBN: 978-0-7566-5195-4

Color reproduction by MDP, UK
Printed and bound by Toppan, China

Discover more at
www.dk.com

ANYTHING

Contributors Lisa Burke, Susan Kennedy,
Kim Bryan, Susan Stott,
Dougal Dixon, Carole Watts,
Jim Pipe, Claire Walker,
Richard Walker,

DK

Space

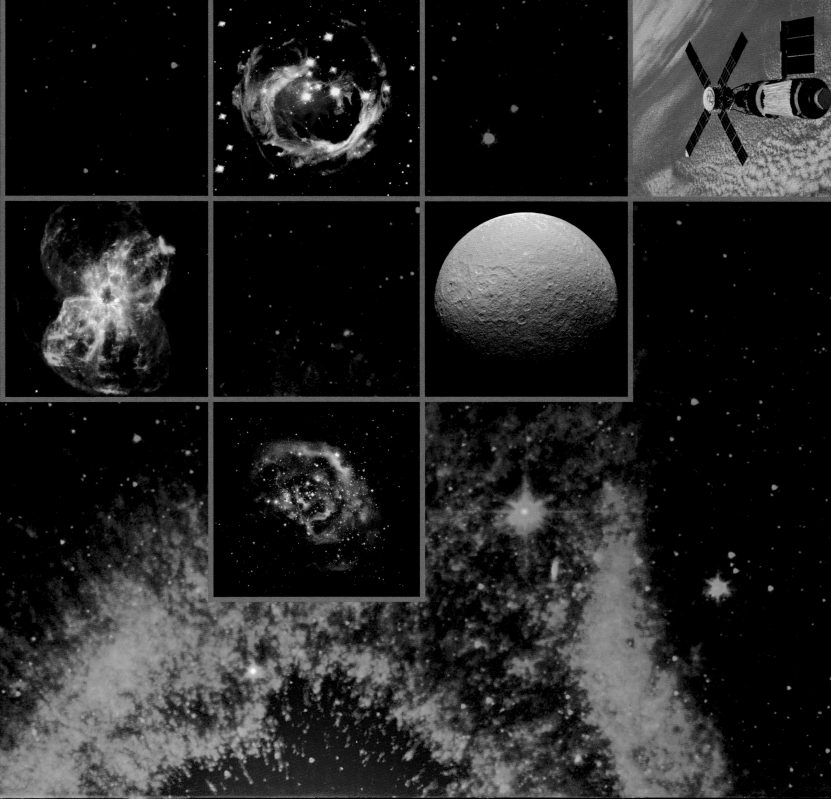

The universe is about 13.7 billion years old. At its beginning it looked nothing like it does today. Yet, everything in today's universe did exist in some form back then. It all started with the Big Bang, a kind of explosion that would not only go on to produce all the matter in the universe, but also marked the start of time.

Sun

06: silicon	0.099%
07: magnesium	0.076%
08: neon	0.058%
09: iron	0.14%
10: sulfur	0.04%

FAST FACTS

Creation of the universe

01: At the start, the universe was a hot and dense ball of radiation energy.

02: In one-thousandth of a second, tiny radiation particles produced tiny particles of matter. These combined to form the first-ever chemical elements, hydrogen and helium.

03: Some regions of the young universe contained slightly more hydrogen and helium than others. These shrank to form the first stars.

04: Nuclear reactions inside the stars produced many other chemical elements, including carbon and oxygen.

05: The elements in the universe today were produced from those elements created in the Big Bang.

How to: **create the universe**

01. Start time with a Big Bang – a massive explosion that lasts for less than one trillionth of a second that will create tiny particles of radiation smaller than the size of a period.

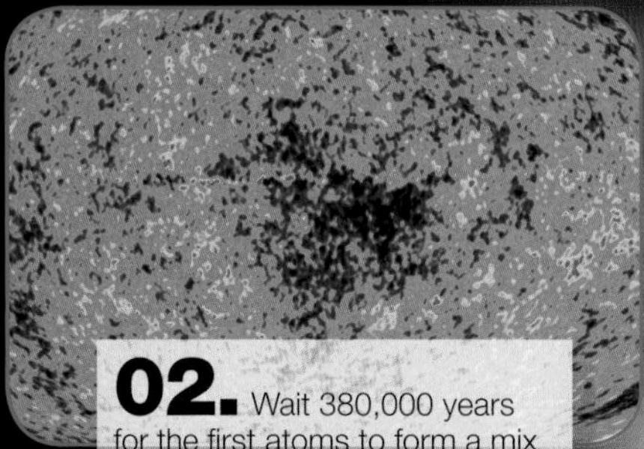

02. Wait 380,000 years for the first atoms to form a mix that is 76 percent hydrogen and 24 percent helium.

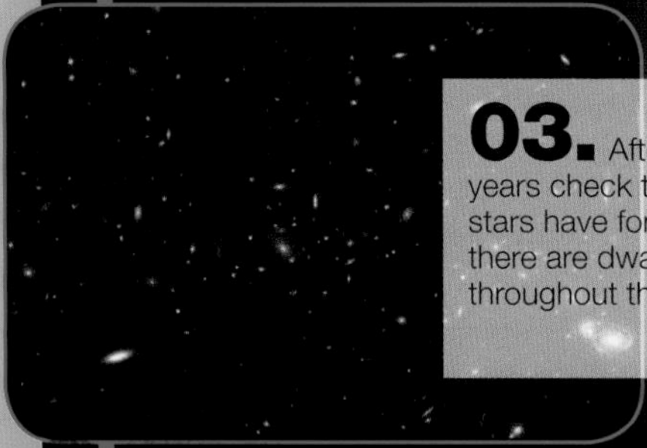

03. After 1 billion years check that the first stars have formed and there are dwarf galaxies throughout the universe.

Everything in the universe produces energy—you produce energy when you exercise, and light energy is produced by nuclear reactions inside stars.

WHAT'S IN A NAME?

The term "**Big Bang**" was coined by Fred Hoyle in 1950 to illustrate to his radio listeners the difference between it and his own theory, "Steady State," where the universe has no beginning.

Hot stuff!

1800000000000000000000000000000000

In the first trillionth of a second of its creation, the temperature of the universe was **18 billion trillion trillion degrees Fahrenheit**—18 and 32 zeros (1 billion trillion trillion degrees Centigrade—1 and 33 zeros).

Blasts from the past

1931
Belgian Georges Lemaître suggests that all material in the universe started as a single condensed sphere that exploded.

1948
Russian-born physicist George Gamow explains the first elements formed in the explosion.

1955
Englishman Fred Hoyle shows how heavier elements are produced by massive stars.

1965
American physicists Arno Penzias and Robert Wilson discover cosmic microwave background radiation, the leftover radiation initially produced by the Big Bang.

1980
American Alan Guth modifies the Big Bang theory by introducing the idea of inflation—a short period of extra expansion within a split second of the start of the universe.

Near, far... and really far

Depending on how far away objects are, distances in the universe are calculated using a variety of measuring units.

★ **Miles or kilometers**
Useful for measuring the distance of relatively near objects in our solar system, such as the planets, moons, and asteroids.

★ **Astronomical units**
Used for measuring planetary distances within the solar system. The distance from the Sun to Earth equals one astronomical unit (AU).

★ **Light-years**
This measurement is useful for distances within our galaxy, the Milky Way, and across the universe. One light-year is the distance light travels in one year—equal to 5.88 million million miles (46 million million km).

Human origins

5 billion years ago
The Sun formed from hydrogen and helium and small amounts of other elements.

4.5 billion years ago
Some of the material not used up in the Sun joined together to form Earth.

About 3.7 billion years ago
Carbon-containing molecules in young Earth's oceans evolved into bacterialike cells; the first forms of primitive life.

1 million years ago
The first humans walked on Earth.

Australopithecus skull

The universe is **expanding** by about 45 miles (70 km) every second.

Looking back

◉ We see objects in space because of their light. Stars produce their own but others, such as the Moon and planets, shine by reflecting light.

◉ Light travels at 186,287 miles per second (299,800 km per second)—faster than anything else.

◉ Distant stars are seen as they were in the past—when the light left them.

◉ The most distant galaxies we see are about 13 billion light-years away, and as they were in the early universe.

What about me?
All the elements on Earth, including all the elements in your body, were produced in stars.

05. When 9 million years old, form our solar system in the Milky Way Galaxy.

04. When the universe is 3 billion years old, merge small galaxies to form massive ones.

Bigger and bigger

Planets
Earth may feel big to us, but at 7,926 miles (12,756 km) across, it is just a speck in an expanding universe.

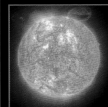

Stars
Planets orbit stars—our star is the Sun. Without it, there would be no life. It measures 870,000 miles (1.4 million km) across.

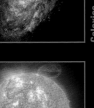

Galaxies
Stars exist in galaxies, colossal star systems that come in a range of sizes and shapes. Earth is in the Milky Way Galaxy.

Cluster
Galaxies exist in clusters—the Milky Way Galaxy is in the Local Group cluster, stretching 10 million light-years across.

Supercluster
Galaxy clusters are within superclusters—we are in the Virgo Supercluster, 200 million light-years from one side to the other.

Voids
The largest structures in the universe are chains of superclusters that are separated by huge empty voids.

How many galaxies are there in the universe?

We don't know. Every time astronomers look into the universe they discover more galaxies. Some parts of the universe have not been looked at yet, and there are other parts that telescopes cannot see. The best estimate by astronomers is that there are at least 125 billion galaxies out there.

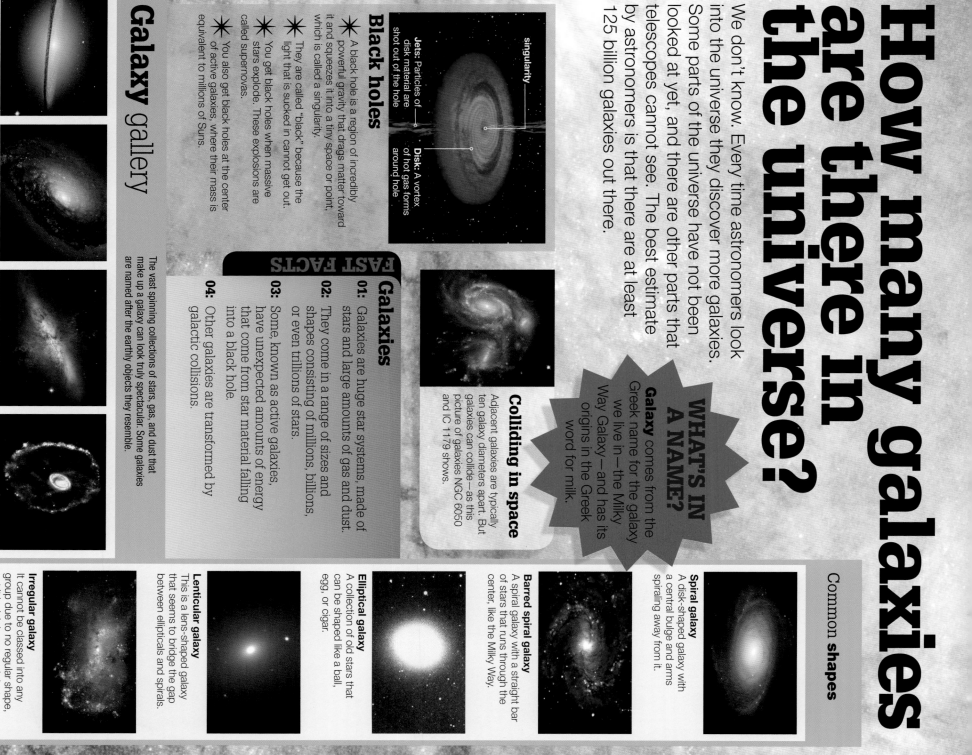

Black holes

Jets: Particles of disk material are shot out of the hole

singularity

Disk: A vortex of hot gas forms around hole

★ A black hole is a region of incredibly powerful gravity that drags matter toward it and squeezes it into a tiny space or point, which is called a singularity.

★ They are called "black" because the light that is sucked in cannot get out.

★ You get black holes when massive stars explode. These explosions are called supernovas.

★ You also get black holes at the center of active galaxies, where their mass is equivalent to millions of Suns.

Galaxy gallery

The vast spinning collections of stars, gas, and dust that make up a galaxy can look truly spectacular. Some galaxies are named after the earthly objects they resemble.

Sombrero Galaxy

Black Eye Galaxy

Cigar Galaxy

Cartwheel Galaxy

FAST FACTS

Galaxies

01: Galaxies are huge star systems, made of stars and large amounts of gas and dust.

02: They come in a range of sizes and shapes consisting of millions, billions, or even trillions of stars.

03: Some, known as active galaxies, have unexpected amounts of energy that come from star material falling into a black hole.

04: Other galaxies are transformed by galactic collisions.

Colliding in space

Adjacent galaxies are typically ten galaxy diameters apart. But galaxies can collide—as this picture of galaxies NGC 6050 and IC 1179 shows.

Common shapes

Spiral galaxy
A disk-shaped galaxy with a central bulge and arms spiraling away from it.

Barred spiral galaxy
A spiral galaxy with a straight bar of stars that runs through the center, like the Milky Way.

Elliptical galaxy
A collection of old stars that can be shaped like a ball, egg, or cigar.

Lenticular galaxy
This is a lens-shaped galaxy that seems to bridge the gap between ellipticals and spirals.

Irregular galaxy
It cannot be classed into any group due to no regular shape, yet it is rich in gas and dust.

Three views of the Milky Way

Orion Arm

Central bar: Arms of stars spiral out from both ends

Disk: Contains arms of younger stars

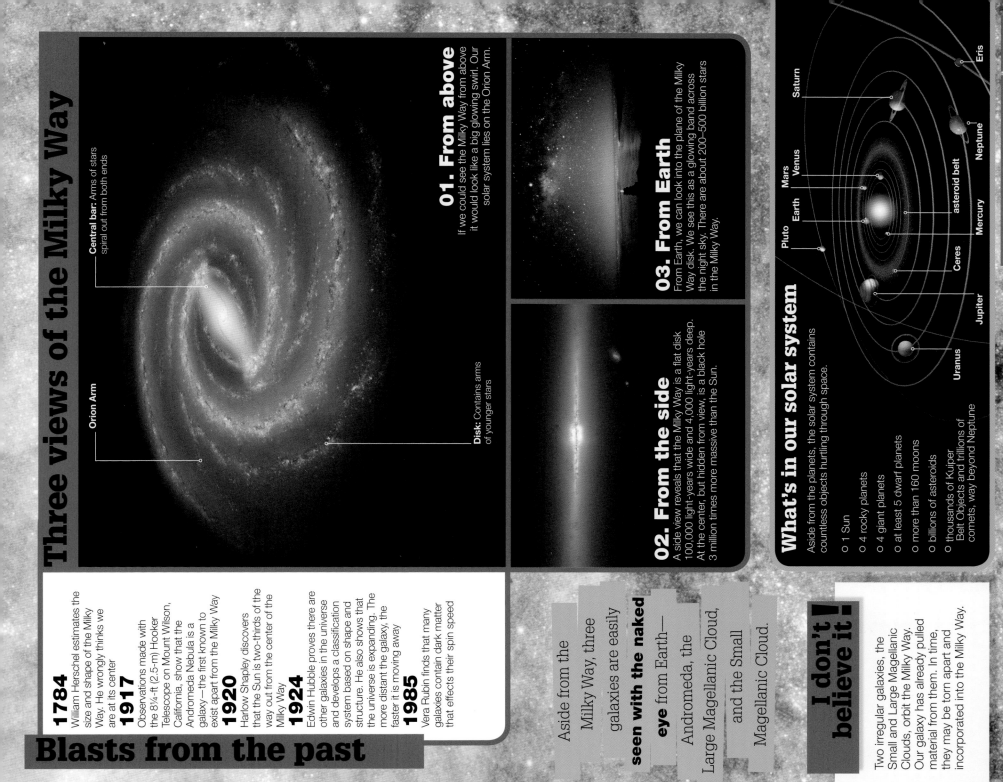

01. From above
If we could see the Milky Way from above it would look like a big glowing swirl. Our solar system lies on the Orion Arm.

02. From the side
A side view reveals that the Milky Way is a flat disk 100,000 light-years wide and 4,000 light-years deep. At the center, but hidden from view, is a black hole 3 million times more massive than the Sun.

03. From Earth
From Earth, we can look into the plane of the Milky Way disk. We see this as a glowing band across the night sky. There are about 200–500 billion stars in the Milky Way.

What's in our solar system
Aside from the planets, the solar system contains countless objects hurtling through space.

- 1 Sun
- 4 rocky planets
- 4 giant planets
- at least 5 dwarf planets
- more than 160 moons
- billions of asteroids
- thousands of Kuiper Belt Objects and trillions of comets, way beyond Neptune

Pluto · Earth · Mars · Venus · Saturn · Eris · Mercury · Neptune · asteroid belt · Ceres · Jupiter · Uranus

Blasts from the past

1784
William Herschel estimates the size and shape of the Milky Way. He wrongly thinks we are at its center

1917
Observations made with the 8¼-ft (2.5-m) Hooker Telescope on Mount Wilson, California, show that the Andromeda Nebula is a galaxy—the first known to exist apart from the Milky Way

1920
Harlow Shapley discovers that the Sun is two-thirds of the way out from the center of the Milky Way

1924
Edwin Hubble proves there are other galaxies in the universe and develops a classification system based on shape and structure. He also shows that the universe is expanding. The more distant the galaxy, the faster it is moving away

1985
Vera Rubin finds that many galaxies contain dark matter that effects their spin speed

Aside from the Milky Way, three galaxies are easily **seen with the naked eye** from Earth— Andromeda, the Large Magellanic Cloud, and the Small Magellanic Cloud.

I don't believe it!
Two irregular galaxies, the Small and Large Magellanic Clouds, orbit the Milky Way. Our galaxy has already pulled material from them. In time, they may be torn apart and incorporated into the Milky Way.

Are all stars the same?

No, every star is unique. With the exception of the Sun, stars are all so far away from Earth that they appear as pinpoints of twinkling light to us. But even though they may look the same to the naked eye, they all have their own characteristics, differing in size, temperature, color, and brightness, depending on how old they are.

How to: **form a star**

01. You will need perfect star forming conditions—vast clouds of mainly hydrogen, helium, and dust.

02. Collapse fragments of the cloud and shrink them to form protostars—the first stage of a star's life.

03. Start nuclear reactions in the star's core so that it is able to shine steadily.

RECORD BREAKER

All stars spin, but some spin much faster than others. The **fastest star** identified as of all is a neutron star identified as XTE J1739-285, which spins around at a head-turning 1,122 times a second.

STAR LIFE

A star's mass—it is made of—determines how long it is going to live; the greater the mass, the shorter the life.

I don't believe it!

Half the stars in the universe are doubles—two stars that orbit each other. In 2008, astronomers found the most massive pair yet; they are known as A1 in the star cluster NGC 3603. One of the pair is 116 times more massive than the Sun.

In numbers

80,000°F
(45,000°C) The temperature of the hottest stars

4,500°F
(2,500°C) The temperature of the coolest stars

6 million
How many times more light is produced by the most luminous stars than by the Sun

10 billion
How many years the oldest stars can live

Closest stars to the Sun

Proxima Centauri

name	distance (light-years)
Proxima Centauri	4.2
Alpha Centauri A	4.3
Alpha Centauri B	4.3
Barnard's Star	5.9
Wolf 359	7.8
Lalande 21185	8.3
Sirius A	8.6
Sirius B	8.6

Five brightest nighttime stars

How bright a star appears in the Earth's sky depends not only on how much light it produces—its luminosity—but also on its distance from Earth.

Sirius
Distance: 8.6 light-years
Brightness scale -1.44

Canopus
Distance: 313 light-years
Brightness scale -0.62

Rigil Kentaurus
Distance: 4.3 light-years
Brightness scale -0.28

Arcturus
Distance: 37 light-years
Brightness scale -0.05

Vega
Distance: 25 light-years
Brightness scale 0.03

BRIGHTNESS

The brightness of a star seen from Earth is described according to a scale of numbers. The smaller the number, the brighter the star. Those with a value of 6 or below can be seen by the naked eye.

Stellar stunners

Despite their name, planetary nebulae actually have nothing to do with planets or star-forming nebulae, but are mature stars whose outer layers of gas have been pushed out to create a spectacular ring of color around the white-dwarf remains of the original star.

Failed star

Brown dwarfs are stars that aren't massive enough to start nuclear reactions in their core. Therefore, these stars don't shine but are instead a dark red-brown color.

Helix Nebula

Eskimo Nebula

Cat's Eye Nebula

Ant Nebula

Three ways to search for life in the universe

01 The Allen Telescope Array in the United States is a group of 42 radio-telescope dishes working as a giant ear listening for signals from extraterrestrial life.

02 Anyone can take part in the Search for Extraterrestrial Intelligence (SETI) by running a screensaver on their computer that looks for data patterns from the Allen Telescope.

03 In 2015, a spacecraft called *Darwin* will be launched to look for Earth-like planets. Onboard telescopes will then analyze light from the planets for signs of gases that might have been produced by living things.

Exoplanets

★ **The Sun is not the only star with planets orbiting around it;** more than 330 planets have been identified beyond the solar system, with new ones being found all the time.

★ The first exoplanet (planet outside the solar system) was discovered in 1992.

★ **Exoplanets found so far are mostly Jupiter-like worlds—massive, giant planets.**

★ For a planet to support life it is thought that it needs to be at a distance from the star where the temperature is right for liquid water to exist.

04. End the life of your massive star with an explosion, leaving behind a supernova remnant, neutron star, or black hole.

Will the Sun shine forever?

The Sun is a star—a vast sphere of luminous gas. Its light is a by-product of gas-fueled nuclear reactions in its core. It shines steadily now, but in about five billion years it will swell up before dying as a cold, dark cinder in space.

Tell me more: the Sun's surface

Flares: These are massive bursts of energy that explode in the Sun's lower atmosphere

Spicules: Short-lived jets of gas shoot out from the surface

Prominences: Sometimes giant clouds of gas loop out hundreds of thousands of miles

Photosphere: The Sun's visible surface looks bumpy here due to hot gas rising up from inside the star

Faculae: The hottest areas, called faculae, look almost white and are highly active regions created by the Sun's magnetic field

In numbers

1.3 million
How many Earths could fit inside the Sun

660 million
(600 million metric tons)
The number of tons of the gas hydrogen converted to helium every second in the core of the Sun

137 miles/sec
(220 km/sec) The speed at which the Sun is moving around our galaxy's center

220 million
The number of years it takes the Sun to orbit our galaxy once

Studying the Sun

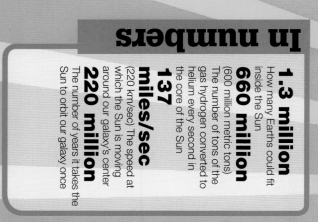

Watching from space...
Spacecraft have observed the Sun since the 1960s. The Solar and Heliospheric Observatory, SOHO, has been watching it continuously since 1995.

...and underground!
Sudbury Observatory in Canada lies 6,800 ft (2,073 m) underground. From it, scientists detect particles from the center of the Sun that are traveling through Earth.

WEIRD OR WHAT?
The Sun's gravity pulls gas inward, but the pressure of the gas at the center pushes outward. The two forces balance to give the Sun its ball shape.

Why does the Moon change shape?

The Moon is a large ball of rock that doesn't change shape—it just looks as though it does. The shape we see in the sky today depends on how much of the Moon's face is lit up. Sometimes we observe a thin crescent, and at other times we see half or three quarters of the Moon, and then a fully lit face—a Full Moon.

Lunar cycle

The view we have of the Moon changes according to the relative positions of the Sun, Earth, and Moon. A complete cycle of shapes, known as phases, takes 29.5 days.

New Moon

Crescent

First quarter

Waxing gibbous

Full Moon

Waning gibbous

Last quarter

Crescent

Tell me more: how the Moon was formed

Most astronomers think that the Moon was formed out of Earth about 4.5 billion years ago. It is known as the giant-impact theory.

01: A Mars-sized asteroid collides into Earth at a speed of 12 miles/sec (20 km/sec).

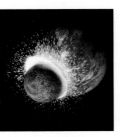

02: Smashed asteroid pieces and material gouged out of Earth's rocky mantle form a ring around the Earth.

03: Over several million years, the pieces of orbiting material bump into each other and join together.

04: They form one large body—the Moon. About a quarter the size of Earth, it slowly moves out to its present orbit.

WHAT'S IN A NAME?

A new mineral discovered on the lunar surface by the Apollo 11 crew in 1969 was named **Armalcolite** in their honor. Armalcolite takes letters from their names: Armstrong, Aldrin, and Collins.

I don't believe it!

In 1835, six articles in the *New York Sun* newspaper described bat-winged humanlike creatures seen on the Moon through a telescope. Amazingly, the stories were believed for several weeks.

There's so little gas in the Moon's atmosphere that the amount was doubled when the *Apollo* craft used its rocket motors to land on the surface.

Blasts from the past

1546
John Heywood suggests the Moon is made of "green cheese." But not the color green—by "green" he means fresh and unmatured

1609
Englishman Thomas Harriot is the first to look at the Moon through a telescope. A few months later Galileo sees lunar mountains, and he estimates their heights by the length of the shadows they cast

1969
On July 20, Neil Armstrong is the first person to walk on the Moon. Buzz Aldrin (pictured below) follows 19 minutes later

Night lights

01: Material streams from the Sun's corona (outer layer) and is known as **solar wind**.

02: Solar wind travels toward Earth at about **280 miles/sec** (450 km/sec).

03: The wind causes gas particles above Earth's polar regions to glow and give colorful light displays called **auroras**.

Tell me more: the Sun

🌞 About 75 percent of the Sun is hydrogen, most of the rest is helium.

🌞 **The Sun is about 4.28 light-years from its nearest starry neighbor, Proxima Centauri.**

🌞 The Sun is about 5 billion years old. That's a lot of candles!

🌞 **It is about 870,000 miles (1.4 million km) across.**

🌞 Eight planets orbit around the Sun—only about 4 percent of the stars in the sky have planets.

Blasts from the past

434 BCE
Greek philosopher Anaxagoras suggests the Sun is a fiery stone about a quarter the size of Greece

270 BCE
The first attempt to measure the Sun's distance is made by Greek astronomer Aristarchus of Samos. He thinks it is 31 times closer than it actually is

1609
Italian astronomer Galileo Galilei realizes that the Sun takes about a month to rotate

1842
French photographer Noël Paymal Lerebours takes the first photograph of the Sun

1869
Englishman Norman Lockyer observes the Sun and discovers a chemical element he calls helium after Helios—the Greek Sun god

How to: watch a total solar eclipse

01. Using an eclipse viewer, observe the Moon passing directly in front of the Sun—a rare occurrence not to be missed!

02. Observe the Moon looking like a dark disk, covering more and more of the Sun's face. Slowly day seems to turn to night.

03. "Totality" occurs when the Moon covers the Sun's face completely, revealing its corona; it lasts 3–4 minutes.

04. As the Moon continues on its path, watch the Sun come back into view. The sky brightens, and distant stars become invisible again.

05. The eclipse is almost over; only a fraction of the Sun remains covered, and the shadow cast on Earth by the Moon has all but gone.

Six layers of the Sun

01. Corona: The outer atmosphere, seen during an eclipse

02. Chromosphere: The inner atmosphere

03. Photosphere: The visible surface of the Sun from which energy is released in a blaze of light

04. Convective zone: The layer through which the Sun's energy travels outward through the Sun by "convection"

05. Radiative zone: The layer through which energy travels outward from the core as radiation

06. Core: The center of the Sun where nuclear reactions convert hydrogen to helium, producing energy

What about me?

You should never, ever, look directly at the Sun. It emits dangerous radiation that can damage cells at the back of your eyes and cause blindness.

Hot, hot, hot

How hot is the Sun?
It depends where you put your thermometer...

Corona: 3.6 million°F (2 million°C)

Transition region (between chromosphere and corona): 36,000°F (20,000°C) to 1.8 million°F (1 million°C)

Chromosphere: from bottom to top, 8,100°F (4,500°C) to 36,000°F (20,000°C)

Photosphere: 10,000°F (5,500°C)

Core: 27 million°F (15 million°C)

FAST FACTS

01: The pull of Earth's gravity keeps the Moon in orbit.

02: The Moon's surface gravity is about one-sixth of Earth's.

03: The Moon's gravity pulls on Earth's oceans to produce tides.

04: The "far side" of the Moon we don't see was first imaged in 1959 by the Soviet spacecraft *Luna 3*.

05: The Moon reflects light like a very dirty mirror. Although the Full Moon looks bright, it is 400,000 times dimmer than the Sun.

06: The Moon is 400 times smaller than the Sun, but since it is 400 times closer they look the same size.

07: The Moon's surface temperature changes every Moon-day from hotter than boiling water to colder than liquid air.

Moon rock

- More than 2,000 samples of rock, sand, and dust were brought back by the six Apollo crews that walked on the Moon between 1969 and 1972.

- Samples were also collected and brought to Earth by three robotic craft sent by the Soviet Union (1970–1976).

- More than 50 pieces of Moon rock have blasted off the Moon's surface by asteroid impact, and then landed on Earth as meteorites.

In numbers

238,855 miles
(384,400 km) The distance between the Moon and Earth

60
How many hours it takes a spacecraft from Earth to reach the Moon

27.32
The number of days it takes the Moon to spin once on its axis, and also to orbit the Earth. This means the same side of the Moon always points toward Earth

1.5 in
(3.82 cm) The annual increase in distance between Earth and the Moon

0.18
How many milliseconds longer a day on Earth becomes every century as the distance between Earth and the Moon grows

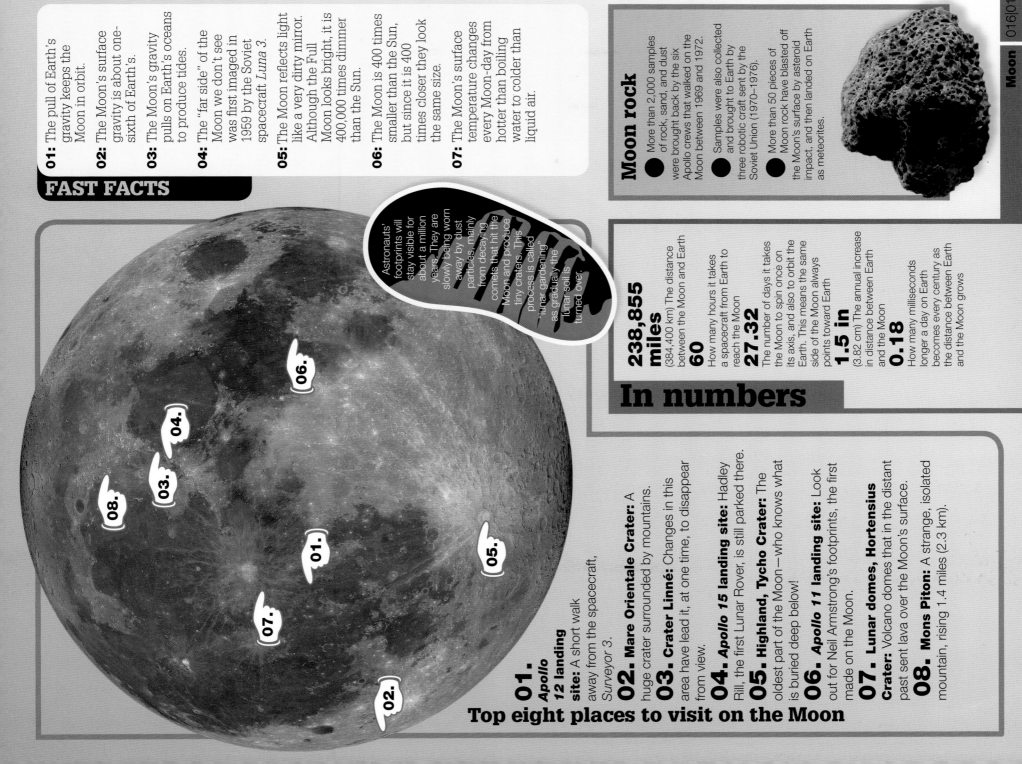

Astronauts' footprints will stay visible for about a million years. They are slowly being worn away by dust particles, mainly from decaying comets that hit the Moon and produce tiny craters. This process is called "lunar gardening" as gradually the lunar soil is turned over.

Top eight places to visit on the Moon

01. *Apollo 12* landing site: A short walk away from the spacecraft, *Surveyor 3*.

02. Mare Orientale Crater: A huge crater surrounded by mountains.

03. Crater Linné: Changes in this area have lead it, at one time, to disappear from view.

04. *Apollo 15* landing site: Hadley Rill, the first Lunar Rover, is still parked there.

05. Highland, Tycho Crater: The oldest part of the Moon—who knows what is buried deep below!

06. *Apollo 11* landing site: Look out for Neil Armstrong's footprints, the first made on the Moon.

07. Lunar domes, Hortensius Crater: Volcano domes that in the distant past sent lava over the Moon's surface.

08. Mons Piton: A strange, isolated mountain, rising 1.4 miles (2.3 km).

Are there other planets like Earth?

No, we don't know of any other planets exactly like Earth, with its unique life-forms. But Earth has similarities to three other planets orbiting the Sun—Mercury, Venus, and Mars. All four are made of rock and metal, orbit close to the Sun, and have relatively hot surfaces. They are known as the terrestrial or rocky planets.

Swift Mercury

- Mercury is named after the Roman messenger to the gods because of its speedy movement.

- It is the smallest planet—Earth is 2.5 times bigger.

- It is also the densest planet, with a huge iron core.

- The temperature on Mercury ranges from 800°F (430°C) in the day to -290°F (-180°C) at night.

- The planet has a dark, dusty, surface, covered with craters and unchanged for a billion years.

Lost in space?

If you could be zapped onto any of the rocky planets, which should you choose?

Mercury: If you arrive at night, you will freeze to death. If you arrive during the day, you will be toast.

Venus: Difficult to know if you will dissolve in the sulfuric acid clouds before you are cooked by the heat.

Earth: Be prepared to swim in case you land in water. If you come across other living things, check if they look friendly or hungry and either smile or run.

Mars: If you have your own oxygen supply and land in the warmest regions you might be fine for a while, but the violent winds and dust storms are unbearable.

Rocky planets

01: The rocky planets were formed about 4.56 billion years ago from a vast cloud of gas and dust that produced the Sun and other bodies in the solar system.

02: Material close to the Sun clumped together, eventually producing four large balls—the rocky planets.

03: The metal sank to the planets' cores and the lighter rock moved to the surface.

04: Over time, the planets cooled and their different surfaces were formed by meteorite bombardment, volcanic activity, water, and movements in their crusts.

Vital statistics

Mercury
Diameter: 3,029 miles (4,875 km)
Distance from Sun: 36 million miles (57.9 million km)
Rotation: 59 days
Orbit of the Sun: 88 days

Venus
Diameter: 7,521 miles (12,104 km)
Distance from Sun: 67.2 million miles (108.2 million km)
Rotation: 243 days
Orbit of the Sun: 224.7 days

Earth
Diameter: 7,926 miles (12,756 km)
Distance from Sun: 93 million miles (149.6 million km)
Rotation: 23.93 hours
Orbit of the Sun: 365.26 days

Mars
Diameter: 4,213 miles (6,780 km)
Distance from Sun: 141.6 million miles (227.9 million km)
Rotation: 24.63 hours
Orbit of the Sun: 687 days

Life on Earth

  Earth is the only place in the universe where life is known.

It is home to 1.5 million distinct forms of life and more are being discovered all the time.

Earth is just far enough away from the Sun for liquid water and life to exist. If it were any closer, Earth would be too hot, any farther away, and it would be too cold.

More than 70 percent of Earth is covered in water. If the planet were perfectly smooth its surface would be covered with a layer 1.7 miles (2.8 km) deep.

Earth has just the right temperature for its water to be liquid. Mercury and Venus are too hot, and their water has evaporated. Most of Mars's water is frozen beneath its surface.

What about me?

Venus is the easiest planet to see in Earth's sky. Look for it in the east just before sunrise and in the west just after sunset. It looks like a brilliant star and is nicknamed the "morning star" and "evening star."

I don't believe it!

A Venusian day is longer than a Venusian year. Venus is the slowest spinner of all the planets, taking 243 days to spin once. But as it spins it travels on its orbit around the Sun once every 224.7 days. The time between one sunrise and the next is 117 Earth days.

Cloudy Venus

01: Venus is named after the Roman goddess of love and beauty.

02: It is surrounded by dense clouds stretching up to 50 miles (80 km) above the surface.

03: The clouds are made of dilute sulfuric acid droplets and reflect 80 percent of the sunlight, making Venus overcast.

04: Heat is trapped by the clouds in the same way glass traps heat in a greenhouse.

Venusian volcanoes

Venus has hundreds of volcanoes and about 85 percent of the planet is covered in volcanic lava. The biggest are shallow shield volcanoes, like those in Hawaii on Earth.

name	height	diameter
Maat Mons	5 miles (8 km)	245 miles (395 km)
Gula Mons	2 miles (3 km)	170 miles (276 km)
Sif Mons	1.2 miles (2 km)	125 miles (200 km)
Sapas Mons	1 mile (1.5 km)	135 miles (217 km)

Martian myths

🍅 **In the 1870s, an Italian astronomer was mistranslated, which led people to believe he had seen canals on Mars built by Martians.**

📻 When a radio version of the H. G. Wells book *War of the Worlds* was broadcast in 1938, listeners panicked because they thought they had turned into a news report and that Martians had landed on Earth.

🔭 **Photographs taken by spacecraft in 1976 seemed to show a 2-mile- (3.2-km-) long human face on Mars' surface. It later proved to be a huge rock formation.**

👽 About 50 years ago, astronomers studying Mars' moon Phobos concluded it was artificial—a metal hollow sphere made by Martians.

Red surface: Mars is named after the Roman god of war because of its bloodlike color

Ascraeus Mons: A giant shield volcano

Atmosphere: This is 95 percent carbon dioxide

Valles Marineris: This is a complex system of canyons more than 2,500 miles (4,000 km) long and on average 5 miles (8 km) deep

Olympus Mons is the **largest volcano** on Mars and in the solar system. It is 15 miles (24 km) high and 403 miles (648 km) across.

I don't believe it!

Just over 100 years ago, a large monetary prize was offered for the first person to communicate with an extraterrestrial. Mars was excluded from the competition, because it was thought that getting in touch with Martians would be too easy.

Which planet is the biggest?

Jupiter is the biggest and is truly giant. It is large enough for 11 Earths to fit across its face and 1,300 to fit inside it. There are four giant planets in our solar system. The next biggest is Saturn, followed by Uranus, and Neptune. They are also known as "gas giants" because of their colorful, ice-cold gas atmospheres.

FAST FACTS

Giant planet structure

01: Temperature and density increase toward the center of the giant planets. This affects the physical state of the material the planets are made up of.

02: In Jupiter and Saturn, squashed gases become fluid and more like liquids. Deeper still, the gases are like molten metal.

03: In the heart of all four giants are round cores of rocky and metallic material.

04: All four giant planets have rings. They look solid from a distance but are made of individual pieces that follow their own orbits around their planet.

Jupiter is named after the king of the Roman gods and ruler of the heavens.

Jupiter
Diameter: 88,846 miles (142,984 km)
Distance from Sun: 483.6 million miles (778.3 million km)
Rotation: 9.9 hours
Orbit of the Sun: 11.9 years

Saturn
Diameter: 74,898 miles (120,536 km)
Distance from Sun: 888 million miles (1.43 billion km)
Rotation: 10.7 hours
Orbit of the Sun: 29.5 years

Uranus
Diameter: 31,763 miles (51,118 km)
Distance from Sun: 1.78 billion miles (2.87 billion km)
Rotation: 17.3 hours
Orbit of the Sun: 84.0 years

Neptune
Diameter: 30,760 miles (49,532 km)
Distance from Sun: 2.8 billion miles (4.5 billion km)
Rotation: 16.1 hours
Orbit of the Sun: 164.8 years

WEIRD OR WHAT?
Jupiter has a powerful **magnetic field**—it is as if there is a large bar magnet inside the planet. It's the strongest field of any planet—about 20,000 times more forceful than Earth's.

I don't believe it!
Jupiter is shrinking. When it was young it was five times its present size. It is cooling and getting smaller by about ¾ in (2 cm) a year.

Tell me more: Jupiter

Zones: White bands of cool rising air

Clouds: Jupiter's stripes are clouds in its violent atmosphere. They are pulled into bands parallel to the equator by the planet's fast spin

Belts: Red-brown bands of warmer, falling air

Tell me more: Saturn

- Saturn is named after the father of the Roman god Jupiter.
- The first to see Saturn's rings was Italian astronomer Galileo Galilei, in 1610. He thought they were handlelike ears fixed to the sides of the planet.
- None of the gas giants are perfect spheres. They are all oblate (squashed balls). Saturn's diameter is almost one-tenth bigger at its equator than at its poles.

Rings: Saturn has seven main rings and hundreds of smaller ringlets

Ringed world

- As Saturn orbits the Sun, its rings can be seen from different angles.
- The rings are made of particles and chunks of dirty ice in orbit around the planet.
- The pieces range in size from dust grains to large boulders several yards across.
- The pieces are also very reflective. The rings shine brightly and are easy to see.

I don't believe it!

Saturn is the least dense of all the planets—if you could put it in a bath of water, it would float.

Uranus

- Uranus is named after the father of the Roman god Saturn.
- Uranus became the seventh planet in the solar system, and the first to be discovered by telescope when it was unexpectedly spotted by astronomer William Herschel on March 13, 1781.
- Uranus rolls around its orbit on its side. The planet is tilted over by 98 degrees, possibly as a result of a collision with a large asteroid when it was young.
- Like the other three gas giants, Uranus's atmosphere is mostly hydrogen. It also contains methane, which absorbs red light and makes the planet blue.

Neptune

- Neptune is named after the Roman god of the sea.
- It's the fourth largest of the gas giants.
- Neptune is about 30 times farther from the Sun than Earth.
- It is the coldest giant, –320°F (–200°C) at its cloudtops and has the fastest winds of any planet, reaching speeds up to 1,340 mph (2,160 kph) near its equator.

I don't believe it!

Neptune was only discovered on September 23, 1846. Although it had been noticed many times before, astronomers thought it was a star.

Spots: Giant weather storms

Great Red Spot: This weather storm is bigger than Earth. It rotates counterclockwise every 6–7 days and has been raging for more than 300 years

What is a dwarf planet?

Astronomers are constantly discovering new objects that they need to describe. In 2006, they decided on a new class—dwarf planets. These are small, almost round bodies that orbit the Sun in a belt of other objects. The solar system is also full of other small bodies, including moons that orbit other planets, asteroids, Kuiper Belt Objects that form a flattened belt beyond Neptune, and comets.

From out of the sky

Rocks from space sometimes make it to Earth and are known as meteorites.

⊛ Most come from asteroids but some originate from the Moon and Mars.

⊛ About 3,000 meteorites weighing more than 2 lb (1 kg) land on Earth every year—most fall into the oceans.

⊛ More than 22,500 meteorites have been collected and cataloged.

⊛ The largest meteorite ever found landed in Hoba West, Namibia, in 1920. It weighed 72 tons (66 metric tons).

⊛ There are three main types of meteorite:

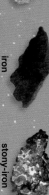

stony

iron

stony-iron

Impact craters

Most extraterrestrial bodies heading for Earth are broken up as they pass through the atmosphere, but sometimes big objects, or parts of them, survive and crash onto the surface as meteorites, gouging out vast craters. The five largest impact craters include the Manicouagan Crater, seen here from space.

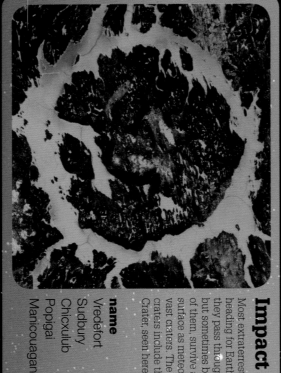

name	location	diameter	age (years)
Vredefort	South Africa	185 miles (300 km)	more than 2 billion
Sudbury	Canada	155 miles (250 km)	1.85 billion
Chicxulub	Mexico	105 miles (170 km)	65 million
Popigai	Russia	60 miles (100 km)	35.7 million
Manicouagan	Canada	60 miles (100 km)	214 million

Dwarf planets

At present we know of five dwarf planets—four in the Kuiper Belt, and Ceres in the Main Belt of asteroids between Mars and Jupiter.

dwarf planet	discovery date	moons
Eris	2005	1
Pluto	**1930**	**3**
Haumea	2005	2
Makemake	**2005**	**0**
Ceres	1801	0

I don't believe it!

Jupiter's biggest moon, Ganymede, and Saturn's biggest moon, Titan, are both larger than the planet Mercury.

STREAKERS

Meteors occur in the sky every night. They are fleeting streaks of light, caused by **comet dust particles** traveling through Earth's atmosphere. They are best spotted during one of the 20 or so annual meteor showers.

Mysterious moons

Miranda

This is the smallest of Uranus's five major moons. Its rugged surface is covered with huge canyons.

Io

This moon of Jupiter is covered in active volcanoes that are constantly renewing its surface.

Titan

The largest of Saturn's moons, it is the only planetary moon to have a thick atmosphere.

Phobos

Mars has two tiny moons. Phobos, the largest, which is 17 miles (27 km) across, and Deimos.

Asteroids

FAST FACTS

01: Asteroids are remains of a rocky planet that failed to form between Mars and Jupiter 4.5 billion years ago.

02: The remains did not stick together but smashed into each other.

03: These rocky and metallic objects were scattered throughout the solar system crashing into planets.

04: Eventually, a belt of rocky pieces, known as the Main Belt, settled between Mars and Jupiter, plus a small number of asteroids on other orbits around the Sun.

05: Some asteroids, known as near-Earth asteroids, travel close to the Earth and have the potential to hit it.

Kuiper Belt

★ The Kuiper Belt is a flat belt of cometlike bodies beyond Neptune that stretches from 3.7 to 7.4 billion miles (6 to 12 billion km) from the Sun.

★ More than 1,000 Kuiper Belt Objects are known and it is suspected at least 70,000 more than 60 miles (100 km) across are awaiting discovery.

★ Four known dwarf planets exist in the belt, and at least 200 more are expected to be found.

★ Most objects in the Kuiper Belt take more than 250 years to orbit the Sun.

Top 10 biggest moons

name	diameter	parent planet
01: Ganymede	3,270 miles (5,260 km)	Jupiter
02: Titan	3,200 miles (5,150 km)	Saturn
03: Callisto	3,000 miles (4,820 km)	Jupiter
04: Io	2,260 miles (3,640 km)	Jupiter
05: Moon	2,160 miles (3,480 km)	Earth
06: Europa	1,940 miles (3,120 km)	Jupiter
07: Triton	1,680 miles (2,710 km)	Neptune
08: Titania	980 miles (1,580 km)	Uranus
09: Rhea	950 miles (1,530 km)	Saturn
10: Oberon	945 miles (1,520 km)	Uranus

Planets and their moons

planet	number of moons
Mercury	0
Venus	0
Earth	1
Mars	2
Jupiter	at least 63
Saturn	at least 60
Uranus	27
Neptune	13

Tell me more: comet anatomy

1 Nucleus: The heart of the comet is an irregular-shaped ball of snow and dust covered in a thin crust of dust.

2 Coma: As the comet moves close to the Sun it forms a huge head of gas and dust.

3 Gas tail: The Sun's heat turns the nucleus snow to gas, which flows out as a blue tail.

4 Dust tail: Dust released from the nucleus trails away from the coma as a white tail.

Cool comets

★ Comets are huge dirty snowballs left over from when the giant planets formed.

★ Their paths take them in all directions as they orbit around the Sun.

★ There are trillions of comets. They make a vast sphere, called the Oort Cloud, which surrounds the planetary part of the solar system.

★ Some comets have left the Oort Cloud and now orbit in the inner solar system returning again and again to the Earth's sky.

How many constellations are there?

There are 88 constellations in the night sky. Each one is a straight-edged area of sky that includes a pattern made from bright stars, and they all fit together like pieces of a jigsaw to make up the entire sky around Earth.

The Compass

PYXIS

θ
λ
κ
δ γ
τo
α
β ζ

Thirteen constellations feature humans. Twelve come from Greek mythology, and the thirteenth is Native American.

There are 15 animal constellations, including a bull and a wolf.

The eight birds include a peacock and a toucan.

A crab, a dolphin, and a sea monster are among nine water-based constellations.

Twenty-eight objects include a harp, a compass, a cross, a clock, and a microscope.

The remaining 15 are a miscellany, from a fly to mythical creatures.

Far, far away

The stars in a particular pattern only appear close together in space. In fact, the stars are totally unrelated and at vastly differing distances from Earth.

Blasts from the past

2000 BCE
The first constellations are devised by Sumerians and Babylonians

150 CE
Greek astronomer Ptolemy lists 48 constellations

1596–1603
Twelve constellations are introduced by Dutch navigators Peter Keyser and Frederick de Houtman

1690
Seven new constellations complete the northern sky

1754
Fourteen constellations are introduced by French astronomer Nicolaus de Lacaille to complete the southern sky

1922
The 88 constellation patterns are sanctioned by the International Astronomical Union

1930
The constellations' straight-edge official boundaries are set

How to: spot Orion

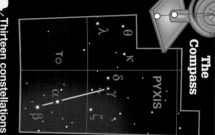

Orion

01. Face the horizon. Hold out your arm with hand outstretched. Orion is a little bigger than your hand. If you are in the southern hemisphere, Orion appears upside down.

02. Look for a row of three bright stars very close together in the sky. This is his belt.

03. At equal distance, one above and one below the belt, are two bright stars. The brightest, with a warm red glow, is Betelgeuse. The whiter star is Rigel.

ORION

Betelgeuse
69
2½·5
μ
ε
69
φ2
α
χ2
χ1
56
51
λ·φ1
32
M78
NGC 2024
IC 434
δ
31·22·
η
ρ
23
15
Bellatrix
ν
11
M 42
σ
κ
29
β
Rigel
π1
π2
π3
π4
π5
o1
o2

Large Dog

CANIS MAJOR
θ
μ
UW NGC 2362
27
NGC 2360
γ
o2
o1
π
ι
α Sirius
15
ε Adhara
M41
ζ1 ζ2
β
ν3
ν2
κ
λ

Tell me more: the celestial sphere

Ancient astronomers imagined the night sky as a giant sphere of stars rotating around the Earth.

The idea of a celestial sphere is still used to describe a star's position.

The sphere is divided into the 88 constellations.

The outline of the Orion constellation (left) is shown in orange.

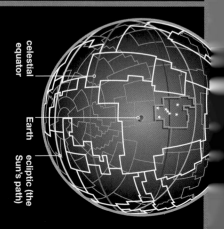

celestial equator

Earth

ecliptic (the Sun's path)

Great Bear

Bear necessities

01 There are **two bears** in the sky, **Ursa Major** (Great Bear) and **Ursa Minor** (Little Bear). They are both found in northern hemisphere skies.

02 One of the most famous stars of all is Polaris, the **North Star**, at the tip of Ursa Minor's tail. It lies above Earth's North Pole.

03 No one knows why both bears are given long tails, since real bears have short stubby tails.

One of the best-known patterns in the night sky, **the Big Dipper**, is not a constellation but a star pattern known as an **asterism**. The seven stars are part of **Ursa Major**, the Great Bear.

URSA MAJOR

THE BIG DIPPER

M82 · M81 · Dubhe · Merak · Phad · Alioth · Mizar · Alcor · Alkaid · M108 · M97 · M109 · M101

Dutch artist Vincent van Gogh shows the Big Dipper in his painting *Starry Night Over the Rhône*.

WEIRD OR WHAT?

The strangest constellation has got to be a **head of hair**. Its official name is **Coma Berenices**, because it is named for the hair of Berenice, the Queen of Egypt.

The Zodiac

Twelve constellations form the backdrop to the Sun's path across the stars. Together, they are known as the Zodiac.

The Sun completes one circuit of the Zodiac in a year, taking about a month to pass through each constellation.

The word "Zodiac" comes from the Greek for animal and, with one exception, is a circle of creatures. Libra, the scales, was introduced long after the others.

Aquarius · Capricorn · Sagittarius · Scorpio · Libra · Virgo · Leo · Cancer · Gemini · Taurus · Aries · Pisces

I don't believe it!

The star patterns aren't going to last for ever, but neither are they going to change any time soon. All stars are moving at about 30–60 miles (50–100 km) a second, but we can hardly tell because they are so far away. Constellation stars are typically 100 light-years away, and so it takes us about 10,000 years before we start to notice a star's changing position.

The biggest constellation is **Hydra**, a water snake that meanders its way across 3.16 percent of the whole sky.

The smallest constellation is **Crux**, the southern cross, which is also the brightest constellation.

Small Dog

CANIS MINOR

Procyon · α · β · γ · ε

Starry dogs

There are four dogs in the sky. Two make the constellation **Canes Venatici**, the hunting dogs. The other two are Orion's hunting dogs, **Canis Major** (Large Dog) and **Canis Minor** (Small Dog).

The star **Sirius**, in **Canis Major**, is the brightest star in the sky. It is sometimes called the **Dog Star**.

The ancient Greeks and Romans called the hottest days of summer "the dog days" because these were the days when Sirius rose in the sky as the Sun set.

Sirius is, in fact, a double star. Its companion, Sirius B, is fondly known as "the pup."

How does a telescope "see" in the dark?

A telescope is a light bucket. It collects light from the objects in space using either a lens or, more usually, a mirror. A main mirror reflects the light to a smaller one, which brings the light to a focus where an image of the object is formed.

Tell me more: inside an observatory

Prime focus: The astronomer originally sat here but today the view is recorded on to a computer

Flashlight: In this time-lapse image, the light is someone walking around with a flashlight

Base: Telescope is mounted on a crushed granite base in case of an earthquake

Mount: Horseshoe-shaped mount supports telescope and turns it to point to a particular part of the sky

Dome: The aluminum and steel dome rotates and opens so the telescope can look at different parts of the sky

Top five telescopes

name and location	main mirror diameter
Gran Telescopio Canarias La Palma Island, Spain	34 ft (10.4 m)
Keck I and Keck II Mauna Kea, Hawaii	33 ft (10 m)
Southern African Large Telescope South Africa	33 ft (10 m)
Hobby-Eberly Mount Fowlkes, Texas	30¼ ft (9.2 m)
Large Binocular Telescope Mount Graham, Arizona	27.6 ft (8.4 m)

WEIRD OR WHAT?

A batch of radio telescopes known as the Allen Telescope Array **listen for signs of alien life**. Together, they will survey a million stars for radio signals generated by extraterrestrial intelligence.

In numbers

34
The number of telescopes at The Kitt Peak National Observatory, Arizona, and the Mauna Kea Observatory in Hawaii

80 ft
(24.5 m) The diameter of the mirror in the Giant Magellan Telescope in Las Campanas, Chile, scheduled for completion in 2017. It will be the biggest telescope ever

36
The number of separate hexagonal pieces, each 6 ft (1.8 m) across, which make up the mirror in each of the twin Keck telescopes at Mauna Kea, Hawaii

Types of telescope

Refracting telescope
Uses a large lens to refract, or bend, the light to form an image of a distant object

Reflecting telescope
Uses a large curved mirror to pick up the faint light from distant stars

Radio telescope
Captures invisible radio waves given out by stars and other objects in space

Space telescope
Controlled by engineers on the ground, it orbits Earth and works 24 hours a day

Blasts from the past

1608
Flemish eyeglass maker Hans Lippershey applies for a patent for his newly invented telescope

1609
Italian scientist Galileo Galilei makes a telescope out of a couple of eyeglass lenses

1668
English scientist Isaac Newton invents a reflecting telescope that uses two mirrors instead of lenses

1838
German astronomer Friedrich Bessel uses a telescope to measure the distance to the star 61 Cygni—the first star distance measured after the Sun

1887
Lick Observatory, Mount Hamilton, California, becomes the first permanent mountaintop observatory

1919
The 8-ft (2.5-m) Hooker Telescope on Mount Wilson, California, shows that most nebulae are distant galaxies, and that the universe is expanding

1962
Ariel 1 is launched. It is the first telescope put into orbit around Earth

Beyond vision

Stars don't just emit light but give off energy in a range of wavelengths. Different types of telescope detect different types of energy, which reveal a whole range of activity in the universe.

gamma ray image
gamma-ray burst

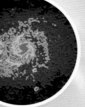

X-ray image
Bullet galaxy cluster

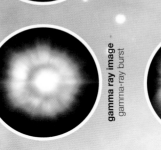

ultraviolet image
the Sun

visible light
Flame nebula

infrared image
Pinwheel galaxy

radio wave image
Whirlpool galaxy

Looking back

Light travels at 186,000 miles (300,000 km) per second, so light from very distant objects takes a long time to reach us.

Light from the Sun takes 8.3 minutes to reach us.

Light from the nearest star after the Sun takes 4.28 years, so we say this star, Proxima Centauri, is 4.28 light-years away.

The Andromeda Galaxy is 2.5 million light-years away from Earth. This means we see the galaxy as it was 2.5 million years ago. We are looking back in time.

What about me?

With the naked eye you can just about make out something 80 miles (130 km) across on the Moon's surface. The best Earth-based telescope can detect objects just over half a mile (1 km) across.

The **largest single radio telescope** is the 1,000-ft (305-m) dish at Arecibo, Puerto Rico.

Built in a hollow in the island's hills, it faces different parts of the sky as the Earth turns.

Working together

Some telescopes work together to produce a more detailed image. The Very Large Array in New Mexico consists of 27 radio dishes, each 82 ft (25 m) across.

Observatories

01: The best observatory sites are high altitude desert regions close to the equator.

02: They are usually about 50 miles (80 km) from a small town—near enough for supplies, but far enough away from light pollution.

03: They are in mountain locations, so clouds won't obscure the view.

04: Telescopes are placed high on the observatory building so they are not affected by the Earth's heat.

Tell me more: Hubble Space Telescope

● **The Hubble Space Telescope was launched into space on April 24, 1990, costing $1.5 billion.**

● The 43.5-ft- (13.2-m-) long telescope orbits Earth every 97 minutes at an altitude of 353 miles (569 km), traveling at 5 miles/sec (8 km/sec).

● **Its main mirror collects light, which is directed to cameras and instruments. The data they record is sent to Earth about twice a day.**

● Hubble's replacement, the James Webb Space Telescope, will launch in 2013. It will be located 930,000 miles (1.5 million km) from Earth.

What is a space probe?

A space probe is the everyday name given to an unmanned spacecraft, and there are several types. Fly-by crafts travel past their target, orbiters fly around it, and landers touch down on it, either standing still or releasing a rover to travel across its surface.

Tell me more: spacecraft anatomy

A probe is a car- or bus-sized robot that is individually designed for a specific purpose. This is *Rosetta*, which will orbit a comet and travel with it as it journeys around the Sun.

Solar panels: Convert the Sun's energy into electrical energy to power the craft. The total wingspan is 105 ft (32 m)

MIRO: The name of the microwave instrument that senses the subsurface temperature of the comet's nucleus

Instruments: *Rosetta* carries 11 instruments. This one tests the comet's environment

Radiator: One in a series of radiators that prevent the craft from overheating

Antenna: The 7 ft- (2.2-m-) wide steerable antenna will send collected data to Earth

Insulation: *Rosetta*'s body is covered with dark thermal insulation to keep its warmth when in the cold outer solar system

Philae: Released by *Rosetta* to land on the comet's nucleus and drill into it for samples

Planetary orbiters

Planet: Mercury
First orbiter: *Messenger*
Date into orbit: March 2011

Planet: Venus
First orbiter: *Venera 9*
Date into orbit: October 1975

Planet: Mars
First orbiter: *Mariner 9*
Date into orbit: November 1971

Planet: Jupiter
First orbiter: *Galileo*
Date into orbit: December 1995

Planet: Saturn
First orbiter: *Cassini*
Date into orbit: July 2004

RECORD BREAKER

The spacecraft *Helios 2* is the **fastest artificial object**. It studied the Sun in the late 1970s, whizzing around it at a staggering 42.72 miles/sec (68.75 km/sec).

I don't believe it!

In 1999, *Mars Climate Orbiter* moved into the wrong orbit around Mars and it was destroyed. The robot wasn't to blame; humans back on Earth had directed it using Imperial measures rather than the metric units it was expecting.

Fly-by tour

The twin *Voyager* craft, which between 1979 and 1989 investigated all four giant planets and 48 of their moons, are together the two most outstanding fly-by missions. They both flew by Jupiter and Saturn; *Voyager 2* continued on past Uranus, then Neptune, and remains the only craft to visit these two planets.

Where are they now?

Unlike astronauts, robotic craft do not have to return home once their work is done. Many "dead" probes still orbit targets or remain where they landed.

- After eight years studying Jupiter and its moons, *Galileo* was deliberately put on a collision course with Jupiter. In September 2003, the craft disintegrated in the planet's atmosphere.

- *Surveyor 3* (pictured) landed on the Moon in 1967. Two years later Charles Conrad and Alan Bean walked from their *Apollo 12* module to *Surveyor 3* and took away a camera, soil scoop, and other pieces of the craft for return to Earth.

- *NEAR-Shoemaker*, the first craft to land on an asteroid, is still there. It was not originally meant to be there, as it was built only to orbit the asteroid.

Sample return

Occasionally, a robotic mission returns from space with a sample of a celestial body, such as:

- ✪ moon soil and rock
- ✪ solar wind particles
- ✪ comet particles

Space debris

An enormous amount of spacecraft debris is orbiting Earth, from whole derelict crafts and pieces of rocket, to flecks of paint.

- There are 17,000 or so chunks floating around larger than 4 in (10 cm).
- More than 200,000 pieces are between ½ in and 4 in (1 and 10 cm).
- Millions of pieces are smaller than ½ in (1 cm).
- Most debris is within 1,250 miles (2,000 km) of the Earth's surface.

RECORD BREAKER

Voyager I is more than 10 billion miles (16 billion km) away—**farther from Earth than any other spacecraft**. What's more, it is more than 100 times farther from the Sun than Earth.

Cassini-Huygens

01: After a seven-year voyage, *Cassini-Huygens*—the most expensive and one of the most sophisticated missions to date—arrived at Saturn in July 2004.

02: It used its 12 instruments to study Saturn and its moons.

03: Smaller *Huygens*, hitching a ride with *Cassini*, parachuted to the surface of Titan, which is Saturn's largest moon.

04: The whole mission cost about $3.26 billion. The United States contributed $2.6 billion, the European Space Agency $500 million, and Italy gave $160 million.

05: A DVD on *Cassini* contains signatures from 616,420 people from 81 nations.

06: The signatures of the astronomers Jean Cassini and Christiaan Huygens, whose names the craft bear, were taken from manuscripts and included in the DVD.

First landers

1959 September
Target: Moon
First lander: *Luna 2*

1970 December
Target: Venus
First lander: *Venera 7*

1976 July
Target: Mars
First lander: *Viking 1*

2001 January
Target: Eros
First lander: *NEAR-Shoemaker*

2005 January
Target: Titan
First lander: *Huygens*

Roving robots

Moving landers—commonly called rovers—have worked on the Moon and Mars.

Lunokhod 1
The first rover to any solar system body, from November 17, 1970, it explored the Moon for about 10 months. Cameras allowed scientists on Earth to direct it.

Sojourner
The first rover to a planet was a microwave-oven-sized buggy. It was carried to Mars by the landing craft *Pathfinder* and worked for almost three months in 1997.

Spirit and Opportunity
Identical crafts that arrived on opposite sides of Mars in January 2004. Five years later, these robot geologists continue to roll across Mars at a speed of 2 in/sec (5 cm/sec).

How many humans have been into space?

About 500 people from nearly 40 nations have traveled into space. However, only three countries have launched astronauts into space—Russia, the United States, and China. The Moon is the farthest destination that any human has been in space.

Where did they go?

⊕ Most astronauts have traveled only as far as a few hundred miles above Earth.

⊕ The first astronauts were launched inside a capsule. They sat in the nose part of a rocket. Once above the ground, the rocket fell away, and the astronauts inside the capsule began their orbit of Earth.

⊕ Today, astronauts are launched by rocket or space shuttle, and the majority are delivered to the International Space Station (ISS).

⊕ Twenty-six astronauts have traveled to the Moon and back, and 12 of these have walked on the surface of the Moon.

Like father, like son

Russian **Alexander Volkov** first flew into space in 1985. His son, **Sergei Volkov**, followed in his footsteps when he flew to the International Space Station in April 2008.

RECORD BREAKER

On March 11, 2001, US astronauts Susan Helms and Jim Voss spent 8 hours 56 minutes working outside the International Space Station, the **longest period of extra vehicular activity** to date.

How to: **fix the Hubble Space Telescope**

01. Get suited up, then pick up the new telescope part and your tools for fixing it in place.

02. With your feet and back attached to the space shuttle's robotic arm, move yourself into position.

03. A second astronaut attached to a tether uses a screwdriver to remove an old part.

04. Use your helmet lights to see as you install the new part. Helmet cameras record every move.

05. Job done. Once you are both back inside the space shuttle, release the telescope into its orbit.

FAST FACTS

How space affects the human body

01: Nearly all astronauts experience space sickness soon after entering space. The symptoms, such as headaches, nausea, and vomiting, last for only a day or two.

02: Body fluids rise to your head and give you a head cold, stuffy nose, and puffy face.

03: Less fluid in the lower body results in a smaller leg circumference called "bird legs."

04: Calcium is lost from the bones and excreted in human waste. Decreased bone density can lead to fractures, but exercise on the treadmill helps to prevent this.

05: The heart shrinks because it does not have to work so hard in space.

06: Dust doesn't settle in space and hangs around in the air. It gets up astronauts' noses and they can sneeze more than 100 times a day!

WHAT'S IN A NAME?

The word **astronaut** comes from the Greek for "star" and "sailor," and it's used to describe all space travelers. Russian space travelers are called **cosmonauts**, and Chinese **taikonauts**.

Five space firsts

Yuri Gagarin
The Russian astronaut was the first human in space. He traveled once around Earth in *Vostok 1* on April 12, 1961, in 108 minutes.

Valentina Tereshkova
On June 16, 1963, the Russian became the first woman in space. She made 48 orbits of Earth in 71 hours.

Neil Armstrong
The first person to walk on the Moon, on July 21, 1969, said "That's one small step for man, one giant leap for mankind."

Alexei Leonov
On March 18, 1965, he became the first person to spacewalk. Attached to a tether, he walked in space for a total of 10 minutes.

Dennis Tito
American Dennis Tito paid $20 million to become the first space tourist on April 28, 2001. In seven days he orbited Earth 128 times.

The planetary geologist Eugene Shoemaker's dream of going to the Moon finally came true after he died, when his **ashes traveled to space** inside the *Lunar Prospector* spacecraft.

Astronauts don't wash dishes; they clean them with wet and dry wipes.

Fun and games

Alan Shepard hit two golf balls on the Moon in 1971 using a club fashioned from lunar tools. His best shot sent the ball 1,200 ft (366 m).

☞ Greg Chamitoff (above) took a chess board to the ISS in 2008 and played long distance against the ground-based control centers. The centers in Houston, Russia, Japan, and Germany took turns making a move.

☞ Since 1985, 50 different toys, including a jump rope, yo-yo, marbles, and a boomerang have been used in space. They are part of a program to educate children about weightlessness.

Astronaut wanted

The European Space Agency enrolls candidates with the following attributes. When they last advertised, in June 2008, 8,413 people applied.

● **Age range:** 27 to 37

● **Height:** 5 ft 1 in–6 ft 2 in (153–190 cm)

● **Language:** Speak and read English

● **Education:** University degree or equivalent in science-based subject

● **Health:** Good, of normal weight, mentally sound

● **Personal qualities:** Good reasoning capability and memory, high motivation, flexibility, emotional stability, manual dexterity

● **Extra assets:** Flying experience, speak Russian

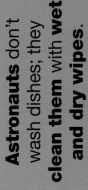

What about me?

Do you want to go into space? For $200,000 you can book a seat on *SpaceShipOne* for a 60-mile (100-km) altitude, edge-of-space trip in 2010, to experience about six minutes of weightlessness.

Tell me more: space missions

Every space mission has an emblem, and these are often produced as embroidered patches. On manned missions the astronauts wear them on their suits. Here are the mission patches from some of the highlights in the story of space exploration. The many space shuttle flights are given STS (Space Transportation System) numbers.

1975 Viking Mission
Two landers are launched to Mars

1988 Buran
Only flight of the Russian space shuttle program

1996 Mars Pathfinder
Launch of robotic rover to Mars

1978 Soyuz 31
The crew on this Russian mission includes the first German astronaut

1989 STS-34
Launch of Galileo probe to Jupiter

1998 STS-95
American John Glenn becomes the oldest astronaut in space at the age of 77

1981 STS-1
First-ever American shuttle mission

1990 STS-31
Launch of Hubble Space Telescope

1999 STS-93
Launch of Chandra X-ray space telescope

1961 Mercury 3
First American astronaut in space

1982 Salyut 7
First French astronaut visits the Russian space station

1990 STS-41
Launch of Ulysses probe to explore the polar regions of the Sun

2000 ISS Expedition 1
Launch of first crew to the International Space Station (ISS)

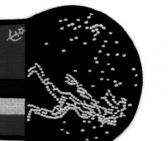

1965 Gemini 4
First American space walk

Space agencies
Astronauts and spacecraft also carry the emblem of their country's space agency.

NASDA: Japanese space agency

ESA: European space agency

MOA: Chinese space agency

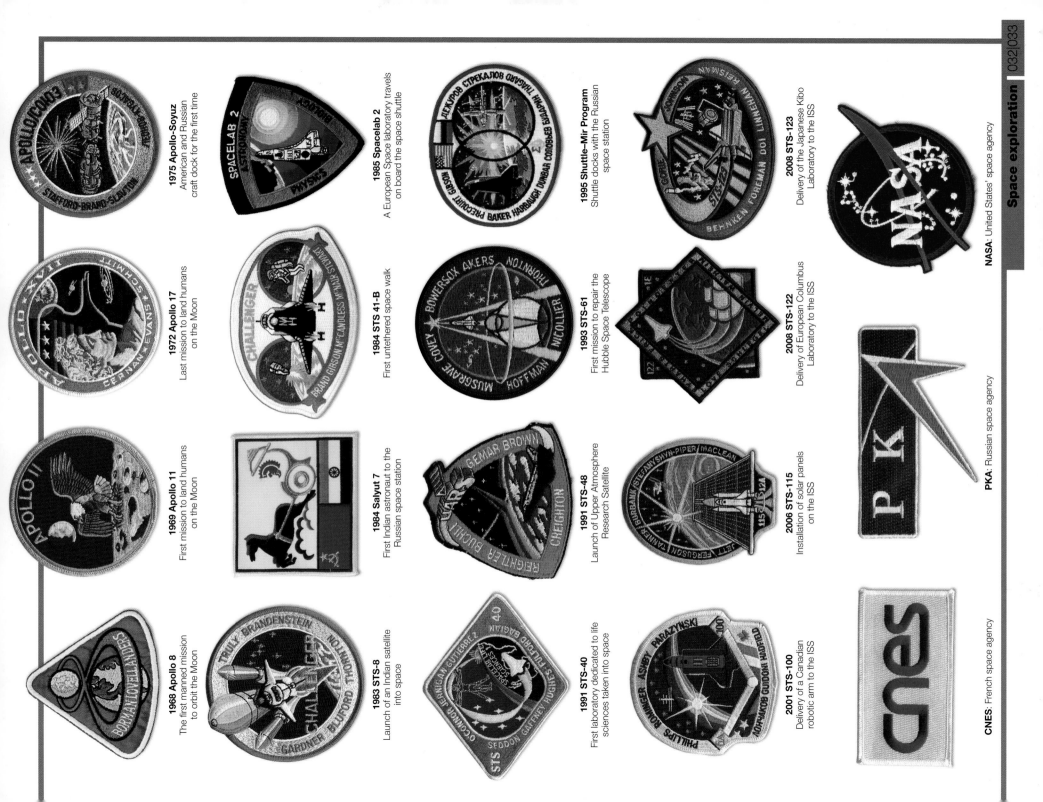

1975 Apollo-Soyuz
American and Russian craft dock for the first time

1985 Spacelab 2
A European Space laboratory travels on board the space shuttle

1995 Shuttle-Mir Program
Shuttle docks with the Russian space station

2008 STS-123
Delivery of the Japanese Kibo Laboratory to the ISS

1972 Apollo 17
Last mission to land humans on the Moon

1984 STS 41-B
First untethered space walk

1993 STS-61
First mission to repair the Hubble Space Telescope

2008 STS-122
Delivery of European Columbus Laboratory to the ISS

1969 Apollo 11
First mission to land humans on the Moon

1984 Salyut 7
First Indian astronaut to the Russian space station

1991 STS-48
Launch of Upper Atmosphere Research Satellite

2006 STS-115
Installation of solar panels on the ISS

1968 Apollo 8
The first manned mission to orbit the Moon

1983 STS-8
Launch of an Indian satellite into space

1991 STS-40
First laboratory dedicated to life sciences taken into space

2001 STS-100
Delivery of a Canadian robotic arm to the ISS

NASA: United States' space agency

PKA: Russian space agency

CNES: French space agency

What do astronauts do on a space station?

A space station is a working laboratory and home for astronauts that permanently orbits the Earth. Astronauts stay for weeks or months at a time and spend their days conducting scientific investigations, such as the effect of space on the human body and growing plants. They also maintain the station.

Blasts from the past

1971
Launch of the first space station, the Russian Salyut 1. Six more Salyuts follow, with Salyut 7 in orbit until 1991

1973
The first US space station, Skylab, is launched

1986
The construction in space of Russian space station Mir begins

1998
The first part of the International Space Station (ISS) is launched

Salyut 1

Skylab

Mir

FAST FACTS

International Space Station (ISS)

01: On November 2, 2000, the first crew moved into the ISS and stayed 138 days.

02: There has been a crew on board ever since—most stay for about six months.

03: There is a crew of three, but this will increase to six as the station grows.

04: The ISS is 356 ft (108.5 m) by 239 ft (72.8 m)—about the size of a football field.

05: The station orbits Earth at 17,500 mph (28,000 kph).

How to: build a space station

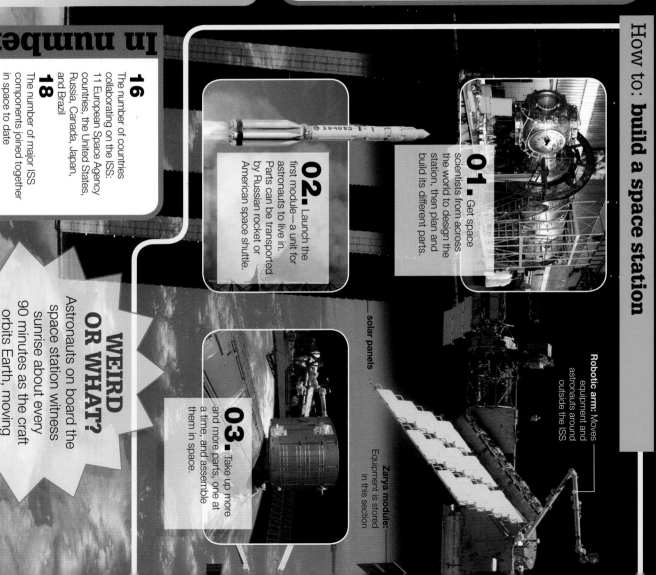

01. Get space scientists from across the world to design the station, then plan and build its different parts.

02. Launch the first module—a unit for astronauts to live in. Parts can be transported by Russian rocket or American space shuttle.

03. Take up more and more parts, one at a time, and assemble them in space.

solar panels

Robotic arm: Moves equipment and astronauts around outside the ISS

Zarya module: Equipment is stored in this section

In numbers

16
The number of countries collaborating on the ISS: 11 European Space Agency countries, the United States, Russia, Canada, Japan, and Brazil

18
The number of major ISS components joined together in space to date

18,000
The number of meals that have been eaten on board the space station

WEIRD OR WHAT?

Astronauts on board the space station witness sunrise about every 90 minutes as the craft orbits Earth, moving between the sunny and dark sides of the planet.

Tell me more: staying in orbit

🌍 A space station is kept in orbit by boosts from visiting craft.

🌍 **Without boosts, the ISS loses about 300 ft (90 m) in altitude each day.**

🌍 If abandoned, initially the station would continue to orbit, though its altitude would decrease.

🌍 **Eventually, it would tumble to Earth, but most of it would break up and burn in the atmosphere.**

🌍 Mir's descent was controlled so that in March 2001, several tons of material plunged into the Pacific Ocean.

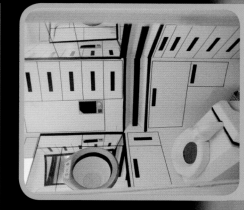

The smallest room

🚽 **For the first ten years there was only one toilet on the ISS, in the Russian-built Zvezda module. Hang on in there!**

🚽 In May 2008, the toilet broke and a new pump had to be rushed from Russia to the US, then delivered by space shuttle. This took two long weeks! While the toilet was out of action the crew used facilities in the Soyuz transport capsule.

🚽 **A second toilet, costing $19 million, was installed in the American side of the ISS in November 2008. Is this the most expensive toilet in the universe?**

🚽 Leg and thigh restraints keep the astronaut in position as fans suck waste away. Urine is collected through hoses attached to personalized funnels.

Day in the life of an astronaut

🔲 Eat breakfast and do housekeeping tasks

🔲 Take blood sample for analysis and check day's schedule with Mission Control

🔲 Do air quality check and start work on allotted experiment

🔲 Exercise for two hours, followed by lunch

🔲 Break, then maintenance and experiment work

🔲 Another hour of exercise

🔲 Finish work tasks, clean up experiments, and check the station's systems

🔲 Evening meal; conference to plan the next day

🔲 Free time, and then bed

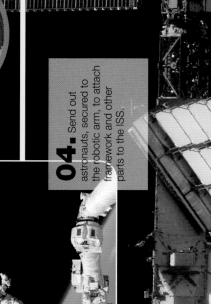

04. Send out astronauts, secured to the robotic arm, to attach framework and other parts to the ISS.

05. Add laboratory modules, where the astronauts can work, and solar panels to power the station.

06. Once the station is complete you'll need to service it regularly to keep things working smoothly.

Radiators: These panels help control the temperature inside the space station

Zvezda module: Here the crew eat and sleep

What about me?

The ISS orbits Earth more than 15 times a day, and so regularly passes over where you live at a height of about 240 miles (390 km).

Russian cosmonaut **Valeri Poliakov** lived on board Mir for a record-breaking 437.7 days between January 1994 and March 1995.

Earth

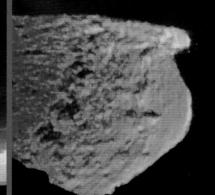
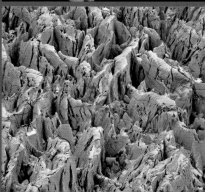

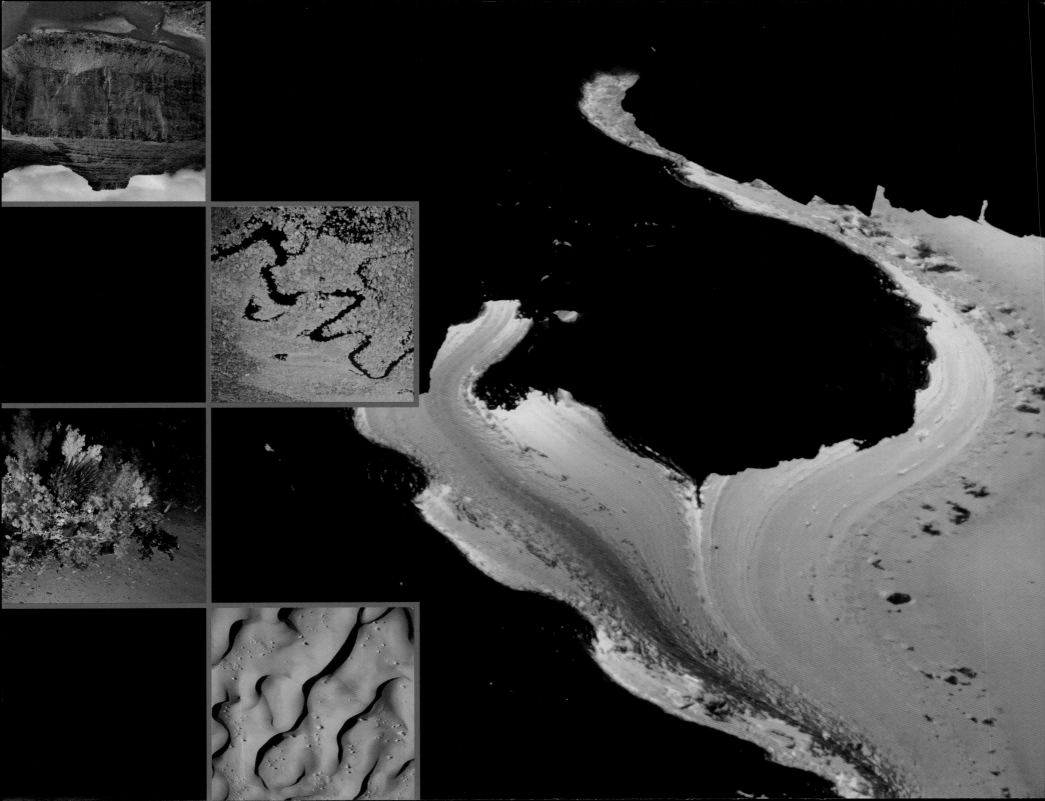

Do the continents really move?

Yes, the continents and oceans are constantly moving on the Earth's crust. More than 200 million years ago, the continents were joined in one huge landmass, but over millions of years this drifted and separated into the seven main continents we know today: Asia, Africa, Europe, Australia, Antarctica, North America, and South America.

Plates move between 1–8 in (2–20 cm) per year—the rate at which fingernails grow.

Tell me more: inside the Earth

Crust: There are two types—continental crust (land) and the thinner oceanic crust (seafloor)

Mantle: A thick layer of rock that begins between 3-45 miles (5-70 km) below the surface. Heat rising from the core keeps the mantle moving slowly

Outer core: At a depth of 3,200 miles (5,150 km), it is made of molten iron with a temperature in excess of 7,200°F (3,980°C)

Inner core: In the solid iron core the temperature reaches 8,500°F (4.700°C)

How to: assemble the Earth

01. Take a large rocky ball as the base. Watch out, since the surface is slowly moving, so when you place the pieces on it they won't stay still.

02. Sort out your crust. There are seven big pieces, and lots and lots of really fiddly small pieces. It will help if you know your geography!

- Australian plate
- Cocos plate
- Scotia plate
- North American plate
- Nazca plate
- Indian plate
- Pacific plate
- South American plate
- Philippine plate
- Eurasian plate
- Arabian plate
- Antarctic plate
- Caribbean plate

Landmass

The proportion of land per continent is:

- **Asia** 30 percent
- **Africa** 20 percent
- **North America** 16 percent
- **South America** 12 percent
- **Antarctica** 9 percent
- **Europe** 7 percent
- **Australia** 6 percent

What's in a name?

Africa comes from the Latin name of the ancient Roman colony in northern Africa.

Australia comes from the Latin meaning "southern," since 18th-century explorers hoped to find a giant landmass in the southern oceans.

Europe may be named after princess Europa, who appears in Ancient Greek mythology.

Antarctica comes from the Ancient Greek word *antarktikos*, which means "opposite of the north."

Asia is first mentioned by the Greek historian Herodotus, writing about 440 BCE, who said it was named after the Lydian prince Asias. The word may have originally meant "land of the sunrise."

African plate

Slide past
Where plates slide past one another, you get what is called a transform fault. They don't slide past smoothly and so you get earthquakes.

Converge
At a convergent boundary two plates move together, forming mountain ranges.

03. Assemble the pieces around the ball. Be careful to fit the edges of the plates correctly—there are three main types of boundary.

Europe is only a continent for political reasons—geographically, it should be part of Asia.

Diverge
You get a divergent boundary when two plates move apart. The huge gaps form the world's oceans.

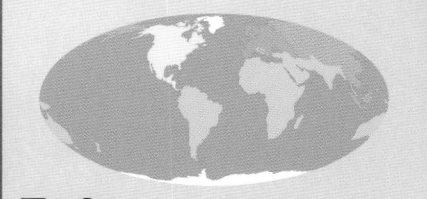

200 million years ago
Many of the continents are locked together in a landmass named Pangaea.

100 million years ago
Divergent plates begin to open up the Atlantic Ocean. South America drifts west, Antarctica heads for the South Pole, and India creeps toward Asia.

Today
India is in place after colliding with the Eurasian mainland. Greenland separates from North America, which has a land bridge with South America. Australia drifts in the Pacific Ocean.

Violent Earth

Exciting new imaging techniques mean that we can see where the continents are crashing into each other, ripping apart, and where new land is forming.

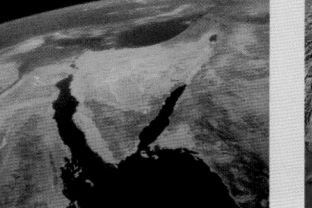

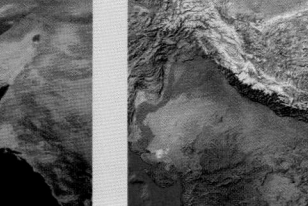

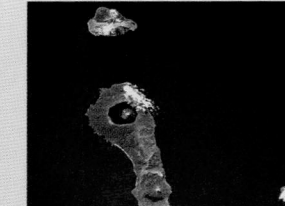

Pulling the ocean apart
Magma rising up into the gap created as the African plate moves east has formed a ridge of undersea mountains down the middle of the Atlantic Ocean.

Splitting from Africa
The Red Sea marks the split where Arabia is breaking away from Africa; it is growing wider all the time.

Crashing into Asia
The mountains of the Himalayas are the youngest mountains on Earth and are still rising as India crashes into the Eurasian plate.

Volcanic hotspot
The islands of Hawaii formed over a "hotspot" in the mantle. Unlike many volcanoes, those over hotspots form chains and are not on plate margins.

I don't believe it!

The deeper down inside the Earth a tunnel goes, the hotter it becomes. The deepest gold mines in South Africa have to be cooled down artificially so that people are able to work in them.

Looking through the **Earth's crust**

This cross-section through the crust along the equator shows how the continents fit together and the rises and falls of Earth's surface.

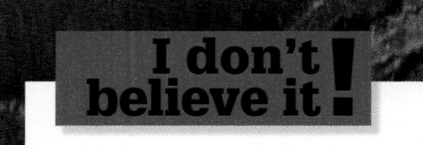

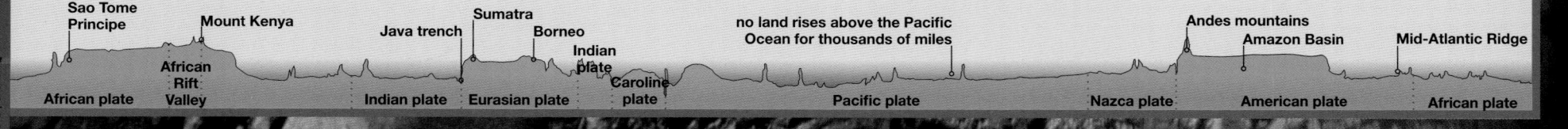

Sao Tome Principe | Mount Kenya | Java trench | Sumatra | Borneo | Indian plate | no land rises above the Pacific Ocean for thousands of miles | Andes mountains | Amazon Basin | Mid-Atlantic Ridge

African plate | African Rift Valley | Indian plate | Eurasian plate | Caroline plate | Pacific plate | Nazca plate | American plate | African plate

How many oceans are there?

Earth is not nicknamed the "Blue Planet" for nothing—no other known planet is as watery. We divide this huge body of water into the Pacific, Atlantic, Indian, Arctic, and Southern oceans, but, in reality, they are all connected as one vast ocean.

The five oceans

Pacific: 96.6 million sq miles (155.6 million sq km)

Pacific Ocean

Atlantic: 51.2 million sq miles (82.4 million sq km)

Atlantic Ocean

Indian: 45.7 million sq miles (73.6 million sq km)

Indian Ocean

Southern: 12.6 million sq miles (20.3 million sq km)

Southern Ocean

Arctic: 8.7 million sq miles (14.1 million sq km)

Arctic Ocean

Tell me more: ocean water

≈ Salt
On average, each 2 pints (1 liter) of water contains about 1¼ oz (35 g) of salt, although shallow, warmer seas are usually saltier.

≈ Light

Sunlight allows plants to grow underwater to a depth of about 650 ft (200 m). Below this, the waters get darker the deeper you get and plants cannot grow.

≈ Pressure

The deeper you go in the sea, the more pressure, or squeezing force, there is. The polystyrene cup on the right was the same size as the one on the left until attached to the outside of a deep-sea submersible and crushed by pressure.

≈ Temperature
The surface temperature of tropical seas is about 77°F (25°C), and in most other seas about 62°F (17°C) in summer and 50°F (10°C) in winter. The temperature at the bottom of the ocean is 36°F (2°C).

≈ Sound
Sound travels at a speed of 5,022 ft (1,531 m) per second under water—four times faster than it does in the air.

Five largest seas

01: South China Sea
1,848,300 sq miles (2,974,600 sq km)

02: Caribbean Sea
1,563,300 sq miles (2,515,900 sq km)

03: Mediterranean Sea
1,559,600 sq miles (2,510,000 sq km)

04: Bering Sea
1,404,900 sq miles (2,261,100 sq km)

05: Gulf of Mexico
936,700 sq miles (1,507,600 sq km)

The **oceans affect climate,** since water warms more slowly than land and cools more slowly than land, so islands and the coasts of continents have cooler summers and warmer winters than inland areas.

I don't believe it!
An underwater mailbox, where divers can send special waterproof postcards, lies 33 ft (10 m) below the waves in Susami Bay, Japan. It's an official mailbox and is emptied every day.

How to: find lunch in the ocean

01. If you're feeling hungry, head for where currents lift nutrients from the ocean floor toward the surface.

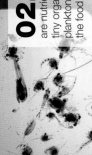

02. Where there are nutrients you'll find tiny organisms called plankton, the first link in the food chain.

03. Wherever you find plankton, small fish such as sardines swarm to feed off them. Enjoy the feast!

04. A word of warning—large predators will be attracted by the fish, so make sure you don't end up as their lunch!

Ocean zones

Our oceans are divided into different zones, depending on their depth. From the sunlit zone to the deepest depths, a variety of marine life can be found.

Sunlit zone
Most sea animals live near the surface where there is lots of light. Fish live off plankton (microscopic plants and animals) and in turn they are eaten by larger predators.

Twilight zone
From 500 ft (150 m) to 3,300 ft (1,000 m) is known as the twilight zone. Many creatures living here produce their own light and glow, either to attract prey or scare predators.

Deep ocean
Even at the greatest depths, 6 miles (10 km) below the surface, strange animals lurk on the dark seafloor waiting for dead things to fall from the water above.

WHAT'S IN A NAME?

The word "ocean" comes from Oceanus, who in Greek mythology was the son of Uranus, god of the sky, and Gaea, goddess of the Earth. Oceanus was also the river they believed surrounded the flat Earth.

FAST FACTS

Seas

01: Seas have specific features and form part of a larger ocean.

02: They are shallower than oceans, with no major currents flowing through them.

03: Seas have salt water, but names can be confusing. One of the world's saltiest seas, the Dead Sea in Israel, is actually a lake because it is not connected to an ocean.

Extreme ocean

The tallest mountain on Earth is Mauna Kea, a volcano in Hawaii. At 33,480 ft (10,205 m), it is much taller than Mount Everest but most of it is under water.

The ocean's deepest point is the Challenger Deep in the Mariana Trench, in the Pacific, at a depth of 36,200 ft (11,034 m).

In the deepest ocean trenches, springs of hot water, called black smokers (pictured), gush clouds of chemicals up to 750°F (400°C) from the seabed.

In numbers

-40°F
(-40°C) The average winter temperature of the Arctic Ocean

70%
The percentage of the Earth's surface covered by oceans and seas

97%
The percentage of the world's water in the oceans—2 percent is ice and 1 percent is fresh water or water vapor in the atmosphere

30,000
The number of islands in the Pacific Ocean. Some are the peaks of underwater volcanoes

How do mountains grow?

Where the plates of Earth's crust crash into each other, land is pushed upward, forming mountains. The Himalayas are the tallest mountains on Earth, and the youngest. They formed over the last 145 million years, as India crashed into Asia. Mountains are also formed when volcanoes erupt and molten rock builds up into steep mounds.

I don't believe it!

From the ground, mountains make the Earth's surface look very bumpy, but if the Earth were reduced to the size of a 3 ft (1 m) diameter ball, Mount Everest would be a pimple no more than 0.03 in (0.69 mm) high!

WHAT'S IN A NAME?

There's no official **definition of a mountain**, though in most places mountains are more than 2,000 ft (600 m) high. Some so-called mountains may just be hills, but a mountain should be steep and have an obvious summit.

Four famous peaks

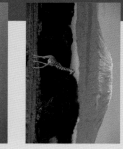

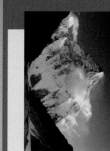

Kilimanjaro, Tanzania
At 19,340 ft (5,895 m), this extinct volcano is the tallest mountain that is not part of a mountain range.

Mount Fuji, Japan
Each year, more than 200,000 people climb 12,388 ft (3,776 m) to the top of the tallest mountain in Japan, also a sacred site.

Matterhorn, Switzerland
At 14,692 ft (4,478 m) high, it's not the tallest mountain in the Alps, but has a classic pyramid-shaped peak.

K2, Pakistan and China
The world's second highest mountain, at 28,253 ft (8,611 m), is said to be the trickiest mountain to climb.

The tallest mountains in every continent

Asia
► Mount Everest, Nepal and China
29,028 ft (8,848 m)

South America
► Aconcagua, Argentina
22,834 ft (6,960 m)

North America
► Mount McKinley, Alaska
20,320 ft (6,194 m)

Africa
► Mount Kilimanjaro, Tanzania
19,340 ft (5,895 m)

Europe
► Mount El'brus, Russia
18,510 ft (5,642 m)

Antarctica
► Vinson Massif
16,066 ft (4,897 m)

Australasia
► Puncak Jaya, New Guinea
16,535 ft (5,040 m)

FAST FACTS

Avalanches

01: You rarely get avalanches (masses of snow rushing down mountains) where the slope is less than 25 degrees.

02: Slab avalanches are the most deadly and occur when a frozen slab of ice on the surface of the snow breaks off.

03: When snow gets heavy because it's saturated with water you get what's known as an isothermal avalanche.

04: As an avalanche shoots down the slope it collects more snow. If it picks up lots of air with the snow it becomes what's called a powder snow avalanche. These are the largest avalanches and can reach speeds of 200 mph (300 kph).

Major mountain ranges

The world's longest mountain ranges usually follow the edges of the Earth's plates.

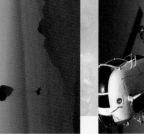

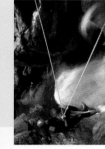

Aleutian Range
1,650 miles (2,650 km)

Rocky Mountains
3,000 miles (4,800 km)

Andes
4,500 miles (7,200 km)

Himalayas
2,400 miles (3,800 km)

Tien Shan
1,400 miles (2,250 km)

Central New Guinea Range
1,250 miles (2,000 km)

West Sumatran-Javan Range
1,800 miles (2,900 km)

Brazilian Atlantic Coast Range
2,000 miles (3,000 km)

Great Dividing Range
2,250 miles (3,600 km)

RECORD BREAKER

The **tallest mountain** on Earth is Mauna Kea in Hawaii, which rises 33,480 ft (10,205 m) from its base on the seabed to its summit.

The **longest mountain range** on Earth is the mid-Atlantic ridge, which runs for nearly 10,000 miles (16,000 km) below the Atlantic Ocean.

Five crazy **mountain sports**

Paragliding
Leap off a mountain harnessed to a fabric wing and soar down on the wind—it's probably the nearest you can get to flying.

Heliskiing
For the ultimate off-trail skiing, take a helicopter to the top of an isolated peak, jump off, and head downhill.

Canyoning
To scramble down a mountain along the path of a river you need to be a confident climber and swimmer.

Ice climbing
This is the sport of hacking your way up a steep wall of ice, such as a mountain icefall or frozen waterfall, using ice axes.

Climbing
There are many ways up a mountain, and some people choose the route up vertical faces and overhanging rocks.

Tell me more: **mountain zones**

As you climb up a mountain the average air temperature drops by about 1.8°F (1°C) for every 650 ft (200 m). There is also less oxygen in the air the higher you go. As a result, mountains can be divided into distinct habitat zones.

The top: High mountain peaks are harsh environments, of either bare rock or snow, where little, if anything, will grow.

High altitude: Above the tree line only specially adapted mountain species, such as Alpine ibex, can survive.

Mid altitude: Foothills are often covered by forests, but these end at a "tree line," beyond which it is too cold and dry for trees to grow.

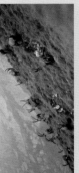

01: Will I make the top?

Of the hundreds of people who attempt to climb Everest each year, only about 30 percent succeed. The biggest problem is bad weather, which can trap climbers at Base Camp or force them to turn back.

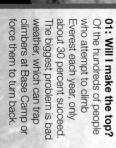

02: Do I need to be fit?

Yes, the route to the summit at 29,028 ft (8,848 m) is over rock, snow, and ice. However, age is no barrier. The youngest to make it was Temba Tsheri, 15; the oldest was Bahadur Sherchan, 76, and both were from Nepal.

03: How long will it take?

It's impossible to predict, but, from Base Camp, four days up and four days down is reasonable. The fastest ascent was by Italian Hans Kammerlander, who got to the top in 16 hours and 45 minutes in 1996.

04: What should I take?

What you take up, you must bring down, so take only the bare essentials. There's an estimated 50 tons of trash on Mount Everest, made up of equipment and supplies left behind—much of it at Base Camp.

05: Will it be cold?

The temperature at the summit averages -33°F (-36°C), but can drop as low as -76°F (-60°C). This can freeze the skin, causing frostbite. Toes are the first to suffer, so warm socks are essential.

06: What is snow blindness?

This is when snow reflects the Sun's rays and it burns the back of the eyes so you can't see. Sun goggles are essential. They absorb the harmful UV rays.

07: What is altitude sickness?

Above 12,000 ft (3,660 m), oxygen levels drop by 40 percent and most climbers gasp for breath. To avoid serious symptoms they need to breathe oxygen from cylinders.

08: Is the climb risky?

Yes, to date, the mountain has claimed 210 lives. Photographer and climber Bruce Herrod fell and died on Everest in 1996. The picture of him above, was developed from his camera, found a year later.

09: What's the Death Zone?

This is the region above 26,500 ft (8,000 m), where there is only half the normal level of oxygen. Even with an oxygen supply, the body starts to shut down and the slightest exertion takes tremendous effort.

10: What's at the top?

From the top of the world you get a unique view over the Himalayas of Tibet, India, and Nepal. You can see for more than 100 miles (160 km) and even make out the curvature of the Earth's surface.

What happens when a volcano erupts?

A volcano erupts when hot molten rock from deep inside the Earth bursts out of the ground. Rivers of liquid rock, called lava, flow down the side of the volcano burning trees, houses, and anything else in their paths. An exploding volcano may also fling out ash, mud, and poisonous gases. Volcanoes are not just destructive, however, and often create new mountains and islands.

Tell me more: Kilauea volcano, Hawaii

2,200°F
(1,200°C) The top temperature of the rivers of basalt lava that flow from Hawaiian volcanoes—12 times hotter than a boiling kettle

200
The number of megatons of energy released when Krakatoa erupted in 1883—the same as 15,000 nuclear bombs

550
The number of volcanoes that have erupted on Earth's surface since records began—about 60 are active each year

90%
The percentage of volcanoes that lie along the Ring of Fire, a circle of volcanic activity around the edge of the Pacific Ocean, at the boundaries of the Earth's plates

Clouds of gas: Water vapor, carbon dioxide, and sulfur dioxide form clouds above the eruption

Inside a volcano

Beneath an active volcano lies a chamber of hot molten rock, called magma. The magma is less dense than the solid rock around it, so rises to the surface through cracks or fissures and a main outlet, called a vent. Magma that contains a lot of dissolved gases will explode at the surface, throwing ash and rocks, known as bombs, into the air. Sometimes, burning gas and ash, known as a pyroclastic flow, pour down the sides. Magma that contains very little gas flows more slowly.

Burning river: Lava flows downhill at speeds of up to 60 mph (100 kph)

Magma: Some of the molten rock hurled into the air forms "bombs"

Crater: Lava, cinders, and volcanic ash build a rocky but fragile ridge around the vent

spreading ash cloud

volcanic bombs

pyroclastic flow

erupting volcanic vent

Red hot: Flowing lava has a temperature of about 1,800°F (1,000°C)

WHAT'S IN A NAME?

Volcanoes are named after **Vulcan**, the Roman god of fire and metalwork, who was said to have had his workshop under Mount Vulcano, an island off the north coast of Sicily.

Cooling surface: A wrinkled or rough skin forms as lava cools

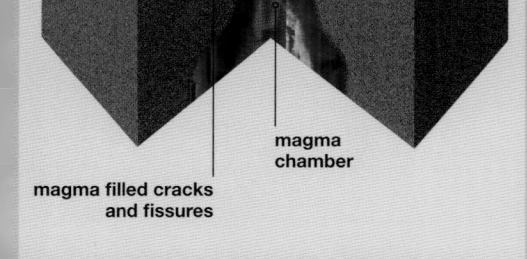

magma filled cracks
and fissures

magma
chamber

Six types of eruption

Hawaiian In this quiet, slow type of eruption, lava streams out of the vent and sometimes collects in great lakes.

Strombolian An eruption with frequent but small explosions releasing gas and sending lumps of lava whirling through the air.

Vulcanian A violent explosion where gas escapes from beneath a crust of lava and forms a dense white cloud.

Vesuvian A huge cloud, thick with ash and gas shoots violently into the air and rises high over the volcano.

Plinian The most powerful type of eruption, since sticky lava explodes violently. Large Plinian eruptions, like that at Mount St. Helens, Washington, in 1980 (pictured) often have pyroclastic flows.

Peléan Highly destructive eruptions where a high-speed avalanche of gas, dust, ash, and burning lava fragments sweeps down the sides of the volcano.

How to: live with an active volcano

01. Wear hard hats. Children living near Sakurajima volcano in Japan, must wear them to school to protect against flying debris.

02. Don't get too settled. If you live next to Mount Etna in Sicily, you need to be ready to evacuate.

03. Drive carefully. Lava flows on Hawaii don't obey road signs, and might appear around any corner.

04. Wear a mask. After the eruption of Merapi in Indonesia the air was filled with ash for days.

Four reasons to like volcanoes

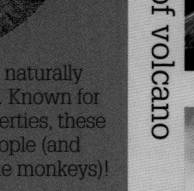

01: Hot springs occur naturally around volcanoes. Known for their healing properties, these are enjoyed by people (and Japanese macaque monkeys)!

02: Geothermal power plants tap the energy from hot magma under the ground.

03: The mineral-rich ash that falls on the soil around volcanoes is ideal for growing crops.

04: Some volcanoes, such as Mount Fuji in Japan and Mount Kilimanjaro in Tanzania, have become sacred sites.

Types of volcano

Cinder cone
These are the smallest but most common type of volcano, such as Parícutin, Mexico, and are made up of loose volcanic rock from repeated eruptions.

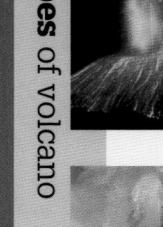

Shield volcano
Runny lava spreads out as it flows from the volcano and, over time, layers of lava build to form a vast low mound, seen here at Puu Oo in Hawaii.

Stratovolcano
Large steep mountains, like Mount Fuji in Japan, are formed from layers of ash and lava from repeated eruptions.

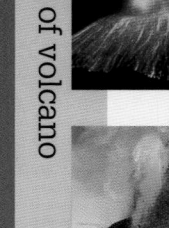

Supervolcano
These vast volcanoes can cause a long-lasting change in weather, threaten the extinction of species, and cover huge areas with lava and ash.

Submarine volcano
Where volcanoes erupt beneath the seabed, the weight of water prevents big explosions, and pillow lava may form, seen here off the coast of Hawaii.

Blasts from the past

c. 1630 BCE
An eruption blows apart the island of Santorini, Greece, creating a tsunami (giant wave) that may be the origin of the legend of the submerged city of Atlantis.

79 BCE
When Mount Vesuvius in Italy erupts, inhabitants of Pompeii are buried by a cloud of cinder and ash (pictured).

1783 CE
Deadly gases at the eruption of Laki, Iceland, poison 200,000 animals, and cause a famine that kills 9,000 people.

1792
When part of Mount Unzen in Japan collapses, it causes a tsunami that kills more than 14,300.

1815
The eruption of Tambora, Indonesia, is the biggest for 1,000 years and kills more than 90,000 people

1883
Krakatoa island, Indonesia, explodes, unleashing a tsunami that kills 36,000 and a cloud of dust that lowers the world's temperature by 1.8°F (1°C)

1985
Some 23,000 people die in Colombia when the eruption of the Ruiz volcano causes massive mudflows, which swamp the town of Armero, 45 miles (70 km) away

I don't believe it!

One day in 1943, a farmer in Mexico was walking through his cornfield when he noticed a strange crack. It turned out to be an erupting volcano, now known as Parícutin. Within a year the volcano was 1,102 ft (336 m) high, and it continued to grow for a decade.

Why does the Earth quake!

The surface of the Earth is like a massive jigsaw puzzle made up of huge rocky pieces called tectonic plates. The pieces of this puzzle are constantly moving around very slowly, but with immense force. If they slide past or crash into each other the Earth shakes and quakes.

How to: survive an earthquake

In earthquake zones, such as California and Japan, schoolchildren regularly practice an earthquake drill. In California, children are taught to "Duck, Cover, and Hold."

01. As soon as you feel the earth shaking, duck or drop down to the floor.

02. Take cover under a desk or table and protect your head and neck with your arms.

03. Hold onto the desk, table, or furniture and move with it, if necessary. Remember to stay put until the shaking stops.

Warning signs?

Some people claim that you can predict an earthquake by spotting changes in some animals' behavior in the days before an earthquake.

- **Hens stop laying eggs**
- Bees leave their hives
- **Rats, weasels, and centipedes leave their homes in large numbers**
- Dogs bark or whine excessively
- **Flamingos abandon their low-lying breeding grounds**
- Toads migrate en-masse to safer ground

Most earthquakes occur at **depths of less than 50 miles** (80 km) below the Earth's surface.

Cracks in the Earth

In some places you can clearly see the cracks, called faults, at the edges of the Earth's plates.

Thingvellir Rift, Iceland
These exposed fault lines show the rift that lies on the boundary separating the American and Eurasian plates.

San Andreas Fault, California
This is a strike-slip fault, which indicates that the rocks move sideways and in opposite directions.

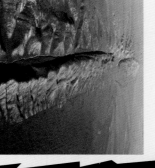

Great Alpine Fault, New Zealand
This fault line runs almost the entire length of New Zealand's South Island and is visible from space.

Moonquake
It's not only the Earth that's shaking—there are quakes on the Moon, too. These "**moonquakes**" happen less often and are of smaller magnitude than those on Earth.

Deadliest earthquakes

- **Tangshan, China**
Date: July 28, 1976
People killed: 830,000+

- **Kansu, China**
Date: December 16, 1920
People killed: 180,000+

- **Toyko-Yokihama, Japan**
Date: September 1, 1923
People killed: 140,000+

- **Gulf of Chihli, China**
Date: September 27, 1290
People killed: 100,000+

- **Catania, Sicily, and Naples, Italy**
Date: January 11, 1693
People killed: 60,000+ (Catania) and 93,000+ (Naples)

- **Shemakha, Azerbaijan**
Date: November 25, 1667
People killed: 80,000+

- **Messina, Italy**
Date: December 28, 1908
People killed: 75,000+

- **Kansu, China**
Date: December 26, 1932
People killed: 70,000+

Date: January 23, 1556
People killed: 242,000+

Tsunami

If an earthquake happens under water it can cause a series of **powerful and destructive ocean waves**. An earthquake in the Indian Ocean on December 24, 2004, triggered a series of tsunamis that killed more than 225,000 people in 11 countries.

Part of Indonesia's coastline before and after the 2004 tsunami

High-rise buildings in California and Japan must be able to **withstand severe earthquakes.** Foundations are equipped with mechanical shock absorbers, which act like the shock absorbers used in cars.

Quake measures

Scientists measure earthquakes in two different ways—by its **magnitude** or its **intensity.** Magnitude means the power of the shock waves, and it's usually measured on the **Richter scale.** The **Modifed Mercalli Intensity scale** measures the effects of an earthquake.

Most powerful earthquakes

- Chile
  Date: **May 22, 1960**
  Richter measure: **9.5**
- Prince William Sound, Alaska
  Date: **March 28, 1964**
  Richter measure: **9.2**
- Indian Ocean
  Date: **December 26, 2004**
  Richter measure: **9.1**
- Andreanof Islands, Aleutian Islands
  Date: **March 9, 1957**
  Richter measure: **9.1**
- Kamchtka, Russia
  Date: **November 4, 1952**
  Richter measure: **9.0**

The Richter scale

magnitude	description	effects
less than 2	micro	not felt
2–2.9	minor	generally not felt, but recorded
3–3.9	minor	often felt, but damage rare
4–4.9	light	noticeable shaking of indoor items, rattling noises
5–5.9	moderate	can cause damage to poorly constructed buildings over small areas. At most, slight damage to well-designed buildings
6–6.9	strong	can be destructive in areas up to 100 miles (160 km) across
7–7.9	major	can cause damage over larger areas
8–8.9	great	can cause serious damage in areas several miles across
9–9.9	great	devastating in areas several thousand miles across
10+	epic	never recorded

Five famous **earthquakes**

1755 Lisbon, Portugal
One of the worst earthquakes in history was followed by a tsunami and many fires.

1906 San Francisco, California
Fires following this massive quake left 3,000 dead and 20,000 homeless.

1964 Alaska
This powerful quake lasted nearly five minutes and was followed by a tsunami.

1995 Kobe, Japan
Lasting barely 20 seconds, this quake killed 6,400 people and caused $200 billion in damage.

2003 Bam, Iran
The city's many mud-brick buildings were destroyed by this massive earthquake.

I don't believe it !

According to the United States Geological Survey, there are more than 3 million earthquakes every year. That's about 8,000 a day, or one every 11 seconds! Most of these are too weak to be noticed.

Could the Amazon River ever run dry?

No. The water that flows down the Amazon River in South America fell as snow or rain in a vast area known as a drainage basin. This drainage basin is the largest in the world and includes eight countries, covering an area three-quarters the size of the United States.

FAST FACTS

Amazon River

01: The water flows at an average speed of 1.5 mph (2.4 kph).

02: The mouth of the river is more than 200 miles (320 km) long.

03: Where the river meets the sea, it discharges 200 billion gallons (770 billion liters) of water an hour. This is enough to fill almost two million bathtubs every second.

04: If you were 60 miles (100 km) from the mouth of the Amazon, way out in the Atlantic Ocean, you could still scoop a pan of fresh Amazon water.

05: There are about 2,500 species of fish in the Amazon—that's more than there are in the Atlantic Ocean.

06: There are no bridges over the Amazon.

I don't believe it!

In winter, all 1,060 miles (1,705 km) of the MacKenzie River—Canada's longest—freezes.

RECORD BREAKER

The world's **shortest river** is the Rose River in Montana. It is just 201 ft (61 m) long.

Nile knowledge

▶ The Nile River in north Africa has two sources. The longer White Nile flows from Lake Victoria in east Africa. It is joined at Khartoum, Egypt, by the Blue Nile, which has its source in the highlands of Ethiopia.

▶ Downstream, beyond Khartoum, the White Nile contributes just 16 percent of the volume of the river's water, and the Blue Nile contributes the rest.

▶ The Nile River floods every year, when heavy summer rain and melting snow in the mountains of Ethiopia swell the river.

▶ Only 22 percent of the Nile is in Egypt.

Top five longest rivers in the world

Nile (Africa)
4,160 miles (6,695 km)

Amazon (South America)
4,007 miles (6,448 km)

Yangtze (Asia)
3,964 miles (6,378 km)

Mississippi/Missouri (North America) 3,870 miles (6,228 km)

Ob (Asia)
3,460 miles (5,570 km)

Great lakes

Lake Titicaca (Peru and Bolivia)
Sitting on the edge of the Andes, Titicaca is 120 miles (195 km) long and about 50 miles (80 km) wide. Reeds that grow in its marshes are used to make boats.

Great Salt Lake (Utah)
The water in this vast salt lake is about five times saltier than seawater. It has three major tributaries that fill the lake with minerals, and the rocky shores are covered with salt crystals.

Lake Manyara (Tanzania)
The water is inhabited by hippopotamuses, and the surrounding national park protects elephants and is famous for tree-climbing lions. The groundwater in the lake is saturated with minerals derived from volcanic rock.

Lake Eyre (Australia)
This salt lake is the lowest point on the Australian continent. It receives water from streams and is fed by erratic rainfall. It is thought to have once dried out completely, but has reached its present size following exceptionally heavy rain at the end of the 20th century.

Top five largest lakes

01: Caspian Sea
central Asia
143,000 sq miles
(371,000 sq km)

02: Michigan/Huron
Canada/United States
45,342 sq miles
(117,436 sq km)

03: Superior
Canada/United States
31,700 sq miles
(82,103 sq km)

04: Victoria
east Africa
26,828 sq miles
(69,485 sq km)

05: Tanganyika
central-east Africa
12,700 sq miles
(32,893 sq km)

The **Caspian Sea** lake in central Asia was **once** cut off from **a sea**. It was cut off from the Mediterranean Sea when sea levels dropped during the last Ice Age and is now **landlocked**. Unlike most lakes, it contains salty seawater.

FAST FACTS

Dams

01: About 15 percent of the world's river water is held back by dams built to control flooding and generate hydroelectric power.

02: Almost one-fifth of the world's electricity is supplied by dams.

03: The Rogun Dam in Tajikistan is the highest in the world. At 1,099 ft (335 m), it is taller than the Statue of Liberty.

04: The largest dam in the world will be the Three Gorges Dam across the Yangtze River, China. It should be fully operational in 2011 and will be 7,661 ft (2,335 m) long and 331 ft (101 m) high.

Lake Baikal in Russia is the **deepest lake in the world** and dips to 5,712 ft (1,741 m) in parts. It is deep enough to **stack five Eiffel Towers** and still not break the surface.

River features

Gorge
The Colorado River carved the steep-sided Grand Canyon. This gorge stretches more than 220 miles (350 km) and measures 18 miles (29 km) at it widest point.

Waterfall
The waterfall with the longest single drop is Angel Falls on the Carrao River, Venezuela. The water plunges 3,212 ft (979 m), with much of the water turning into mist as it falls.

Meander
The snaking pattern of a river forms when the moving water erodes on the outer of bends and deposits on the inner. This widens the valley, creating a looping, S-shaped curve in the river.

Delta
This is a flat plain where a river meets the sea. The world's largest is where the Ganges, Brahmaputra, and Meghna rivers of India and Bangladesh empty into the Bay of Bengal.

River cities

Many great cities lie on rivers. Can you match the rivers with the right city? Watch out, one river passes through two major cities. You'll find the answers below.

CITY	RIVER
St. Petersburg, Russia	Nile
Montreal, Canada	Tigris
Rome, Italy	Danube
Paris, France	Plate River
Shanghai, China	St. Lawrence
Vienna, Austria	Tiber
New York City	Neva
Ho Chi Minh City, Vietnam	Huangpu
Baghdad, Iraq	Vistula
Alexandria, Egypt	Seine
Warsaw, Poland	Saigon
Budapest, Hungary	Hudson
Buenos Aires, Argentina	

ANSWERS: Nile—Alexandria, Tigris—Baghdad, Danube—Budapest and Vienna, Plate River—Buenos Aires, St. Lawrence—Montreal, Tiber—Rome, Neva—St. Petersburg, Huangpu—Shanghai, Vistula—Warsaw, Seine—Paris, Saigon—Ho Chi Minh City, Hudson—New York City

How much ice is there on Earth?

About one-tenth of the Earth's land surface is covered in ice. Built up over thousands of years, most ice occurs in thick ice sheets that cap the land at the North and South poles. Ice also tops the peaks of high mountains, and rivers of ice called glaciers gouge deep valleys in polar and mountain regions.

Tell me more: icebergs

❋ Icebergs form, or "calve," when huge chunks of ice from glaciers and ice caps break off and fall into the ocean.

❋ Seven-eighths of an iceberg's mass is below water. The one-eighth you see is just the "tip of the iceberg."

❋ Just like ice cubes in your drink, icebergs float because the density of ice is less than water.

Iceberg shapes

Tabular
Steep sides with a flat top, like a huge tablet

Blocky
Box-shaped with steep vertical sides

Wedge
The top narrows to a pyramidlike point

Dome
A very rounded and smooth top

Pinnacle
One or more spires rise very high

Drydock
A U-shaped opening in the middle due to erosion

Top 10 coldest places in the world

01: Vostok, Antarctica: -129°F (-89°C)

02: Plateau, Antarctica: -119°F (-84°C)

03: Oymyakon, Russia: -96°F (-71°C)

04: Verkhoyank, Russia: -90°F (-68°C)

05: Northice, Greenland: -87°F (-66°C)

06: Eismitte, Greenland: -85°F (-65°C)

07: Snag Yukon, Canada: -81°F (-63°C)

08: Prospect Creek, Alaska: -80°F (-62°C)

09: Fort Selkirk, Yukon, Canada: -74°F (-59°C)

10: Rogers Pass, Montana: -70°F (-57°C)

airborne snow

snow (85–90% air)

I don't believe it!

Sometimes when moving icebergs scrape past each other they produce a sound like barking dogs or screeching monkeys—but a lot louder! Some of these "icequakes" are as deafening as the tremors caused by a large earthquake.

Ocean hazard

In 1912, the luxury passenger liner **Titanic** struck an **iceberg** and **sank**. More than 1,500 people lost their lives in the disaster.

Tell me more: glacier anatomy

✳ A glacier is a huge, slow-moving river of ice.

✳ As a glacier moves downhill it carves steep-sided, U-shaped valleys.

✳ There are two main types of glaciers. Valley glaciers are streams of flowing ice that are confined within steep-walled valleys. Continental glaciers resemble huge chunks of ice and can cover a large part of a continent, like Antarctica.

Medial moraine: Created when two glaciers meet

Englacial debris: Rocks that were once carried along with a glacier

Crevasse: Deep crack in a glacier caused by motion

Cirque: Deep recess in a mountain with steep walls

Rock-fall: Fragments of loosened rock fall from the face of cliff

Ice-fall: Glacier flows over a steep slope

Rock avalanche: Ground movement causes rocks to fall

Lateral moraine: Pile of rocks that forms alongside the glacier

Terminal moraine: Rock debris that forms at the end of a glacier

Glacial lake: Lake formed by a melting glacier

Outwash plain: Sand, gravel, and mud that has washed out from a glacier

Five glacial features

Meltwater cave
Cave formed by melted snow or ice

Crevasse
Vertical crack in the ice as a glacier moves

Iceberg
Floating ice that has broken away

Retreating glacier
Thinning of snow and ice on a glacier

Ice pinnacle
Large piece of ice that juts out from a glacier

In numbers

7.2 million cubic miles
(30 million cubic km) The volume of the largest piece of ice on Earth—the Antarctic ice sheet

70%
The percentage of fresh water frozen in the Antarctic ice sheet

2.5 miles
(4 km) The depth of the ice cap covering the South Pole

RECORD BREAKER

In 1953, the Kutiah Glacier in Pakistan set the record for the fastest glacial surge, covering more than 7 miles (12 km) in three months and averaging a distance of 368 ft (112 m) per day.

Snow to ice

Snow falls to the ground and compresses into small, round ice particles called granular ice. As the ice compacts it contains less air and forms larger granules, known as "firn." With the pressure of further snow, the firn welds into solid, glacial ice, called "blue ice."

granular ice (30–85% air)

firn (20–30% air)

blue ice (less than 20% air)

Greenland

Despite its name, Greenland is mostly covered in a layer of ice averaging 5,900 ft (1,790 m) thick. A single glacier makes up most of this ice.

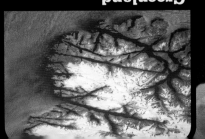

How dry is a desert?

The dry conditions in deserts occur due to the lack of rain and snow, which is usually less than 10 in (25 cm) in a year. The driest desert on Earth is the Atacama, Chile, where in many parts there has not been any rainfall in living memory.

Tell me more: hot and cold places

■ **Hot deserts** are found close to the tropics, where the Sun's rays are strongest.

■ Hot deserts are **freezing at night** because there are no clouds to trap the Earth's heat.

■ **Cold deserts** have hot summers but extremely cold winters—in the Gobi desert, in Central Asia, temperatures can drop to -40°F (-40°C).

Five things to do in deserts

Grow things
Large-scale desert irrigation makes it possible to grow fruits and vegetables.

Test probes
NASA tested the Viking lander space probes in the Atacama Desert, Chile.

Harvest salt
A vast amount of salt is harvested in the Salar de Uyini desert in Bolivia, South America.

Run a race
In Alice Springs, Australia, people race in bottomless boats down a dry riverbed.

Store planes
The Sonoran Desert in the United States is a graveyard for thousands of disused planes.

Top five largest deserts

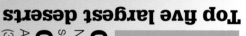

01. Sahara
Northern Africa, 3,514,000 sq miles (9,100,000 sq km)

02. Australian
Australia, 1,313,000 sq miles (3,400,000 sq km)

03. Arabian Peninsula
Southwest Asia, 1,004,000 sq miles (2,600,000 sq km)

04. Turkestan
Central Asia, 734,000 sq miles (1,900,000 sq km)

05. Gobi
Central Asia, 502,000 sq miles (1,300,000 sq km)

How to: identify a desert

01. Check the rock features around you. They should be eroded by very strong winds and extreme temperatures.

02. Examine the terrain. It should be bleak—sand, rocks, and stones and, in polar deserts, snow.

03. Try to find surface water. No luck? That's a good sign you are in a desert.

Striking landmarks

Erg
Arabic word for an extensive area of sand dunes, such as those found in the Sahara.

Playa
An almost flat area in the center of a basin in which lakes form periodically.

In numbers

1,525 ft
(465 m) The height of the sand dunes in the Algerian Sahara

330,000 tons
(300,000 metric tons) The weight of sand sucked up by a giant sandstorm in the Gobi desert in 2006 and then dumped on Beijing, China, more than 1,000 miles (1,600 km) away

169°F
(76°C) The temperature of the ground in Death Valley, in the Mojave Desert of California and Nevada. This is hot enough to burn the skin off your feet

The mighty Sahara

The world's largest hot desert is the size of the United States and covers 11 North African countries.

Algeria
Chad
Egypt
Libya
Morocco
Mauritania
Mali
Niger
Sudan
Tunisia
and **Western Sahara**

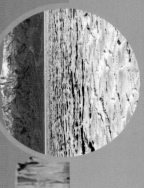

Not everyone agrees that **Antarctica is a desert**, but it's certainly dry—some valleys here have **not had rain for 4 million years**. It is bigger than the Sahara, with an area of 5.3 million sq miles (13.7 million sq km).

Spooky desert names

☠ **Death Valley, United States** The country's hottest landscape is breathtaking

☠ **Takla Makan, China** Means "you can get in, but you'll never get out"; it is also nicknamed "Sea of Death."

☠ **Skeleton Coast, Namibia** Named after the wrecks of ships, not people, that line the dunes where desert meets the sea.

☠ **The Empty Quarter, Saudi Arabia** An area of sand the size of France.

Survival tips

Cover up
Wear light clothes and a hat to protect you from the sun and insects, and to reduce evaporation of sweat.

Keep drinking
Dehydration (loss of water) and overheating are the greatest dangers.

Find some shade
Don't shelter inside a hot, stuffy vehicle, but in its cooler shadow.

Do not travel
Stay put in the heat of the day, and only travel at dusk or dawn.

Keep off the ground
Try not to sit or lie on the ground where it's hot, and where scorpions, spiders, and snakes may lurk.

RECORD BREAKER

The **highest temperature** ever recorded was at Al'Aziziyah, Libya, in the heat Sahara Desert when a head-melting soared to a 136°F (57.8°C).

05. Look up. You should see clear blue skies with not a rain cloud in sight.

04. Make sure there is little or no vegetation—just tough desert plants.

I don't believe it!

More people drown in deserts than die of thirst! When rain falls in a desert, it comes suddenly, and dried up riverbeds can turn into surging rivers in just a few minutes.

Inselberg
An isolated hill with steep sides that stands out above the plains of the desert.

Arch
Stunning creation formed by whirling winds blasting at rock and wearing it away.

Butte
A flat-topped hill with steep sides capped with a layer of resistant rocks.

Wadi
A steep-sided valley formed by a river in a semiarid or arid desert region.

How many trees make a **forest?**

The definition of a forest varies around the world, but the main characteristics are the same—it is an area that is densely planted with tall trees and covers a large area. More than 50 percent of Earth's animal and plant species can be found here.

Types of forest

Rain forest
Lush tropical forests are found in hot regions with high rainfall, usually around the tropics of Cancer and Capricorn.

Tropical dry forest
Vegetation that can survive the long, parched months of a dry season grow in these forests.

Coniferous forest
Vast areas of coniferous forest stretch across the cold regions of North America, northern Europe, and Asia.

Temperate forest
In areas with distinct cool and warm seasons grow broadleaved trees that lose their leaves in the winter months.

How to: reach the top of a rain forest

04. Arrive at the top, known as the emergent layer. Here the very tallest trees reach the sky, sometimes at a height of 230–262 ft (70–80 m) above ground.

03. Stop off at the canopy, where the tops of taller trees spread out to form a dense canopy that traps sunlight.

About 300 million people are born, live, and die in the world's forests, and 60 million of them are almost totally dependent on the forests to maintain their lifestyles.

The trees of the Amazon rain forest have their roots in nine different countries:

Brazil
Peru
Colombia
Venezuela
Ecuador
Bolivia
Guyana
Suriname
French Guiana

Tell me more: **deforestation**

The clearing away of trees, known as deforestation, affects our planet in a variety of ways.

- It destroys forest habitats and kills the animals living there. Two-thirds of all species on Earth need forests for shelter or food.

- The lower number of trees to convert carbon dioxide into oxygen contributes to global warming.

- Trees give off water vapor, so the fewer trees there are, the less water there is in the atmosphere.

- Without tree roots to hold the soil together, there is an increased chance of soil erosion, flooding, and landslides.

US: Many of the United States' forested areas are protected as national parks

Canada: Almost one million Canadians are involved in the country's forest industry

Russia: About 20 percent of the world's forests can be found in the largest country on Earth

Brazil: The Amazon rain forest covers more than half of Brazil and is the largest remaining tropical rain forest on Earth

Central Africa: This tropical rain forest is home to 11,000 plant species and more than 400 species of mammal

China: Forests in China grew by 1.2 percent every year between 1990 and 2000, the highest growth rate in the world

About 30 percent of Earth's total land area is forested.

In 1908, in Tunguska, Russia, about 830 sq miles (2,150 sq km) of forest—that's **80 million trees**—in Siberia were **flattened**. No one knows why for sure, but most people now agree that a meteor or comet burst in the air above the Tunguska River.

02. Climb up to about 50 ft (15 m) from the floor. You're now in the understory, where small trees can branch out.

01. Start in the damp, shady forest floor. In some forests, only two percent of light reaches this area, which is covered in leaves and roots.

In numbers

The Amazon rain forest contains an amazing variety of flora and fauna.

1 million
insect species

40,000
plant species

3,000
fish species

428
amphibian species

427
mammal species

378
reptile species

1,294
bird species

I don't believe it!

Stretching 367 ft (112 m) into the skies, a redwood sequoia tree in Montgomery State Reserve near Ukiah, California, can claim to be the tallest tree. However, it is not the tallest tree in history. Two trees in Australia measured 470 ft (143 m) and 492 ft (150 m) before they died.

Not all rain forests are hot and steamy. The cool west coast of North America can get up to 132 in (350 cm) of rain each year, and here you find dense rain forests of giant conifers, such as redwoods covered with thick mosses.

Forest fires

Fires can sweep through forests causing huge devastation to trees, plants, and animal life. However, they can also help regenerate a habitat by clearing the area for new growth and leaving a layer of rich ash where new seeds will flourish. The main causes of forest fires are these:

⚡ **human activity or deliberate fire-starting (arson)**

⚡ **lightning**

⚡ **excessively hot and dry conditions that help the fire spread**

More than five million native Indians once lived in the Amazon rain forest, but now only about 200,000 remain.

Is a coral reef animal, vegetable, or mineral?

It's animal, vegetable, and mineral! A coral reef is a colony of millions of tiny animals called polyps. As they grow, each polyp produces a hard, limestone skeleton, on which the next generation of polyps grow. Corals also contain an algae, which is essential for their survival.

Tell me more: inside a polyp

Tentacles: These catch food and push it into the cuplike mouth.

mouth

Gut cavity: Tissue around the gut cavity lays down limestone on the rock below.

Limestone skeleton: A hard coral skeleton builds up.

Living coral looks like an upside-down jellyfish, with a tubular body and tentacles around its mouth. Tropical reef-building corals use their tentacles to catch plankton from the water.

How to: grow a tropical coral reef

01. Choose a sea that is clear, well lit, and free of any pollutants.

02. Check the depth—a reef won't grow below 100 ft (30 m), because there's not enough sunlight.

03. The water must be just the right temperature—no colder than 70°F (21°C) and no warmer than 86°F (30°C).

04. The sea should be low in nutrients, otherwise algae thrive and the coral suffocates.

Scientists have discovered a **freaky stony coral** at depths of nearly 20,000 ft (6,000 m). Little is known about it but, unlike tropical coral, they live in total darkness.

Name the coral

There are two main types of coral—hard, stony corals that build reefs, and soft corals that don't. They often have very descriptive names—what do you think?

Brain coral
The wrinkled ridges of this hard coral make it look like a giant brain.

Fan coral
The polyps of fan coral link together to form a large lacy skeleton.

Dead-man's-fingers
The tentacles of these polyps look like decomposing fingers.

Staghorn coral
This antlerlike coral is one of the speediest growers on the reef.

Great reefs of the world

01: The Great Barrier Reef, Australia
About 3,000 reefs combine to form the largest living structure on Earth, more than 1,250 miles (2,010 km) long.

02: Kwajalein, Marshall Islands
The world's largest atoll surrounds a lagoon 60 miles (97 km) long.

03: Bikini Island, South Pacific
In 1946, the bikini swimsuit was named after this atoll.

04: Lighthouse Reef, Belize
At the center of this Caribbean atoll lies the Great Blue Hole, 480 ft (145 m) deep.

Threats to coral reefs

Global warming
If the temperature of the ocean rises, the algae in coral dies. This kills the coral, which is dependent on it.

Rising seas
Global warming is also causing sea levels to rise, which will have a dramatic effect on coral reefs.

Pollution
Reefs are damaged by pollution from untreated sewage, mining, fertilizers, pesticides, and oil spills.

Aquarium trade
Some fishermen in Indonesia and the Philippines use cyanide poison to stun fish. They then use crowbars to rip apart the coral to get at the fish.

Overfishing
The overfishing of sea urchins—the spiny predators of coral-eating starfish—leaves corals vulnerable.

Reefs of all shapes and sizes

Fringing reefs
These reefs follow the shorelines of continents and islands in tropical seas and are found close to shore.

Barrier reefs
Lying farther offshore, barrier reefs are separated from land by a deep lagoon.

Atoll reefs
A ring of coral that grows on top of a sunken volcano, forming a lagoon, is called an atoll.

Patch reefs
Patches of young coral commonly grow at the bottom of the sea in the lagoon behind a barrier or atoll reef.

Platform reefs
When coral reaches the surface of the sea and branches out, growing horizontally, a platform reef is formed.

I don't believe it!

Many corals on the Great Barrier Reef spawn (produce eggs) once a year. They all do it at exactly the same time—four to five days after the Full Moon in October or November—to create a spectacular "underwater snowstorm" as the sea is filled with eggs.

Why we need reefs

Although coral reefs cover less than 1 percent of the Earth's surface, they are home to 25 percent of all marine fish species.

Reef fish and mollusks feed between 30 and 40 million people every year. An estimated 500 million people rely on coral reefs for their food or livelihoods.

Chemical compounds found in reefs are used to make several important medicines.

Coral polyps turn the carbon dioxide in water into limestone. Without coral, the amount of carbon dioxide in the water would rise, destroying precious habitats.

Coral reefs form natural barriers that protect nearby shorelines from strong waves or currents.

Australia's Great Barrier Reef is home to...
500 species of coral
400 species of seaweed
1,000 species of sea sponge
175 species of bird
1,500 species of fish
30 species of mammal

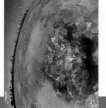
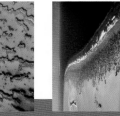

Blasts from the past

500 million years ago
The world's first coral reefs appear

230 mya
Modern corals first develop in the Early Triassic era

199 mya
Mass extinction—two-thirds of coral types are wiped out by climate change, at the end of the Triassic era

18 mya
The formation of Australia's Great Barrier Reef begins. Its growth will stop and start several times

18,000 years ago
Temperatures on the Earth fall and seawater becomes trapped as ice in enormous glaciers, causing sea levels to fall to their lowest levels ever. Any coral reefs exposed during this period die

10,000–8,000 years ago
The reefs we can see today begin to develop at the end of the last great Ice Age. Glaciers melt and sea levels rise to the position they are still at today

Why does the wind blow?

The Earth's weather is caused by the Sun heating the atmosphere, oceans, and the Earth's surface. The hot air rises, and the cool air sinks and all this activity gets air moving across the globe. The Sun also evaporates water in lakes, rivers, and seas to make clouds and rain.

It takes about a million cloud droplets to make one raindrop.

Global warming

☀ Earth's climate is heating up faster than ever before.

☀ Most scientists believe this is due to a buildup of greenhouse gases in the atmosphere. These are gases produced by power plants, factories, and cars that trap heat around the Earth.

☀ If the polar ice caps melt on a large scale, sea levels will rise, putting at risk islands such as the Maldives, which lie only 3 ft (1 m) above sea level.

☀ Global warming may also cause more extreme weather, such as storms, droughts, and hurricanes.

WHAT'S IN A NAME?

Monsoon means season in Arabic, because the monsoon winds always bring heavy rainfall to southern Asia in the summer.

Stormy weather

Tropical storm
Cyclones, also known as hurricanes or typhoons, start at sea.

Sandstorm
In desert regions, winds often whip up sand and dust into thick clouds.

Ice storm
This occurs when half-frozen rain freezes in a thick layer on and around the ground.

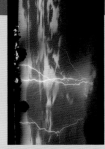

Thunderstorm
Electricity in thunder clouds causes flashes of lightning and loud booms.

I don't believe it!

In 1930, a German glider pilot got caught in a hailstorm and had to bail out. Tragically, he was sucked up into the storm and covered with heavy layers of ice to become a human hailstone and fell 7 miles (11 km) to his death.

The water on our planet gets used over and over again.

When your sweat evaporates, it comes back as rain about 10 days later! The raindrops falling on your head contain the same water that fell on the dinosaurs more than 65 million years ago.

Weather black spots

🌡 **Coldest**
The coldest temperature ever was a brain-numbing -123.8°F (-89.6°C), recorded at Vostok Research Station, Antarctica, on July 21, 1983.

🌧 **Wettest**
Cherrapunji in northeastern India receives an annual rainfall of 500 in (1,270 cm).

🌀 **Windiest**
Port Martin in Antarctica has an average wind speed of 108 mph (174 kph), but gusts can blow at speeds up to 200 mph (320 kph).

❄ **Most snow**
Between February 18, 1972, and February 19, 1971, 102 ft (31.1 m) of snow fell on Mount Rainier, Washington.

FAST FACTS

Clouds

01: Clouds form when warm air rises.

02: High in the sky, invisible water vapor in the warm air cools and turns into water droplets.

03: High-level clouds float at 40,000 ft (12,000 m), while clouds that touch the ground create fog and mist.

04: An average cloud weighs as much as a jumbo jet, but luckily this weight is spread out over a large area!

Beaufort scale

Wind speeds are based on the Beaufort scale, which ranges from 0–12.

0 Calm Smoke rises vertically, the surface of the sea is like a mirror

1 Light air Smoke drifts in the wind, ripples are seen on the surface of water

2 Light breeze Wind is felt on face, leaves rustle, small wavelets produced

3 Gentle breeze Small twigs move, flags flutter, waves break

4 Moderate breeze Dust is raised, small branches move, small waves form

5 Fresh breeze Small trees begin to sway, waves form "white horses"

6 Strong Breeze Large branches move, large waves form

7 Near gale Whole trees move, sea whipped up to form white foam

8 Gale Twigs broken off trees, difficult to walk against the wind, waves are high

9 Severe gale Chimney tops and slates fall, crests of waves topple

10 Storm Trees uprooted, damage to houses, sea white with foam

11 Violent storm Widespread damage, small ships hidden by waves

12 Hurricane Extensive damage, huge waves, air filled with foam and spray

Five ways to predict the weather

In the past, farmers and sailors used natural signs to predict the weather.

◆ **Hang a piece of dry seaweed up—when rain is on the way it will feel sticky.**

◆ Your hair is longer on a damp day because it takes in water from the air and expands!

◆ **Look out for the storm petrel, a sea bird that flies inshore when a storm is on its way.**

◆ Oak and maple trees have leaves that curl when the humidity is very high and the wind is blowing strongly, both signs that a storm is coming.

◆ **There's a saying that "when chairs squeak, it's about rain they speak," because wooden chairs absorb moisture from the air, causing them to squeak.**

In numbers

6,000
The number of lightning flashes around the world each minute

21
The number of people killed by the same lightning bolt when it struck a hut in Zimbabwe in 1975

730
The average number of tornadoes each year in the US, causing more than 100 deaths annually

44,000
The number of storms that can rumble over the Earth each day

120 miles
(190 km) The length of the longest lightning bolt ever recorded

Four snowflake facts

01: All snowflakes have six sides, but each snowflake is unique.

02: In cold air, snowflakes tend to be needle-shaped, while in warmer air, they are star- or plate-shaped.

03: The largest snowflakes can be 2 in (5 cm) across.

04: The average snowflake falls at a speed of 3 mph (5 kph).

Tell me more: tornadoes

Dark skies: A tornado begins when air inside a thundercloud starts to spin

Funnel-shaped cloud: When the funnel of wind hits the ground, the tornado moves off across the countryside—it can reach speeds of up to 70 mph (115 kph)

Rising air: The whirling air spins faster and faster, sucking dust and objects as big as cars from the ground and destroying everything in its path

Base of tornado: This usually measures around half a mile (1 km) across

What are rocks made of?

Every type of rock has its own "recipe" of one or more minerals. There are about 4,000 minerals found on Earth, each with its own unique shape and color. Earth's rocks are like buried treasure—they are full of valuable minerals and contain metals, gemstones, fossils, and fuels, such as coal and gas.

Rocks

01: Earth started as a fiery mass of molten rock, but about 4 billion years ago the outer layer began to cool and form a hard crust.

02: There are many types of rock, formed in three main ways.

03: Most igneous rocks appear on the surface as melted rock (magma) brought to the Earth's surface by volcanoes. When this cools, it crystallizes into solid rock.

04: Sedimentary rocks are made from loose rocks and the ancient remains of animals and plants. Carried by wind and water, they compact and harden into solid rock over millions of years.

05: Metamorphic rocks are rocks that change when they are baked and crushed by the heat and pressure deep below the Earth's surface.

Tell me more: the rock cycle

Sediment: Layers build up on the seabed

Sedimentary rock: Forms from compressed sediments

Rivers: Carry sediment down to the sea

Mountaintop: Ice and snow in mountains create sediments

Erosion: Rivers create valleys and make sediments

Igneous rocks: Formed by lava cooling at the surface

Magma: Heats and changes surrounding rocks into metamorphic rock

Metamorphic rock: Forms when sedimentary rocks are heated and crushed

Mineral ID

To identify a mineral you need to test for:

01 **Color, luster, and habit** The color of a mineral's crystal, its surface shine (luster), and the form (habit) of its crystals

02 **Streak** The color of a streak left by the mineral when rubbed across a tile

03 **Cleavage** How the mineral breaks when hit with a hammer

04 **Hardness** Measured on the Mohs scale, from 1 (very soft) to 10 (very hard)

05 **Crystal system** The basic geometrical shape of the mineral's crystals

WHAT'S IN A NAME?

Scientists in the 19th century came up with the **Wrinkled Apple Theory** when they saw the folded rocks in some mountains. They thought the Earth's crust was wrinkling, like an old apple skin!

Five famous **rocks**

Uluru
In central Australia lies one of the world's largest single pieces of rock, 1,256 ft (383 m) high and 1.2 miles (2 km) long.

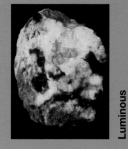

Ship Rock
The Ship Rock in New Mexico is a giant pillar of stone that rises 1,640 ft (500 m) out of the plain.

Mount Rushmore
Four American presidents' faces were carved out of a rock in South Dakota.

Sugar Loaf Mountain
The majestic Sugar Loaf Mountain in Rio de Janeiro, Brazil, rises to 1,300 ft (396 m).

Delicate Arch
This 53-ft- (16-m-) high sandstone arch has worn away over time by weathering and erosion.

Weird or what?

Although both are forms of the element carbon, graphite is dark gray and one of the softest minerals, while diamond is clear and the world's hardest natural substance.

Rocks with strange powers

Magnetic
Minerals, such as magnetite, are naturally magnetic.

Radioactive
Uraninite is a radioactive mineral from which uranium is extracted.

Luminous
Some minerals, such as sodalite, glow when ultraviolet light is shined over them.

Crystal clear

Crystals are minerals that grow into regular shapes with smooth, flat faces and sharp edges.

A crystal's shape is known as its habit. Salt crystals are like tiny cubes, zircon crystals (used in jewelry) are like pyramids, while asbestos grows in long strands.

Millions of tiny crystals can cluster together to make a chunk of rock.

Given enough room, crystals can grow underground to an incredible length of 36 ft (11 m).

I don't believe it!

About 110,000 tons (100,000 metric tons) of uranium ore produces 28 tons (25 metric tons) of radioactive uranium, the annual amount used by a nuclear power plant.

RECORD BREAKER

The **largest gold nugget** ever found weighed 158 lb (72 kg). Discovered in Moliagul, Australia, in the 1869 gold rush. It was named the "Welcome Stranger."

The size of a gem is given by weight units called **carats**. One carat is the same as 0.007 oz (200 mg).

Five famous **diamonds**

Star of Africa (530.2 carats)
In 1908 this diamond was mounted in the Royal Sceptre, part of the British crown jewels.

Millennium Star (203 carats)
Discovered in 1990, it took three years for lasers to cut and shape this pear-shaped diamond.

Regent (140.5 carats)
Found in 1698 by an Indian slave who hid it in a wound in his leg, it was stolen by an English sea captain. In 1812, it was used to decorate Napoleon's sword.

Koh-i-noor (105.6 carats)
Since 1304, it has belonged to various Indian and Persian rulers, but became part of the British crown jewels after Queen Victoria became Empress of India in 1877.

Blue Hope (45.5 carats)
One of the most famous owners of this cursed diamond (pictured), Marie Antoinette, wife of King Louis XVI of France, was beheaded in 1793 during the French Revolution.

Tell me more: **minerals and rocks**

The Earth's landscape is made up of rocks and minerals, some precious and rare, others plentiful. Many are useful in our day-to-day lives.

agate

wulfenite

diaspore

cuprite

halite

wavellite

augite

magnetite

artinite

azurite

crystalline adamite

brochantite

garnet

malachite

olivine

tourmaline

carnallite

daisy gypsum

cassiterite

hematite

jadeite

botryoidal hemimorphite

turquoise

flourite

graphite

cinnabar

marcasite

pyrite crystal (fool's gold)

quartz

lazurite

galena

sphalerite

sulfur

chalcopyrite

calcite

rhodochrosite

barite

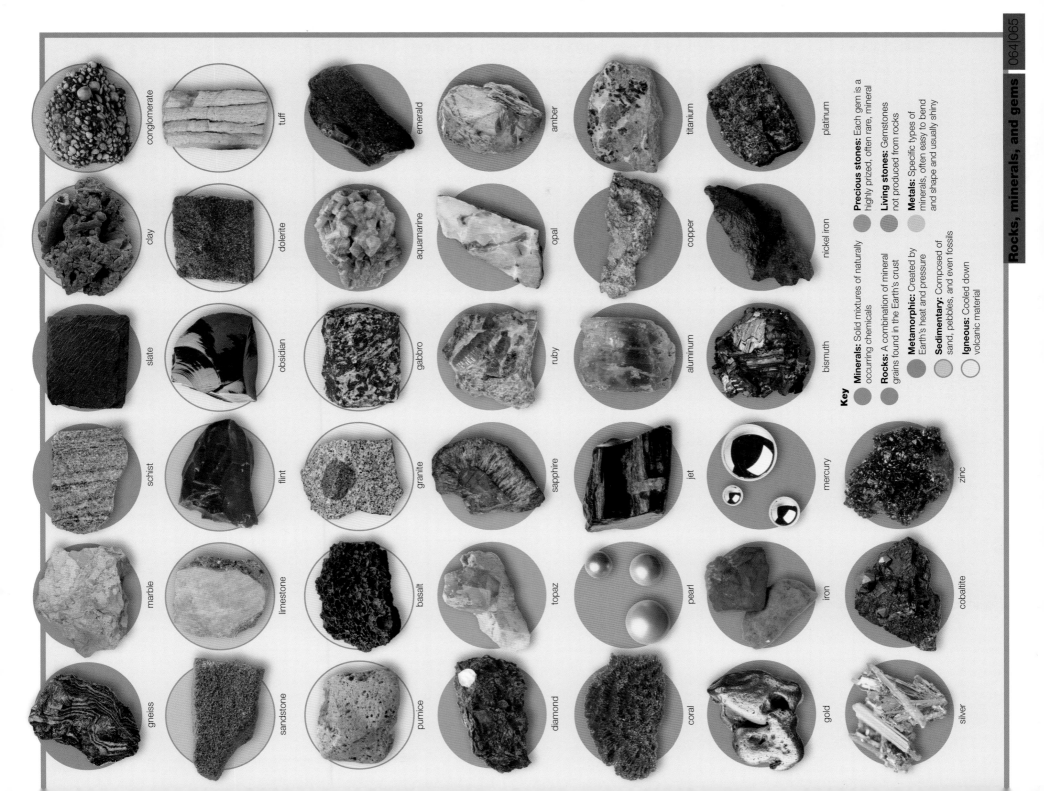

conglomerate

tuff

emerald

amber

titanium

platinum

clay

dolerite

aquamarine

opal

copper

nickel iron

slate

obsidian

gabbro

ruby

aluminum

bismuth

schist

flint

granite

sapphire

jet

mercury

zinc

marble

limestone

basalt

topaz

pearl

iron

cobaltite

gneiss

sandstone

pumice

diamond

coral

gold

silver

Key

Minerals: Solid mixtures of naturally occurring chemicals

Rocks: A combination of mineral grains found in the Earth's crust

Metamorphic: Created by Earth's heat and pressure

Sedimentary: Composed of sand, pebbles, and even fossils

Igneous: Cooled down volcanic material

Precious stones: Each gem is a highly prized, often rare, mineral

Living stones: Gemstones not produced from rocks

Metals: Specific types of minerals, often easy to bend and shape and usually shiny

Where does the world's energy come from?

Solar power converts sunlight to electricity. We also release energy when we burn fuels such as oil, gas, and coal. Wind and water are examples of renewable resources, since they never run out.

Top 10 users of electricity (2007)

01: United States
3,717,000,000,000 kWh

02: China
2,494,000,000,000 kWh

03: Japan
946,300,000,000 kWh

04: Russia
940,000,000,000 kWh

05: India
587,900,000,000 kWh

06: Germany
3524,600,000,000 kWh

07: Canada
522,400,000,000 kWh

08: France
482,400,000,000 kWh

09: Brazil
415,900,000,000 kWh

10: United Kingdom
345,200,000,000 kWh

kWh stands for kilo Watt hour and is a unit of energy, measuring the amount of power used in one hour.

Odd one out

a) umbrella   b) metal nails   c) soap   d) dice   e) CD   f) balloon   g) nonstick pan   h) lipstick

Oil is an important resource. Not only does it produce energy, but it also contains chemicals that are used to make all kinds of things. It's used in all the objects below except one. Can you spot the odd one out? (answer opposite page)

FAST FACTS

Energy resources

01: Coal makes up 24 percent of the world's energy

02: Gas supplies 21 percent of the world's energy

03: Oil is used more than any other fuel, supplying 35 percent of the world's energy

04: Solar power can be harnessed directly using special solar-electric cells

05: Wind can turn into electricity using machines called turbines

06: Tide movement and the waves in oceans can be used to make electricity

07: Nuclear energy involves splitting atoms, which causes a nuclear explosion that generates huge amounts of power

08: Hydroelectric power is the energy generated by rushing water harnessed by special dams

09: Geothermal means "hot rock," and its energy can be tapped where heat from deep inside the Earth rises to the surface

10: Biomass is the use of natural materials and waste to make energy

In numbers

70 million
The number of barrels of oil that are pumped from the ground each day

1.3 million
The number of people who receive electric power from the Hoover Dam, on the Colorado River

2050
The year that oil is expected to run out in 2100, and coal by 2250

75%
The percentage of fuel wasted by cars in generating unnecessary heat and noise

WHAT'S IN A NAME

Coal, oil, and gas are known as **fossil fuels** because they are formed from plants and plankton that lived up to 300 million years ago.

US: Uses one-third more than it produces

Canada: Produces 52% more than it uses

South America: Produces 42% more than it uses

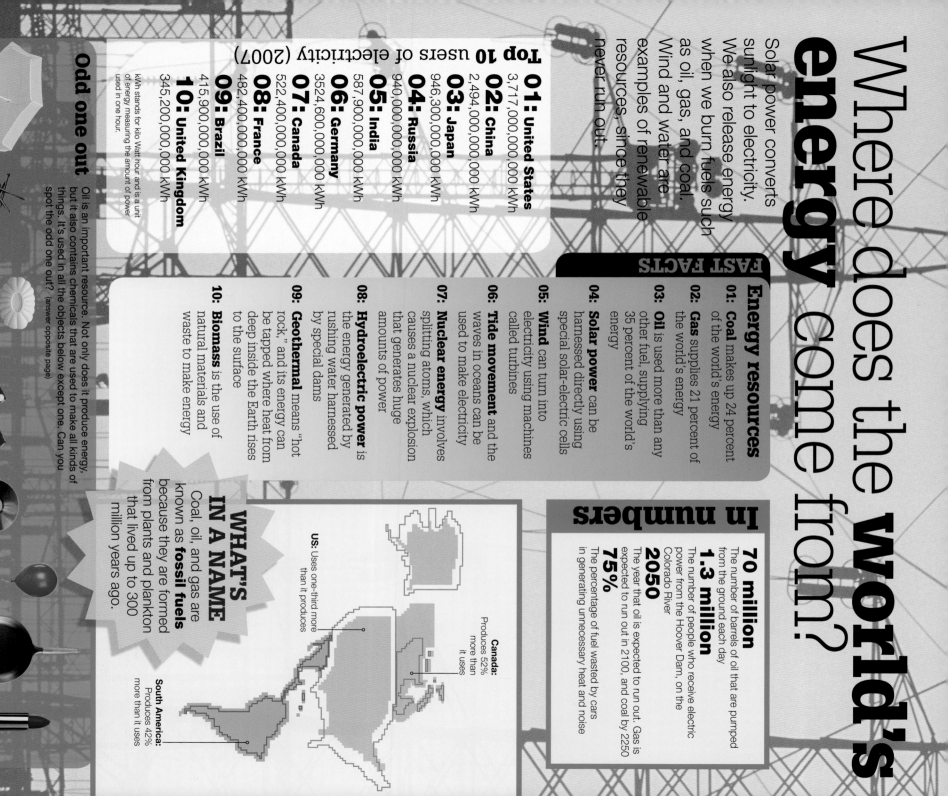

Blasts from the past

500,000 BCE
Early humans discover fire

200 BCE
Chinese first mine coal

644 CE
The first windmill recorded is in Persia (now Iran)

1740
Commercial coal mining begins in the United States

1765
James Watt invents the steam engine

1821
First natural gas well drilled in Fredonia, New York

1840s
Joule, a unit of energy used to show the energy value of many foods, is invented by British scientist, James Prescott Joule

1859
First oil well drilled by Edwin Drake in Pennsylvania

1860
Etienne Lenoir invents the internal combustion engine

1880s
First coal power plants are built to provide energy for factories

1882
A waterwheel supplies first hydroelectric power to two paper mills in Appleton, Wisconsin

1888
Charles F. Brush builds first automatic wind turbine in Cleveland, Ohio

1891
First natural gas pipeline built from Indiana to Chicago

1904
First geothermal power plant is built in Laderello, Italy

1941
Solar cells are invented

1944
First nuclear reactor begins operation in Richland, Washington

1954
Better design allows for more efficient solar panels

Six ways to save energy

Walk or cycle instead—it costs nothing and is good for you.

Use energy efficient lightbulbs instead of traditional bulbs, since they use one-fifth of the energy and last up to 10 times longer.

Turn your heat down by reducing the thermostat in your home by just 2°F (1°C)—this will knock 10 percent off the heating bill.

Insulate your home, especially your attic. Windows should be double-paned.

Don't overfill your kettle, and boil only the water you need.

Reusing products saves the energy used to make replacements.

What is biomass?

Biofuels, such as ethanol, are liquid fuels made from biomass. This includes organic materials that can be burned to provide heat and produce steam.

crops, such as sugar, hemp, or rapeseed

garbage, such as cardboard

animal manure

corn stalks

woodchips or pellets

seaweed

Tell me more: world energy producers and consumers

The colored-in regions show energy production, and the outlined areas show energy use. If the colored area spills over the outline, it means they make more than they use.

Russian Federation: Produces 60% more than it uses

China: Uses as much as it produces

Japan: Uses five times more than it produces

Australia: Produces twice as much as it uses

UK: Produces 11% more than it uses

France: Uses twice as much as it produces

South Africa: Produces nearly one-third more than it uses

The Middle East: Produces almost three times as much as it uses

I don't believe it!

In August 2003, around 50 million people in cities from New York City to Toronto, Canada, were affected by a mass power outage. People were trapped in elevators and subway cars, and the loss of power in pumping stations led to sewage spills.

The population of China is **four times bigger** than that of the US, but it uses **less than half** the amount of energy.

Three ways to cook an egg

1. Sunny side up
The energy given off from the Sun in a scorching desert can heat rocks high enough to fry an egg.

2. Boiling hot
Water erupting from an overheated geyser can reach a scalding 204°F (95°C)—anyone for boiled eggs?

3. Light a fire
The heat energy from burning wood will ensure a tasty treat.

Dinosaurs

Why were some dinos so huge?

With necks as long as 36 ft (11 m) and bodies the size of buses, sauropods were the most distinctive dinosaurs to roam throughout the Jurassic and Cretaceous Periods, 200 to 65 million years ago. These giant vegetarians were able to browse leaves high up in trees and their huge size deterred predators.

How to: **survive as a Jurassic plant-eater**

01. Grow thick skin like *Barosaurus*—it will help protect you from predators.

02. You will need a long, muscular, whiplike tail for balance and protection.

03. Large, elephantlike feet will help support your heavy body.

04. Your intestinal system needs to be extensive enough to digest large amounts of low-quality leaves. Swallow stones to help mash up the food inside the stomach.

Dinosaur skulls are made up of delicate bones that do not often fossilize. Scientists did not find a skull of the most famous sauropod, *Apatosaurus* (or *Brontosaurus* as it was known then), until a hundred years after the first skeletons had been found.

SAUROPOD SALAD

(crunchy) **conifers**

(low-calorie) **cycads**

(glorious) **gingko**

(sumptuous) **seed ferns**

(mushy) **moss**

Sauropod myths

MYTH: It was once believed that sauropods lived in water because they were so heavy they would not have been able to support their weight on land.
TRUTH: Scientists can tell now from their footprints that they did not live in water, but were land-dwelling animals.

MYTH: It was once thought that their necks could have been used as snorkels, so they could breathe while submerged under water.
TRUTH: The long neck as snorkel idea would never have worked, since water pressure would not have allowed the lungs of the submerged animal to expand, leading to breathing problems.

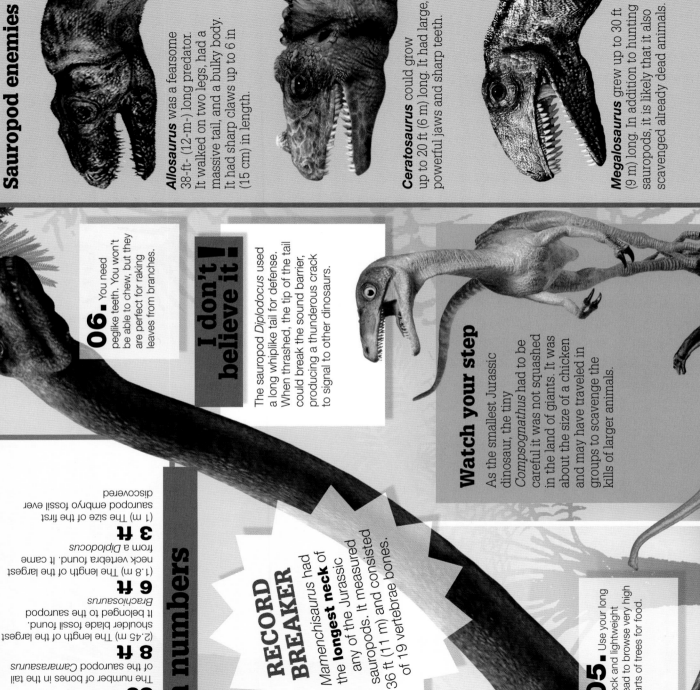

Sauropod enemies

Allosaurus was a fearsome 38-ft- (12-m-) long predator. It walked on two legs, had a massive tail, and a bulky body. It had sharp claws up to 6 in (15 cm) in length.

Ceratosaurus could grow up to 20 ft (6 m) long. It had large, powerful jaws and sharp teeth.

Megalosaurus grew up to 30 ft (9 m) long. In addition to hunting sauropods, it is likely that it also scavenged already dead animals.

06.
You need peglike teeth. You won't be able to chew, but they are perfect for raking leaves from branches.

I don't believe it!

The sauropod *Diplodocus* used a long whiplike tail for defense. When thrashed, the tip of the tail could break the sound barrier, producing a thunderous crack to signal to other dinosaurs.

Watch your step

As the smallest Jurassic dinosaur, the tiny *Compsognathus* had to be careful it was not squashed in the land of giants. It was about the size of a chicken and may have traveled in groups to scavenge the kills of larger animals.

In numbers

53
The number of bones in the tail of the sauropod *Camarasaurus*

8 ft
(2.45 m) The length of the largest shoulder blade fossil found. It belonged to the sauropod *Brachiosaurus*

6 ft
(1.8 m) The length of the largest neck vertebra found. It came from a *Diplodocus*

3 ft
(1 m) The size of the first sauropod embryo fossil ever discovered

RECORD BREAKER

Mamenchisaurus had the **longest neck** of any of the Jurassic sauropods. It measured 36 ft (11 m) and consisted of 19 vertebrae bones.

05.
Use your long neck and lightweight head to browse very high parts of trees for food.

Super **sauropods**

Camarasaurus 60 ft (18 m)
Probably fed by swinging its strong neck stiffly sideways and down to strip tough leaves from shrubby trees

Brachiosaurus 100 ft (30 m)
Long, spoon-shaped teeth capable of pulling twigs and needles from the highest conifer trees

Paralititan 90 ft (27 m)
Its neck accounted for one-third of its entire body length; estimated to have weighed 80 tons

Saltasaurus 90 ft (27 m)
Like many of the later sauropods, *Saltasaurus* had thick, armorlike skin along its back

Why did some dinos have crests?

Craziest crests

Hadrosaur crests came in a wide range of shapes and sizes. *Parasaurolophus*'s sticklike crest was up to 6 ft (1.8 m) long.

Tsintaosaurus

Saurolophus

Parasaurolophus

Corythosaurus

Hadrosaurs are a group of dinos famous for their flat beaks. Not all of them had head crests, but those that did could have been a real hoot. Some scientists believe that when the dino blew air through its crest, it made a noise like a trombone. Other theories are that crests made it easier to recognize one another, or perhaps worked as a cooling system.

Three good reasons to make a noise

01 Warn the herd of predators.

02 Keep the herd grouped together.

03 Attract a mate. (Who could resist a booming trombone?)

How to: **qualify as a hadrosaur**

01. Check out how you look. As an *Edmontosaurus*, you should have a long face and a broad, flat snout.

02. Grind any rough vegetation and digest your food using the teeth along the inside of your cheek.

03. Your large eyes, excellent hearing, and a good sense of smell help you to avoid predators.

04. Support your weight and forage for food using your forelimbs.

05. Walk comfortably using your hooflike nails.

06. Use your hind legs to run, and all four legs to walk slowly or graze.

07. Keep warm and protect yourself with your tough skin.

08. Your bulky body will come in handy against any predators, like T. rex.

09. Balance and support yourself using your long, stiff tail.

10. Run faster with the help of your large and powerful hind legs.

Eight amazing *Maiasaura* facts

01: *Maiasaura*'s name means "good mother lizard."

02: They grew up to 30 ft (9 m) long, and weighed about 3 tons.

03: *Maiasaura* lived in the late Cretaceous Period, about 80–65 million years ago.

04: They lived in herds with possibly up to 10,000 individuals.

05: A colony of *Maiasaura* nests was discovered in Montana.

06: Their nests were made of scooped out soil and contained eggs the size of grapefruits.

07: The mother did not sit on her eggs, but probably covered them in rotting vegetation to keep them warm.

08: Newborn hatchlings were about 1 ft (30 cm) long.

Survival tips
(for hadrosaurs)

01 Hang out in a herd. There is safety in numbers.

02 If you spot a predatory carnivore, like a *Tyrannosaurus rex*, hoot loudly to alert the herd and hoof it.

03 Keep an eye on any old or sick herd members in case the *T. rex* tries to isolate them from the herd.

04 Run as quickly as possible until you are a safe distance from the predator.

05 Continue to graze vegetation—you need to keep you energy levels boosted!

Daily grind

Hadrosaurs had hundreds of teeth in their cheeks, which ground and chopped their vegetarian food before they swallowed it. The teeth wore out because of the constant grinding action, but there were always new teeth growing to replace the old.

Hadrosaur cuisine

Breakfast
Lip-smacking leaves with fragrant flowers

Lunch
Tasty twigs with a side of sumptuous seeds

Dinner
Prickly pine needles washed down with fresh water from the lake

WHAT'S IN A NAME?

Hadrosaur means "duck-billed" because they had broad and flat beaks, a little like that of a duck. But while a duck's bill is soft and sensitive, hadrosaurs had tough, horny beaks.

I don't believe it!

In 1999, a teenage palentologist found the remains of the most intact hadrosaur ever in North Dakota. The dinosaur had been mummified before it was fossilized and so soft tissue, such as skin and muscle, were preserved. The rare fossil was analyzed by a huge scanner usually used to examine aircraft.

RECORD BREAKER

Bigger than a bus at 50 ft (15.5 m), the *Shantungosaurus* was the **largest hadrosaur.** It weighed around 20 tons (18 metric tons)—about ten times heavier than an elephant.

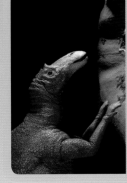

Meet (some of) the family

Corythosaurus
Lived: 80–65 million years ago
Where: Alberta, Canada
Length: 35 ft (10 m)
How to spot: Hollow crest like half a dinner plate

Saurolophus
Lived: 72–68 million years ago
Where: Canada and Mongolia
Length: 35 ft (10 m)
How to spot: Long, pointed tail and bony head spike

Maiasaura
Lived: 80–65 million years ago
Where: Montana
Length: 30 ft (9 m)
How to spot: Flat skull with small crest in front of eyes

Lambeosaurus
Lived: 83–65 million years ago
Where: Alberta, Canada
Length: 50 ft (15 m)
How to spot: Two-part crest with spike behind

Brachylophosaurus
Lived: 83–75 million years ago
Where: Alberta, Canada
Length: 30 ft (9 m)
How to spot: Flat, platelike crest and long forearms

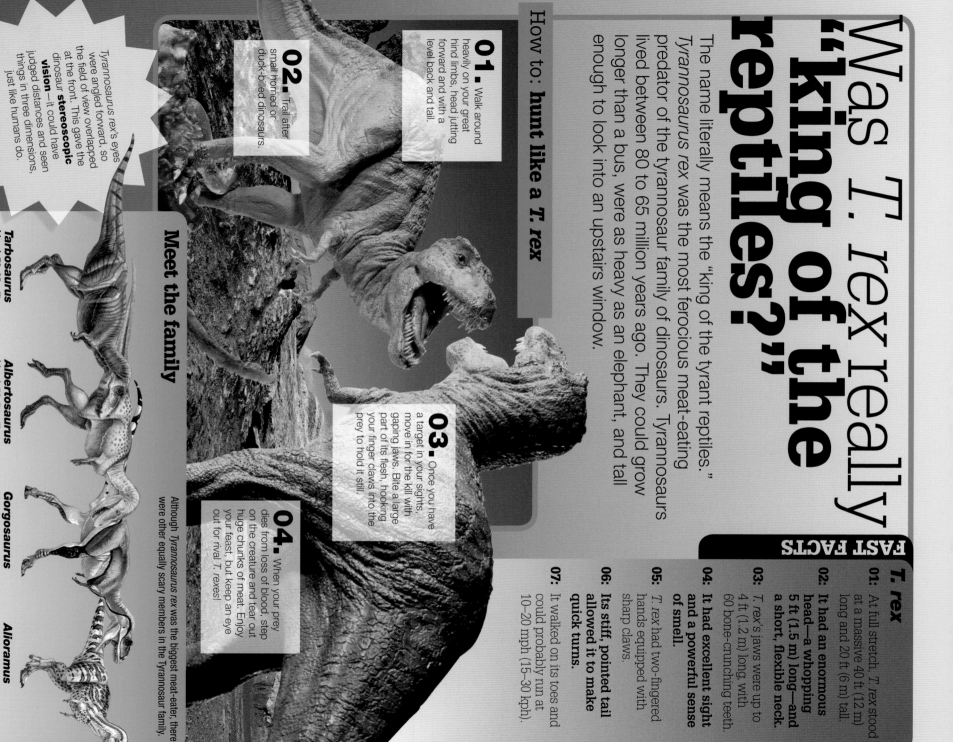

Was *T. rex* really "king of the reptiles?"

The name literally means the "king of the tyrant reptiles." *Tyrannosaurus rex* was the most ferocious meat-eating predator of the tyrannosaur family of dinosaurs. Tyrannosaurs lived between 80 to 65 million years ago. They could grow longer than a bus, were as heavy as an elephant, and tall enough to look into an upstairs window.

How to: **hunt like a *T. rex***

01. Walk around heavily on your great hind limbs, head jutting forward and with a level back and tail.

02. Trail after small horned or duck-billed dinosaurs.

03. Once you have a target in your sights, move in for the kill with gaping jaws. Bite a large part of its flesh, hooking your finger claws into the prey to hold it still.

04. When your prey dies from loss of blood, step on the creature and tear out huge chunks of meat. Enjoy your feast, but keep an eye out for rival *T. rexes*!

Tyrannosaurus rex's eyes were angled forward, so the field of view overlapped at the front. This gave the dinosaur **stereoscopic vision**—it could have judged distances and seen things in three dimensions, just like humans do.

Meet the family

Although *Tyrannosaurus rex* was the biggest meat-eater, there were other equally scary members in the Tyrannosaur family.

Tarbosaurus
Lived: 70–65 million years ago
Where: Mongolia and China
Length: 40 ft (12 m)

Albertosaurus
Lived: 76–74 million years ago
Where: Canada
Length: 33 ft (10 m)

Gorgosaurus
Lived: 76–68 million years ago
Where: North America
Length: 30 ft (9 m)

Alioramus
Lived: 70–65 million years ago
Where: Mongolia
Length: 20 ft (6 m)

Five good reasons **NOT to invite a *T. rex* to dinner**

01: You'll need an awful lot of meat to keep your guest happy: *T. rex* can tear off 500 lbs (230 kg) of meat in one bite.

02: Expect bad table manners. With such tiny short arms, *T. rex* would guzzle straight from the plate.

03: It won't be a pretty sight. *T. rex* eats with its mouth open, chopping up food with teeth like giant spikes.

04: Your other guests might be a tad nervous—and some may end up as an extra course if your meat supplies aren't sufficient.

05: With rows of teeth where meat can get caught and rot, and no sign of a Cretaceous toothbrush, you can guarantee that this guest would have fearsome breath.

What about me?

One of the largest parts of the *T. rex*'s brain was the area that identified odors—so it would have no trouble sniffing you out. You would, however, be just a light snack!

I don't believe it!

A coprolite (fossilized dropping) belonging to *Tyrannosaurus rex* has given scientists clues about the diet of these feared predators. Nearly as long as a man's arm and weighing as much as a six-month-old baby, this dropping contained chewed bits of bone from a plant-eating dinosaur as big as a cow.

Superstar Sue

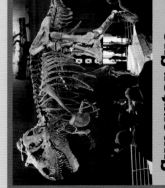

The most complete *T. rex* fossil ever found is on display at the Field Museum in Chicago, and she's known as Sue.

🦖 **The fossil was discovered on August 12, 1990, by the Cheyenne River, South Dakota.**

🦖 We don't know if Sue is male or female; the fossil is named after Sue Hendrickson, the fossil hunter who discovered it.

🦖 **The fossil was bought by the museum for nearly $8.4 million.**

🦖 Sue died 67 million years ago.

🦖 **When she was alive, she would probably have weighed 7 tons.**

🦖 She was 42 ft (12.8 m) long from snout to tail.

🦖 **Her skeleton is made up of more than 200 bones.**

🦖 She had 58 teeth in her awesome jaws.

🦖 **The skull in the display is a replica—the real skull is just too heavy to hold in place.**

🦖 Her brain is just big enough to hold a quart (liter) of milk.

Fright bite

T. rex had a mouth full of teeth of different sizes. Some teeth have been found as long as 13 in (33 cm).

Movie star

T. rex has appeared many times on the silver screen, although, sadly, he only gets to play the villain. Here are just a few of his most recent movies.

■ *Jurassic Park* (1993) and II (1997), and III (2001)
■ *King Kong* (2005)
■ *Night at the Museum* (2006)
■ *Journey to the Center of the Earth* (2008)

How did dinosaurs defend themselves?

Different dinosaurs reacted in different ways when they came across predators. *Iguanodon* would blend into its surroundings—its skin patterns and color camouflaging it. *Gallimimus* used its speed to escape predators such as *Tyrannosaurus rex*, reaching speeds of 35 mph (56 kph). Others relied on sturdy body armor.

How to: be indestructible

01. As a *Protoceratops* you have nothing to fear: swing around to face the danger. Your shield will protect your neck.

02. Stand and face your enemy so that the bright colors of your neck shield can be seen.

03. Have your sharp beak ready to snap at limbs or soft underbellies if your enemy comes too close.

04. It is best to go around in a herd, so that you are less likely to be picked on.

WEIRD OR WHAT?

Euoplocephalus may have used its clublike tail as a decoy head.

Tail tales

■ *Scelidosaurus* may have used its tail for balance while it reared itself up on its hind legs to flee predators.

■ *Euoplocephalus* had tail bones that were fused together to make it straight, so it could swing its tail club from side to side like a mace.

■ *Gastonia* had big spines all over its tail, which made it a formidable weapon. The rest of its body was also studded with sharp defensive spines.

Sticking together

Growing family
In a big group with lots of females, the dominant *Pachycephalosaurus* male was able to find many mates, increasing the herd.

Child-minding
Hypacrosaurus raised young in large groups—greater numbers meant better defense against predators.

Protection
Big dinosaurs that couldn't run fast, like *Centrosaurus*, found safety in numbers.

Hunting in herds
Small, fierce dinosaurs, like *Deinonychus*, made up for their size by hunting in packs, like lions.

Scary horns

Horns on dinosaurs may have been used for defense against meat-eaters, fighting for leadership of a herd, and for showing off.

Triceratops
Three horns, one on the nose and two above the eyes

Styracosaurus
One horn on the nose and six around the rim of the neck

Centrosaurus
One crooked horn on the nose

What to do if you meet a...

Triceratops
Keep behind the frill where it can't see you. But beware, *Triceratops* move around in herds, so there may be another one creeping up behind you!

Euoplocephalus
Vulnerable parts lie underneath, so hide on the ground until it walks over you, and strike from below.

Stegosaurus
Keep clear of the tail and watch out. Even after a fatal blow to the head, *Stegosaurus* (pictured) could still be active since nerves in the hip keep the hind legs and tail working for a while.

Most plant-eating dinosaurs had **eyes on the sides of their heads**. This gave them a wide field of vision, allowing them to scan the landscape for predators.

Killer claws

Deinonychus grabbed its prey with its jaws and hands. It then balanced on one leg and slashed the claws of the other foot back and forth, to disembowel its victim.

Claws: Rose up and flicked forward with brutal force

Skin deep
The armor-plated skin of some dinosaurs provided extra protection. Predators would find slashing or biting the tough skin hard going.

Three ways to **catch your prey**

01: Sudden ambush
Hiding in trees, the massive *Giganotosaurus* (pictured) probably waited patiently until a slow-moving herbivore passed by, then grabbed it in its jaws.

02: Chasing down prey
Compsognathus was a fast sprinter and used its speed and agility to pursue its prey.

03: Snatch and grab
Baryonyx snatched unsuspecting fish in its narrow jaws and hooked thumb claw, piercing the prey with its teeth.

Tell me more: *Gorgosaurus teeth*

Front teeth: Short and stout for clamping on to struggling prey

sharp serrated edge

Back teeth: Bladelike and serrated to slice the flesh

Jaw: Hinged to open wide and engulf prey

Were dinosaurs able to fly?

Dinosaurs could not fly, but their reptile relatives, pterosaurs, soared high above them. Pterosaurs ruled the skies, flying over land and sea while the dinosaurs stalked the Earth. These majestic winged reptiles died out at the same time as the dinosaurs, 65 million years ago.

How to: fly like a *Dimorphodon*

07. Steer yourself through the air using the flap of skin at the end of your tail as a rudder.

RECORD BREAKER

The **biggest flying creature** ever to soar the skies was the pterosaur *Quetzalcoatlus*. Its wingspan was 40 ft (12 m)—as big as a small aircraft.

01. Keep your head warm with just a few short, fine threads of hair.

04. Stretch out your neck while flying to reduce drag from air resistance.

06. To keep airborne, flap your leathery wings, which are made of skin and muscle. When not flying, fold your wings against your body.

02. Spot prey far away using your large, probing eyes.

I don't believe it!

In 1856, builders constructing a railroad tunnel claimed to see a large creature resembling a *Pteradactyl*. It apparently fluttered its wings before dropping down dead and turning to dust. Hmm. With no evidence to corroborate the story, was it really a flying reptile or just a flight of fancy?

05. Support your wing with your long fourth finger. Use the other three sharp, hooklike fingers for defense.

03. Dive toward the sea and use your sharp teeth to spear fish.

Walking on wings

The biggest pterosaurs, the azhdarchids, liked to walk as well as fly. They had strong back legs, and at the front they used their wing "hands" as front legs.

High flyers

Winging it through the skies with the pterosaurs was a collection of animals that had evolved from therapod dinosaurs. These animals, not pterosaurs, are considered to be the first birds.

Dimorphodon

Peteinosaurus

Lived: 220 million years ago
Habitat: Swamps and river valleys
Where: Southern Europe
Length: 24 in (60 cm)
Diet: Flying insects

Pterosaurs

01: The first pterosaurs were small flappers, but over millions of years they evolved into giant gliders.

02: **Slim, hollow bones made pterosaurs very light for flying.**

03: Pterosaur skulls contained air sacs to make them lighter.

04: **Some pterosaurs had curious head crests, possibly for courtship displays.**

05: Some pterosaurs gathered together in huge colonies to mate and breed.

06: **A fossil pterosaur egg contained an unhatched baby inside a soft eggshell, like that of a modern reptile.**

What's the difference?

pterosaurs	birds
furry body	feathered body
most had teeth	most are toothless
claws on the wings	no claws on the wings
membrane-type, batlike wings	feathered wings

Like pelicans, pterosaurs had long, narrow heads and **throat pouches**. They plunged their beaks beneath the water to grab fish, which they stored in their pouches.

goshawk

Pterodactylus

Lived: 150 million years ago
Habitat: Lake shores
Where: Europe
Length: 3 ft (1 m)
Diet: Fish

Giant jaws

■ Birds have beaks, but pterosaurs mostly had toothy jaws.

■ A few had crests, possibly for cleaving (passing through) the water as they dipped for fish.

■ Sharp, pointed, widely spaced teeth were good for seizing fish or other slippery prey.

■ Some crests were brightly colored.

■ Some pterosaurs were toothless.

Pteranodon

Lived: 88 million years ago
Habitat: Oceans, shores
Where: North America
Length: 6 ft (1.8 m)
Diet: Fish

Dinobirds

It is believed that today's birds are not the descendants of pterosaurs, but of dinosaurs that took to the air. The reason is the discovery over the last 150 years of fossils of animals that were half-bird and half-dino, such as *Caudipteryx*.

Pterodactylus

Could dinosaurs swim?

No, but while dinosaurs ruled the land, marine reptiles ruled the sea. These ichthyosaurs, pliosaurs, plesiosaurs, placodonts, and mosasaurs were carnivores—preying on other sea creatures as well as each other. They needed air to breathe, so they had to swim to the surface to refill their lungs, before disappearing back into their underwater world.

How to: live like an *Elasmosaurus*

01. Use your four paddle-shaped flippers to help you swim.

02. Slide slowly through the water. It takes a lot of energy to move a body that weighs up to 3 tons.

03. Use your tail to stabilize and steer your body.

04. Keep afloat using the small stones in your stomach as a ballast (a weight to keep your body stable).

05. Protect your chest and support your powerful paddle muscles using your large platelike shoulder bones.

I don't believe it!

In 1997, the skeleton of a giant ichthyosaur *Shonisaurus* was found in a mountain stream in British Columbia, Canada. It was 69 ft (21 m) long, but the only way paleontologists could get a good look at the whole thing was through aerial photography!

In numbers

10 in
(26 cm) The width of each eye of some ichthyosaurs

46 ft
(14 m) The length of *Elasmosaurus*, which lived in oceans 66 million years ago

72
The number of vertebrae bones in an *Elasmosaurus*'s neck. This is more than any other animal

6 ft
(1.8 m) The length of the skull of *Deinosuchus*— a giant distant cousin of modern crocodiles

5 tons
The weight of *Deinosuchus*

WEIRD OR WHAT?

Some scientists think that small plesiosaurs crawled onto sandy beaches to lay their eggs, just like turtles.

Sea monsters

Tylosaurus
This 36-ft (11-m) mosasaur predator hunted fish, squid, and turtles.

Ichthyosaurus
Females gave birth to live young, tail first. Adults grew to 6½ ft (2 m) and weighed up to 200 lb (90 kg).

Kronosaurus
This 33-ft (10-m) long, 7-ton giant pliosaur had winglike flippers and huge, powerful jaws.

Nothosaurus
This slender, 46-ft (14-m) long reptile fed mainly on fish.

Tell me more: pliosaur anatomy

Pliosaur fossils, like this *Liopleurodon* skeleton, suggest that these vast creatures glided through the waters like a sea lion. But, at around 82 ft (25 m) long and weighing around 165 tons (150 metric tons), it was 10 times bigger.

Backbone: Long, arched back

Back flippers: Enabled them to swim at speed

Huge front flippers: Measuring up to 10 ft (3 m), they propeled the reptile underwater

Bony plates: The underneath of the reptile is protected by broad chest bones and hip bones

enormous head

Daggerlike teeth: Fish were impaled on the sharp points

Like divers, marine reptiles sometimes suffered from a disease called "the bends," which occurs when **bubbles of nitrogen** appear in the blood stream after surfacing too quickly.

Seafood (and eat it)!

There was a wide and tantalizing menu for marine reptiles to feed on.

Ammonites: Coiled shell-baring squid relatives, eaten by ichthyosaurs and mosasaurs

Fish: A wide variety eaten by sharp-toothed plesiosaurs and ichthyosaurs

Squid: Soft-bodied animals were a lip-smacking favorite of toothless ichthyosaurs

Shellfish: Eaten by broad-toothed, strong-jawed ichthyosaurs, mososaurs, and early walruslike placodonts

Fossil finds

01 Fossils of marine reptiles were found before anything was known about the dinosaurs.

02 The first complete ichthyosaur skeleton was discovered in 1791.

03 At first, scientists thought ichthyosaurs were a type of extinct dolphin or crocodile—or even a sea dragon!

06. Use your long, snaking neck to give you strength and flexibility.

07. Use your sharp teeth and strong jaws to catch slippery prey, like fish and squid.

08. Use your excellent vision to spot prey.

What on Earth can digging unearth?

WHAT'S IN A NAME?

A **paleontologist** is a scientist who studies rocks and fossils. Paleontology literally means **"the study of prehistory,"** which is life before humans began recording events.

If you know where to look, you might find a fossil—the word fossil even comes from the Greek for "dug up." Fossils are the ancient remains of organisms that have been preserved in rocks. From them, scientists are able to find out about the different life-forms that existed millions of years ago.

LIFE ON EARTH

Earth's history is divided up into four main periods:

- **EARLY PALEOZOIC 545–417 million years ago**
  Living things that have been living in the seas for 3 billion years develop hard shells. Plants begin to colonize the land.

- **LATE PALEOZOIC 417–248 million years ago**
  More life-forms evolve. Amphibians, reptiles, and insects inhabit the land, living on the plants. Many species die out in a mass extinction at the end of this period.

- **MESOZOIC 248–65 million years ago**
  Dinosaurs stalk the land, pterosaurs rule the skies, and marine reptiles lurk in the waters. The first flowering plants and small mammals appear. Another mass extinction wipes out many species, including all dinosaurs.

- **CENOZOIC 65 million years ago to present day**
  Mammals and flowering plants become more varied and dominate the land, while bony fish thrive in the seas. Humans evolve.

Fossil finds

Sometimes insects get engulfed in sticky pine tree resin and become fossilized as it hardens into **amber**.

In some rare instances **dinosaur skeletons** may be found intact, with the bones still connected.

A heap of bones gives scientists freedom to cut up the skeleton for further investigation.

An **isolated bone** is the most common find and must be examined for clues about what it is and where it's from.

Tell me more: becoming a fossil

01: For a dead animal to become a fossil, before it is eaten or decomposes, it needs to be buried quickly, by falling into a muddy riverbed, or by a sandstorm, for example.

02: Soft tissue rots away, but the skeleton remains to be replaced by minerals and turned to rock over millions of years.

03: Over time, mud and river sediments build up over the fossil, forming layer upon layer of sedimentary rocks.

04: Over more millions of years, erosion and movements in the Earth's crust can expose the fossil, and, with luck, a paleontologist may find it.

How to: excavate a dinosaur

01. Remove the soil and rock from above the dinosaur skeleton until you are just above the level of the fossil.

02. Delicately remove the last layer with knives, needles, and brushes, until the skeleton is exposed.

03. Place a grid over the exposed skeleton, and draw a map of the bones. This will help to determine how the dinosaur died.

04. Protect the bones with varnish, then wrap in plaster, like a broken leg, to keep them whole until they get to the laboratory.

The **world's oldest fossils** are of minute bacterialike cells **3.5 billion years old**.

PLANT LIFE

Plant fossils help to draw a picture of the lands through which animals like the dinosaurs roamed.

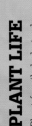

Ferns and club mosses: The first plant types

Cycads: Palmlike plants related to conifers

Conifers: Trees such as the giant redwood and monkey puzzle

Broad-leaved trees: First appear at the end of the Age of the Dinosaurs

Dinosaur **eggs** and nests are also fossilized. At a site in Spain, 300,000 eggs were found.

Fossilized dinosaur **footprints** can help reveal an animal's height and how fast it moved.

Some very detailed **fossil casts** can reveal an animal's skin texture, as well as its bones.

Fossilized dung (a coprolite) is a trace fossil. These reveal how the animal lived and what it ate.

sea fossils

Marine fossils are the most common because dead sea creatures are quickly covered by silt and sand when they fall to the seafloor.

Belemnite: An animal like a squid, but with a pencil-shaped internal shell

Ammonite: An octopus-like animal in a coiled shell, now extinct

Shark's teeth: Commonly preserved as fossils because they are so hard

Trilobite: An ancient jointed animal that crawled on the seafloor

Fish: Primitive vertebrates that first appeared about 500 million years ago

Top five fossil sites

01: Dinosaur National Monument, Utah
Hundreds of dinosaurs have been found in an ancient floodplain.

02: Liaoning, China
Fine lake sediments have preserved tiny dinosaurs and early birds in detail.

03: Mt. Kirkpatrick, Antarctica
The first site to reveal that dinosaurs lived in Antarctica.

04: Egg Mountain, Montana
The site of a dinosaur nesting colony.

05: Patagonia, Argentina
The biggest dinosaurs ever, both meat-eaters and plant-eaters, have been found here.

Four famous fossil hunters

William Buckland
In 1824, Buckland became the first to describe a dinosaur as a "big reptile" or *Megalosaurus*.

Sir Richard Owen
In 1841, this British scientist first came up with the name "dinosaur," meaning "terrible lizard."

Mary Anning
A professional fossil hunter, Anning excavated marine reptiles for scientists in the early 19th century.

Roy Chapman Andrews
This scientist and explorer made the first dinosaur discoveries in Asia.

Who ruled the world after the dinos died out?

Sixty-five million years ago, a mass extinction wiped out the dinosaurs. Mammals had been around since the Jurassic Period. Living alongside the dominant dinosaurs, they were just a small group of tiny, rodentlike creatures. When the dinos died out, so did many of the mammals, but the survivors evolved to become the most successful type of animal around.

Andrewsarchus
A wolflike creature with a wide head, the largest known carnivorous land mammal ever

Canis dirus
Wolflike creature with a wide head, strong jaws, and large teeth—perfect for breaking and eating bones

Smilodon
Far-from-friendly feline with enormous gnashers

Daeodon
"Killer buffalo pig"—the name says it all, really

How to: **be a prehistoric mammal**

01. You will need your wits about you, so a large brain is a must-have.

02. Use your sensory whiskers to aid navigation.

03. A covering of fur will help keep you warm.

04. Catch and eat prey using your specialized teeth.

05. Your warm-blooded metabolism will keep you alert and active.

06. Make sure your limbs are tucked beneath your body instead of sprawling like a lizard's legs.

What about me?
Modern humans evolved 200,000 years ago, when woolly mammoths still stalked the icy plains.

Newcomers
New groups of animals that soon appeared on the scene included big plant-eaters like elephants, hoofed mammals like pigs and tapirs, sea mammals like whales and dolphins, and the first bats.

Five strange new species

Moetherium
A primitive elephant with a massive body, short legs, and a long, thick neck.

Arsinotherium
A heavy, rhinolike plant-eater with massive horns, which were covered in skin.

Macrauchenia
This animal had a body like a horse, a neck like a camel, and a short trunk like a tapir.

Phenacodus
Like a wild boar, it had a skeleton suited to a lifestyle of running in open woodlands.

01: Mammoths lived from around 4.8 million years ago until most died out in the last Ice Age, 10,000 years ago.

02: One group of pygmy woolly mammoths still existed in the Arctic until 1650 BCE.

03: Several woolly mammoths have been found preserved in the frozen ground of Siberia, with pieces of fur, skin, and even stomach contents intact.

04: The woolly mammoth could grow to 11 ft (3.3 m) tall and was covered in hair up to 3 ft (90 cm) long.

WHAT'S IN A NAME?

Basilosaurus sounds like a dinosaur, but was actually a kind of **whale**. The scientist who first studied it thought it was a reptile, and the rules of scientific naming meant that the name he gave it had to stick.

Extinction winners and losers

Reptiles
All species of dinosaur, pterosaur, and plesiosaur were wiped out, along with 36 percent of crocodilians, 27 percent of turtles and tortoises, and 6 percent of lizard and snake species.

Mammals
All types of mammals lost species, but the marsupials were hit the hardest, with 75 percent of species wiped out.

Birds
Seventy-five percent of bird species disappeared.

Fish
Fish got off lightly, with only 15 percent of species lost forever.

Amphibians
The amphibians hopped off the winners—no species were lost.

I don't believe it!

Modern-day bowhead whales are thought to be the exact same species as certain fossilized whales that have been found to date back to between 1.8 and 10 million years ago. That's some staying power!

Meteorite strike!

When the dinosaurs were wiped out, so were around 70 percent of all animal and plant species. Many scientists believe this mass extinction was caused by a meteorite crashing into Earth.

1 The shock wave destroyed every living thing in the immediate area.

2 Heat of the impact produced extensive forest fires.

3 Tsunamis swept across low-lying lands.

4 Smoke and ash cut out sunlight and killed plants.

5 Acid rain from the clouds also destroyed many plants.

Top of the tusks

Mammoth
This woolly creature's long, curving tusks were used as snowplows.

Gomphotherium
Four tusks, two at the top and two at the bottom, were used for all kinds of tasks, such as digging and scraping.

Dienotherium
Its tusks curved downward from the lower jaw and were used as picks.

Phiomia
Resembling an overgrown warthog, it had lower tusks like shovels for digging.

Why don't some plants have flowers?

Although many plants use flowers to reproduce, some do not. There are more than 30,000 types of these nonflowering plants. Mosses, for example, release tiny spores that are spread by the wind. Conifers make seeds inside scaly cones. Both spores and seeds grow into new plants.

Spore producers

11,000 species

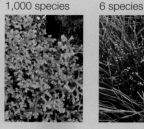

Ferns
A familiar spore producer, armed with tough stems and complex leaves.

15 species

Horsetails
This plant's cylindrical stems and rings of narrow leaves look like brushes.

1,000 species

Club mosses
These plants are notable for their flat or upright stems with spiraling leaves.

6 species

Whisk ferns
The ferns are the simplest plants to have internal plumbing. Tiny tubes carry food and water.

9,500 species

Mosses
Small, leafy upright plants, they can usually be found in bogs and damp woodlands.

100 species

Hornworts
Resemble liverworts, and live in damp places; they can grow on the bark of trees.

8,000 species

Liverworts
These simple plants live in damp or wet places and lack proper stems, roots, or leaves.

Seed producers

70 species

Gnetophytes
Pronounced "neat-o-fights", they include shrubs, trees, and the desert welwitschia.

1 species

Ginkgo
Also known as the Maidenhair tree, it has fan-shaped leaves that drop off in the fall.

140 species

Cycads
They resemble palm trees, live in warm places, and can be male or female.

550 species

Conifers
They are mostly trees and include pines, cedars, spruces, larches, and firs.

I don't believe it!

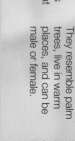

If wet sphagnum moss is dried out, it becomes very absorbent. In the past it was used in babies' diapers to soak up urine, and in hospitals to dress wounds in order to soak up blood.

RECORD BREAKER

Bristlecone pines are the **oldest trees** on the planet. Growing slowly on cold, windswept mountainsides in the western US, they can live for thousands of years. The oldest specimen is known as Methuselah, and is about 4,800 years old.

Can a cone predict rain?

01: Find a pine tree and collect a fallen cone.

02: Put the cone somewhere convenient at home.

03: Look at your cone when you get up in the morning.

04: If the cone's scales have opened up, it's likely to be a dry day.

05: If the cone's scales have closed, it will probably be drizzly or rainy.

Which of these are *not* plants? (answers at bottom of page)

a) Green seaweed

b) Green stain mushroom

c) Reindeer moss

d) Brown seaweed

e) Staghorn coral

FOUR USES FOR NONFLOWERING PLANTS

01: Horsetails were used—and still are in some places—as pan scourers. Hard silica (from sand grains) in their stems makes them abrasive.

02: Some people believe that an extract made from gingko tree leaves helps memory.

03: If lycopodium powder—from the spores of club mosses—is thrown into the air and ignited it creates an amazing fireball. Don't try at home!

04: Edible pine nuts (the seeds produced by certain pine trees) have been eaten for thousands of years, and are a key ingredient of Italian pesto.

Sunlight to sugars

All plants make their own food by a process called photosynthesis, whether they have flowers or not. Plant leaves contain **chlorophyll**, which makes them green. Chlorophyll "captures" energy in sunlight and uses it to make glucose, energy-rich sugars, like glucose, from simple raw materials.

How to: **make food if you're a plant**

01. Make sure the Sun is shining.

02. Take plenty of water in from the soil using your roots.

03. Transport the water up the stem and to your leaves.

04. Take the gas carbon dioxide from the air into your leaves.

05. Use sunlight to combine with carbon dioxide and water to make energy-rich glucose (sugars). Yum!

06. Release the waste gas oxygen from your leaves into the air.

KEY
glucose
carbon dioxide
water
oxygen

Why welwitschia is weird

- It lives in the arid Namib Desert, Africa, and gets water from morning dew.
- It can live for more than 1,000 years.
- It has just two long, curly, and hard leaves that split as they grow.
- Older specimens look more like a pile of garbage than plants.

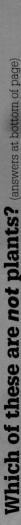

Why do some plants have flowers?

Flowering plants are the most successful and numerous plants on the planet and grow just about everywhere. Whether it's a cactus, daisy, maple tree, or rice plant, every flowering plant produces flowers. At the center of each flower are ovaries that make the seeds that will grow into that plant's offspring.

Five ways to get pollinated

Bats
They feed on nectar and pick up pollen.

Hummingbirds
Hovering in front of flowers, hummingbirds feed on nectar and pick up pollen.

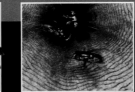

Flies
Flowers that smell of dead meat will attract flies.

Butterflies
By feeding on flowers, butterflies pick up pollen.

Wind
Willow catkins blowing in the wind release lightweight pollen.

How to: pollinate a flower

01. Find a suitable flower, land on the petals, and locate the nectar. Petal patterns will guide you in the right direction.

02. Stick out your proboscis (tongue) and use it to suck up sweet nectar from the nectary.

03. While feeding, you will accidentally pick up pollen grains on your hairy back from the flower's anthers.

04. Leave that flower and buzz through the air carrying pollen grains until you find another flower.

05. Land on the new flower, look for nectar, and unknowingly transfer pollen to the flower's sticky stigma. Job complete!

Life cycle of a flowering plant

1. Flower opens up and attracts insects that carry pollen from the same type of flower

2. Fertilization happens, seeds grow inside the ovaries, and the petals fall off. The seeds scatter and fall to the ground

3. Seeds germinate and grow if the soil is warm and moist

4. Young plant grows out of the soil, and its leaves use sunlight energy to make food

5. Plant matures and produces one or more flower heads

Types of flowering plant

There are more than 250,000 species of flowering plant, which are divided into two groups—monocots and dicots.

Monocots usually have narrow leaves with parallel veins, and three (or multiples of three) petals.

grass

lily

orchid

palm

Dicots have broad leaves with a central midrib that connects to a smaller network of veins. They have four or five (or multiples of four or five) petals, and also include trees, such as oaks and maples.

magnolia

poppy

buttercup

lupin

RECORD BREAKER

The **world's tallest flower** is the *titan arum*, which rises to 10 ft (3 m). Smelling of rotting meat to attract the tiny bees that pollinate it, it is short-lived and rarely seen.

Most of our plant food comes from flowering plants. We eat many different parts, including roots, stems, leaves, fruits, and seeds.

I don't believe it!

Some species of bamboo grow so fast you can almost watch it happening. Bamboo belongs to the grass family, and the fastest growing specimens can add more than 3 ft (1 m) in height every day.

Tell me more: parts of a flower

Flowers vary enormously in shape and size, but all have the same basic parts.

Sticky stigma: Collects pollen from visiting insects

Petal: Attracts and guides insects toward the flower

Anther: Makes pollen containing male cells and dusts it onto visiting insects

Flower stalk: Holds up the flower

Ovary: Contains female cells that will develop into seeds once they are fertilized by male cells

In numbers

130–140 million
How many years ago the world's first flowers began to bloom. They would have been similar in appearance to today's magnolia.

21,000 ft
(6,400 m) The altitude of the highest living flowering plant, *Ranunculus lobatus*, which is found in the Himalayan mountain range

150
How many years it takes the slowest flowering plant, *Puya raimondii*, to flower. It is found high up in the Andes mountain range of Bolivia and Peru

305 ft
(93 m) The height of the tallest flowering plant—the Australian majestic mountain ash tree

6¹⁄₂ ft
(2 m) The size of the largest floating leaves, which belong to the Amazon water lily and are able to support the weight of a child

What are fruits?

To reproduce, a flowering plant makes seeds inside each flower's ovary. Around a seed or seeds, the ovary grows into a fruit. Fruits come in all shapes and sizes and can be juicy and succulent or dry and hard. They protect the seeds and help them disperse far away from the parent plant so new plants don't compete for water and light.

Fruit fight!

- The Battle of the Oranges takes place in the Italian town of Ivrea. Every February, thousands of locals, divided into teams, throw oranges at each other—although nobody is really sure why.

- La Tomatina (pictured) is the world's biggest food fight. For just one hour every August in the small Spanish town of Buñol, tens of thousands of people throw tons of ripe, squishy tomatoes at each other.

How to: **turn a flower into fruit**

01. Attract insects to your flower's brightly colored petals.

02. Allow an insect to pollinate your flower. After pollination, seeds form inside your flower's ovary.

03. No longer required, your petals should fall off and the ovary begin to swell.

What about me?

If you eat fruits such as apples, or oranges, get a juicy treat, you not only of essential vitamins and minerals.

Foul fruit

The durian is a large fruit that grows on trees in southeast Asia. Although it is prized for its sweet flesh, it gives off a **disgusting smell!** In Singapore, it is forbidden to take durians on public transportation because of the unbearable stink.

How seeds **spread**

Raspberries
Eaten by animals, the seeds come out in droppings

Burrs
Their spines or hooks stick to animal fur

Pea pods
Pods dry out and explode, launching seeds into the wind

Poppy seeds
The head of a poppy acts like a pepper pot to release seeds

Maple seeds
These have "wings" that spin through the air like a helicopter

Coconuts
Fall into the sea and are carried by the currents

Brazil nuts
Seeds are buried by animals, such as agoutis (a type of rodent)

Squirting cucumber
Explode under high pressure, showering seeds

How to: **grow a bean seed**

01. Begin to sprout. You need fertile soil, ample water, and warm weather.

02. Begin to expand. Your outer covering splits, and your radicle (root) grows outward and down into the soil.

03. Grow upward. After three days, a plumule (young stem) should sprout up, using energy from the cotyledons (seed leaves).

04. Use your roots to take in water. Your stem lengthens, and "true" leaves appear above the soil. They use sunlight energy to make food. Just watch out for that slug!

true leaf
network of roots
radicle
seed case
plumule
cotyledon

04. Congratulations! You've grown a bright orange pumpkin. Who wants soup?

Fruit or not?

Do you know your fruits from your vegetables? Look at the list below, and see if you can pick out which are the fruits.

a. banana
b. sweet potato
c. cucumber
d. chili pepper
e. eggplant
f. asparagus
g. strawberry

(answer below)

Smallest seed

The world's smallest seed-bearing plant, the watermeal, is 0.039 in (0.1 cm) wide. It produces fruits that are tinier than salt grains.

Biggest seed

The biggest seed is produced by the coco de mer, or double coconut palm. It weighs 44 lb (20 kg) and grows in the Seychelles Islands in the Indian Ocean.

ANSWER: a, c, d, e, and g are fruits; b is a root vegetable; f is a plant stem

---

RECORD BREAKER

The **heaviest cultivated fruit** is the pumpkin. It can reach an astonishing weight of 1,300 lb (600 kg) — the same as the combined weight of eight adult men.

How long do **trees** live?

Trees can live for an extremely long time—tens, hundreds, even thousands of years. Most trees have a single woody stem called a trunk that supports a mass of branches carrying leaves. There are an estimated 100,000 tree species worldwide.

My Year, by A. Tree

In northern Europe and North America, deciduous (leaf-shedding) broadleaved trees follow the seasons.

Spring
As days lengthen and temperatures increase, buds burst open to produce new growth, leaves, and flowers.

Summer
Trees are in full leaf, and a variety of fruits develop from flowers pollinated by insects, or by the wind.

Fall
Fruits fall or are eaten, leaves change color and drop from trees, and tiny buds remain dormant until spring.

Winter
During the short days of cold winter months, the trees "rest" and the branches are bare of leaves.

Leaf types

Simple
Like most trees, the sweet chestnut has simple leaves with single blades (the "leafy" part).

Compound
The false acacia tree has compound leaves made up of many leaflets sprouting from a long stalk.

Needle
Pine trees have thick, tough needles that thrive in the extreme cold climates that would damage other leaves.

How to: **be a tree**

02. Support leaves. flowers, and fruits with a mass of twigs growing from branches.

01. Trap sunlight and make food using thousands of leaves.

03. Spread out branches from your trunk to form a "crown."

04. Use your strong trunk to support the weight of the branches so you can sway in the wind.

05. Protect inner tissues from bugs and cold with hard bark covering.

Five top tree careers

01: Tree surgeon
Treats old trees to preserve them

02: Lumberjack
Fells trees for lumber

03: Dendrochronologist
Dates events by counting tree growth rings

04: Forester
Manages and maintains forest areas

05: Topiarist
Clips trees or shrubs into interesting shapes

Six good reasons not to cut down trees

01 Trees release oxygen into the air. Every year, 2.5 acres (1 hectare) of mature trees release the oxygen needed by 45 people.

02 Trees store the carbon dioxide breathed out by all living things and released by burning fossil fuels. Since carbon dioxide is a greenhouse gas (a gas that contributes to climate change), without trees global warming would be far worse.

03 Trees clean the air by removing tiny airborne particles and polluting gases.

04 Trees provide shade from the sun, and in cities act as natural "air-conditioners" to reduce summer temperatures.

05 Tree roots stabilize the soil and prevent it from being eroded (blown away) by wind, or washed away by heavy rain.

06 Trees provide homes for thousands of animals, including insects, birds, frogs, and monkeys.

06. Fix yourself in the ground by strong roots that also take in vital water and minerals.

Bonsai is the ancient Japanese art of growing miniaturized trees in pots. These are normal trees, but their branches and roots are pruned in a specific way to resemble fully grown trees.

In numbers

15,000 ft (4,600 m) The altitude at which the Silver fir grows, in southwest China—higher than any other tree

2,500 tons The weight of the heaviest tree, the giant sequoia, which grows in California

400 ft (1200 m) The depth of the roots of the Himalayan wild fig tree

79 ft (24 m) The size of the world's largest leaves, which are found on the African raffia palm

2 in (5 cm) The size of the dwarf willow, the world's smallest tree, which grows in the Arctic tundra region

-85°F (-65°C) The lowest temperature that the most cold-tolerant tree, Tamarack larch (found in northern North America), continues to grow

RECORD BREAKER

Growing in California, the **world's tallest tree** is a coast redwood, rising to the dizzying height of 370 ft (112 m)—taller than the Statue of Liberty.

I don't believe it!

If African acacia trees are chewed by a giraffe or other hungry plant-eater, they immediately boost levels of nasty-tasting chemicals inside their leaves to deter the diners. What's more, they release a gas that tells neighboring acacia trees to do the same thing.

Three types of tree

Broadleaved
There are about 25,000 species of broadleaved tree, including birch, oak, and maple. They are flowering plants and have broad, veined leaves. Many are deciduous, losing their leaves in winter.

Palm
The 3,000 species of palm tree are flowering plants. They include coconut and oil palms and most grow in warm places. The trunks are fibrous, not woody, and are topped with tufts of large leaves.

Conifer
The 550 species of conifer include pines, firs, and spruces. They are nonflowering plants that produce seeds inside cones. They have slender trunks and tough evergreen leaves.

Tell me more: inside the trunk

Sapwood: Consists of vertical tubes called xylem that carry water from the roots

Bark: The trunk and branch's outer protective layer

Phloem: Vertical tubes that carry sugary sap from the leaves

Cambium: Thin layer of cells that divide to let the trunk grow and widen

Annual growth ring: Shows the amount of growth that takes place in one year

Heartwood: Mature xylem (carrying water and minerals from the roots) that support the trunk and branches

How do plants survive?

Survival means different things to different plants. Parasitic plants survive by stealing water and nutrients from other plants. Other plants depend on their ability to defend themselves against hungry animals. Desert plants must endure extremely dry conditions, while plants in mountain regions cope with extremely cold temperatures.

What about me?

You should never touch or eat any plant that you are unsure about, because it may be poisonous.

Plant parasites

More than 4,000 plant species have stems or roots that enter other plants and then, like vampires, suck out sugars, minerals, and water from their hosts.

Plant survival techniques

Plant armor
Sea holly consists of tough, spine-tipped leaves that keep most plant-eaters at bay.

Stinger
Nettles are covered with sharp hairs. The hairs jab into the skin of any animal that brushes past.

Defensive hairs
Lamb's ears is a herb covered with tiny hairs that stop small insects from eating it.

Camouflage
The fleshy, mottled leaves of living stones make them look like pebbles.

Fearsome fluid
Fireglow spurges can ooze a milky fluid called latex, which is dangerous for animals to eat.

Chemical weapons
Dumb cane contains sharp crystal chemicals that can stick in an animal's throat.

How to: **survive as a cactus**

01. Reduce your leaves to spines to cut down on water loss.

02. The spines will also protect you against hungry plant-eaters.

03. Make food by trapping sunlight in your green stem.

04. When it rains, store water in your stem for later use.

RECORD BREAKER

Rafflesia—a parasitic plant from southeast Asia—has the world's **heaviest flower.** It weighs up to 15 lb (7 kg) and can reach more than 3 ft (1 m) in diameter.

Epiphytes

01: Epiphytes are plants that grow high up on trees and other plants. This gives them a share of the sunlight without having to spend lots of energy growing tall.

02: They are common in rain forests, but they also grow in cool, damp woodlands.

03: Epiphytes include liverworts, mosses, lichens, as well as flowering plants.

04: Epiphytes aren't parasites, they just use their roots to hold on to the tree.

05: They get water from rain and food from airborne particles, or things that drop onto them.

06: Some large epiphytes, called bromeliads, collect water in a tanklike hollow at the center of the plant.

07: Bromeliad tanks are important habitats. Some frogs lay their eggs in them and tadpoles hatch in them, high up in the tree.

WHAT'S IN A NAME?

The ants that live in the swellings at the base of the **whistling thorn tree** ward off animals that try to eat its leaves. On windy days, the swellings make a whistling sound, which is how the tree got its name.

Surviving the snow

The dogtooth violet is able to grow through a blanket of snow. The snow forms a protective layer that shields the plant from the worst of the cold and wind. As spring arrives and the snow begins to melt, the dogtooth violet's flower begins to bloom.

I don't believe it!

In October 2006, visitors to the Botanical Gardens in Lyon, France, reported an unpleasant stink from a group of pitcher plants native to the Philippines. Staff discovered the smell was a part-digested mouse in one of the pitchers.

Poisonous plants

Cherry laurel
A fast-growing garden shrub, the cherry laurel has thick, evergreen leaves that are well protected from insects because they give off cyanide if they are pierced or crushed.

Poison ivy
A thick, sticky poison called urushiol causes severe swelling if it touches bare skin.

Foxgloves
If a mammal eats this plant's leaves, it risks a heart attack. When administered with care, however, digitoxin (the poison found in a foxglove) can be used as a medicinal drug to treat people with heart failure.

Deadly nightshade
A family containing hundreds of plants that produce poisons called alkaloids. Although important in medicines, in large amounts they can kill.

castor-oil plant

Castor-oil plant
The world's deadliest plant releases ricin, a poison that is 10,000 times more deadly than the venom of a rattlesnake.

Four **parasitic plants**

Instead of growing on their own, parasitic plants live by stealing from other host plants.

Dodder (devil's thread) Slender brown stems twist around and penetrate their host plant.

Broomrape Its roots attach to the roots of neighboring plants to rob them of nutrients.

Mistletoe Grows latching on to branches of its host tree and steals water and minerals.

Australian Christmas tree It can flower during the hot, dry southern Christmas because it taps in to nearby plant roots.

Desert survival

The sack-of-potatoes tree grows in the desert on the island of Socotra in the Indian Ocean. Its fat, sacklike trunk stores water and is topped with several short, stubby branches that produce pink flowers.

06. Spread your long roots wide and deep to collect water.

05. Waterproof yourself with your stem's waxy covering.

How to: **catch a fly**

Carnivorous (meat-eating) plants, such as the brightly colored pitcher plant, live in boggy soils that are low in nutrients. They get extra nutrients by trapping insects and other small animals. Pitcher plants lure insects to pitcher-shaped traps on the ends of their leaves.

A sticky end

Sundews have a very sticky weapon—their hairs. Lured in by the plant's attractive colors, an unsuspecting fly soon finds itself stuck to beads of glue at the tips of the sundew's hairs.

Snatch: The fly is attracted by the glistening, sticky droplets, but soon finds itself stuck.

Grab: Now it's in big trouble. As the fly struggles to free itself, the sticky hairs curl around it.

01. Use your colorful appearance to lure all kinds of insect, from large cockroaches to tiny, tasty flies.

02. Produce nectar around the rim. This attracts insects to walk on and over the rim as they search for the source of the nectar.

Snappy trap

The Venus flytrap's hinged trap imprisons an unwary damselfly. After about a week, the trap reopens, letting the dead remains fall to the ground. Each trap digests several meals and then withers away.

Touch down: Once the damselfly lands on the plant, three small bristles in the middle of each pad activate the trap.

No escape: The pads snap together when the damselfly touches two of the triggers.

Meal time: Digestive enzymes break down the damselfly's body.

03. Make the rim slippery so the unwary fly loses its grip and falls into your trap.

04. Make sure you have a sufficient amount of fluid to drown the fly. A sea of other insect victims will be the last thing it sees.

05. Release digestive enzymes. Fluids released from your walls, aided by bacteria, turn the fly's soft parts into a mushy goo.

06. Absorb the nutrients that are released by the insects inside the pool then let their hard, indigestible parts sink to the bottom of your pitcher.

Feed: The sundew digests the fly and absorbs nutrients. Any indigestible parts remain stuck to the leaf.

Are bacteria important?

Bacteria are the most plentiful living organisms on the planet. They are also the smallest, each consisting of a simple, single cell. A few types of bacteria, often called germs, cause disease in humans. But most bacteria are harmless, and some are very useful, including those used in making foods and drugs.

Tell me more: anatomy of a bacterium

Loop of DNA: Contains instructions for building and running bacterium

Cytoplasm: Contains chemicals that bring the bacterium to life

Cell membrane: Controls substances that enter and leave

Capsule: Slimy jacket helps to protect bacterium

Ribosomes: Produce bacteria-building proteins

Cell wall: Rigid and shapes bacterium

Flagellum: Rotates to propel bacterium through its surroundings

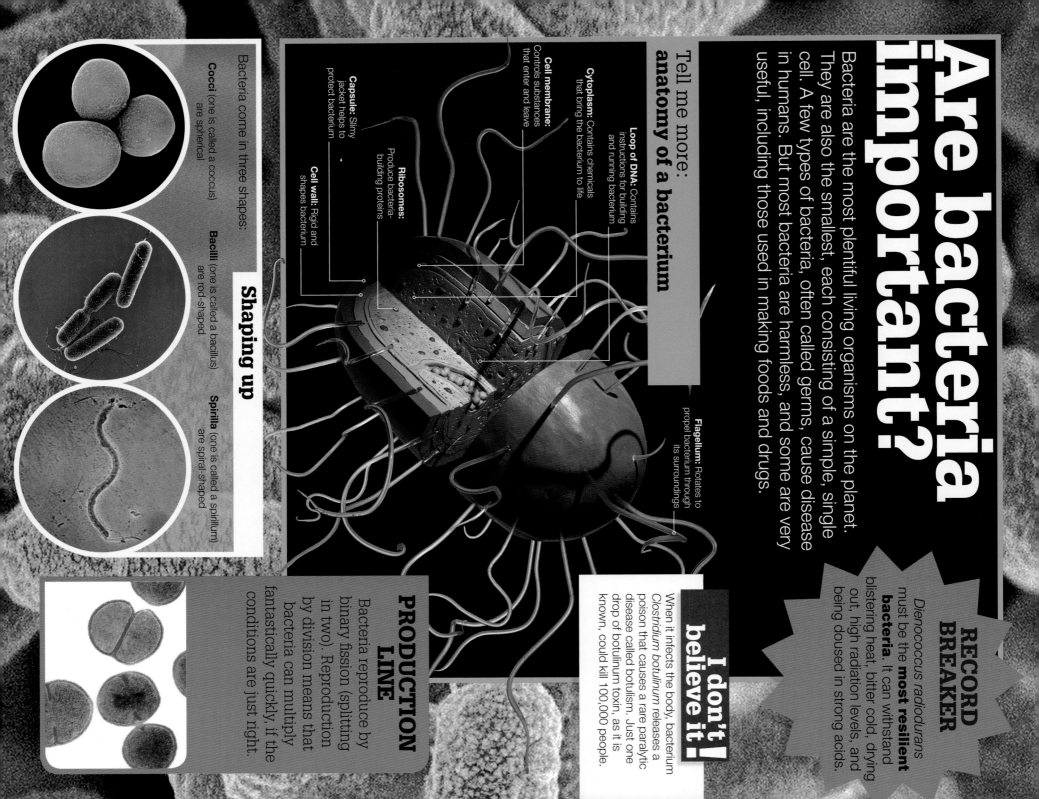

Shaping up

Bacteria come in three shapes:

Cocci (one is called a coccus) are spherical

Bacilli (one is called a bacillus) are rod-shaped

Spirilla (one is called a spirillum) are spiral-shaped

PRODUCTION LINE

Bacteria reproduce by binary fission (splitting in two). Reproduction by division means that bacteria can multiply fantastically quickly, if the conditions are just right.

RECORD BREAKER

Dienococcus radiodurans must be the **most resilient bacteria**. It can withstand blistering heat, bitter cold, drying out, high radiation levels, and being doused in strong acids.

Five diseases that bacteria cause in humans

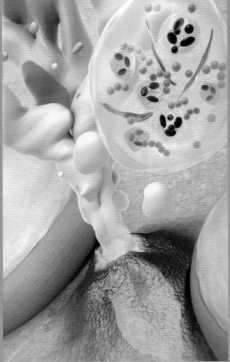

Acne Pimples can be sore and erupt (pictured)

Dental caries Tooth decay that form cavities

Cholera The major and most deadly symptom is severe diarrhea

Diphtheria A terrible, but rare, respiratory illness

Tetanus Serious disease causing muscle spasms

Lucky break

In 1928, British scientist Alexander Fleming was studying harmful bacteria by growing them in glass dishes. Returning from a vacation, he noticed that some dishes were infected with a blue penicillin fungus. This fungus released a chemical that killed harmful bacteria. The discovery lead to the development of penicillin—the first bacteria-killing drug, or antibiotic.

Clear zone: Where penicillin has killed harmful bacteria

penicillin fungus

harmful bacteria

In numbers

0.0004 in
(0.0001 cm) The average length of a bacterium

99%
The percentage of bacterial species that don't cause disease

10,000
The number of bacteria-laden droplets that you will breathe out in the next five minutes

100,000
The number of bacteria living on 0.16 sq in (1 sq cm) of your skin

2.5 billion
The number of bacteria in 0.04 oz (1 g) of soil

1,000 trillion
The number of bacteria on and inside the human body

5 billion trillion
The number of offspring that, in theory, a single bacterium dividing every 20 minutes produces in 24 hours

What about me?

Always remember to wash your hands after a trip to the restroom. Around half the weight of your feces (poop) is made up of bacteria, some potentially harmful.

Where don't bacteria live?

Bacteria appear in many places, but not everywhere. Can you guess where they don't appear?
(answers below)

a) Inside your brain and kidneys

b) In the Dead Sea, which is 10 times saltier than the Atlantic Ocean

c) In Antarctica, where the temperature can plummet to −76°F(−60°C)

d) On your teeth

e) In solid rock, 2 miles (3 km) below the Earth's surface

f) In clouds

g) On a sandwich

h) On the planet Mars

i) In hot springs, where the water temperature is near boiling point

Answers: a) and (probably) h)

Reasons to like bacteria...

✔ They are used to make yogurt and cheese.

✔ **Chemicals made by bacteria are used in the processes of baking.**

✔ Some bacteria produce antibiotics that are used to kill other harmful bacteria.

✔ **Bacteria in sewage processing help to break down smelly human waste.**

✔ Soil bacteria break down dead organisms so their components can be recycled.

✔ **Some bacteria release life-giving oxygen into the air.**

WEIRD OR WHAT?

Light-producing bacteria live inside the Hawaiian squid. At night, the **bacteria mimic moonlight** shining through the water, making the squid invisible to nearby, hungry predators.

Blasts from the past

3.6 billion years ago
First bacteria appear, more than 900 million years after Earth forms

2.7 billion years ago
Cyanobacteria use sunlight energy to make food, releasing oxygen into the atmosphere

1683
Dutch scientist, Antoni van Leeuwenhoek, using his homemade microscope, becomes the first person to see bacteria (in scrapings from his teeth)

1860s
French scientist Louis Pasteur shows that some bacteria cause disease

1990s
Scientists research genetically modified bacteria to produce useful substances, including anticancer vaccines

How do mushrooms grow so fast?

Mushrooms belong to a unique group of living things called fungi. They consist of a network of hairlike threads called hyphae, which spread unseen through the soil. When the conditions are right, hyphae push upward out of the soil with incredible speed to form a mushroom.

How to: qualify as a mushroom

01. You will need a cap that, like an umbrella, protects your gills from the rain.

02. Make sure you have gills to produce and shed millions of tiny spores. This is how you reproduce.

03. You should have a stem ring, which is the remnant of the membrane that covered the young gills as you were growing.

04. Your stem should lift the cap and gills above the ground so that spores can be carried away by the wind.

05. From your stem base, a network of hairlike threads, called hyphae, will penetrate the soil.

There are more than **100,000 species** of fungi in three main groups:
* black bread molds
* spore shooters
* spore droppers

Hidden hyphae

The fine threads of the hyphae spread through whatever it is feeding on, be it dead leaves, stale bread, rotting fruit, or damp skin.

Hyphae release enzymes that digest their surroundings into a soupy mix of nutrients.

The nutrients are absorbed by the hyphae, which provides the fungus with energy and building blocks for growth.

Gone in a puff

A puffball is a type of fungus that releases billions of spores. A slight tap from, say, a raindrop causes clouds of spores to puff out through a hole in the puffball's cap.

Menacing mushrooms

The Death cap may look harmless but less than 1 oz (28 g) can kill a person in just a few hours. Likewise, Coffin web cap, Destroying angel, and False morel are all poisonous mushrooms and should never be eaten.

What about me?

Only handle wild fungi if an adult with expert knowledge checks that it is OK first—and always wash your hands after touching fungi.

Five reasons fungi can be bad

01: Some fungi are highly poisonous and can even kill.

02: Dry rot fungus destroys wood and timber in houses.

03: Fungi cause diseases such as athlete's foot and ringworm.

04: Fungi can attack paper, clothes, and other household items.

05: Mildews, smuts, and rusts infect and destroy valuable crops.

Five reasons fungi are good

01: Some types of fungi are delicious to eat.

02: Molds put the blue into blue cheeses, and the rind on brie and camembert.

03: Yeast makes bread rise and the alcohol in wine and beer.

04: Some molds produce bacteria-killing antibiotics, such as penicillin.

05: Cyclosporin, isolated originally from a fungus, is a drug used to stop the body from rejecting transplanted organs, such as kidneys.

vs

I don't believe it!

The most valuable fungus is the white truffle. Prized by chefs for its pungent smell, by weight it is five times more expensive than silver.

How to: fill a balloon with yeast breath

01. Take the top off a bottle of cola and allow it to go flat overnight. Blow up a balloon and let the air out to soften it.

02. Put a teaspoon of dried yeast into the bottle and shake. Stretch the mouth of the balloon over the mouth of the bottle and place in a warm spot.

03. The yeast feeds on the sugar in the cola. As it feeds it breathes, releasing carbon dioxide, which inflates the balloon.

Four curious fungi

Bridal veil fungus
Although they do not smell nice, they are eaten in some parts of southern China.

Scarlet elf cup
Bright in appearance, these fungi are easily visible in damp woodlands in winter.

Devil's fingers
Native to Australia, this strange red fungi has an unpleasant rotting meat smell.

Jelly Antler
Usually found on roots and trunks of conifer trees, Jelly antlers look like sea coral.

A rotten job

One of the most important functions of mold is to break down dead animal and plant remains. Without these fungi we would be knee-deep in dead organisms. As this pepper shows, mold breaks down the remains, leaving it to rot.

day 1   day 5   day 10

RECORD BREAKER

The **world's biggest fungus**—and, possibly, biggest living organism—is a specimen of honey fungus known as the "humongous fungus." It grows beneath a forest in Oregon, covering an area of 3.5 sq miles (9 sq km), and may weigh up to 600 tons.

What's the connection between a slug and an octopus?

Both animals are members of a diverse group of animals called mollusks, which also includes mussels, oysters, limpets, whelks, periwinkles, and squid. There are more than 100,000 species of mollusk. Many live in the sea, but some live in fresh water or, like the garden snail, on land.

Tell me more: mollusks

Most mollusks have three body parts: a head, a soft body, and a muscular foot.

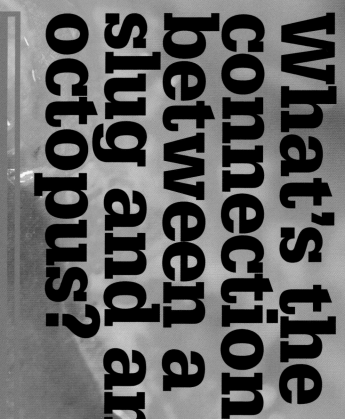

Shell: Many mollusks have shells to protect their soft bodies

soft body

Mouth: Contains a rasping radula (tooth-lined tongue)

Eyes: The snail has eyes on the end of its tentacles

Foot: The snail has no legs but a single muscular foot

head

Tongue: A microscopic image reveals rows of teeth

Record breakers

🐚 The **largest of all mollusks** is the aptly named colossal squid, which can reach 46 ft (14 m) in length. That's one scary predator.

🐚 The **biggest bivalve** (a mollusk with a shell in two parts) is the giant clam, which can reach 5 ft (1.5 m) in width. In the past, its half shell was used as a baby bath.

🐚 The **largest gastropod** is the giant African land snail, which can reach 12 in (30 cm) in length.

🐚 The **fastest mollusk** is the squid, which can speed away from danger at 22 mph (35 kph).

🐚 One of the **slowest land mollusks** is the garden snail, which travels at 0.03 mph (0.05 kph). That means it covers a distance of just over half a mile (1 km) every 20 hours.

🐚 The world's **oldest living animal** is a mollusk—it's a type of clam called an ocean quahog. In 2006 and 2007 scientists found specimens off Iceland that are estimated to be between 405 and 410 years old.

Five types of mollusk

Mollusks are invertebrates (animals without backbones) and come in a wide range of shapes and sizes.

Chitons
A family of marine grazers with an armadillo-like shell

Tusk shells
These marine burrowers have a long, tapering shell

Bivalves
Mollusks with a shell in two hinged parts, called valves

Gastropods
Most gastropods have a spiral shell, tentacles, and a muscular foot

Cephalopods
Big, intelligent, fast-moving animals with tentacles

How to: **be a master of disguise**

For self-defense, the cunning mimic octopus changes its shape, color, and texture in order to appear like dangerous or unappetizing animals.

01. If a hungry mantis shrimp is on the prowl, change from your natural form (pictured) and turn yourself into one as well, by pulling in your tentacles and changing color.

02. If predators are lurking nearby, then change quickly to look like an unfriendly sea snake to scare them off.

03. If that doesn't work, try looking like a starfish—they are not very pleasant to eat.

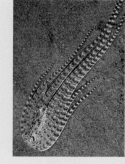

04. Try impersonating a flat fish—you really are a camouflage expert!

Spectacular shells

Nautilus
Inside this shell are pearly chambers of air that help the mollusk float.

Spiny oyster shell
Archeologists believe these shells were used 5,000 years ago to make ornaments.

Venus comb murex
The spines of this shell may prevent it from sinking into sandy mud.

Giant clams
The leaflike scales of these shells are used for shelter by crabs and others.

Cuban land snails
Now protected by law, overcollecting of these shells once threatened their future.

Cowries are sea-dwelling gastropods with pretty round shells that were used in many places as a form of **currency**, from the time of the pharaohs in Ancient Egypt up to the 20th century.

What about me?

If you spot a small, cute octopus with blue rings in the rock pools off the Australian coast, don't pick it up. The blue-ringed octopus is one of the world's most venomous animals and one bite could kill you.

I don't believe it!

Shipworms are not worms at all, but weird-looking bivalves with their shells at the front end of their bodies. Also called boring clams, shipworms burrow into and weaken any wooden structure in the sea. Their handiwork has even sunk boats!

Feeding methods

Gastropods use a radula (tooth-lined tongue) to eat algae or plants, or to dig into other animals.

Bivalves open and shut their shells and filter tiny food particles from the water.

Cephalopods stalk their prey and then grab it and pull it into their mouths with tentacles and suckers and crush it with their horny beaks.

Three cuttlefish facts

01 Cuttlefish can change color at will in less than a second. They do this to hide from predators and communicate their mood.

02 Their brown ink, which they squirt at enemies when making an escape, has been used by artists for centuries.

03 Pet birds are given cuttlefish skeletons to peck for their calcium content.

Mollusk moves

- Slugs and snails creep and glide on a muscular foot
- Some sea snails simply float on the ocean's surface
- Bivalves like cockles burrow into sand or mud using their muscular feet
- Scallops (above) push themselves through the water by opening and closing their valves
- Cuttlefish and squid swim by rippling their fins
- The octopus swims by pulling his arms and suckers through the water
- Octopus and squid can also make a quick getaway using jet propulsion, squeezing water out of their bodies at high speed

Which are the most successful animals on Earth?

There are more insects living and flying inside an area the size of a small town than there are human beings on Earth. They live just about everywhere—only the oceans are insect-free. Insects have six legs, four wings, and a body divided into three parts.

Tell me more: wasp anatomy

Cuticle: A hard, waterproof exoskeleton that supports and protects the body

Thorax: Middle section of the body, with two pairs of wings attached

Abdomen: Contains the intestines and reproductive organs, and is long and slender to help with balance when in flight

Compound eye: Made up of lots of tiny lenses to give a wide field of vision

Antenna: One of two, flexible antennae, used to feel, smell, and taste

Head: Houses the brain and sense organs

Leg: One of six jointed legs, attached to the thorax

Wing: One of two pairs of wings, attached to the thorax

A BIGGER GROUP

Insects, along with crustaceans, arachnids, and centipedes, belong to an even bigger group of invertebrate animals called **arthropods**. All arthropods have a hard outer skeleton (exoskeleton) and flexible legs with joints.

in numbers

10 quintillion*
Estimate of how many insects there are on Earth

300,000,000
Number of years ago that the first flying insects appeared

30,000,000
Estimate of how many insect species there actually are

1,017,018
Number of named insect species (this is increasing all the time)

*10,000,000,000,000,000,000

10 types of insect

Dragonflies and damselflies
5,500 species
Large eyes and wings, and slender bodies

Grasshoppers and crickets
20,000 species
Powerful hind legs and chewing mouthparts

Mantises
2,000 species
Triangular head, large eyes, extendable front legs for catching prey

Cockroaches
4,000 species
Oval, flattened bodies with a leathery casing

Light show

Fireflies are beetles with an unusual ability: they have a special organ in their abdomens that produces flashes of light. As fireflies fly around at night they flash signals to attract mates.

Insect snacks

Insects are cheap, plentiful, and rich in protein. Here's a sample of insect snacks.

Jumiles
Stink bugs, used as a taco filling in Mexico.

Mopani worms
These moth larvae are eaten sun-dried or in tomato sauce.

Fried queen termites
From Africa, they are rich in fat as well as protein.

Seven insect movies

Deadly Mantis (1957)
The Fly (1958, remade 1986)
The Swarm (1978)
Antz (1998)
A Bug's Life (1998)
Bugs (2003)
Bee Movie (2007)

How to: change from an egg into a butterfly

01. As a newly laid egg, find yourself stuck on the leaf of a plant that will provide you with constant food when you hatch.

02. Hatch from your egg and enjoy the leafy feast in front of you. You need your strength for all the coming changes to your body. Shed your outer coat several times so that your body can keep expanding.

03. On your last and final molt you'll find it difficult to move, since a hard outer coat forms around you in the pupa stage. Over the next week or so, your body tissues reorganize into those of an adult insect.

04. Split open the pupa casing and emerge as a beautiful butterfly. Wing it over to a flower and use your new sucking mouthparts to drink its nectar.

Three insects to avoid

Mosquitoes
Suck blood and may spread diseases such as malaria and dengue fever

Bed bugs
These suckers feed on the blood of people sleeping in bed

Botflies
They lay eggs that hatch into maggots under your skin

I don't believe it!

Some doctors use specially bred blowfly larvae (maggots) to treat flesh wounds. The maggots clean a wound by eating dead tissue and harmful bacteria.

Ants, bees, and wasps
198,000 species
Many live in colonies, but some are solitary

Butterflies and moths
165,000 species
Special feeding mouthparts, scales on body and wings

Beetles
370,000 species
Toughened front wings encase and protect hind wings

True flies
122,000 species
Single pair of wings, with small balancing organs called halteres

Bugs
82,000 species
Two pairs of wings and long "beaks" that pierce and suck

Termites
2,750 species
Soft bodies, chewing mouthparts and short antennae. Live in colonies

What are arachnids?

This is the group of invertebrates (animals without backbones) that includes spiders, scorpions, harvestmen, mites, and ticks. There are about 65,000 species of arachnid, half of which are spiders.

How to: qualify as an arachnid

01. You will need a tough outer skeleton (exoskeleton), like insects and crustaceans.

02. Eat other animals.

03. Have eight legs.

04. Make sure your body is divided into two parts with the legs attached to the front part, and, in spiders, silk-making glands in the back part.

05. See using up to eight eyes.

Top five biggest spiders

01: Goliath bird-eating spider (right)
leg span: 12 in (30 cm)

02: Honduran curly hair spider
leg span: 12 in (30 cm)

03: Bolivian pink bird-eating spider
leg span: 8 in (20 cm)

04: Goliath pink toe spider
leg span: 7 in (18 cm)

05: King baboon spider
leg span: 6¾ in (17 cm)

Good enough to eat

Male spiders, which are usually smaller than females, sometimes get eaten by their partners after mating. It's not a lover's tiff—it's usually because the female mistakes her mate for prey.

WHAT'S IN A NAME?

Bird-eating spiders do occasionally eat birds, but usually they go for insects, frogs, mice, and lizards. Tasty!

Hair flair

Spiders sense the world around them through their hairs, which can detect tiny vibrations, and some are even able to taste. If threatened, a tarantula brushes its legs against its body to send tiny barbed hairs into the eyes, nose, or mouth of the predator. So never stroke a tarantula! They use their hairs for:

* sensing the world around them
* courtship displays
* moving around
* self-defense
* catching prey

RECORD BREAKER

A **spider web** in Lake Tawakoni State Park in Texas covered 2,000 sq ft (180 sq m) of trees and bushes. What was once a white web soon turned dark when hundreds of mosquitoes got caught in it.

I don't believe it!

Spider's silk is five times stronger than a steel strand of the same width. It's also elastic, stretching to four times its original length before breaking. A pencil-thick strand of spider silk could, in theory, stop a jumbo jet in flight.

Hunting techniques

Trapdoor spiders hide in burrows concealed under a trapdoor, which flies open when the spider leaps out to grab prey.

Orb web spiders make circular webs to catch prey.

Jumping spiders stalk and jump on prey.

Wolf spiders are nighttime hunters.

Spitting spiders squirt sticky stuff at prey to trap it.

Hairy tarantulas and **bird-eating spiders** ambush prey as big as lizards and mice.

Funnel web spiders lure their prey into a funnel-shaped web.

Five super scorpion facts

01: Scorpions glow in the dark. They glow bright blue or yellow-green under ultraviolet light.

02: The largest scorpion, the African, can grow to more than 8 in (20 cm).

03: Scorpions grab prey with their claws and crush them into a mush that they then suck up.

04: The sting in a scorpion's tail is used mainly for self-defense.

05: Several thousand people die each year from scorpion stings.

Top five most dangerous spiders

01: Funnel web spider Australia

02: Black widow spider North America

03: Red back spider Australia

04: Brown recluse spider US

05: Brazilian wandering spider Central and South America

Five tasty arachnid dishes from around the world

Central America: Char-grilled bird-eating spider with pepper sauce
China: Fried crispy scorpion
Cambodia: Fried Thai zebra tarantula
China: Scorpion soup
Brazil: Roasted tarantula eggs

Scary spider stats

01: Some large spiders lay more than 2,000 eggs in a single egg sac.

02: The average spider can weave a web in less than one hour.

03: An empress of China once demanded a robe made entirely out of spider web silk. It took 8,000 spiders to make her coat.

04: Out of about 20,000 species of spider in the United States, only 60 are capable of causing harm to humans.

05: The black widow spider's bite is reported to be 15 times stronger than that of a rattlesnake.

What about me?

Arachnophobia is an excessive fear of spiders, and it's the world's most common phobia—even though most spiders are harmless.

How to: spin a spider's web

01. Climb to a suitable spot and use the glands on your abdomen to release a length of thread into the wind.

02. If the thread catches and sticks to another surface, walk across the thread and release a second, looser thread.

03. Lower yourself onto the second thread and then rapel down on a vertical thread to form a Y-shape.

04. Attach threads to the corners of the web to build up the frame.

05. Spin more radius threads out from the center. Strengthen the web with five circular threads.

06. Add a sticky spiral of threads to complete the web. You are now ready to trap unlucky prey.

Why do crabs walk sideways?

A crab has eight walking legs. The joints on the legs on one side push, producing the sideways-scuttling movement they're famed for. Like their lobster and shrimp relatives, crabs are crustaceans—a group of animals that are extremely numerous in seas, rivers, and ponds.

Three cunning crustaceans

Valet service
Cleaner shrimps team up with fish like this moray eel to get food. They use their tiny pincers to perform a valet service by picking off parasites, dead skin, and scraps of uneaten food.

Camouflage
Decorator crabs collect tiny shells, bits of seaweed, sponges, sea anemones, and other small animals, which they attach to the hooks that cover their shells for the perfect camouflage.

Lopsided male
Male fiddler crabs have one very big claw and one tiny one. They signal to females that they will make good mates by waving the big claw up and down, and use it in ritual fights with rival males.

Odd one out

goose barnacle

brine shrimp

common shrimp

horseshoe crab

pill woodlouse

There are more than 40,000 different species of crustacean. Can you tell at a glance from this lineup of creatures which one is not a crustacean? (answers on opposite page)

How to: **qualify as a lobster**

01. You will need a jointed abdomen ending in a telson (tail fan) that flicks downward for rapid swimming.

02. Have four pairs of jointed walking legs, just like those of crabs and prawns.

RECORD BREAKER

With a leg span of up to 13 ft (4 m) and weighing up to 44 lb (20 kg), the giant spider crab is the **biggest crustacean.**

FAST FACTS

Crustaceans

01: This very diverse group of animals includes crabs, lobsters, shrimp, prawns, barnacles, and woodlice.

02: Like insects and arachnids, crustaceans are arthropods—invertebrates with a hard outer skeleton and jointed limbs.

03: The outer skeleton (cuticle) in many species is reinforced by chalky calcium carbonate.

04: More than 40,000 species live in the sea and fresh water, and a few species are land-dwellers.

05: Crustaceans range in size from microscopic water fleas to giant spider crabs.

Planktonic performers

Plankton is made up of tiny living things that float in the surface waters of oceans, ponds, and rivers. Crustaceans make up an important part of plankton.

- Crab larvae float in the sea before settling on the seabed to mature.

- Copepods (tiny crustaceans) are superabundant in the plankton and are an important source of food for fish, seabirds, and whales.

- Tiny shrimp provide food for small fish.

Mantis shrimp

- This marine crustacean is a ferocious predator that lives in tropical oceans.

- Its second pair of legs is hinged and normally folded up, just like a praying mantis insect.

- It hides in crevices and ambushes prey by flicking out its folded limbs with lightning speed.

- In captivity, it has smashed through thick aquarium glass.

How to: **move house** (if you are a hermit crab)

01. Realize that you have outgrown your present home (a mollusk shell) and need to find somewhere bigger.

02. Clamber out of your shell and look for a new home. You're a walking snack for passing predators, so beware.

03. Identify a potential new shell. Tentatively probe the new, bigger shell with a pincer to make sure it isn't occupied.

04. Curl your abdomen into the spiral shell for protection. Fully retreat into your new home if danger threatens.

Antarctic krill

- These 2-in- (6-cm-) long, shrimplike crustaceans live in the nutrient-rich ocean around Antarctica, feeding on tiny plantlike phytoplankton.

- They live in massive swarms that provide a major source of food for many animals, including seals, penguins, and massive baleen whales, which filter krill out of the water.

- The total weight of all Antarctic krill in the oceans is more than 500 million tons. It is the most successful species on Earth.

- Krill have tiny light-producing organs that flash pinpoints of yellow-green.

- A blue whale, which is 10 billion times bigger than its prey, can eat more than 2.5 tons of krill daily.

03. Make sure you have a carapace (shield) covering the front part of your body (cephalothorax).

04. Have two compound (many-faceted) eyes on stalks.

05. Use your two pairs of antennae to feel your way around and detect food.

06. Break up and handle food with your powerful pincers.

I don't believe it!

Christmas Island in the Indian Ocean is home to 1.2 million red crabs. In November they walk en-masse through houses, stores, and across roads to breed at the coast.

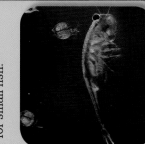

How do fish breathe?

Fish are vertebrates (animals with backbones) that live in the sea and in fresh water. Like all animals they have to breathe in oxygen. Lungs would simply fill up with water, so instead, fish have feathery gills at the back of the head that extract oxygen from water as it flows over them.

Tell me more: fish features

Streamlined body: The ideal shape to move through water

Overlapping scales: These form a smooth surface for water to flow over

Tail fin: The tail gives forward thrust to push fish through the water

Slimy mucus: This makes fish slippery and protects against parasites

Dorsal fin: This controls how much the fish rolls to one side or the other

Lateral line: Sensors here detect sound vibration and water movement

I don't believe it!

The eel-like pearlfish has a strange relationship with sea cucumbers, sausagelike relatives of starfish. The fish hunts for food at night and lives inside the sea cucumber by day, going in and out of the creature's bottom!

Fish families

"Fish" is a general name given to a range of vertebrates with streamlined bodies that live in water. There are three types of fish.

Jawless
These long, thin fish have a sucking mouth to grasp food. The group includes lampreys (pictured) and hagfish.

Cartilaginous
Rays (pictured), skates, and sharks all have a skeleton made of flexible cartilage instead of bone.

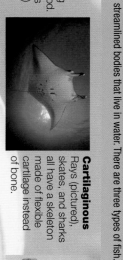

Bony
This is the largest group of fish. They have a skeleton made of bone and come in all shapes and sizes.

Reef life

Many fish that live on coral reefs have bright colors and patterns to break up their outlines, making it harder for predators to catch them or for prey to see them coming.

Monsters of the deep

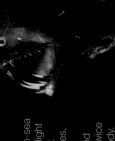

Down in the cold, dark gloom of the ocean depths lurk some very strange fish. This deep-sea **anglerfish** can emit light in order to attract prey. It also has flexible bones, allowing the jaws and stomach to expand and create room for prey twice the size of its entire body.

Seahorses

- Seahorses are slow movers and never exceed 0.001 mph (0.0016 kph).

- To anchor themselves in strong currents, they can wind their tails around a piece of weed.

- The male has a pouch in his body into which the female lays up to 600 eggs. He incubates the eggs in his pouch until they hatch.

- Although seahorses are bony fish, their skin is not covered with scales.

Electric shockers!

Electric eels live in the murky waters of South American rivers and produce 500 volt electric pulses to stun prey and deter predators.

Electric catfish from tropical Africa are nocturnal hunters that use their electric organs to generate 300 volts to stun prey.

Electric rays can release 220 volts to stun other fish.

Elephantnose fish produce weak electrical currents to help with navigation.

Sharks and rays detect the weak electric currents produced by some prey and go in for the kill.

Sharks are more at **risk** from humans than we are from them. Shark **fishing**, especially for shark fins, has seriously depleted **numbers** of some species.

Slithery slime

Hagfishes are jawless fish that are also known as slime eels. Here's why:

- An average sized hagfish can produce enough gooey mucus to fill an 14-pint (8-liter) bucket.

- They use slime as a defense against predators while they feed on dead and dying fish.

- Hagfish get rid of their own mucus by tying a knot in their bodies and then sliding it forward.

Four sharks to avoid

Great white shark
This scary predator does attack humans, although it doesn't really like the taste.

Hammerhead shark
With widely spaced eyes, this shark is prone to making unpredictable attacks.

Tiger shark
A striped scavenger found in coastal waters and known to attack people.

Blue shark
The most widespread of all sharks, the blue commonly circles prey before attacking.

In numbers

43 ft
(13 m) The length of the whale shark, the world's biggest fish

0.3 in
(.8 cm) The length of *Paedocypris progenetica*, the world's smallest fish. It lives in peat swamps on the Indonesian island of Sumatra

70 mph
(110 kph) The speed of the sailfin

12,500 miles
(20,000 km) The distance the great white shark migrates on its return trip between South Africa and Australia

140
The age in years of the longest-living fish—the rougheye rockfish

Eyes: Vision is important for navigation and to find mates and food

powder-blue surgeonfish

Operculum: A flap that covers the gills and opens to let water flow out

Pelvic fin: Used to steer the fish

Pectoral fin: Used to control the direction of movement

The **stonefish**, found in the Indian and Pacific Oceans, has **spiny fins** **filled with venom** that can be fatal to people who step on them.

How does a toad differ from a frog?

Most frogs are active jumpers that live near water, have long back legs, webbed feet, and smooth, moist skins. Toads are generally less active, have dry, warty skins, and prefer to live on land. Frogs and toads are amphibians—animals that typically prefer moist surroundings, spend part of their lives in water and part on land, lay their shell-less eggs in water, and breathe through lungs and their skin.

Tell me more: amphibians

Wide mouth: Accommodates large prey

Eardrum: Enables salamander to hear mates and rivals

Bulging eye: Provides a wide range of vision to look for prey

Leg: Each of four legs ends in toes and are webbed in frogs

Skin: Smooth and moist skin to take in oxygen

fire salamander

In numbers

½ in
(9.8 mm) The length of the tiny Brazilian gold frog

13 in
(33 cm) The length of the massive goliath frog, which is found in west Africa

6 ft
(180 cm) The length of the biggest amphibian, the Japanese giant salamander—that's as tall as an adult human

Types of amphibian

tiger salamander

great crested newt

Newts and salamanders
Number of species: 360
Features: slender bodies; long tails; legs the same length

South American horned toad

red-eyed tree frog

Frogs and toads
Number of species: 3,500
Features: short, compact bodies; long powerful hind legs; no tail

caecilian

Caecilians
Number of species: more than 200
Features: wormlike; legless; burrowers and swimmers; resemble snakes and live mostly underground

Five fantastic frogs and tremendous toads

Asian horned toad
It looks like a leaf and is perfectly camouflaged in its forest home.

Madagascan tomato frog
No surprise where it gets its name.

Darwin's frog
From Chile, the male carries young in its vocal sac.

Budgett's frog
A scary looking frog from Argentina, it screams and grunts to frighten off attackers.

Chilean red-spotted toad
This small toad can be found as high as 13,000 ft (4,000 m) in the Andes mountains.

WHAT'S IN A NAME?

If you look underneath a **glass frog**, its skin looks as though it is made of frosted glass. You can even see the frog's heart, liver, and intestines through it.

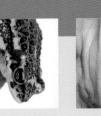
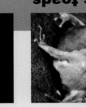

HIP HOP
A group of frogs is called a "chorus."

Don't lick them!
Poison dart frogs from Central and South America and mantellas from Madagascar have bright colors to warn predators that their skin is deadly poisonous.

strawberry poison dart frog

green mantella

green and black poison dart frog

Panamanian golden frog

painted mantella

Big mistake
The big South American cane toad was introduced to Australia in 1935 to eat beetles that were destroying sugar cane crops. It didn't eat the beetles, but managed to snaf down lots of other animals, including native frogs, snakes, and mammals, making some extinct.

FAST FACTS
Newts
Newts spend most of their lives on land, but return to water to breed.

Newt eggs hatch into larvae with small feathery gills.

The larvae lose their gills and switch to using internal lungs to breathe air. They then take to the land.

Newts can regenerate damaged eye tissue and heart tissue.

Many newts produce toxins as a defense against predators.

How to: grow up if you're a frog

01. Start your life as one of a mass of fertilized eggs called frog spawn.

02. After a few days, start to wiggle inside your transparent egg.

03. By day six it is time to hatch from the egg. Stick on to pond weed to feed and breathe through external gills.

04. After a few more days start swimming around—but look out for predators, such as ferocious dragonfly larvae.

05. Your external gills should disappear after seven weeks and your back legs pop out. Eat small animals.

06. Grow front legs during the next nine weeks so you look like a frog with a tail.

07. Your tail disappears, and you hop out of the pond to join the other froglets. The growing up process, called metamorphosis, is over.

I don't believe it!
Snakes are not the most venomous animals in the world. This title belongs to the gold poison dart frog, which carries enough poison to kill 20 people or two bull elephants!

WEIRD OR WHAT?
The male midwife toad winds strings of fertilized eggs around his legs and back and carries them until they are ready to hatch.

Do snakes feel slimy?

No, their scaly skin feels cool and dry, a feature snakes share with other reptiles including lizards, turtles, and crocodiles. Reptiles have backbones and are cold-blooded. This means they rely on the Sun's heat to warm them up. Most reptiles lay eggs with waterproof shells, although some snakes give birth to live young.

Tell me more: **chameleons**

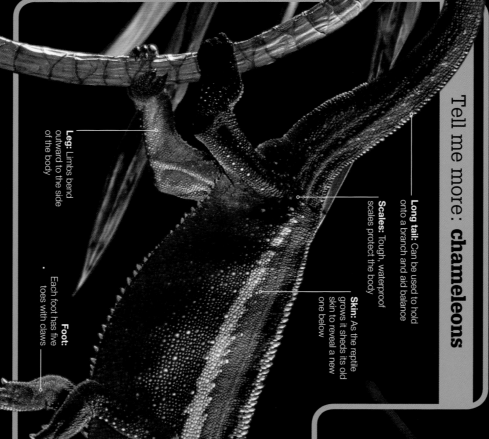

Long tail: Can be used to hold onto a branch and aid balance

Scales: Tough, waterproof scales protect the body

Skin: As the reptile grows it sheds its old skin to reveal a new one below

Leg: Limbs bend outward to the side of the body

Foot: Each foot has five toes with claws

Five reasons not to fall asleep under a tree on Komodo Island

01: The Indonesian island is home to the Komodo dragon, at 10 ft (3 m) long, the world's biggest lizard.

02: Although it prefers rotting flesh, the lizard is not averse to fresh meat, even human flesh!

03: The lizard has a great sense of smell, flicking its tongue to detect scent molecules in the air.

04: If it finds you dozing, the dragon will use its sharp, serrated teeth to bite off chunks of flesh.

05: The incredibly toxic bacteria in its saliva can kill you simply by infecting a wound.

One in the eye

A snake that you should definitely avoid is the spitting cobra, which can open its mouth and squirt venom droplets into the air from tiny openings in its fangs. This venom can cover a distance of 6 ft (2 m), and if the venom spray hits a predator's eyes it can cause permanent blindness. They also bite!

Types of **reptile**

There are four different groups of reptile:

Lizards and snakes
Lizards, snakes, and amphisbaenians (worm-lizards that live underground) are all closely related.

Crocodilians
This group of semi-aquatic predators includes alligators, crocodiles, caimans, and the gharial.

Tortoises and turtles
These reptiles have a bony shell to protect the soft parts of the body, four limbs, and a toothless beaky mouth.

Tuataras
Only found on islands off New Zealand, tuataras look a lot like lizards but can put up with colder conditions.

How to: eat lunch if you're a python

01. Sneak up to your prey and, before it can get away, coil your muscular body around it.

02. Each time your victim breathes out, tighten the coils a bit more.

03. When your prey stops breathing, loosen the coils and find its head.

04. Open your mouth wide by unhinging your jaws, and swallow the prey head first. Lie still and digest.

In numbers

3/4 in
(1.6 cm) The length of the smallest reptile, the dwarf gecko of the Dominican Republic

2
The number of species of tuataras, ancient lizardlike reptiles

33 ft
(10 m) The length of the longest snake, the reticulated python, found in southeast Asia

23
The number of species of crocodile and alligator

175
The age of the longest lived reptile, the Galápagos tortoise

294
The number of species of turtle and tortoise

2,900
The number of species of snake

4,500
The number of species of lizard

Big bite

Crocodiles have amazingly powerful jaws, with the strongest bite in the whole animal kingdom. The force of their bite is:

- **six times** that of a bone-crushing hyena dismembering its prey
- **thirteen times** that of a great white shark in a feeding frenzy
- **fifteen times** that of a Rottweiler dog eating meat

Tongue: A long, sticky tongue flicks out to catch prey

Eye: Each eye moves independently, so the animal can look in opposite directions at the same time

---

Top five most deadly snakes

If you want to avoid the snakes with the deadliest poison, don't go to Australia!

01: Taipan
(Australia)
The most poisonous snake in the world; prey is paralyzed the instant it is bitten.

02: Brown snake
(Australia)
Though less poisonous, the brown snake is more common than the taipan.

03: Tiger snake
(Australia)
Just to confuse you, this snake sometimes has stripes, but often does not.

04: Beaked sea snake
(Arabian Sea to coast of northern Australia)
Will attack and bite divers if disturbed.

05: Malayan krait
(southeast Asia and Indonesia)
This snake is slow to strike, but its poison can be fatal.

Diary of a green turtle

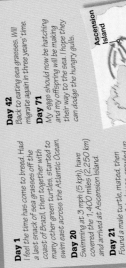

Day 1
I feel the time has come to breed. Had a last snack of sea grasses off the coast of Brazil, then together with many other green turtles, started to swim east across the Atlantic Ocean.

Day 20
Swimming at 3 mph (5 kph), have covered the 1,400 miles (2,250 km) and arrived at Ascension Island.

Day 21
Found a male turtle, mated, then under cover of darkness, crawled up the beach. Dug a hole with my flippers, laid 150 eggs, covered them up, and headed back to sea.

Day 22
Swam home to Brazil using the stars and Sun to navigate.

Day 42
Back to eating sea grasses. Will migrate again in three years' time.

Day 71
My eggs should now be hatching and my offspring will be making their way to the sea. I hope they can dodge the hungry gulls.

Ascension Island

Brazil

Why do birds have feathers?

Tell me more: bird features

Feathers help to keep birds warm and enable them to fly. Their wings are equipped with stiff flight feathers to provide both lift and, when the wings are flapped, forward thrust to propel these masters of flight through the air. Something else common to all birds is that they lay eggs with hard shells.

Wings: Powerful chest muscles move the wings

Tail: Short tail has feathers growing from it

Legs: Two scaly legs for walking, and for taking off and landing

Body: Shaped by a lightweight skeleton

Feet: Adapted to bird's lifestyle, and can be used to run, perch, and grasp

Feathers: Cover the body

Beak: Lightweight, and without any teeth

Eyes: Provide bird with a keen sense of vision

Flight checklist

- You will need a strong but light skeleton with hollow bones
- Your wings, carefully curved by their feathers, give you lift when air flows over them
- Strong wing muscles to power your wings, and create the thrust that pushes you forward
- Strong leg muscles to launch you into the air
- Contour feathers make flying more efficient by streamlining your body
- A tail that works as a rudder so you can change direction as you fly through the air

In numbers

1.5 billion
The number of red-billed quelea in Africa that form a flock. It takes five hours for this huge flock to fly past.

10,000
Species of bird

25,000 miles
(40,000 km) The distance of the Arctic tern's incredible migration. Every year, it flies from its Arctic breeding grounds to the Antarctic and back again

60%
The percentage of all birds that belong to the Passeriformes group (perching birds)

Bird life

Birds come in all shapes and sizes. Their behavior is also wonderfully diverse. Here is just a sample of the types of birds that are found throughout the world.

Flightless birds
What ostriches lack in flight, they make up for in running speed.

Gamebirds
These birds include wild turkey and pheasants and are often hunted for food.

Penguins
Flightless birds found in the Southern Hemisphere spend equal time on land as water.

Waterfowl
They are strong swimmers and include ducks, geese, and swans.

Weird or what?
An ostrich's eyeball is bigger than its brain and as wide as the bee hummingbird—the world's smallest bird—is long.

Right beak for the job

Finch
Tough and sharp to crack open seeds

Parrot
Hook pulls flesh off fruit and beak cracks open nuts

Flamingo
Acts as a filter to strain out tiny animals

Gull
All-purpose beak catches fish and tears food apart

Eagle
Hooked to rip flesh of prey that cannot be eaten whole

RECORD BREAKER

The Ostrich is the **biggest bird**, growing to a height of 9 ft (2.7 m). It also lays the **biggest egg**, up to 7 in (18 cm) long, and is the **fastest runner**, reaching speeds of up to 45 mph (72 kph).

Diary of a duck egg

Day 1
Just laid—I'm an embryo resting on a yolk food store.

Day 12
It's safe and warm in this hard shell, and at last I'm beginning to feel like a bird.

Day 20
I've been growing fast and things are getting a bit cramped in here—I'm planning to break out, but I can't find the door.

Day 21 morning
In desperation, I have begun to bash my way out with a toothy piece on my beak—I can see the light at last.

Day 21 afternoon
I'm free! My feathers have dried out, and I've found my legs and am running around. I am starting to feel a bit hungry, so will start looking for food.

Nesting materials

Some birds just lay their eggs on the ground, but most build a nest to keep them safe. The materials birds use to make their nests include the following:

- **spiders' webs (for glue)** • moss
- **lichen** • grass • **feathers** • mud
- **animal hair** • old snake skin
- **sticks** • stones • **dead beetles**
- anything useful humans leave behind like string and soft materials

I don't believe it!

Australian lyrebirds are fantastic mimics. They copy not only other bird songs to attract mates, but also cell phone ring tones, camera shutters, chainsaws, crying babies, barking dogs, and even car alarms.

Four feathers

Wing
Stiffer feathers that cover the wings

Tail
Stiffer feathers that help in flight

Contour
Cover the body to give a streamlined shape

Down
Grow close to the skin to keep the bird warm

Perching birds
They are also known as songbirds because of their whistling tunes.

Swifts and swallows
These graceful flyers both catch their insect prey in flight.

Parrots
Their ability to imitate human voices makes them popular pets.

Owls
Most owls are night hunters, using their sharp hearing and eyesight to catch food.

Wading birds
Flamingos often stand on one foot, but no one knows why.

Shorebirds
Thought to have an internal compass to help them migrate over long distances.

Why do cats have fur?

Cats, like all other mammals, are warm-blooded, and a furry coat helps to insulate the body and keep them warm. Mammals produce milk to feed their young, and look after them until they are able to fend for themselves. Many mammals have different types of teeth, for cutting, piercing, and grinding food.

Meet the family

The closest relatives of humans, apes are highly intelligent mammals, adept at performing tasks with their flexible limbs.

Gorilla: Lives in mountains and lowland forests of central Africa; eats leaves and fruit

Chimpanzee: Lives in the forests of west and central Africa; eats leaves, fruit, insects, and small mammals

Bonobo: Lives in the rain forest of central Africa in female-dominated societies; eats vegetation

Orangutan: Lives in the forests of Borneo and Sumatra; eats fruit

Tell me more: mammal anatomy

female lion and cubs

Fur: Most mammals have a covering of fur or hair

External ear: Pinna (ear flap) directs sounds into the inner ear

Nipples: Young feed on milk produced by their mother

Toes: Tipped with nails, claws, or hooves

Nostrils: Lead to nasal cavity, allowing for a good sense of smell

Mouth: Contains teeth used to break up food

Types of mammal

There are 21 different groups of mammal. Here are some of the major ones.

Monotremes
Include the platypus and echidna and are the only mammals to lay eggs

Marsupials
Produce undeveloped young that grow in mother's pouch

Rodents
Small mammals with paired chisel-like incisor teeth

Primates
Intelligent, long limbed, with flexible fingers and toes

Bats
The only mammals capable of sustained flight

Insectivores
Small, nocturnal, and feed on invertebrates, especially insects

Five facts about feeding

01: An adult **elephant** munches its way through 550 lb (250 kg) of vegetation daily. Sixty percent of that comes out of the other end undigested.

02: Blue whales can filter up to 8,000 lb (3,600 kg) of shrimplike krill from the sea every day.

03: Hyenas can swallow a third of their body weight in half an hour.

04: Shrews have to consume their own weight in food every day.

05: A **star-nosed mole** can snaffle an insect larva in a quarter of a second.

RECORD BREAKER

Snow leopards are the world's **greatest leapers.** Found in central Asia, they can hurdle over ravines and pounce on their prey, such as sheep and deer, over a distance of 50 ft (15 m).

I don't believe it!

Arabian or dromedary camels can go for months without drinking and then consume 16 gallons (60 liters) of water in just a few minutes.

In numbers

20 million
The number of Brazilian free-tailed bats that group together to form one colony

6,600 ft
(2,000 m) The depth to which a sperm whale can dive, staying there while it hunts for squid and other prey

1,300 lb
(600 kg) The weight of the biggest land carnivore (meat-eater), the polar bear

12 tons
The weight of an African elephant, the biggest land mammal

180 tons
The weight of a blue whale, the biggest animal that has existed on Earth. They can be as long as 110 feet (33.6 m)

60 mph
(100 kph) The top running speed of the cheetah—the fastest land mammal

0.1 mph
(0.16 kph) The speed of the three-toed sloth—the world's slowest mammal

18 ft
(5.5 m) The height of the tallest mammal, the giraffe

Furry patterns

Some mammals have distinctive coat markings that help camouflage them in their native environments

jaguar | zebra | giraffe | eastern chipmunk | tiger

WEIRD OR WHAT?

Male Dayak fruit bats from southeast Asia are the only **male mammals** known to **lactate** (produce milk) and suckle their own young.

How to: find food like a giant anteater

01. Using your sense of smell (your sight isn't too good), find a nice big termite or ants' nest.

02. Use your strong front legs and big, sharp claws to break open the nest (but don't destroy it—you'll probably pay a return visit).

03. Put your lengthy, toothless snout near the nest and extend your 2-ft (60-cm) long tongue to probe for prey.

04. Flick your sticky, spiked tongue in and out of the nest 150 times a minute to trap insects.

Carnivores
Active hunters and meat-eaters with sharp, cutting teeth

Pinnipeds
Aquatic carnivores that breed on land and feed on marine life

Hoofed: even-toed
Have feet with two toes capped with hooves, such as gazelles and camels

Cetaceans
Aquatic mammals that spend their lives in water; blubber keeps them warm

Hoofed: odd-toed
One or three toes on each hooved foot, such as zebras and rhinos

Elephants
Large mammals that collect food with a trunk

Do animals have a sixth sense?

Yes, while humans traditionally have five senses—sight, hearing, taste, touch, and smell—many animals possess one or more extra senses. These might include detecting electrical fields or heat to find prey, or magnetic fields in order to navigate.

Listen up

Big ears
Mammals collect sound using large external ear flaps. Hares can even turn their ears to scan for sound.

Dish face
The great gray owl's large dish-shaped face channels sound waves into its ears.

Eardrums
Frogs do not have protruding ears, but large eardrums behind each eye.

Insect ears
The cricket has an "ear" just below the knee of both its front legs.

Keep in touch

👉 Animals use touch to find food, communicate, or navigate in the dark.

👉 **The sensitive hairs on a spider's legs help it detect prey.**

👉 The star-nosed mole (pictured) uses the 22 pink, fleshy tentacles on its nose to hunt for worms and leeches.

👉 **Snakes press their lower jaws to the ground to sense vibrations.**

👉 A raft spider sits on dry land and dangles its four front legs in the water to detect prey.

👉 **Mammals like to caress each other for comfort.**

WHAT'S IN A NAME?

Many animals have what is called a **Jacobson's organ** located on the roof of the animal's mouth. This organ **senses chemicals in the air** and is named after Danish scientist Ludwig Jacobson.

A tasty smell?

✴ A sense of smell helps animals to find food or sniff out a mate from a distance, while taste helps them to check things out up close.

✴ **Flies have taste receptors all over their bodies, from their wings to their feet.**

✴ A catfish's whiskers are covered in taste buds and it can identify another catfish by smell alone.

✴ **Whales have no sense of smell, but a very good sense of taste.**

✴ Rats smell in stereo and, in a single sniff, can figure out exactly where a smell is coming from because the odor reaches one nostril around 50 milliseconds before the other.

Tell me more: finding the way

Migrating animals often travel on long, dangerous journeys from breeding to feeding grounds. They rely on a variety of senses to find their way.

◆ **Sight:** Using visual clues such as coastlines and mountain ranges, bar-headed geese (pictured) fly over the Himalayas twice a year to avoid storms in winter and monsoon rains in summer.

◆ **Smell:** Salmon use their excellent sense of smell to find the stream they were born in, which can be up to 2,000 miles (3,200 km) inland.

◆ **Sound:** Baleen whales listen to the sound of waves crashing on beaches to help them navigate around islands.

◆ **Heat:** When spiny lobsters feel the waters cooling, they know it is time to move to deeper waters to avoid the stormy fall season.

◆ **Touch:** Boree moth caterpillars leave a trail of silk for their siblings to follow as they swarm off in search of food.

Why senses make sense

An animal's survival depends on it being able to sense what is happening around it.

Finding food
The duck-billed platypus uses receptors in its bill to sense the electric fields of underwater prey.

Hibernating
Feeling chilly is the sign for some animals, like the dormouse, that it is time to hibernate.

Avoiding predators
Sensitive whiskers help nocturnal mammals, like the rat, avoid predators in the dark.

Detecting injury
Senses inform this duck its wing is broken, so its body can begin healing processes.

Finding a mate
Hyenas stick out their tongues to taste information about other individuals.

Migrating
The migration of monarch butterflies is triggered by changes in temperature and the length of the day.

I don't believe it!

Scientists have discovered that cats can heal themselves by purring, since vibrations between 20–140 Hz can help heal fractures, mend torn muscles, and relieve pain.

How to: **see in the dark (like a bat)**

01. Produce a loud, incredibly high-pitched sound by rushing air from your lungs past your vibrating vocal chords.

02. The squeaky sound wave you've created rushes forward at the speed of sound—741 mph (1,193 kph)—and bounces back off any objects around you.

03. Direct the echo into your inner ear using the strange folds on your nose and ears.

04. Figure out how long it takes the noise to return to build up a picture of how far away objects are and if any of them are prey.

05. Keep calling until you are close enough to grab yourself a tasty snack.

WEIRD OR WHAT?

Bats' calls are **ultrasonic**, which means they're so high-pitched human ears can't hear them. The calls are also so loud the **bats risk deafening themselves**, so their ears have special muscles that close to protect the ear and then open to listen to the echo.

Hot stuff
Pit vipers have heat-sensitive organs between the eyes and the nostrils with around 7,000 nerve endings. Using these heat organs, they create a "heat-blooded picture" of warm-blooded prey when hunting at night.

Eye to eye

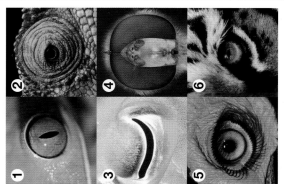

① The large red eyes of the **nocturnal tree frog** help it to see in the dark and may startle predators if the frog is disturbed during the day, giving it a split second to leap away.

② The **chameleon**'s protruding eyes can roll from side to side, each independent of the other, so the animal can figure out exactly where prey is.

③ The eyes of the **cuttlefish** are very similar to human eyes, except for the distinctive curved black pupil. Cuttlefish have excellent vision.

④ Like many insects, the **hoverfly** has a compound eye made up of thousands of lenses, which enable it to spot the slightest movement.

⑤ The **southern ground hornbill** has long eyelashes to protect the eye from the sun and dust as it forages for food on the ground with its beak.

⑥ Cats, such as the **tiger**, are able to see well in the dark because they have a mirrorlike layer in their eyes.

Can animals talk?

Animals can pass on all kinds of messages using touch, smells, and sounds, or visual signals, such as light, color, and body language. Some signs are clear, like a gorilla smiling at her baby, or subtle, such as a female wolf spider leaving a trail of silk woven with her scent to lure mates.

Reasons to communicate

Make an impression
Wolves howl to declare their territory, to call to each other, and to show they are part of a pack.

Find a mate
Polar bears in the vast Arctic wilderness won't bump into each other by accident, they need to leave behind a trail of smells.

Defend your territory
Tigers urinate on trees to mark their territory and avoid competition.

Warn of danger
Prairie dogs have a range of warning calls to tell others what the threat is and how fast it's approaching.

Care for young
A chick taps its parent's beak to say "Feed me!"

Intimidate opponents
A male gorilla beats its chest to show how big and strong it is.

Cool call
The howl of a coyote reveals its identity, its gender, and how it is feeling.

How to: **read the signs**

01. Feel threatened if a hippopotamus yawns to show off its teeth.

02. Get even more worried if it splashes or scoops the water to add to the effect.

03. If you notice the hippo is shaking its head, lunging forward and then rearing back, prepare to flee.

04. When you hear roaring and grunting it is time to run away!

Male Madagascan ring-tailed lemurs compete for mates by trying to outstink each other.

Causing a stink

Most animals (except birds) give off chemicals known as "pheromones." These trigger a reaction in other members of the species and can even affect how their bodies grow.

Once given off, pheromones can travel very long distances when carried by the wind.

Leaving chemical messages behind is a good way to let other animals know you're in the neighborhood.

This **poison dart frog**'s colors say: "Don't eat me—I'll poison you!"

The **firefly**'s bright colors tell predators it tastes bad and should be left alone.

The male leader of a troop of **mandrill** has a vivid red stripe on his nose, reminding the rest of the troop who's boss.

A **skunk**'s black and white colors warn of its foul-smelling spray.

A male **frilled lizard** fans out a huge flap of skin to show females how attractive he is.

I see what you're saying!

A guide to making faces

Much like humans, chimpanzees use facial expressions to communicate with each other.

Fear grin
This is a nonthreatening signal used to diffuse an explosive situation.

Pout
By pouting its lips, a chimp expresses anxiety, frustration, or distress.

Play face
An open mouth is a sign that the chimp wants to play.

Making a noise

01: Amphibians, reptiles, birds, and mammals combine lung power and vibrating or echoing body parts to produce an amazing range of cries and calls.

02: Fish scrape their gills together, birds flutter their wings, while insects buzz, squeak, and click by vibrating wings or rubbing body parts against their hard outer skeletons.

03: Low sounds travel farthest and forest animals often have deeper calls than creatures living out in the open.

04: Birdsong travels up to 20 times farther in the early morning when the air is stiller and cooler than it is in the middle of the day.

Keeping in touch

Touch is used by social animals, such as ants, spiders, and crabs, and especially mammals and birds that care for their young.

Bugs vibrate plants to communicate with other bugs, burrowing animals make the ground vibrate, while alligators produce a deep sound that can travel more than half a mile in still waters.

Licking and grooming keeps a mammal family clean, but also shows affection.

Scout honey bees perform a complicated "waggle dance" to direct other members of the hive to a good patch of flowers. Wing vibrations pass on the message even in the dark.

Showing off

Coloring and pattern are used by most animals to tell male from female. Different markings also help avoid confusion when similar species live in the same habitat.

Body language is great for scaring off predators or attracting a mate, such as the intricate courtship dance of the Japanese crane (pictured). Intelligent species use body language to deal with complicated family relationships.

Flashing signals on and off attract more attention, such as a sudden display of peacock feathers or the flash of the brightly colored patch of skin under an anole lizard's neck.

Highs and lows

Sounds are pressure waves traveling through the air. When they disturb air particles close to us, the vibrations are picked up by ears and translated back into sound. These vibrations are measured in Hertz (Hz). 1 Hz is one vibration in a second. The more vibrations there are, the higher the sound.

elephants rumble at 8 Hz

human ears hear sounds from 20 Hz to 20,000 Hz

dogs can hear sounds up to 45,000 Hz

dolphins communicate with sounds well over 100,000 Hz

moths can hear sounds as high as 240,000 Hz

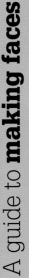

What is a food chain?

All animals must have food to give them the energy they need to survive, and they get it by eating other living things. This transfer of energy from one living thing to another is called a food chain. Every animal is either a predator or prey for other animals. Those at the top of the food chain are called top predators.

Who eats whom?

↑ Secondary consumers: Plant-eating animals are eaten by carnivores, called secondary consumers. They are at the top of the food chain.

↑ Primary consumers: Animals that eat plants are called herbivores. They may have many different predators.

↑ Primary producers: At the bottom of most food chains are plants, which get their energy from the Sun.

How to: **be a top predator**

01. Locate your prey, then watch, wait, and try to look invisible while you figure out what's going on.

02. Identify a likely victim and try and isolate it from the rest of the herd. Slowly approach.

03. Move in, with only your eyes showing above the surface of the water, until close enough to launch your attack.

04. Seize the prey with your massive jaws and drag it into the water. Hold until it has drowned, then tear apart and eat.

A frogfish can open its mouth and snap it shut in just 6 milliseconds. **Gulp!**

In numbers

69 billion
The estimated number of locusts in a swarm that devastated parts of northwest Africa in 2004

50,000
The number of bees in a typical domestic beehive

30
The number of minutes a marine iguana can hold its breath while grazing on seaweed underwater

99%
The percentage of a giant panda's diet that is bamboo

Horrible ways to die

01: Dismembered
The tough jaws of a praying mantis (pictured) slice through its victim's body with ease.

02: Strangled
Lions clamp their jaws around a zebra's throat and throttle it to death. Anacondas squeeze prey until it stops breathing.

03: Impaled
The cone snail impales its prey by firing a harpoon with explosive speed.

04: Poisoned
Jellyfish, spiders, and scorpions are all master poisoners.

05: Stunned
An electric eel can stun or kill its prey with a powerful 500V shock.

06: Crushed
Secretary birds stamp on large prey to kill it.

07: Thumped
The tiny peacock mantis shrimp thumps its prey with its clublike limbs, with a force thousands of times its body weight.

08: Wrapped
The uloborid spider wraps its prey in silk so tightly that it breaks their legs and bursts their eyes.

I don't believe it!

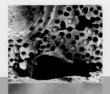

About 140 species are known to eat their own kind. Some insects, fish, and amphibians eat their relatives when food is rare, and the female black widow spider, praying mantis, and scorpion eat the males after mating.

Koalas eat almost nothing but eucalyptus leaves. These aren't very nutritious, so they need to **sleep 16 hours a day** to save energy.

Dinner is served

🍽 Spiders inject flies with juices that **turn their insides to mush, then suck out the resulting soup.**

🍽 Snakes can't chop or chew their food so they have highly flexible necks and jaws that dislocate, so they can swallow prey whole.

🍽 **Killer whales, polar bears, and big cats all play with their prey before or after killing it.**

🍽 Leopard seals shake a captured penguin's body and smash it against the surface of the water to break it up into manageable pieces.

🍽 Crocodiles sometimes store **drowned prey underwater, waiting for its body to rot before eating it.**

Full pantries

Acorn woodpecker
These sensible birds drill holes in a tree trunk and fill them with acorns for winter.

Red-backed shrike
Also known as the butcher bird, this shrike keeps its food on thorns or barbed wire.

Honeypot ants
Worker honeypot ants are living pantries, storing nectar in their huge bellies to regurgitate later.

Honey bees
Bees turn nectar to honey, which they hoard in the hexagonal cells of their hive.

FAST FACTS

Plant-eaters

01: Many animals get energy from plants, not other animals.

02: Animals eat all parts of plants—the leaves, nuts, seeds, fruits, roots, and nectar.

03: Fruits, seeds, and nectar are rich in energy, but leaves and grasses are not very nutritious, so animals need to consume large amounts of them.

04: To try to keep from being eaten, some plants have developed toxic leaves or thorns.

05: Some plants benefit from being animal food—animals pollinate flowers, help seeds to germinate by digesting their tough coatings and softening their seeds, and disperse seeds in their droppings.

Choose your weapon

Animals use a wide variety of weapons to grab their prey.

The great white shark has several rows of serrated **teeth**. New ones move to the front to replace teeth that fall out.

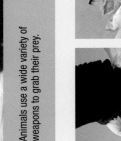

The scorpion grabs prey in its claws, then arches its tail forward to stab the victim with its venom-filled **sting**.

A heron uses its **beak** to pluck a fish from the water, knock it out, and then flip it head first down its throat.

The bald eagle has the hooked **talons** and often snatches its prey feet first, before ripping it apart with its beak.

Crabs use their powerful **claws** to crack and prize open the tough shells of their seafood.

10 masters of disguise

In the animal kingdom everyone is hungry and only the strongest, or most cunning, survive. To snap up an unsuspecting meal or escape from becoming lunch yourself, the best advice is to lay low and blend in, like these cool customers… if you can spot them.

02: Stalking through long grass in search of a tasty meal, tigers go unnoticed as their irregular stripes blend with their surroundings.

01: The Arctic fox's winter coat is white so it blends in with the snow, but for the summer season, its fur turns brown so it merges with the earth and rocks.

03: The great gray owl perches on a tree, safe in the knowledge that its mottled markings merge with the bark.

04: Even at close range the stick insect is easily mistaken for a twig or leaf. In a really sticky situation, they will also pretend to snap off and drop to the ground.

05: The devil scorpion fish hides motionless in reefs looking like a rock or piece of dead coral. Its skin can even change color to blend in with its surroundings.

10: The beautiful orchid mantis is disguised to resemble a flower. Pastel pink with petal-like legs, it waits to catch insects, untroubled by predators.

09: Also known as bush crickets, katydids are easily mistaken for leaves, and even have specks of mold, chewed corners, pretend blemishes, and fake veins.

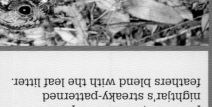
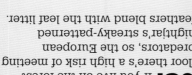
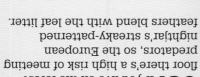

08: If you live on the forest floor there's a high risk of meeting predators, so the European nightjar's streaky-patterned feathers blend with the leaf litter.

07: Clever camouflage provides extra protection for the leafy seadragon. The fish looks like seaweed and is ignored by predators.

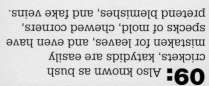

06: Tree trunks in bright sunlight spell danger, but the leaf-tailed gecko's skin texture and color means he disappears into the bark background.

How do animals reproduce?

In most animal species, males and females mate to reproduce. This is called sexual reproduction. Some animals can reproduce without mating. They simply "split" themselves into two or more individuals. This is asexual reproduction. There are also a few species where the female can produce young on her own.

Best buddies

A sea anemone can reproduce asexually by a process called budding. This means that the offspring grow as small parts attached to the mother's body, before dropping off.

Ways to make a good impression

Horns and antlers
Male stag beetles battle with their horns to win the right to mate. Deer, antelope, and other hoofed mammals sport a range of spectacular horns.

Shouting match
Red deer stags bellow day and night to prove how strong they are.

Put on a show
The long-tailed manakin bird judges pairs of hopeful males on a 20-minute display of singing and gymnastics. She may rule out as many as 80 males before making her final choice.

Presents
The male wolf spider catches a fly, then wraps it up in silk before offering it to the much larger and fearsome female. This food will help her to lay more eggs.

A dangerous game

☠ **Crushed**
One in 1,000 female elephants are crushed to death by heavy partners during mating.

☠ **Munched**
The female praying mantis inflicts a fatal "love bite" on her male partners, eating his head while his body continues mating.

☠ **Suicide**
During mating, a male red-back spider somersaults so that his abdomen is right between the female's fangs. She can't resist and usually impales him before sucking his body dry.

☠ **Stabbed**
A male rattlesnake attaches hooks to a female during mating. These injure the female, preventing her from mating with a rival.

Tell me more: **how a blue-footed booby finds a mate**

Sky-pointing: By pointing his bill to the sky and raising his tail, the male blue-footed booby shows the female that he's a bird to be reckoned with

Wings: The male spreads and rotates his wings

Territory: The male chooses a small nesting territory and parades around it to warn rivals and advertise himself to females

Dancing: A stately dance is a good way to show off his feet

Feet: Color is vital—males with the bluest feet stand the best chance of finding a partner

I don't believe it!

Male Kobs (a type of African antelope) gather in groups of 12–40 and wait for females to come to them. The females are attracted less by the male's body and more by the amount of urine sprinkled on his home patch, which reveals how popular he is.

FAST FACTS

Eggs

01: Birds and most reptiles lay eggs with a protective shell that allows them to survive outside water.

02: Fish and amphibians lay their jellylike eggs in water since they don't have a shell and would dry out in the air.

03: A female cod fish can produce 4–6 million eggs in one spawning. The eggs are usually left to develop on their own.

04: Some snakes and lizards keep their eggs inside their bodies until they are just about to hatch.

05: Nearly all birds incubate (warm) their eggs with their own bodies. Meanwhile, the developing embryo inside feeds on the egg yolk.

06: When hatching, some chicks have an egg tooth to crack the eggshell.

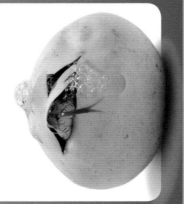

How to: move in... and move out

01. Get your mother cuckoo to lay your egg in the nest of a likely family, like a reed warbler. Don't worry that your new mom will spot that your egg is bigger, since they never suspect a thing.

02. Once you have hatched, you must toss out any rival eggs. There's only room in this nest for one—and it's got to be you.

03. Eat everything and never stop screeching for more. Strangely, your new mom still won't spot that something's up, even though you're larger than she is and growing all the time.

04. You'll know when it's time to leave home—the nest will collapse under your great weight. Don't bother to say thank you.

Top breeder
Female aphids (greenfly) can reproduce both sexually (by mating with a male) and asexually (by producing perfect clones).

Mobile home

Marsupials, such as kangaroos, wallabies, possums, koalas, and wombats keep their young safe in pouches.

A newborn kangaroo is the size of a peanut and squirms through its mother's fur until it reaches her warm pouch.

Safe inside the pouch, the youngster feeds on her milk and grows bigger.

By six months old, the youngster, or joey, hops in and out of the pouch.

Reasons to stick together

01: Breeding
From sea birds to fish, gathering together in large numbers in the breeding season makes it easier to find a partner.

02: Feeding
Wolves, hyenas, and lions coordinate their hunting in order to make it easier to catch prey to feed their young.

03: Babysitting
Adult meerkats (pictured) take turns looking after all the young pups in their group, feeding them and teaching them new skills.

Home, sweet home

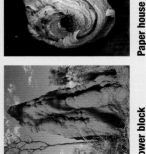

Tower block
Worker termites attend the egg-laying queen and transport the eggs through the mound to the nurseries.

Paper house
Common wasps chew dry wood into a pulp to make their waterproof nests. The cells inside each house an egg.

Warm nest
Pairs of white storks build a huge nest from sticks, rags, and paper. Fresh cattle dung helps to keep the nest warm.

Dam builders
Inside the beaver's lodge is a sleeping chamber above water where the mother nurses her young.

Underground
Moles burrow tunnels underground. Females breed and give birth in chambers lined with soft grass.

Why worry about extinction?

There have been five mass extinction events in Earth's history (the last time, 65 million years ago, the dinosaurs vanished). A sixth mass extinction is taking place thanks to humans. As we drive more animals and plants to extinction, we destroy the life-support systems that all species depend on—including us.

Levels of risk

The World Conservation Union ranking, with each listing giving examples of affected species:

Extinct Tasmanian tiger, dodo

Extinct in the wild
South China tiger

Critically endangered
Arakan forest turtle, Javan rhino, Brazilian merganser

Endangered blue whale, snow leopard, tiger, albatross

Vulnerable cheetah, lion

Near threatened
blue-billed duck, solitary eagle

Least concern pigeons, spiny dogfish

Paths to extinction

✗ Growing population
The more people there are, the less space there is for animals.

✗ Habitat destruction

✗ Pollution

✗ Hunting and fishing

✗ Alien invaders
When humans bring alien animals or plants into a new habitat, the native species often can't compete or will catch diseases they can't fight.

✗ Climate change
Global warming is attacking animals and plants in many ways—from melting the sea ice that polar bears need for hunting to bringing tropical rains early so plants blossom too soon to feed the animals that depend on them.

Tell me more: endangered animals

Bison
Millions were shot in the 19th century and there are now only 3,000 truly wild bison. They are being saved from extinction by a breeding program.

Polar bear
Global warming is a serious threat as their natural habitat melts away.

Iberian lynx
With just 150 left in the wild, this is the most threatened cat species in the world.

A quarter of all mammal species may disappear in the next 100 years.

Giant armadillo
Hunted for food, up to 50 percent of the population have been killed in the last 10 years.

Mountain gorilla
Expanding farms have left their forest homes isolated and they are also threatened by poaching. There are less than 700 in the wild.

Aye-aye
This nocturnal Madagascan primate is threatened by the destruction of rain forests.

WHAT'S IN A NAME?

The phrase "**dead as a dodo**" refers to a flightless bird native to the island of Mauritius in the Indian Ocean that was wiped out little more than a century after it was first discovered by humans in 1581.

Amazing animals you'll never see

Irish elk
Extinct for 7,700 years, this was the largest deer that ever lived. It was 7 ft (2.1 m) tall at the shoulders and its giant antlers measured 12 ft (3.65 m) across.

Mammoth
Due to climate change and hunting, woolly mammoths vanished from Europe around 10,000 BCE. A small group survived on Wrangel Island (Siberia) until 1,650 BCE.

Great auk
This flightless bird had white and black feathers. It was once numerous along North Atlantic coastlines, but the great auk was eventually hunted to extinction in 1844.

Quagga
A zebra with stripes at the front of the body, it roamed South Africa's Cape Province in large numbers until the 1840s, when it was hunted to extinction by Boer settlers.

Five ways to save a species

01 Setting up nature reserves and parks so that enough numbers of rare animals live in the wild to survive on their own.

02 Building up populations of rare animals in zoos through captive breeding so that they can be released into the wild.

03 International agreements on hunting can protect endangered animals such as blue whales.

04 Using alternatives in place of products from rare animals, like the rhino horns used in some Chinese medicines.

05 Storing an animal's genetic material in a gene bank so that in future scientists may be able to "grow" a new animal of an extinct species.

Back for good

From time to time extinct animals are rediscovered:

■ The **La Gomera giant lizard** (pictured) was thought to be long extinct, but it was rediscovered in 1999, living on two cliffs on the island of La Gomera.

■ The **Cyprus spiny mouse** was thought to be extinct, but four were caught in 2007.

■ The **Barkudia limbless skink lizard** has no legs and looks like a giant earthworm. It was seen again in 2003 after a gap of 86 years!

■ A scientific expedition in 2003 rediscovered the **Rancho Grande harlequin frog** breeding along a mountain stream in Venezuela—the first time it had been seen since 1982.

I don't believe it!

Could an extinct species, like a mammoth, be brought back to life? Scientists are looking at many different ways this might work, including combining the DNA from a frozen mammoth and an elephant to create an elephant-mammoth creature.

Bengal tiger
A growing human population has hunted out the tiger's natural prey. The tigers are also poached for the illegal fur trade and Asian medicine market. There are now less than 1,500 in the wild.

Orangutan
Poaching and massive deforestation due to oil palm plantations means just 60,000 survive in the wild.

Blue whale
Almost wiped out by whaling ships in the 1960s, less than 5,000 remain. Populations have recovered since a whaling ban was implemented.

Poaching for the **pet trade** threatens apes such as orang-utans, as well as small creatures like reptiles, fish, and spiders. The poachers usually kill the adult apes and **steal their babies** because they are small and easier to manage.

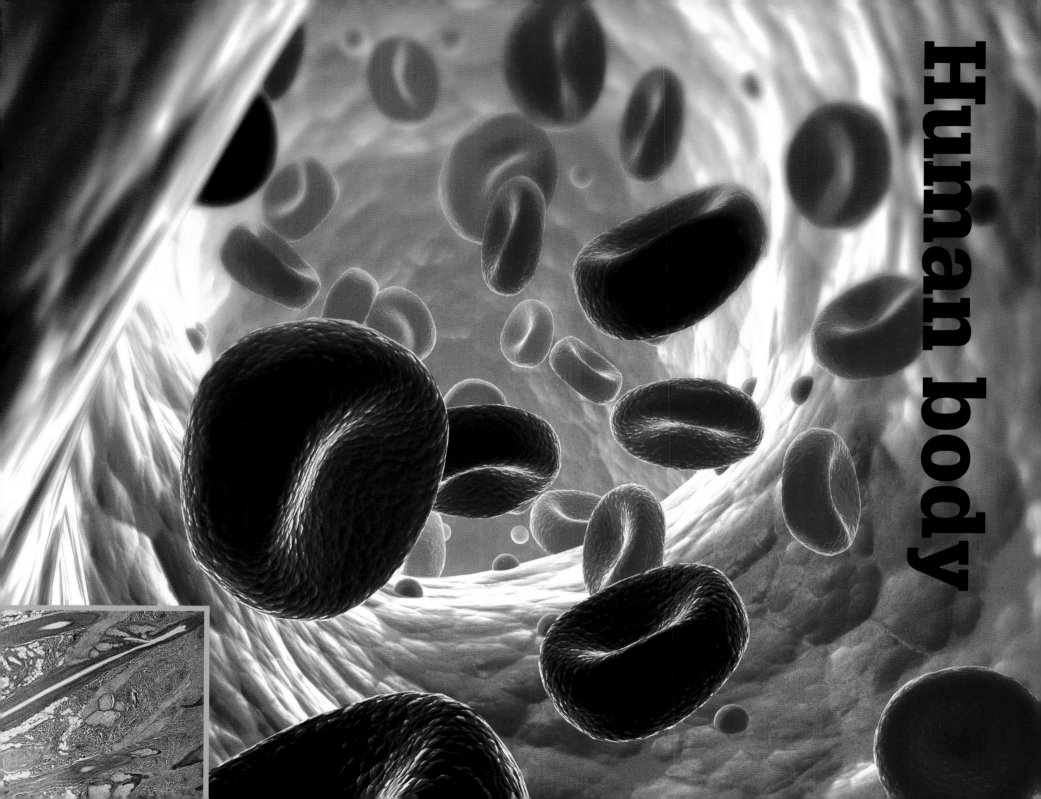

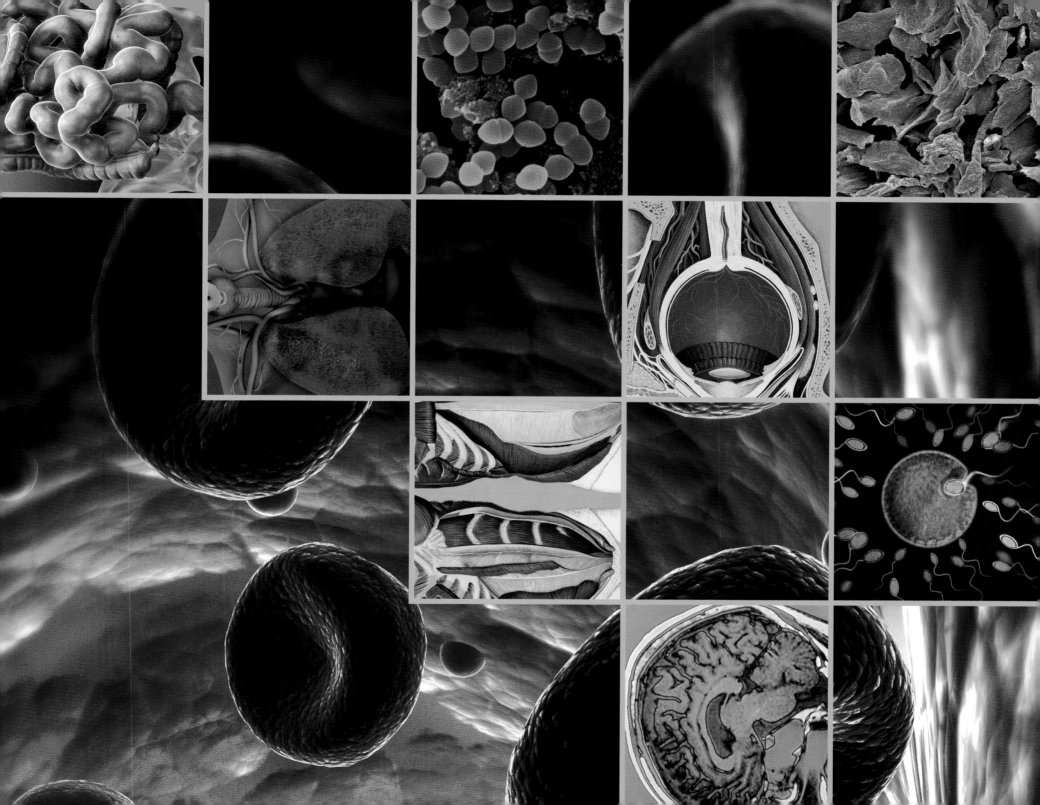

Why don't haircuts hurt?

Because hairs are made of dead cells, so you don't feel a thing. The dead hair cells are filled with a tough, waterproof protein called keratin, as are nails, and the skin flakes that you lose daily in their millions from your skin's surface. All these things are part of the fantastic protective overcoat that covers and protects your body.

Six reasons you need skin

01 It provides a waterproof covering around your body.

02 It forms a barrier between your delicate tissues and the harsh outside world.

03 It stops germs from getting into your body.

04 It filters out harmful ultraviolet radiation in sunlight that can damage your cells.

05 It helps your body maintain a steady temperature.

06 It houses receptors that enable you to detect touch, pressure, vibrations, heat, and cold.

In an average lifetime **a man will shave 20,000 times** (unless, of course, he has a beard).

Tell me more: what's in skin?

Skin is really thin but also very complex. It's made of two layers: The epidermis provides protection and is constantly worn away and replaced. The dermis glues the epidermis to the rest of the body and deals with feeling, temperature control, and food and oxygen supplies.

Hair shaft: Grows above the skin's surface

Nerve ending: Detects touch and other sensations

Lower part of the epidermis: Produces new cells to replace those lost from the surface

Blood vessel: Supplies oxygen and food to skin cells

Hair follicle: A pit in the skin from which hair grows

Sebaceous gland: Releases oily sebum, which keeps hair and skin moist and flexible

Sweat gland: Produces sweat, which is released onto the skin's surface

Upper part of the epidermis: Made of dead cells

Epidermis: The thin, upper layer of skin

Dermis: The thicker, lower part of the skin

What about me?

Zits form when oily sebum blocks a hair follicle. Bacteria move in and their activities alert the body's defenses, so the zit becomes inflamed. Zits are common during puberty, when the skin is more oily.

How to: warm up

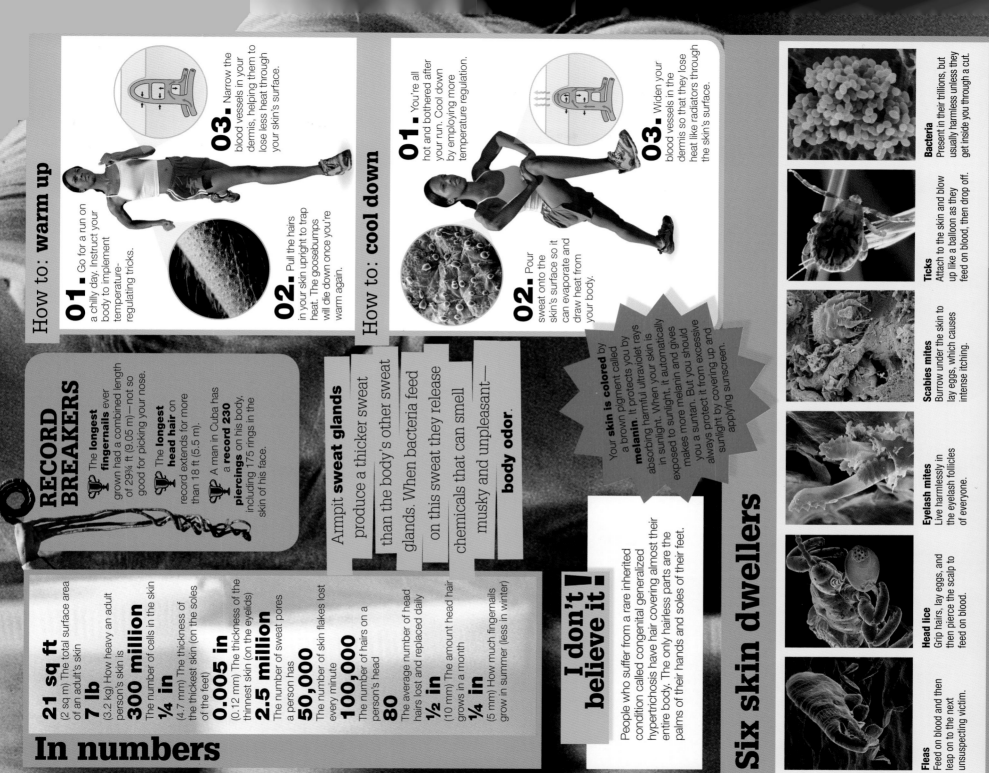

01. Go for a run on a chilly day. Instruct your body to implement temperature-regulating tricks.

02. Pull the hairs in your skin upright to trap heat. The goosebumps will die down once you're warm again.

03. Narrow the blood vessels in your dermis, helping them to lose less heat through your skin's surface.

How to: cool down

01. You're all hot and bothered after your run. Cool down by employing more temperature regulation.

02. Pour sweat onto the skin's surface so it can evaporate and draw heat from your body.

03. Widen your blood vessels in the dermis so that they lose heat like radiators through the skin's surface.

RECORD BREAKERS

🏆 The **longest fingernails** ever grown had a combined length of 29¾ ft (9.05 m)—not so good for picking your nose.

🏆 The **longest head hair** on record extends for more than 18 ft (5.5 m).

🏆 A man in Cuba has a **record 230 piercings** on his body, including 175 rings in the skin of his face.

In numbers

21 sq ft
(2 sq m) The total surface area of an adult's skin

7 lb
(3.2 kg) How heavy an adult person's skin is

300 million
The number of cells in the skin

¼ in
(4.7 mm) The thickness of the thickest skin (on the soles of the feet)

0.005 in
(0.12 mm) The thickness of the thinnest skin (on the eyelids)

2.5 million
The number of sweat pores a person has

50,000
The number of skin flakes lost every minute

100,000
The number of hairs on a person's head

80
The average number of head hairs lost and replaced daily

½ in
(10 mm) The amount head hair grows in a month

¼ in
(5 mm) How much fingernails grow in summer (less in winter)

Armpit **sweat glands** produce a thicker sweat than the body's other sweat glands. When bacteria feed on this sweat they release chemicals that can smell musky and unpleasant—**body odor.**

Your **skin is colored** by a brown pigment called **melanin.** It protects you by absorbing harmful ultraviolet rays in sunlight. When your skin is exposed to sunlight, it automatically makes more melanin and gives you a suntan. But you should always protect it from excessive sunlight by covering up and applying sunscreen.

I don't believe it!

People who suffer from a rare inherited condition called congenital generalized hypertrichosis have hair covering almost their entire body. The only hairless parts are the palms of their hands and soles of their feet.

Six skin dwellers

Fleas
Feed on blood and then leap on to the next unsuspecting victim.

Head lice
Grip hairs, lay eggs, and then pierce the scalp to feed on blood.

Eyelash mites
Live harmlessly in the eyelash follicles of everyone.

Scabies mites
Burrow under the skin to lay eggs, which causes intense itching.

Ticks
Attach to the skin and blow up like a balloon as they feed on blood, then drop off.

Bacteria
Present in their trillions, but usually harmless unless they get inside you through a cut.

Why do **bones** remain for centuries after a person dies?

Bones are made of two main materials: calcium salts make bones hard, and collagen fibers make them strong but also a little flexible. After death, the collagen rots away, leaving just the durable hard parts behind. In life, the bones of a person's skeleton support the body and protect its internal organs.

Tell me more: **inside a bone**

The bones in your skeleton are moist, living organs with their own blood supply. If you look inside a bone you can see that it is not solid. If bones were solid they would be so heavy you would not be able to move.

Spongy bone: Made of bony struts and spaces filled with bone marrow. It is strong but light

Bone marrow: Jellylike substance that fills the spaces inside bones; yellow bone marrow stores fat, while red bone marrow makes blood cells

Compact bone: Made of parallel tubes of bony tissue. It is dense, strong, and forms the outer layer of the bone

Blood vessels: Supply osteocytes (bone cells) with food and oxygen

Periosteum: The outer layer of tissue that surrounds the bone

Skull and crossbones

Because bones endure after death, skeletons—and the skull and cross bones—have for centuries been symbols of disease, danger, and death.

TWO SKELETONS

Axial (central) skeleton (the skull, backbone, and ribs): Consists of 80 bones that run down the center of the body and protect the heart and lungs

Appendicular skeleton (the arms, legs, shoulder girdle, and hip girdle): Consists of 126 bones that hang on to the axial skeleton and move the body

I don't believe it!

The Paris Catacombs are underground bone storage units that contain many thousands of skulls, femurs, and other bones. In fact, the walls of the catacombs are made from bones! They were brought there for storage in the 18th century, from cemeteries that were overflowing with dead people.

In numbers

206
The number of bones in an adult skeleton

300
The number of bones in a newborn baby's skeleton (as a baby grows, some bones fuse together)

106
The number of bones in hands and feet—more than half the number of bones in the body

99%
The percentage of calcium in the body, found in bones and teeth

6
The number of times a living bone is stronger than a piece of steel of the same weight

Blood-making bones

In babies, blood cells are made by red bone marrow inside all bones. In adults, they are made only in certain bones, shown here.

- cranium
- collar bone
- shoulder blades
- top end of each humerus
- breast bone
- ribs
- vertebrae
- top end of each femur

BONE HEAD

There are 22 skull bones, 21 of which have wiggly edges that lock together in sutures (immovable joints) like pieces in a jigsaw puzzle. Sutures stop skull bones from moving, making the skull really strong. The only skull bone that does move freely is the mandible or lower jaw. If it didn't, you would not be able to eat, drink, or speak.

How to: fix a fracture

01. Allow blood to clot, stopping bleeding inside the break and starting the process of self-repair.

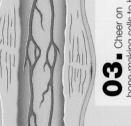

02. Link up the broken ends of the bone so that blood vessels can invade the area along with bone-making cells.

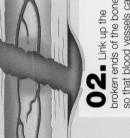

03. Cheer on bone-making cells to build new compact and spongy bone. Within months the fracture is repaired.

FAST FACTS

Bone

01: The smallest bone in the body is the stapes or stirrup bone. Found inside the ear, it is smaller than a grain of rice.

02: The femur or thighbone is the body's longest bone, at about a quarter the body's total length.

03: The skull is the body's most complex bone.

04: Our most complex joint is the knee.

Your "funny bone" isn't a bone at all; it's a spot on the outer part of your elbow that if you hit or knock it gives you a weird tingly pain. This is because the ulnar nerve crosses the bone at that point.

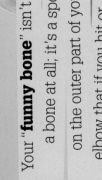

NECK BONES

Humans and giraffes have the same number of neck bones. They both have seven, or cervical vertebrae. Although each of the giraffe's vertebrae are much longer!

Six flexible joints

Ball and socket joint
Allows movement in any direction and is found in the shoulder and hip

Ellipsoidal joint
Allows movement from side to side, backward and forward, and is found in the wrist and knuckles

Hinge joint
Allows movement in just one plane, like a door hinge, and is found in knees and elbows

Pivot joint
Allows the end of one bone to rotate in or on another, found between the top two vertebrae to allow the head to turn

Plane joint
Allows short sliding movements and is found in the wrist and ankle bones

Saddle joint
Provides rotation in all directions, found at the base of the thumb, allowing it to touch the other fingers

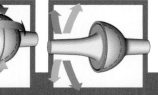

Skull: Protects the brain and gives shape to the head and face

Temporal bone: Encloses the inner part of the ear, which enables us to detect sounds and maintain balance

Mandible: Lower jaw bone is the only moveable part of the skull. It enables us to chew our food

Cervical vertebra: One of seven vertebrae that make up the neck, the uppermost of which allow the head to nod and shake

Clavicle (collar bone): Connects the scapula to the sternum

Scapula (shoulder blade): Forms a joint with the humerus that attaches the arm to the body

Ribs: 12 pairs surround and protect the heart and lungs

Frontal bone: Forms the forehead

Parietal bones: Two bones that together form the sides and top of the skull

Suture: Immovable joint that locks the skull bones together

Occipital bone: Forms the rear and base of the skull

Humerus (upper arm bone): Connects the forearm bones to the shoulder joint, a ball-and-socket joint that allows the arm to move in all directions

Sternum (breast bone): Forms a plate to protect the heart

Backbone: Flexible column of 26 bones called vertebrae that forms the main axis of the body and supports the head

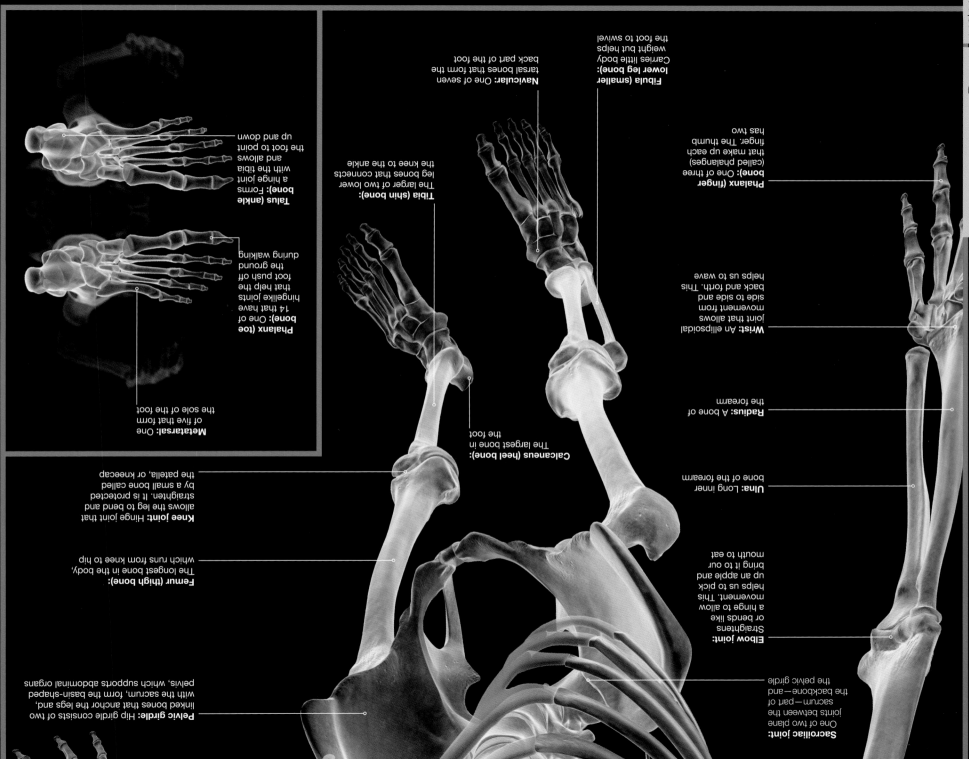

Navicular: One of seven tarsal bones that form the back part of the foot

Fibula (smaller lower leg bone): Carries little body weight but helps the foot to swivel

Phalanx (finger bone): One of three (called phalanges) that make up each finger. The thumb has two

Tibia (shin bone): The larger of two lower leg bones that connects the knee to the ankle

Talus (ankle bone): Forms a hinge joint with the tibia and allows the foot to point up and down

Phalanx (toe bone): One of 14 that have hingelike joints that help the foot push off the ground during walking

Metatarsal: One of five that form the sole of the foot

Wrist: An ellipsoidal joint that allows movement from side to side and back and forth. This helps us to wave

Radius: A bone of the forearm

Calcaneus (heel bone): The largest bone in the foot

Knee joint: Hinge joint that allows the leg to bend and straighten. It is protected by a small bone called the patella, or kneecap

Femur (thigh bone): The longest bone in the body, which runs from knee to hip

Ulna: Long inner bone of the forearm

Elbow joint: Straightens or bends like a hinge to allow movement. This helps us to pick up an apple and bring it to our mouth to eat

Pelvic girdle: Hip girdle consists of two linked bones that anchor the legs and, with the sacrum, form the basin-shaped pelvis, which supports abdominal organs

Sacroiliac joint: One of two plane joints between the sacrum—part of the backbone—and the pelvic girdle

Why does your head flop **when you sleep?**

When you are awake the muscles in your neck and back hold you and your head upright. When you nod off, those muscles relax and your head falls to one side. Muscles do more than just support you—by pulling your bones they produce every movement from lifting a pen to running a marathon.

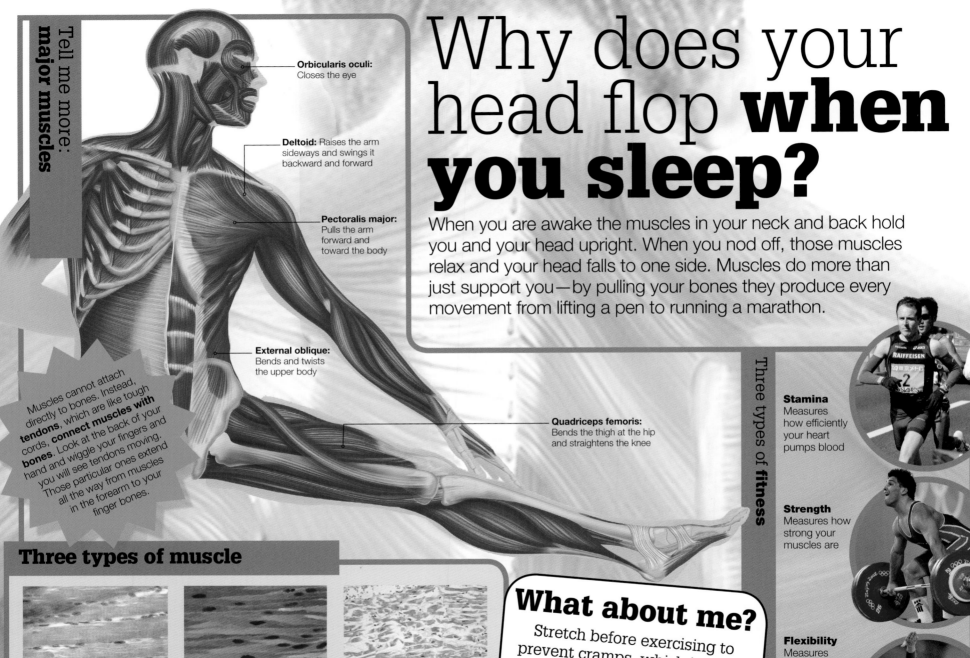

Orbicularis oculi: Closes the eye

Deltoid: Raises the arm sideways and swings it backward and forward

Pectoralis major: Pulls the arm forward and toward the body

External oblique: Bends and twists the upper body

Quadriceps femoris: Bends the thigh at the hip and straightens the knee

Muscles cannot attach directly to bones. Instead, **tendons**, which are like tough cords, **connect muscles with bones**. Look at the back of your hand and wiggle your fingers and you will see tendons moving. Those particular ones extend all the way from muscles in the forearm to your finger bones.

Three types of fitness

Stamina Measures how efficiently your heart pumps blood

Strength Measures how strong your muscles are

Flexibility Measures how flexible your joints, tendons, and muscles are

Three types of muscle

Skeletal muscle Pulls on bones so you can move your body

Smooth muscle Found in the walls of hollow organs, such as the bladder

Cardiac muscle Found in the wall of the heart, it constantly contracts to pump blood

What about me?
Stretch before exercising to prevent cramps, which is when a muscle stays contracted when it should have relaxed and causes pain.

How to: **straighten and bend your arm**

biceps

01. Straighten your arm with your triceps muscle, which will pull your forearm downward.

triceps

02. To bend your arm, contract (shorten) your biceps so it pulls your forearm upward.

04. Your biceps is now fully contracted and your arm bent… time to straighten it again?

03. As your biceps keeps contracting (feel the bulge!), relax your triceps muscle to enable your arm to keep bending from the elbow.

In numbers

640 The number of skeletal muscles in the human body

20 in (50 cm) The length of the longest muscle in your body, the sartorius, which is a thigh muscle

40–50% The proportion of the male body's weight that is made up by muscles

30–40% The proportion of the female body's weight that is made up by muscles

¼ in (0.5 cm) The length of the shortest muscle in your body, the stapedius, which is located in your ear

Latissimus dorsi: Pulls the arm downward, inward, and backward

Triceps brachii: Straightens the arm from the elbow

Gluteus maximus: Straightens the hip by pulling the thigh back

Hamstrings: Straighten the thigh at the hip and bend the knee

Gastrocnemius: Pulls the Achilles tendon to point the foot downward

Achilles tendon

Tell me more: **inside a muscle**

Muscles are made up of long cylindrical cells called fibers.

Nerve fibers: Carry signals from the brain that make the muscle fibers contract

Blood vessels: Carry oxygen and food to the muscle fibers

muscle contracts to pull bones

bundle of parallel muscle fibers

Five facial expressions

More than 30 small muscles pull on the skin of the face to produce the expressions that reveal how we feel.

Fear
Muscles pull the lower jaw downward to open the mouth wide.

Anger
Muscles pull the eyebrows downward, making them wrinkle.

Joy
Muscles pull and lift the corners of the mouth.

Surprise
Muscles raise the eyebrows and make the forehead wrinkle.

Sadness
Muscles pull the corners of the mouth downward.

Why is blood red?

Blood is red because most of its cells are packed with a red-colored substance called hemoglobin. Using this, the red blood cells pick up vital oxygen and deliver it to the body's cells. To achieve this and other roles, such as removing waste, blood is pumped along blood vessels by the heart.

Tell me more: circulation

Blood travels through blood vessels, from the heart, to all parts of the body. Oxygen-poor blood (blue) is pumped to the lungs, where it picks up oxygen. This oxygen-rich blood (red) is then pumped to the rest of the body.

01: Oxygen-poor blood arrives in the heart

02: Oxygen-poor blood flows from the heart along a pulmonary artery to one of the lungs

03: Newly oxygenated blood zooms along a pulmonary vein to the heart's left side

04: Oxygen-loaded blood gets the big push out of the heart and into the aorta—the body's biggest artery—for carrying around the body

05: Small arteries branch off to the body's organs, where blood travels along tiny capillaries and gives up oxygen to the organs' cells

06: Inferior vena cava—a large vein—carries oxygen-poor blood back to the heart to start its journey again

Labels: right lung · left lung · upper body · lower body · liver · stomach · right side of heart · left side of heart · pulmonary artery · aorta

WHAT'S IN A NAME?

In the past, people of noble birth were described as being "**blue-blooded**." Back then, only poor people who worked outdoors had suntans. Rich people had pale skin through which you could see their blue-colored veins, hence, "blue-blooded."

Blood composition

If blood is poured into a glass tube and spun in a centrifuge (a spinning device), its main components separate into three layers.

Plasma (55 percent): A watery liquid containing food, wastes, hormones, and many other substances

White blood cells and platelets (1 percent): White blood cells fight infection, and platelets prevent bleeding by causing blood clots

Red blood cells (44 percent): Transport oxygen from lungs to tissues

Five creatures **that want your blood**

Sheep ticks
These balloon after feeding and can cause Lyme disease in humans.

Leeches
Use their slicing mouthparts to cut through the skin.

Tsetse flies
Biting flies that feed on blood and spread the sleeping sickness disease.

Kissing bugs
These come out at night and suck your blood while you're asleep.

Dracula
A fictional vampire created by Victorian novelist Bram Stoker.

How to: pump blood through the heart

Your heart is mainly made of a special kind of muscle that never tires. It has two sides—left and right—each divided into an upper chamber called an atrium, and a larger, lower chamber called a ventricle.

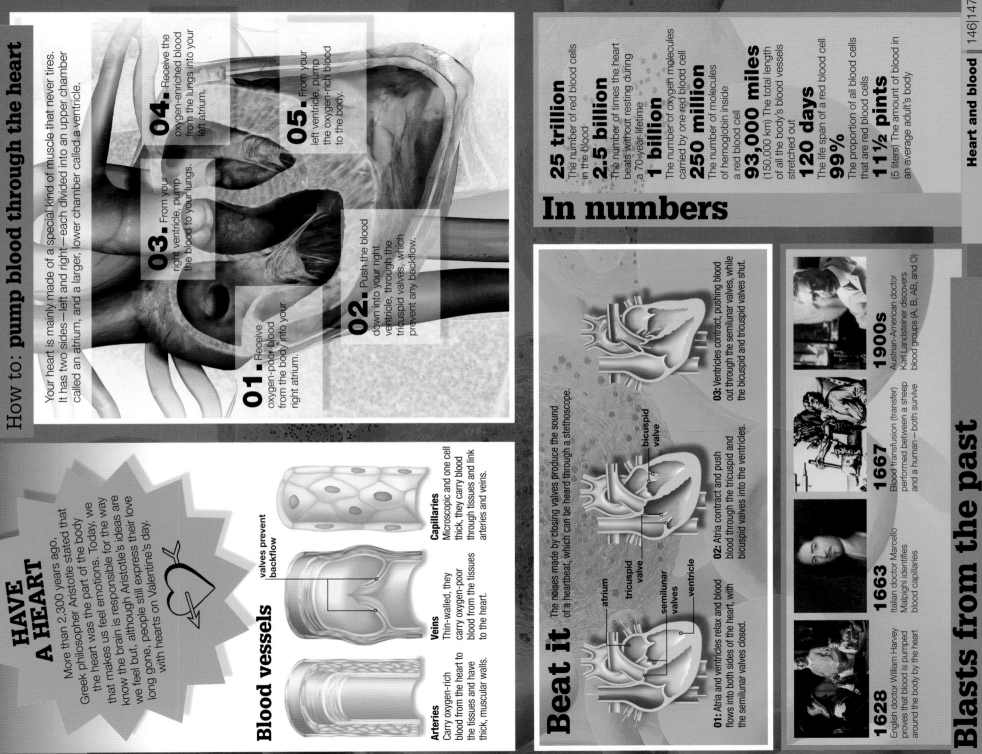

01. Receive oxygen-poor blood from the body into your right atrium.

02. Push the blood down into your right ventricle, through the tricuspid valves, which prevent any backflow.

03. From your right ventricle, pump the blood to your lungs.

04. Receive the oxygen-enriched blood from the lungs into your left atrium.

05. From your left ventricle, pump the oxygen-rich blood to the body.

HAVE A HEART

More than 2,300 years ago, Greek philosopher Aristotle stated that the heart was the part of the body that makes us feel emotions. Today, we know the brain is responsible for the way we feel but, although Aristotle's ideas are long gone, people still express their love with hearts on Valentine's day.

Blood vessels

Arteries
Carry oxygen-rich blood from the heart to the tissues and have thick, muscular walls.

Veins
Thin-walled, they carry oxygen-poor blood from the tissues to the heart.

valves prevent backflow

Capillaries
Microscopic and one cell thick, they carry blood through tissues and link arteries and veins.

In numbers

25 trillion
The number of red blood cells in the blood

2.5 billion
The number of times the heart beats without resting during a 70-year lifetime

1 billion
The number of oxygen molecules carried by one red blood cell

250 million
The number of molecules of hemoglobin inside a red blood cell

93,000 miles
(150,000 km) The total length of all the body's blood vessels stretched out

120 days
The life span of a red blood cell

99%
The proportion of all blood cells that are red blood cells

11½ pints
(5 liters) The amount of blood in an average adult's body

Beat it

The noises made by closing valves produce the sound of a heartbeat, which can be heard through a stethoscope.

atrium

tricuspid valve

semilunar valves

ventricle

bicuspid valve

01: Atria and ventricles relax and blood flows into both sides of the heart, with the semilunar valves closed.

02: Atria contract and push blood through the tricuspid and bicuspid valves into the ventricles.

03: Ventricles contract, pushing blood out through the semilunar valves, while the bicuspid and tricuspid valves shut.

Blasts from the past

1628
English doctor William Harvey proves that blood is pumped around the body by the heart

1663
Italian doctor Marcello Malpighi identifies blood capillaries

1667
Blood transfusion (transfer) performed between a sheep and a human—both survive

1900s
Austrian-American doctor Karl Landsteiner discovers blood groups (A, B, AB, and O)

Why do I need to eat?

Your body's trillions of tiny cells work day and night to keep you alive. To keep going they need energy, which comes from the food you eat. Food also provides the building materials that your cells use to make you grow, but first your body must digest the food, releasing the simple nutrients that your body can use.

What about me?

Digestion begins the moment you put food in your mouth. If you chew on some white bread for a few minutes, an enzyme in your saliva breaks down starch—a bland-tasting carbohydrate in the bread—into sweet-tasting sugars. You've just witnessed digestion in action!

I don't believe it!

The world's human population deposits an incredible two million tons of feces every day, equivalent to the weight of 5,000 completely full jumbo jets.

How to: eat and digest your food

01. Use your teeth to chop and crush food into small pieces.

02. Release watery, slimy saliva into your mouth from the salivary glands. Try not to dribble!

03. Really put your food through the mix, using your tongue to swill it in saliva and push it into the throat for swallowing.

04. Squeeze food along your esophagus, running from your throat to your stomach.

05. With food in your stomach, churn it into creamy liquid chyme (partially digested food).

06. Release bile from your liver and process any digested food here, storing some of the nutrients and dispatching the rest to the body's cells.

07. Squirt bile, stored in your gall bladder, into the small intestine to help digest any fats.

08. From your pancreas, release more digestive enzymes into the small intestine for breaking down food even further.

Four tooth types

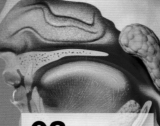

Canine: Grips and tears food

Incisor: Cuts and chops food

Molar: Crushes and grinds food into small pieces

Premolar: Crushes food

WEIRD OR WHAT?

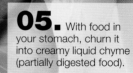

Michel Lotito (1959-2007), better known as **Monsieur Mangetout** ("Mister Eat Everything"), was a man who consumed indigestible items such as metal and glass. His crowning achievement was to eat a Cessna 150 aircraft—a feat that took him just over two years. Oddly, bananas and hard-boiled eggs made him sick.

01: Processing digested food

02: Controlling levels of glucose (sugar) in your blood

03: Storing and transporting fats

04: Processing amino acids (protein building blocks) and making proteins

05: Making green bile, which flows into the small intestine to help digest fats

06: Storing vitamins A, B_{12}, D, E, and K

07: Removing hormones (chemical messengers) from the blood once they've done their job

08: Removing and breaking down drugs and poisons

09: Removing bacteria (germs)

10: Removing worn-out red blood cells

Your **small intestine** is the most important part of the digestive system. Its ridged lining is covered with tiny, fingerlike villi that increase the surface area for absorbing nutrients from the semidigested food passing through.

10. With food remnants now entering the final part of your digestive system—the large intestine—absorb any water from them into the blood, leaving behind solid feces.

09. With semidigested chyme working its way through your sausage-shaped small intestine, absorb any remaining nutrients into your blood, which speeds them along to the liver for processing.

11. Store the feces in your rectum until such time as you can get to a restroom…

12. …and now open your anus, pushing the feces out of your body. Job complete!

Nutrients you need from food

what?	why?	which foods?
carbohydrates	to provide energy	pasta, bread, rice, potatoes
proteins	growth and repair	meat, fish, beans
fats	energy, insulation	dairy foods, plant oils, meat, fish
vitamins	to help cells work	fruit, vegetables, eggs, meat, fish
minerals	to help cells work	dairy foods, meat, fish, nuts, beans
fiber	to help intestines work	fruit, vegetables
water	essential for life	all foods and drinks

Fart facts

- Farts are made up of air that you swallow and gases released by bacteria in the intestines.
- Farts smell because of certain stinky gases released by bacteria.
- Eating cauliflower, eggs, or meat produces the smelliest farts.
- Eating beans produces the largest volume of farts. Bacteria love beans!
- An average person farts 14 times a day.

100 trillion
The number of bacteria living in your colon

3½ fl oz
(100 ml) The volume of water a person loses in their feces each day

20
The number of teeth in a set of baby teeth, which are replaced from age six onward

32
The number of teeth in a full set of adult teeth

30 tons
The weight of food eaten in an average lifetime

24 pints
(11.5 liters) How much food, liquid, and digestive fluid flow through your digestive system every day

WHAT'S IN A NAME?

Borborygmi is the name used by doctors to describe stomach rumblings and other digestive noises because, if you say it, it sounds like the odd noises coming from your belly region.

Vomiting step-by-step

01: An unsuspecting person eats food that contains nasty bacteria or toxins (poisons).

02: The stomach lining becomes irritated by the intruders.

03: The irritated lining sends signals to the "vomiting center" of the brain.

04: The person feels sick and makes for the nearest bathroom. Quickly.

05: The abdominal muscles contract and squeeze the stomach.

06: Soupy food is forced up the esophagus and out of the mouth. Yuck!

Why can't you ever take a break from breathing?

Breathing takes air in and out of your lungs, and that air contains the gas oxygen. Every one of your trillions of body cells needs a constant supply of oxygen, 24 hours a day, and oxygen is something your body cannot store—so, no break! Breathing also removes carbon dioxide from the body—a waste gas that your cells are releasing all the time.

Five ways the nose freshens air

01: Nostril hairs work like a net to catch pollen, insect parts, and skin flakes.

02: Sticky mucus lining the nasal cavity traps bacteria, viruses, and dust particles.

03: Hairlike cilia in the nasal lining move from side to side to waft germ-laden mucus to the throat, where it is swallowed and treated to an acid bath in the stomach.

04: Blood vessels lining the nasal cavity act like radiators to warm the air—especially useful on cold days.

05: The nasal lining loses water vapor to make even the driest air moist.

In numbers

600 million
The number of alveoli in our two lungs

25,000
The average number of breaths we take each day

2,000 gallons
(9,000 liters) The volume of blood that flows through the lungs to pick up oxygen every day

1,900 gallons
(8,500 liters) The average volume of air breathed in and out daily

1,100 sq ft
(100 sq m) The area of the lungs' alveoli, which is equivalent to the area of a tennis court

12–15
The number of breaths a person makes each minute when at rest. This can double during exercise

1 pint
(0.5 liters) The amount of water we lose from the body each day in breathed-out air

RECORD BREAKER

Freedivers dive under water to considerable depths without an air supply. American **freediver** Tanya Streeter has descended to a lung-crushing 524 ft (160 m) and has held her breath for more than six minutes.

Tell me more: the respiratory system

Nasal cavity: Split in two by cartilage running down its middle, it warms and cleans the air flowing through it

Nostril: One of two hairy entrances to the nasal cavity

Larynx (voice box): Produces sounds

Trachea: Carries air to and from the lungs and is held open by cartilage rings

Intercostal muscles: Connect and move neighboring ribs

How to: make sounds and speak

01. Breathe normally so that the vocal cords that stretch across your larynx are wide open to let air pass through.

02. Now pull your vocal cords taut so that they close like curtains.

03. Breathe controlled bursts of air from your lungs through the closed vocal cords so that they vibrate.

04. Using your tongue, teeth, and lips, shape the sounds that the vibrations produce into understandable speech.

FAST FACTS

Cell respiration

01: Inside every body cell are small, sausage-shaped structures called mitochondria.

02: These mitochondria use oxygen to release energy from fuels, such as glucose, that you get from food.

03: The released energy is used to power the cell activities that keep you alive and healthy.

04: This energy release process, called cell respiration, produces waste carbon dioxide.

Throat: Carries air to and from the larynx

Epiglottis: Closes the entrance to the larynx during swallowing

---

Alternative **breathing movements**

Coughing
To clear mucus and other matter from the upper airways, air from the lungs builds up behind the closed vocal cords and is forced out through the mouth.

Sneezing
This movement is the same as for a cough, but air is forced out through the nasal cavity (instead of the mouth) to clear mucus or relieve an irritation.

Hiccupping
An irritation to the diaphragm (perhaps due to eating too quickly) makes it contract suddenly, causing air to rush into the lungs and the vocal cords to slap shut noisily.

Yawning
A deep breath taken into the lungs when you are tired, probably to "flush out" excess carbon dioxide from the blood.

Bronchus: Branch of the trachea that branches repeatedly into smaller bronchi

Bronchiole: Very fine branch of the smallest bronchi

Alveoli: Microscopic air sacs clustered at the end of each bronchiole, through which oxygen enters the bloodstream

Diaphragm: Dome-shaped muscle sheet under the lungs

No choke
Why can't you swallow food and breathe at the same time? A built-in safety device—a flap called the epiglottis—automatically covers the entrance to your trachea. If it didn't, food would get into your trachea, preventing air from reaching your lungs and causing you to choke.

I don't believe it!

Setting the record for nonstop sneezing, a British girl sneezed more than one million times in 978 days between January 1981 and September 1983.

Why do I feel pain if I step on a pin?

Because as the pin sticks into your skin, receptors send signals along nerves to your spinal cord and brain where those signals are analyzed, causing you to feel pain. Your nervous system enables you to move, think, feel, and controls all the activities going on inside your body.

In numbers

2%
The weight of the brain compared to the weight of the body

20%
The proportion of the body's oxygen supply that is used by the brain

100 billion
The number of neurons (nerve cells) in the brain

83%
The proportion of the brain that the cerebrum makes up

100 trillion
The number of connections between the brain's neurons

218 mph
(350 kph) The speed impulses travel along the fastest neurons

2,500
The number of times the fastest neurons "fire" each second

80%
How much of the brain is made up of water

Tell me more: nervous system

Brain: The control center of your nervous system

Cerebrum: The main part of the brain. It is divided into linked left and right halves (hemispheres)

Brain stem: Controls automatic activities such as heart and breathing rates

Cerebellum: Coordinates muscle movement and balance

Nerves: Bundles of long neurons (nerve cells) that relay signals between all parts of the body, and the brain and spinal cord

Spinal cord: A downward extension of the brain that relays signals to and from the brain

WEIRD OR WHAT?
An explosion shot a rod that went through mild-mannered Phineas Gage's left cheek and out through the front of his brain. He survived but became bad-tempered, proving that the front of the brain controls personality.

Tell me more: cerebral cortex

The cerebral cortex is the thin outer layer of each of the brain's hemispheres. It is within the cortex that incoming information is processed and stored and instructions sent out. Each part of the cortex has a particular job to do.

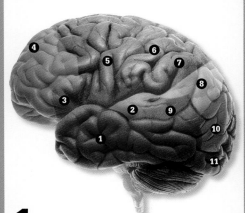

1. Auditory association cortex identifies sounds

2. Primary auditory cortex receives signals from the ears

3. Broca's area controls speech production

4. Prefrontal cortex is involved in planning, problem solving, and thinking

5. Premotor cortex controls complex movements such as riding a bike

6. Motor cortex tells muscles to contract to move the body

7. Primary sensory cortex receives signals from receptors in the skin

Four types of memory

You forget many of the things you experience, but important things are stored in long-term memory. Without memory you would not be able to learn, think, or create.

1: **Working (short-term) memory** provides you with an awareness of your surroundings to help you function.

2: **Procedural memory** stores skills such as riding a bike.

3: **Semantic memory** deals with facts, learned words, and languages.

4: **Episodic memory** remembers life events such as holidays and birthdays.

How to: test your reflexes

05. Before you realize what's happening your upper arm muscle will automatically pull your hand away. Good reflexes!

06. Message reaches your brain and you feel pain. Ouch!

03. When the nerve signal hits your spinal cord, relay it to a motor neuron, plus send on to the brain.

02. Touch a spike! This alerts receptors in your skin to send nerve impulses along sensory neurons to your spinal cord.

04. Send the nerve message to your upper arm muscle through the motor neuron.

01. Locate a cactus with sharp spikes.

KEY
- sensory neurons
- relay neurons
- motor neurons

Left is right and right is left

The left cerebral hemisphere controls the right side of the body, and the right cerebral hemisphere controls the left. Each hemisphere also has its own specialities. The left side is usually dominant, which is why most people are right-handed.

Left hemisphere
- written and spoken language
- numbers and math
- problem solving and logical thinking

Right hemisphere
- thinking spatially (visually)
- appreciation of art and music
- recognizing faces and objects

What about me?

Although it's at the center of your nervous system, your brain cannot feel pain. A headache is not your brain aching; headaches are commonly caused by muscle tension in the neck and under the skin of the scalp.

I don't believe it!

A nerve impulse takes just one-hundredth of a second to travel from the spinal cord to the big toe.

8. Sensory association cortex interprets skin sensations

9. Wernicke's area makes sense of written and spoken language

10. Visual association cortex forms images

11. Primary visual cortex receives signals from the eyes

Top five types of intelligence

01: **Spatial intelligence**
The ability to use the mind to turn around shapes. It is useful in map-reading and understanding how machines are put together.

02: **Verbal intelligence**
This measures how good someone's writing and reading skills are and how rapidly they can take in information.

03: **Numerical intelligence**
Someone who is good at mathematics, with a logical kind of mind that's good at analyzing things, has a high level of numerical intelligence.

04: **Lateral intelligence**
With this aplenty, a person can easily solve problems using the imagination; this person is probably creative, too.

05: **Emotional intelligence**
Scoring well in this department means that you are good at understanding how other people think or feel.

Why is ice cream sweet, smooth, and cold?

Receptors in your tongue's surface detect tastes and they pick up the sweetness of the ice cream. Touch receptors detect the ice cream's smooth texture, and other receptors sense how cold it is. They all send signals to your brain, which allows you to feel the sweet, smooth, and cold sensations.

Tell me more:
anatomy of an eye

Ciliary muscle: Adjusts the thickness of the lens so it can focus light from any distance

Fovea: The point on the retina that produces the most detailed images

Iris: Automatically controls the size of the pupil

Cornea: Lets light into the eye and helps to focus it

Pupil: Lets light into the back part of the eye

Lens: Fine focuses light onto the retina

The five senses

Vision
Eyes detect light and send signals to the brain, which produces moving images of your surroundings.

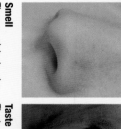

Hearing
Ears detect sounds and send signals to the brain, which identifies them as sounds you can hear.

Smell
The nose detects odor molecules in the air and sends signals to the brain so that you can smell them.

Taste
The tongue's taste buds detect taste molecules in food and send signals to the brain so that you taste what you're eating.

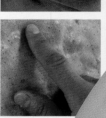

Touch
Receptors in your skin sense different types of touch and send signals to your brain so that you feel your surroundings.

Tell me more: skin sensors

Free nerve ending: Detects pain, heat, or cold

Meissner's corpuscle: Detects light touch

Ruffini's corpuscle: Detects deep and continuous pressure

Pacinian corpuscle: Detects vibrations and deep pressure

Merkel's disk: Detects light touch and pressure

What about me?

Have you eaten anything spicy lately? Chili peppers contain a substance called capsaicin, which triggers pain receptors in your tongue when you eat them. That's why they feel painfully hot.

In numbers

10,000
The number of taste buds on the tongue

5
The number of tastes detected by the tongue

10,000
The number of odors detected by the nose

25 million
The number of smell receptors in the nose

10,000
The number of times more sensitive that the sense of smell is than taste

70%
The proportion of the body's sensory receptors that are in the eyes

10,000
The number of different colors that the eyes can distinguish

120 million
The number of rods (light-sensitive receptors that work in dim light and cannot detect color) in each eye

7 million
The number of cones (light-sensitive receptors that work in bright light and detect colors) in each eye

1 mile
(1.6 km) The distance over which an eye can detect a burning candle in the dark

Five tastes your tongue's taste buds pick up

Sweet
Cakes, cookies, peaches, mangoes

Sour
Lemons, vinegar, fresh orange juice

Salty
Potato chips, bacon, pizza, prepared meals

Bitter
Coffee, dark chocolate

Umami
The savory taste of meat, meaty stocks, and cheese

I don't believe it!

Sometimes people who have had an arm or leg amputated (cut off) can still feel pain in the body part that's missing. This weird and ghostly phenomenon is called phantom pain. And phantom itches are even more frustrating—there's nothing to scratch!

What color is that word?

Approximately 1 in 23 people experience **synesthesia**, which means their **senses intermingle**. They might see words or music as colors, taste sounds, or hear a picture.

Vitreous humor: Semisolid jelly that shapes the eye

Optic nerve: Carries nerve signals to the visual cortex in the brain, which produces the images you "see"

Retina: Thin layer that contains rods and cones (light detectors)

Sclera: Tough, white outer layer of eye

The muscles that move your eyes are the body's most active muscles. **They contract (pull) 100,000 times a day.**

Why do identical twins look exactly the same?

Identical twins happen when a single sperm (male cell), fertilizes a single egg (female cell) that then splits in two. Each one goes on to grow into a baby, but both cells share exactly the same genetic instructions (DNA).

Born July 25, 1978 in Oldham, England, **Louise Brown was the world's first baby to be conceived by IVF** (in vitro fertilization). One of Louise's mother's eggs was fertilized by Louise's father's sperm in a laboratory, and the resulting embryo transferred back to the uterus (womb) of Mrs. Brown.

Little men?

In the 17th century it was thought by some that the head of a sperm contained a tiny, fully formed person (or "homunculus," meaning "little man") that was placed inside a woman's body to grow into a baby.

Reproduction

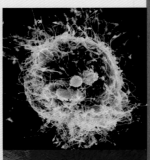

Fertilized egg
Travels toward the uterus, ready to start dividing

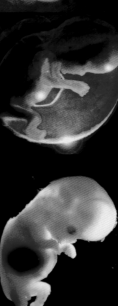

16-cell stage
Three days after fertilization, the egg has become a ball of 16 cells

Embryo at 4 weeks
Pea-sized embryo is embedded in the lining of the uterus

Fetus at 8 weeks
All its organs in place and it has a beating heart and arms and legs

Fetus at 12 weeks
The lemon-sized fetus has recognizable facial features and separate fingers and toes

All humans follow the same path through life. We are born, go through childhood, get older, and eventually die. Reproduction makes sure that we produce children to succeed us when we are no longer here. This sequence reveals how the resulting baby grows inside its mother's uterus, from fertilized egg through the embryo and fetus stages, until it is ready to be born.

Bony bits

A baby's bones have lots of flexible cartilage in them. As he or she grows, the cartilage is replaced by hard bone tissue—which looks dark on an X-ray.

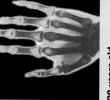

1 year old
There are wide spaces of cartilage between each finger bone.

3 years old
Wrist bones are starting to form and palm bones are thickening.

13 years old
Bones are nearly fully formed, although some bone ends are still separated by cartilage.

20 years old
The bones are fully grown; the only cartilage is covering the ends of the bones.

Where are the **instructions for making a human?**

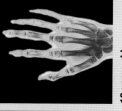

Cell
One of a hundred trillion microscopic living units inside your body

Nucleus
The cell's control center, which contains the instructions to build and run it

Chromosome
One of 46 instruction packages (23 came from your mother and 23 from your father) inside the cell

DNA
A very long molecule that is coiled up to form a chromosome

Gene
A short section of DNA that controls one of your features, such as eye or hair color

Peak ages

Childhood and teens: Peak age for learning

Mid-20s to 30s: Peak age for fitness

Mid-20s to early 30s: Peak age for fertility

In numbers

6.72 billion
The number of humans in the world in November 2008

16 million
The number of living direct male descendants of Genghis Khan (1162–1227)

300 million
The daily number of sperm produced by a man's testes

800,000
The number of eggs in a girl's ovaries when she is born

69
The number of children born to one Russian woman between 1725 and 1765

122 years, 164 days
The longest (confirmed) human lifespan, lived by Louise Calment (1875–1997)

Brain growth

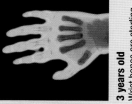

At birth: All of its 100 billion neurons (nerve cells) are in place, but communication between them is poor. Gaps between the skull bones allow it to expand.

At six years: After a rapid growth due to lots of connections being made between neurons, the brain is now nearly full size. Gaps between the skull bones are closed.

At 18 years: The full-sized brain has a complete network of neuron connections.

That's life!

6 months: Baby sits up unsupported, eats semisolid food, and can pick up small objects

12 months: Infant can walk with help, understand simple commands, drink from a cup, and will speak his/her first words

2 years: Child can walk, speak about 300 words, and recognize itself in a mirror

3 years: Child can run, kick a ball, open doors, and speak simple sentences

5 years: Child can catch a ball, dance in time to music, start to read and write, and form more complex sentences

10 years: Child develops a sense of identity, starts to reason, and can perform skills such as cycling

11–17 years (girls): Puberty and adolescence sets in (when her body becomes adult)

13–17 years (boys): Puberty and adolescence sets in (when his body becomes adult)

20s–30s: Young adult at his/her fittest and healthiest

40s–50s: Older adult begins to show the first signs of aging

60s–80s: Visible signs of aging include wrinkles, thinning and graying hair, weaker muscles, poorer sight and hearing

I don't believe it!

The average weight of a newborn baby is 7½ lbs (3.5 kg), but one baby, born in Italy in 1955, weighed a massive 22 lbs (10 kg)! There doesn't seem to be anything to prevent unborn babies from growing bigger and bigger; instead, the onset of labor is linked to the unborn baby's maturity.

Fetus at 20 weeks
Starts to kick, can be felt by its mother, and can hear sounds

Fetus at 30 weeks
The eyes are open and it can hear the sound of its mother's voice

Newborn after about 40 weeks
The baby is born and can breathe, suck, and swallow immediately

What makes the body stop working normally?

Your body is made from trillions of cells that work together within tissues, organs, and systems to keep you alive. Keeping healthy helps ensure that cells work normally. But sometimes things go wrong and you get sick. Usually, modern medicine can treat and cure these malfunctions.

Tell me more: a balanced diet

Follow the guidelines of the food pyramid! The proportion of space in the pyramid given to each category shows how much of each food type the body needs to provide it with energy and to keep it working and healthy.

Sugary foods: Fats, sugars, and junk foods

Dairy: Milk, yogurt, cheese, and butter

Proteins: Meat, fish, eggs, and nuts

Fruits and vegetables: Include apples, bananas, carrots, and cabbage

Starchy foods: Potatoes, bread, pasta, rice, and grains

Blasts from the past

1796
First vaccination (against deadly smallpox) is carried out by English doctor Edward Jenner

1846
First anesthetic (to make a patient unconscious) is used during an operation in Boston

1860
French scientist Louis Pasteur shows how bacteria cause infectious diseases

1865
English doctor Joseph Lister uses antiseptics to prevent wound infection during operations

1895
German physicist Wilhelm Roentgen discovers X-rays

1928
Scottish bacteriologist Alexander Fleming discovers penicillin—the first antibiotic (drug that kills bacteria)

1967
South African surgeon Christiaan Barnard performs the first heart transplant

1980
Introduction of "keyhole" surgery to perform operations through tiny openings in the body

Six key branches of medicine

Anatomy: The structure of the body and its diseases

Epidemiology: How diseases are caused and spread

Immunology: The immune system and its disorders

Neurology: The nervous system and its diseases

Physiology: How cells, tissues, organs, and systems work

Psychiatry: Mental illness and its treatment

I don't believe it!

Testing urine using chemical tests to look for signs of disease is routine these days. Centuries ago doctors examined a patient's urine by smelling it, looking at its color, and seeing if it was cloudy or not—and they also tasted it. Yuck!

Bleeding used to be employed as a (useless) way of treating illness, by **cutting a vein** or by applying a **bloodsucking leech**. Today, leeches have made a comeback, used by doctors to stimulate blood flow where, for example, severed body parts have been sewn back on.

How to: vaccinate against a nasty disease

01. Make a vaccine—a liquid that contains a pathogen that has been made harmless so that it doesn't make you sick.

02. Inject the vaccine into your body.

03. Muster up your body's immune system, which will react to the harmless pathogen and make billions of antibodies, ready to disable it.

04. Cheer on the antibodies surging around your body, mopping up the harmless pathogens.

05. Be amazed when your body becomes infected by the "real" nasty, disease-carrying pathogen and...

06. ...your fully prepared immune system pours out antibodies to combat the pathogen and prevents you from becoming sick.

Four types of pathogen

Pathogens are microorganisms that cause disease.

Viruses Colds, influenza (flu), measles, chicken pox

Bacteria Dental caries (tooth decay), whooping cough, tuberculosis (TB)

Protists Malaria, sleeping sickness, giardiasis (severe diarrhea)

Fungi Athlete's foot, ringworm, candidiasis (thrush)

Alternative therapies

Acupuncture: Sticks fine needles into the skin at specific points to treat disorders

Aromatherapy: Uses scented plant oils to treat disorders or help relaxation

Chiropractice: Manipulates the joints of the backbone to give pain relief

Herbalism: Uses certain plants and their extracts to treat illnesses

Homeopathy: Patients given incredibly dilute doses of a remedy that undiluted produces symptoms similar to the illness being treated

Naturopathy: Holistic (whole body) treatment by changing the patient's lifestyle or diet

Reflexology: Massaging specific parts of the feet that are supposed to be linked to the afflicted body parts

RECORD BREAKER

Before pain relief and anesthetics, the best surgeons were regarded as the ones who worked **fastest.** On December 21, 1846, Scottish surgeon Robert Liston performed a thigh **amputation** in just 25 seconds.

Five ways to improve your health

01 Eat a balanced diet with the right mix of foods in the right quantities.

02 Only eat small amounts of fatty, sugary, or salty foods.

03 Exercise regularly.

04 Avoid spending hours in front of a television or computer.

05 Avoid alcohol, cigarettes, and all other types of drug.

Looking inside the body

These imaging techniques allow doctors to see inside the body without having to cut it open.

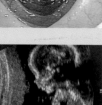
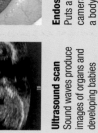
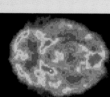
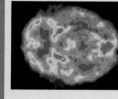
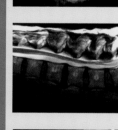

X-ray Passes X-rays through the body to show its bones

Angiogram A special kind of X-ray, used to show arteries

CT scan Uses X-rays and a computer to show body tissues

MRI scan Uses magnets and radio waves to show body tissues

PET scan Uses radioactive substances to show the brain at work

Ultrasound scan Sound waves produce images of organs and developing babies

Endoscopy Puts a tiny camera inside a body opening

Science and technology

What's the matter?

Everything! Well, not quite. Matter is everything in the universe that takes up space and has mass. An atom is the simplest part of matter. It can't be split apart by normal chemical or physical processes—only by a nuclear reaction.

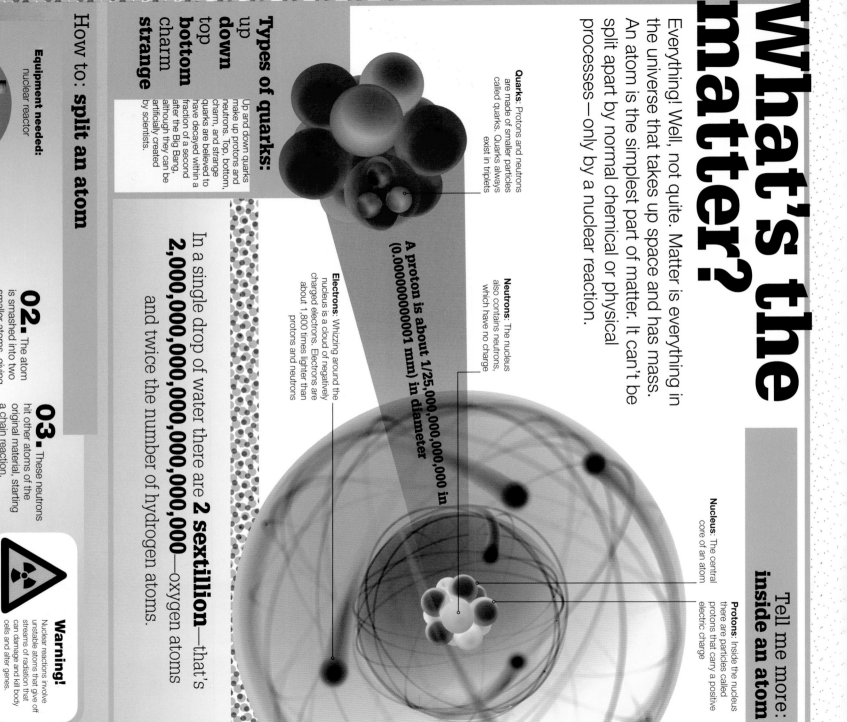

Quarks: Protons and neutrons are made of smaller particles called quarks. Quarks always exist in triplets

Neutrons: The nucleus also contains neutrons, which have no charge

Electrons: Whizzing around the nucleus is a cloud of negatively charged electrons. Electrons are about 1,800 times lighter than protons and neutrons

A proton is about 1/25,000,000,000,000,000 in (0.00000000001 mm) in diameter

In a single drop of water there are **2 sextillion**—that's **2,000,000,000,000,000,000,000**—oxygen atoms and twice the number of hydrogen atoms.

Tell me more: inside an atom

Nucleus: The central core of an atom

Protons: Inside the nucleus there are particles called protons that carry a positive electric charge

Types of quarks:

up
down
top
bottom
charm
strange

Up and down quarks make up protons and neutrons. Top, bottom, charm, and strange quarks are believed to have decayed within a fraction of a second after the Big Bang, although they can be artificially created by scientists.

How to: **split an atom**

Equipment needed:
nuclear reactor

01. Fire neutrons at high speed at the nucleus of a large atom.

02. The atom is smashed into two smaller atoms, giving off energy and more neutrons.

03. These neutrons hit other atoms of the original material, starting a chain reaction.

⚠ **Warning!**
Nuclear reactions involve unstable atoms that give off streams of radiation that can damage and kill body cells and alter genes.

Nuclear reactions produce massive amounts of energy. A lump of uranium about the size of a tennis ball will produce as much energy as about 4 million liters (1 million gallons) of gasoline—that's about enough to fill two Olympic-sized swimming pools.

Blasts from the past

5th century BCE
Greek thinker Democritus guesses that everything must be made from very tiny particles too small to be seen and that could not be destroyed or split into anything smaller. The word "atom" comes from the Greek for "uncuttable"

1661
Irish philosopher Robert Boyle argues that matter is made up of different "corpuscules" (atoms) rather than the classical elements of air, earth, fire, and water

1803
English scientist John Dalton comes up with an atomic theory: that all elements are made up of tiny particles called atoms and that the atoms of each element are different from the atoms of every other element

1897
British scientist Joseph John Thomson discovers the electron

1911
New Zealander Ernest Rutherford shows that atoms have a dense, positively charged nucleus, with negatively charged electrons surrounding it

1913
Danish scientist Niels Bohr explains how atoms share or exchange electrons to make chemical bonds

1932
English physicist James Chadwick discovers the neutron

1963
American physicist Murray Gell-Mann suggests the existence of quarks

What about me?
A human hair is about 1 million atoms wide. You have around 100,000 hairs on your head, so that makes... You do the math!

Most of an atom is made of empty space.

If the atom were the size of a sports stadium, the nucleus would be a pea at the center, with the electrons orbiting at the outer stands.

You can't see atoms because they are **invisible**. They are thousands of times smaller than the wavelengths of light, so they don't reflect light. If you really want to observe individual atoms, try a **scanning tunneling microscope**.

An atom usually has exactly the same number of positively charged protons as it does negatively charged electrons.

Sand grains are made of two kinds of atom—oxygen and silicon. Humans are made of about 28 different kinds of atom.

Most of the atoms that exist on Earth today were present when the solar system formed 4.6 billion years ago.

Thinking big

Atoms make up about 4 percent of the total matter of the universe.

The remaining 96 percent is made up of dark matter, which scientists can so far only observe by seeing how known matter reacts to it.

For every type of particle of matter a corresponding type of particle of antimatter exists, which is like a mirror image of it.

Light, heat, and sound do not take up space or have mass so are not made of matter but are forms of energy. Even though it isn't matter, don't waste energy, since that does matter.

I don't believe it!

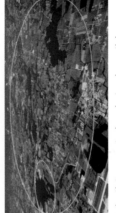

Scientists can study subatomic particles using a **particle accelerator**.

01: Beams of subatomic particles are sent around in circles by powerful electromagnets and speeded up by pulses of electricity.

02: When the particles are traveling fast enough (at almost the speed of light), they are extracted and smash into each other to create smaller particles.

03: The world's largest particle accelerator is run by CERN (the European Organization for Nuclear Research) and is a 17-mile- (27-km-) long underground loop on the border of Switzerland and France.

What is an element?

An element is a pure substance made up of only one type of atom. The atoms of every element are different from the atoms of every other element. 117 elements have so far been discovered or created. Of these, 91 occur naturally on Earth. The others can be created in laboratories. The atoms of one element can combine with atoms of other elements to form compounds. For example, hydrogen and oxygen can combine to form water.

Tell me more: element symbols

Each element has a one- or two-letter symbol as well as its name. Some of the elements have symbols that come from Latin words. For example, the symbol for iron is "Fe," since the Latin word for iron is *ferrum*. Elementary!

Tell me more: the periodic table

The periodic table arranges elements according to their atomic number (the number of protons each element has in its nucleus). This arrangement results in elements with similar properties (characteristics) being grouped together.

Atomic number: How many protons are in the atom's nucleus

Symbol: Used as shorthand when writing chemical equations

Mass number: The total number of protons and neutrons in the nucleus of each atom

28
Ni
Nickel
58

Key

The elements in the Periodic Table can be color coded to show the nine different groupings. Hydrogen does not belong to any one group.

- alkali metals
- alkali-earth metals
- transition metals
- rare earths
- radioactive rare earths
- other metals
- semimetals
- nonmetals
- noble gases
- hydrogen

The symbol for **tungsten**, "W," comes not from Latin, but from its alternative name: **wolfram**.

Periodic Table

1 H Hydrogen 1																	2 He Helium 4
3 Li Lithium 7	4 Be Beryllium 9											5 B Boron 11	6 C Carbon 12	7 N Nitrogen 14	8 O Oxygen 16	9 F Fluorine 19	10 Ne Neon 20
11 Na Sodium 23	12 Mg Magnesium 24											13 Al Aluminum 27	14 Si Silicon 28	15 P Phosphorus 31	16 S Sulfur 32	17 Cl Chlorine 35	18 Ar Argon 40
19 K Potassium 39	20 Ca Calcium 40	21 Sc Scandium 45	22 Ti Titanium 48	23 V Vanadium 51	24 Cr Chromium 52	25 Mn Manganese 55	26 Fe Iron 56	27 Co Cobalt 59	28 Ni Nickel 58	29 Cu Copper 63	30 Zn Zinc 64	31 Ga Gallium 69	32 Ge Germanium 74	33 As Arsenic 75	34 Se Selenium 80	35 Br Bromine 79	36 Kr Krypton 84
37 Rb Rubidium 85	38 Sr Strontium 88	39 Y Yttrium 89	40 Zr Zirconium 90	41 Nb Niobium 93	42 Mo Molybdenum 98	43 Tc Technetium 97	44 Ru Ruthenium 102	45 Rh Rhodium 103	46 Pd Palladium 106	47 Ag Silver 107	48 Cd Cadmium 114	49 In Indium 115	50 Sn Tin 120	51 Sb Antimony 121	52 Te Tellurium 130	53 I Iodine 127	54 Xe Xenon 132
55 Cs Cesium 133	56 Ba Barium 138	57–71	72 Hf Hafnium 180	73 Ta Tantalum 181	74 W Tungsten 184	75 Re Rhenium 187	76 Os Osmium 192	77 Ir Iridium 193	78 Pt Platinum 195	79 Au Gold 197	80 Hg Mercury 202	81 Tl Thallium 205	82 Pb Lead 208	83 Bi Bismuth 209	84 Po Polonium 209	85 At Astatine 210	86 Rn Radon 222
87 Fr Francium 223	88 Ra Radium 226	89–103	104 Rf Rutherfordium 262	105 Db Dubnium 262	106 Sg Seaborgium 266	107 Bh Bohrium 264	108 Hs Hassium 277	109 Mt Meitnerium 268	110 Ds Darmstadtium 271	111 Rg Roentgenium 272	112 Uub Ununbium 285	113 Uut Ununtrium 284	114 Uuq Ununquadium 289	115 Uup Ununpentium 288	116 Uuh Ununhexium 292	117 Uus Ununseptium 210 (undiscovered)	118 Uuo Ununoctium 294

57 La Lanthanum 139	58 Ce Cerium 140	59 Pr Praseodymium 141	60 Nd Neodymium 142	61 Pm Promethium 145	62 Sm Samarium 152	63 Eu Europium 153	64 Gd Gadolinium 158	65 Tb Terbium 159	66 Dy Dysprosium 164	67 Ho Holmium 165	68 Er Erbium 168	69 Tm Thulium 169	70 Yb Ytterbium 174	71 Lu Lutetium 175
89 Ac Actinium 227	90 Th Thorium 232	91 Pa Protactinium 231	92 U Uranium 238	93 Np Neptunium 237	94 Pu Plutonium 244	95 Am Americium 243	96 Cm Curium 247	97 Bk Berkelium 247	98 Cf Californium 251	99 Es Einsteinium 254	100 Fm Fermium 257	101 Md Mendelevium 258	102 No Nobelium 255	103 Lr Lawrencium 256

ELEMENTARY FACTS

Mercury and bromine are the only elements that are liquid at room temperature.

Silver has antibacterial properties—you can buy silver-treated socks to control foot odor.

Lasers using the gas **xenon** can cut through materials so tough that diamond-tipped blades cannot cut them.

Gold is so soft that people used to bite coins to check that they were real—if they were, the bites left teeth marks.

Burning **potassium** gives off a violet flame.

Helium is lighter than air, which is why it's used to fill balloons.

Osmium is used to make durable points on fountain pens.

Elements named after scientists

Mendelevium
Dmitri Mendeleyev
Invented the Periodic Table of elements

Seaborgium
Glen Seaborg
Created 10 new elements

Curium
Marie Curie
Discovered radium and polonium

Bohrium
Niels Bohr
Figured out how atoms bond

Record Breakers

Hydrogen is the simplest and lightest of all the elements. If it is not attached to other elements, hydrogen on Earth floats away into space.

A 1-ft (30-cm) cube of osmium weighs 1,410 lb (640 kg). That's the same as ten 140-lb (64-kg) adults!

Lithium is so soft it can be cut with a knife and is light enough to float on water.

Most common elements in Earth's atmosphere
(estimated percentage of atoms)

nitrogen 78%
oxygen 21%
argon 0.93%
carbon 0.03%
neon 0.0018%
helium 0.00052%

Most common elements in the universe
(estimated percentage of atoms)

hydrogen 92.4%
helium 7.4%
oxygen 0.06%
carbon 1.03%
nitrogen 0.01%
neon 0.01%

I don't believe it!

Want to buy some of the element californium? You will need to win the lottery first, since it costs $27 million for just one gram! Elements at the end of the Periodic Table have to be artificially created in a nuclear reactor and some last for only a fraction of a second, hence the high price tag.

Elements in a human

phosphorous 0.13%
sulfur 0.13%
calcium 0.23%
nitrogen 2.4%
carbon 10.5%
oxygen 26%
hydrogen 61%

In numbers

10,104.8°F
(5,596°C) The boiling point of rhenium

6,422°F
(3,550°C) The melting point of carbon

-452.074°F
(-268.93°C) The boiling point of helium

Why are most gases invisible?

In the air around us, the molecules of gases are usually so far apart that our eyes can't detect them—although with a few, it's possible to detect them by smell. Gases have no firm shape or form. Their molecules move rapidly in every direction to fill whatever container they are in, or escape if the container has no lid.

Tell me more: states of matter

Solid
The molecules in a solid object are tightly packed together. Solids have a fixed volume and a definite shape that is not easy to change.

Liquid
Molecules in a liquid can move past each other, allowing the substance to flow. Liquids have a fixed volume but no definite shape.

Gas
Molecules in a gas are free to move around, filling all the space around them. Gases have no fixed shape or volume.

When a **gas condenses** into a **liquid**, on average, the liquid takes up **1,300 times less space** than the gas.

What about me?

Sound travels three times faster in helium gas than in air. So if you take a gulp from a helium balloon, the resonant frequency (speed of vibrations) of your voice increases, making it sound squeaky.

How does popcorn pop?

Inside each kernel of corn there is a small amount of moisture. When the corn is heated, the moisture changes to steam and expands. The pressure from the expanded gas creates an explosion and the kernel is blown inside out.

How to: fly a hot-air balloon

01. Inflate the envelope of the balloon using a large fan.

02. Blast the burner to heat the air in the envelope. The heat causes the air molecules to move faster and farther apart, causing the envelope to swell.

03. While ground crew hold the balloon's basket down, climb aboard.

04. Hot air rises because it is less dense than the colder air around it and this causes the balloon to lift off. Enjoy your flight!

05. Fire the burner to heat the air more so the balloon lifts higher.

06. When ready to land, open a valve in the balloon's envelope to release the air. The balloon will descend to the ground.

Greenhouse gases

✦ Gases in the atmosphere, such as water vapor, carbon dioxide, and methane, let radiation from the Sun through to warm the Earth and trap some of the heat, which would otherwise be reflected back into space.

✦ This "greenhouse effect" has always happened and is vital in keeping the planet warm enough for life to exist.

✦ As the amount of greenhouse gases in the atmosphere increases due to pollution, burning fossil fuels, and cutting down forests, more heat is trapped and global temperatures rise.

Ever wondered how your soda drink gets its fizz?

Carbon dioxide gas is dissolved in the drink at low temperatures under pressure. When the bottle or can is opened, the pressure is released and the gas escapes in bubbles of fizz.

The gases in a fart

nitrogen **20–90%**
hydrogen **0–50%**
carbon dioxide **10–30%**
sulfur compounds **(they stink!)**
oxygen **0–10%**
methane **0–10%**

Your nose, knows!

Gases travel very fast and mix rapidly and completely with one another in a process called diffusion. So when you open a bottle of something strong-smelling—or let rip with a fart—the scent molecules diffuse into the air and soon reach your nose.

Fart power!

The flatulence of a single small sheep could power a day. sheep could power (40 km), which 25 miles gas, for truck It contains methane gas, as fuel. can be burned

DON'T TRY THIS AT HOME!

If you shake a carbonated soda bottle, the dissolved gas is released and rises to the top of the bottle, creating enormous pressure. When the lid is released, the gas—together with quite a lot of the soda—shoots out!

I don't believe it!

Gas particles move at more than 1,000 mph (1,600 kph) at room temperature—that's faster than the speed of sound.

What is a force?

A force is a push or a pull that gets something moving or changes the way it moves. Flicking a marble creates a force that sends the marble rolling across the table. Putting out your hand to stop it from falling off the table's edge creates a force that sends it spinning in another direction. If the marble rolls off the table, gravity pulls it to the ground—another force, of course!

Newton's first law

An object will stay still or move along at the same speed and in the same direction unless a force acts upon it. This law is sometimes referred to as the law of inertia.

In action: If you brake too hard on your bike, you may go flying over the handlebars. The force exerted by the brakes has stopped the bike, but you keep moving forward at the same speed.

Newton's second law

The amount an object's speed or direction changes depends on its mass and the size of the force acting upon it.

In action: If you exert a force on a marble by pushing it, it begins to move. But it takes more force to move a heavier object or to move something faster. So if you push a giant boulder it won't move so far.

Newton's third law

Whenever a force acts, an equal force acts in the opposite direction.

In action: When you jump, you push the ground with your feet, and the ground pushes back, propelling you into the air.

WHAT'S IN A NAME?

Sir Isaac Newton's three laws of motion, often called **Newton's Laws**, explain how forces make objects move. Legend has it that an apple fell on Newton's head while he was sitting under a tree, which led to his discoveries about motion and gravity.

Tell me more: friction

According to Newton's first law, a rolling ball ought to go on rolling forever, but it actually slows down and stops. That's because there's another force stopping it—**friction**. Friction is the rubbing force created between a moving object and whatever it touches.

Drag snag

Vehicles moving through air or water are affected by friction caused by the air or water around them—this is called **drag**. Giving the vehicle a smooth surface and **streamlined shape**, designed to make air or water flow over the vehicle smoothly, can reduce drag.

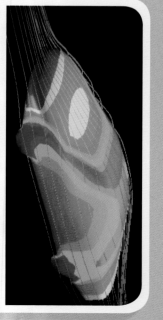

Four reasons why **friction** is useful

Friction produces heat. For thousands of years, humans have rubbed dry sticks together to **make fire**.

The patterned tread on tires creates a rough surface to increase friction, so they **don't slip** on smooth surfaces.

The ridges of your fingerprints create friction between your fingers and whatever you are holding, **helping you grip**.

Brakes rubbing against moving wheels create friction, which causes the wheels to **slow down**.

Every time a roller coaster changes speed or direction, g-force affects every part of your body. As you plummet down, your stomach is pushed up against the base of your lungs—let's hope you haven't eaten too many hot dogs!

When you go up in a lift you feel your body's **inertia** acting downward as it resists the change in its direction. This makes you feel heavier. When you go down, inertia acts upward, making your body feel lighter. You are actually feeling the **acceleration** (the change in speed or direction) your body is experiencing, but because it feels like the force of gravity, it is called a **g-force**.

You can beat **friction** by coating the moving parts of machines with slippery substances called **lubricants**. Lubricants such as oil prevent moving parts from sticking and wearing out due to friction. Also creates heat, lubricants also stop machines from **overheating**.

I don't believe it !

Snow is made up of such tiny particles sliding past each other that they act as a lubricant—that's why you can ski down it.

While you are reading this book, you might think you're not moving at all... but think again!

- You are sitting on the Earth, which is spinning at 1,000 mph (1,600 kph).
- The Earth is going around the Sun at more than 70,000 mph (110,000 kph).
- The solar system is traveling through space at 1,300,000 mph (2,000,000 kph).

How to: **move the tablecloth and not break anything**

01. Find a table, a large cloth, and some cheap objects.

02. Lay the cloth on a table and place the objects on it.

03. Hold the end of the cloth with both hands and give it a quick, firm tug.

04. You should be able to pull out the cloth, leaving the objects where they are. Their inertia stops them from moving with the cloth.

05. If you can't do it the first time, try again with heavier objects or a cloth with a smoother texture.

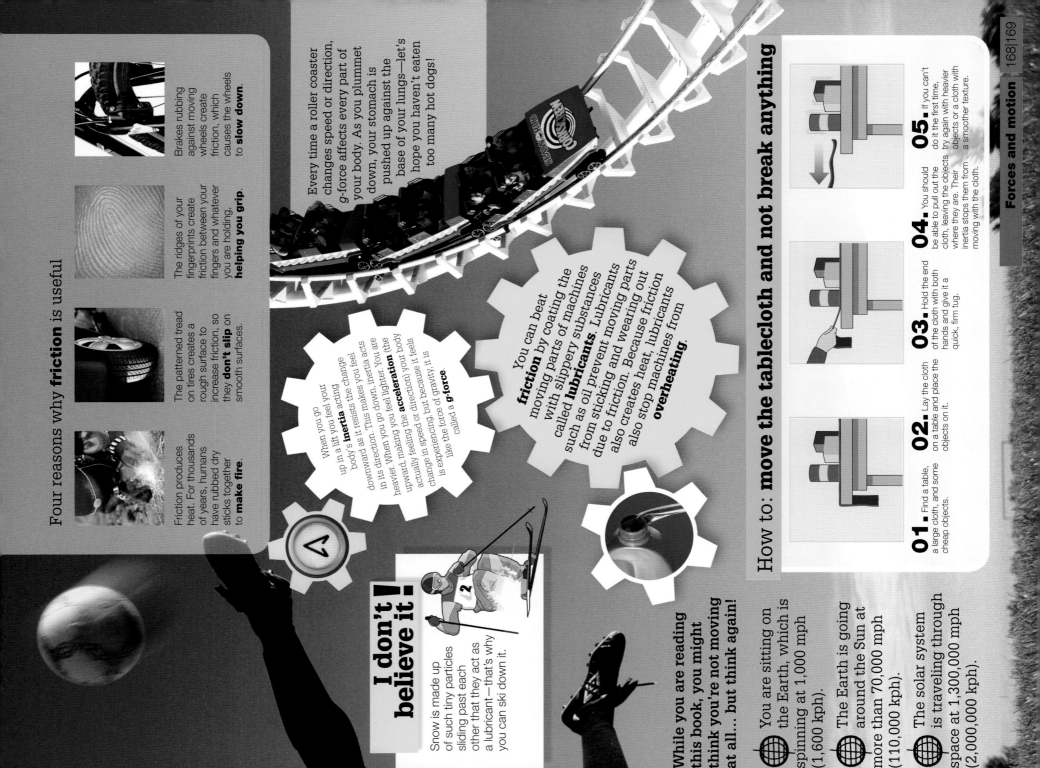

need gravity!

Yes! Without it there would be no universe as we know it.

Gravity is what keeps you, and everything else, on Earth. It is the tendency of objects with mass to be attracted to each other. An object's mass is the amount of material it contains. The bigger the mass of an object, the stronger its force of gravity.

Five reasons why gravity is good

01 Gravity makes things fall when they are dropped. At least you know where to start looking for your socks!

02 It's the force that keeps the water snow fall to the planet's surface.

03 The Earth's gravity holds the atmosphere in place.

04 The Sun's gravity keeps the Earth and other planets in orbit around it.

05 Gravity keeps everything else in the universe in orbit around some other object. Without it there would just be a chaos of floating matter.

Great escape

The speed needed to break free of an object's gravitational pull is called **"escape velocity."** Escape velocity from the Earth is 7 miles/sec (11.2 km/sec).

Zero gravity

Zero gravity does not really mean no gravity at all—that's impossible, since there are always objects with mass exerting gravity, even in space.

⬅ It is the feeling of weightlessness when a person is falling freely without ever reaching the ground.

Watch your weight

The pull of gravity varies across the universe, so your weight (your mass in the presence of gravity) will vary depending on where you are. Multiply your weight by the figure below to find out how heavy you'd be in other parts of the solar system.

Sun	multiply by 28	**Jupiter**	multiply by 2.54
Mercury	multiply by 0.38	**Saturn**	multiply by 1.08
Venus	multiply by 0.91	**Uranus**	multiply by 0.91
Mars	multiply by 0.38	**Neptune**	multiply by 1.19
Moon	multiply by 0.17	**Pluto**	multiply by 0.06

Four ways to achieve zero gravity

01 Orbit around Earth in a spacecraft.

02 Travel to the center of the Earth.

03 Ride in a "vomit comet"—a specially modified aircraft that zooms downward toward the Earth.

04 For a fraction of a second, while you're at the top of your jump, just before you start to come back down, you experience weightlessness.

Brain boxes

Galileo Galilei
Italian scientist Galileo Galilei, who lived from 1564-1642, knew that there was a mysterious force making things move, but he just couldn't figure out what it was.

Isaac Newton
In 1687, English scientist Sir Isaac Newton did the math and told the world it was a force called gravity that made things fall to Earth, and planets move through the night sky.

Albert Einstein
In the early 20th century, German-born genius Albert Einstein was developing revolutionary theories to explain gravity and the universe. Mind-boggling stuff!

Some of the biggest brains in history have struggled to understand the invisible force of gravity.

How to... fly

01. Jump out of a plane (make sure you have a parachute strapped to your back first!) You will at first accelerate then, as drag (resistance) balances the pull of gravity, you will reach a steady speed called terminal velocity.

02. Keep your limbs spread wide to maintain terminal velocity of about 125 mph (200 kph). To change speed, reduce drag by altering body posture.

03. By standing straight up or diving headfirst with your arms and legs behind you, you can reach speeds of 180 mph (290 kph).

04. To slow down for landing, you will need to increase the drag and reduce your speed to around 12 mph (20 kph). To do this, pull the parachute cord to open the canopy.

05. As soon as your toes make contact with the ground, slightly bend your knees, tuck your elbows in close to your body and allow yourself to safely fall.

X300

Mars's moon, Deimos, has such a small force of gravity that if you were standing on it and you jumped hard, you could achieve escape velocity.

What about me?

You may not know it, but you regularly experience big g-forces. A sneeze exerts a force of 3 g on your body, and a cough can punch a mighty 3.5 g.

I don't believe it!

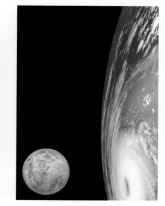

On a diet? Well then plan the weigh-in for a night with a full Moon overhead. The weak pull of the Moon's gravity works against the pull of the Earth's gravity, reducing your weight very slightly. Every little bit helps!

Problems with living in zero gravity...
as experienced by astronauts

- Drinks must be kept in sealed containers and drunk through a straw or they'll float off.

- **Avoid crumbly food since crumbs float away around the spacecraft and can get into everything.**

- When you sleep you have to be strapped tightly into a sleeping bag attached to the wall.

- **It's confusing—there's no up or down in zero gravity, so ceilings, walls, and floors are all the same.**

- You have to be firmly attached to a space toilet with Velcro and a good air seal so nothing floats away! The toilet is flushed with a jet of air.

- **Long-term weightlessness causes weakening of a person's muscles and bones. You need to exercise, or you'll be too weak to walk out of the spacecraft when you get back to Earth.**

In numbers

The g-force is the force you feel under acceleration. It is measured in "g," but you experience it as the heavy feeling when you swoop up the curve of a roller coaster. Hold on tight!

0 g
Weightlessness

1 g
Force of gravity at Earth's surface

2–3 g
Space shuttle astronauts experience between 2–3 g on launch

3 g
Roller coasters are designed not to exceed 3 g, though there are a few hair-raising exceptions

4–6 g
Fighter pilots, who often have to make sharp turns, may wear anti-g suits to protect them from the effects of high g-forces. If forces between 4–6 g are experienced for more than a few seconds a person might lose consciousness

5 g
Experienced by Formula One racing drivers when braking

9 g
Pilots pulling out of a dive may experience as much as 9 g

Why do objects look different colors?

The white light around us is made up of a mixture of different colors of light. The surfaces of objects absorb some colors and reflect others back. Our eyes see only the colors that are reflected. An object that reflects all the colors of light appears white. An object that absorbs all the colors looks black. A tomato absorbs all the colors except red, which it reflects back to us. You get the picture!

Tell me more: electromagnetic spectrum

Light is part of a continuous band of energy called the electromagnetic spectrum, which is made up of waves of radiation with different wavelengths (distance between two peaks or troughs of the waves). Aside from light, all electromagnetic waves are invisible to the human eye.

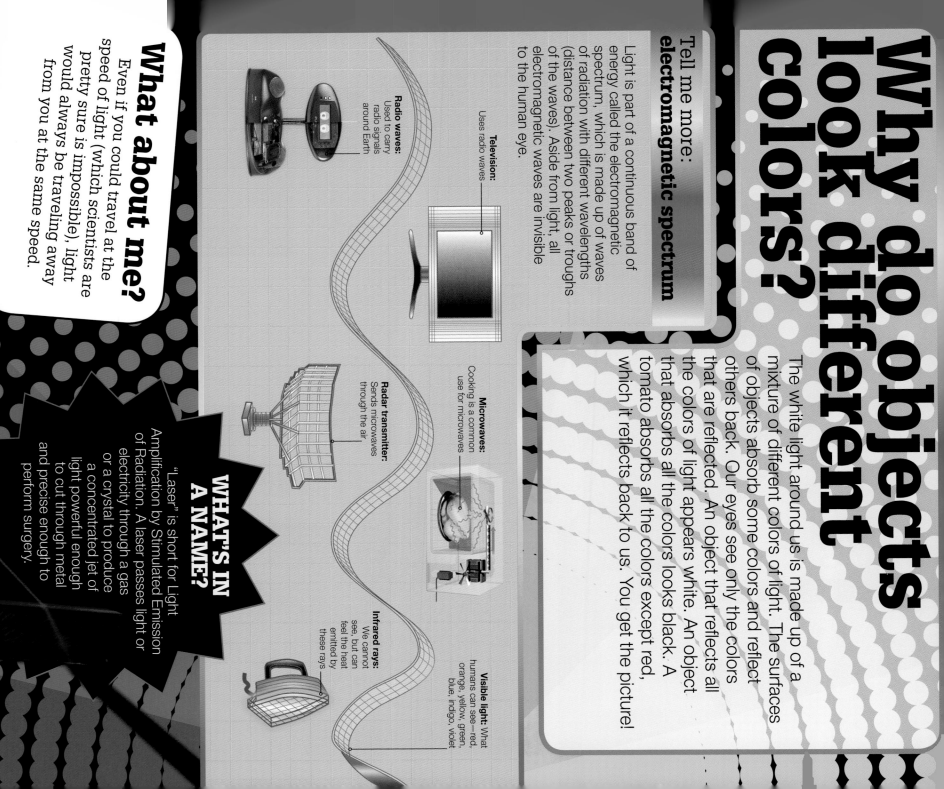

Radio waves:
Used to carry radio signals around Earth

Television:
Uses radio waves

Radar transmitter:
Sends microwaves through the air

Microwaves:
Cooking is a common use for microwaves

Infrared rays:
We cannot see, but can feel the heat emitted by these rays

Visible light: What humans can see—red, orange, yellow, green, blue, indigo, violet

What about me?

Even if you could travel at the speed of light (which scientists are pretty sure is impossible), light would always be traveling away from you at the same speed.

WHAT'S IN A NAME?

"Laser" is short for Light Amplification by Stimulated Emission of Radiation. A laser passes light or electricity through a gas or a crystal to produce a concentrated jet of light powerful enough to cut through metal and precise enough to perform surgery.

Rainbows

01: A rainbow appears when light passes through raindrops.

02: Inside each raindrop, the sunlight is bent and split into the colors of the spectrum:

- **red**
- **orange**
- **yellow**
- **green**
- **blue**
- **indigo**
- **violet**

03: You can only see a rainbow when the Sun is behind you and the rain is falling in front of you.

04: From an airplane, a rainbow forms a complete circle.

05: There are "mnemonic" word tricks to help you remember the colors of a rainbow:

- *Richard Of York Gave Battle In Vain*
- *Roy G. Biv (the rainbow guy)*

FAST FACTS

Colorful triangle

Just like a raindrop, a prism (triangle of glass) changes the direction of light passing through it. This is called **refraction**. The prism bends the wavelengths, splitting the white light into a spectrum of colors.

Primary colors of light

- When beams of all three of the primary colors are mixed together in equal quantities they form white light.

- By combining the primary colors in different proportions any color can be made. This is how the color is produced on a TV screen.

red   **green**   **blue**

Printing color

We can see the different colors in this book because the ink pigments absorb and reflect others. Printers mix yellow, magenta, and cyan ink to create colors. Mixing all three together creates a muddy brown, so printers must also use a black ink.

Secondary colors of light

When mixed together in equal quantities, the primary colors of light form the secondary colors.

red + green = yellow

blue + red = magenta

green + blue = cyan

red   **green**   **blue**   magenta   yellow   cyan

Ultraviolet rays: Invisible rays that can cause damage to our eyes and skin

Gamma rays: Harmful, cancer-causing rays produced by radioactivity

X-rays: High-energy rays used in medicine to check people's bones

In numbers

2000
The number of light waves that would fit in a millimeter (0.04 in)

20
The number of times that more men than women are affected by red/green color blindness. The ability to detect color depends on cells in the retina at the back of the eye that detect particular parts of the spectrum. Some of these are missing or inactive in a color-blind person

8
The number of minutes it takes for the Sun's light to travel the 93,000,000 miles (149,000,000 km) to reach the Earth. We see the Sun the way it looked eight minutes ago

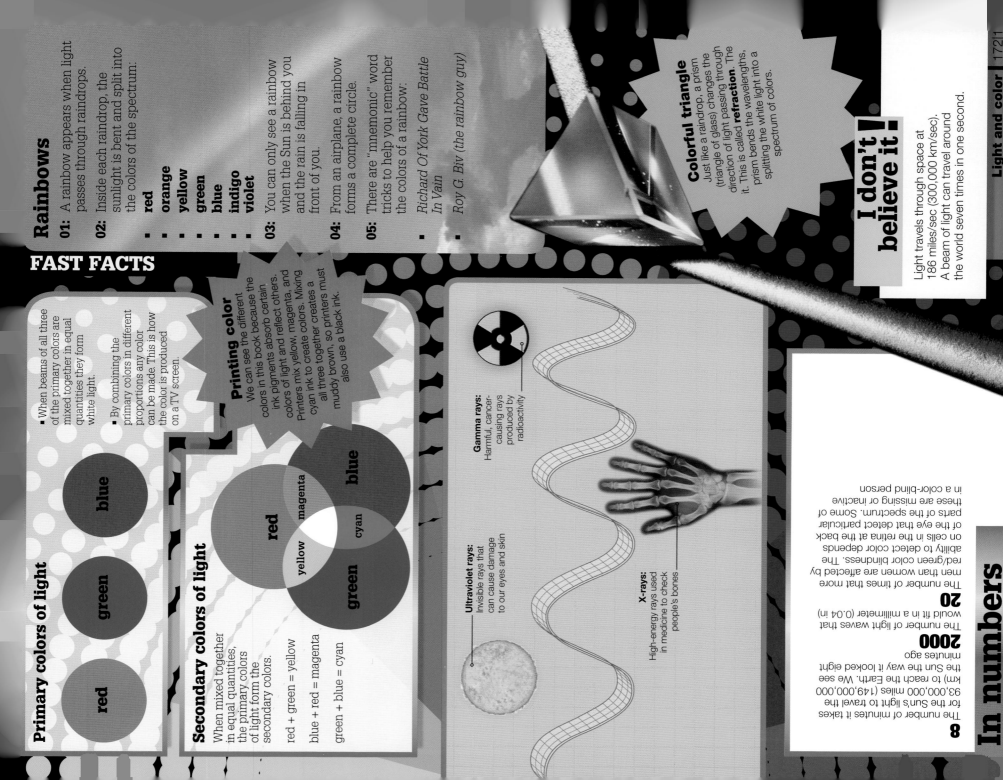

What is electricity?

The word "electricity" comes from Greek elektron, meaning amber. The Greeks noticed that when a piece of amber is rubbed with wool it attracts light objects. This is static electricity.

Inside all atoms, there are particles called protons, which have a positive electric charge, and particles called electrons with a negative charge. Usually there are equal numbers of protons and electrons, so the charges cancel each other out. But sometimes an atom gains or loses electrons, giving it a positive or negative charge. Electricity is the presence or flow of this electric charge.

What about me?

Combing hair can strip it of negatively charged electrons, giving it a positive charge of static electricity. Like charges repel, causing your hair to stand on end.

Static electricity makes plastic wrap clingy.

Conductors

are materials where the electrons are free to move, creating an electric current. Some good conductors:

silver

magnesium

aluminum

steel

copper

lead

gold

mercury

Insulators

are materials where electrons cannot move as freely as they can in a metal, so they cannot conduct electricity. Some good insulators:

rubber

ceramic

fiberglass

plastic

wool

Lighten up!

As night falls the lights go on. Energy-saving lightbulbs use less energy and last longer than regular lightbulbs. Here's how they work.

Visible light: Produced when UV light passes through tube's phosphor coating

Electrons: Interact with mercury gas in tube, producing ultraviolet (UV) light

Tungsten electrodes: Generate electrons from electric current

Wires: Carry electricity to electrodes

Fitting: Connects to mains electricity supply

Bright sparks

These scientists have all had electrical measurements named after them.

André Marie Ampère
(1775–1836)
amp
electric current

Charles Coulomb
(1736–1806)
coulomb
charge

James Joule
(1818–1889)
joule
energy

Georg Ohm
(1789–1854)
ohm
resistance

Alessandro Volta
(1745–1827)
volt
electric pressure

James Watt
(1736–1819)
watt
power

I don't believe it!

When different types of metals come into contact, they can generate an electric current. Biting aluminum foil when you have metal fillings can give you an electric shock!

In numbers

25%
The amount of power a disposable battery may lose in a year even if it is not taken out of its packaging

600 volts
The amount of electricity an electric eel can produce by mixing different chemicals in its body

268 mph
(432 kph) The speed of the electric currents that send messages via the nerves to and from the human brain

10%
The amount of electricity wasted by items left in standby mode in households in the US

What's the point?

Earth is a giant magnet with a magnetic field driven by molten material circulating beneath its surface. Any magnet hanging so that it can move freely—including the needle of a compass—will point in a north–south direction, attracted by Earth's magnetic field.

RECORD BREAKER

At 13½ ft (4.11 m) tall, the world's **biggest lightbulb** sits on top of the Edison Memorial Tower in New Jersey. It marks Thomas Edison's role in inventing the lightbulb.

Weird or what?

Earth's magnetic north pole is not the same as the geographical North Pole. At the moment it's in northern Canada, but it is gradually moving northwest at a rate of 25 miles (40 km) per year.

Tell me more: magnets

- A magnet is a material that will attract objects made of iron and certain other materials.

- **Magnets attract and repel other magnets.**

- Every magnet has two ends called the north and south poles where its magnetic forces are strongest.

- **Like poles (north and north or south and south) repel each other.**

- Unlike poles (north and south) attract.

- **When an electric current moves through a wire it creates a magnetic field around it. A magnet created in this way is called an electromagnet.**

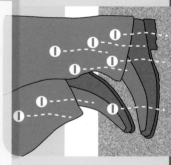

How to: get a shock

01. Walk across a nylon carpet with shoes on. As you do so, your shoes rub electrons off the carpet.

02. These electrons collect on your body, giving it a negative electric charge.

03. When you touch something that is an electrical conductor, such as a metal door handle, the electrons flow away into the handle very quickly, giving you a tingling shock. Ouch!

Why has my bicycle gotten rusty?

You probably left it out in the rain again, didn't you? A chemical reaction took place as the iron in the bike reacted with oxygen in rainwater and in the air to create a new substance called iron oxide—also known as rust.

Chemical equation

2H₂
$$2H_2$$
- two hydrogen molecules
- hydrogen molecules usually contain two hydrogen atoms

+
- plus sign shows that the molecules are reacting together

O₂
$$O_2$$
- oxygen molecule contains two oxygen atoms

→
- arrow shows reaction has taken place

2H₂O
$$2H_2O$$
- the product of the reaction is two molecules of water
- water molecules contain two hydrogen atoms
- water molecules contain one oxygen atom

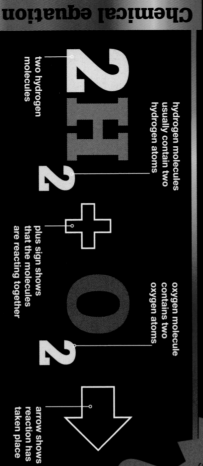

Hydrofluoric acid will dissolve glass.

Tell me more: chemical reactions

01: The atoms that make up matter are joined together in clumps called molecules.

02: In a chemical reaction, the bonds that join the atoms in molecules are broken apart and new molecules are formed.

03: The starting materials in a chemical reaction are called reactants and the materials that are formed are called the products.

04: Chemical reactions never create or destroy atoms, they only rearrange them.

05: There are chemical reactions going on around you all day, every day, in the kitchen, in car engines, and inside you.

What about me?

When things burn they react with oxygen and give out energy in the form of heat. What does this have to do with you? The food you eat combines with oxygen in your body, and the heat released provides you with the energy you need to live.

pH scale

A substance's pH is a measure of how acid or alkaline it is.

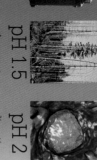

car battery acid	the worst acid rain	digestive juices	vinegar	lemon juice	orange juice	tomato juice	normal rainfall	milk	pure water
pH 1	pH 1.5	pH 2	pH 2.8	pH 3	pH 3.7	pH 4.3	pH 5.6	pH 6.5	pH 7

Chemicals that make you look good

chemical	found in	what it does
mica	eye shadow	provides sparkle
ammonium lauryl sulfate	shampoo	removes dirt and grease
calcium carbonate	toothpaste	grinds away plaque by being abrasive
sodium fluoride	toothpaste	strengthens teeth enamel
hydrated magnesium silicate	face powder	known as talc, gives a smooth sheen
aluminum chlorohydrates	deodorant	controls perspiration

FAST FACTS

What a blast!

A firework display is really a series of dramatic chemical reactions. The rainbow of sparks is produced by using compounds that burn with different colors.

strontium or lithium compounds

calcium compounds

sodium compounds

barium compounds

copper compounds

potassium or strontium with copper compounds

aluminum, titanium, or magnesium compounds

Explosive reactions

- **Alkali metals such as potassium, sodium, rubidium, cesium, and francium are so reactive that just putting them in water makes them explode.**

- Salt (sodium chloride) and vinegar (acetic acid) is an explosive combination when mixed in large quantities.

- **If you set light to thermite (a mixture of aluminum and iron oxide), the reaction produces extremely bright light containing dangerous levels of UV and can reach temperatures of 4,350°F (2,400°C). As the reaction produces its own oxygen, it will even burn in water!**

- When nitrogen compounds revert to nitrogen gas in chemical reactions, masses of energy are released. The nitrogen compound nitroglycerine is often used in explosives.

How to: write a secret message

01. Dab a cotton swab or small paint brush into a bowl of lemon juice. Use the swab or brush to write a message on a piece of white paper and let dry.

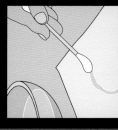

02. Pass your secret message to a friend and instruct them to hold the paper up to a heat source, such as a lightbulb.

03. The lemon juice is slightly acidic and when the paper is held near heat, the acidic parts of the paper turn brown before the rest of the paper does, revealing the hidden message.

Six ways to make a reaction go faster

Reactions happen when molecules bump into each other. Increasing the rate at which molecules collide speeds up the reaction. You can do this by:

01: Using more concentrated solutions, which means there are more molecules in a smaller space.

02: Increasing the pressure of gases, which forces more molecules into a smaller space.

03: Heating, which makes molecules move faster.

04: Shining light, which makes some molecules move faster.

05: Breaking a solid up to increase the surface area exposed to other reactants.

06: Adding a substance called a catalyst, which speeds up a chemical reaction by reducing the energy needed for the reaction to take place but does not itself change during the reaction.

pH 7.3 human blood

pH 8 sea water

pH 9 toothpaste

pH 9.5 bleach

pH 10.5 milk of magnesia

pH 11 household ammonia

pH 12 soap

pH 12.8 hair remover

pH 13.8 oven cleaner

How do we measure time?

By observing the Earth's movements relative to the Sun. One complete spin of the Earth on its axis takes a day. Approximately 365.26 spins (days) make one complete revolution of the Sun, or one solar year. Units of time smaller than a day, such as hours, minutes, and seconds, are measured using clocks. Weeks, months, and years, are measured using calendars. Time to find out more...

Tell me more: time zones

If everyone in the world set their clocks to the same time, when it was midnight it would be daylight in one part of the world and the middle of the night in another. To avoid this, Earth is divided into time zones.

🕐 Time zones generally follow lines of longitude (imaginary lines running from pole to pole), but usually bend to include entire countries or states in one time zone.

🕐 There are 24 time zones, each 15° of longitude and one hour apart.

🕐 India straddles more than one time zone but has chosen a time zone halfway between those on either side so that the whole country can use one time.

🕐 Russia has 11 time zones—more than any other country.

🕐 China stretches across four time zones but uses only one time.

🕐 Countries east of the date line are a day ahead of those to the west.

🕐 The International Date Line dividing one day from the next follows the 180° meridian (longitude line) on the globe.

🕐 The International Date Line runs mostly through the ocean, but where it would pass through or near land it bends to keep from dividing a region into two days.

Areas that adopt a time halfway between two time zones

-11 -10 -9 -8 -7 -6 -5 -4 -3 -2 -1 0 +1 +2 +3 +4 +5 +6 +7 +8 +9 +10 +11 +12

GREENWICH MERIDIAN

INTERNATIONAL DATE LINE

ARCTIC OCEAN

PACIFIC OCEAN

ATLANTIC OCEAN

ATLANTIC OCEAN

ARCTIC OCEAN

INDIAN OCEAN

PACIFIC OCEAN

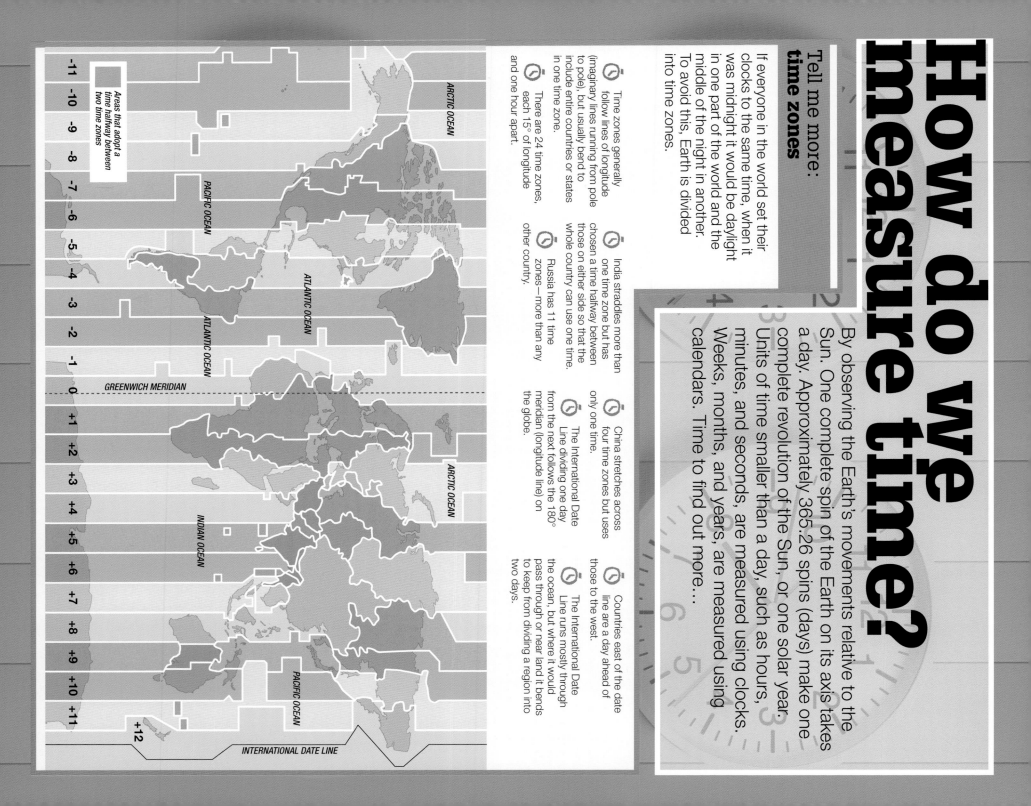

Blasts from the past

1500 BCE
Sundials are used in Egypt to define time periods such as morning and afternoon, and measure the longest and shortest days of the year

1400 BCE
Water clocks are used in Egypt. Water drains from a vessel, reaching different levels that represent periods of time

1000s CE
Arab engineers invent the first mechanical clocks driven by weights and gears

1100s
Monks use the hourglass to show the times of prayer

1325
The first clock with a dial is installed in Norwich Cathedral, England

1335
The first clock to strike the hours is made in Milan, Italy

1350
The oldest known alarm clock is made in Würzburg, Germany

1650
Dutch scientist Christiaan Huygens invents a pendulum clock with an error of less than one minute per day

1759
British clockmaker John Harrison makes an accurate marine chronometer. Timekeeping is vital at sea for calculating position

1949
The first atomic clock is built. This precise timekeeper measures the vibrations of an atom

TICK TOCK!

Clocks keep time by measuring a **constantly repeating motion**. This may be the swing of a pendulum or the vibrations of atoms.

A.M. is short for the Latin phrase *ante meridiem* meaning "before noon."

P.M. is short for the Latin phrase *post meridiem* meaning "after noon."

COUNTING TIME

picosecond = 0.000,000,000,001 seconds
nanosecond = 0.000,000,001 seconds
microsecond = 0.000,001 seconds
millisecond = 0.001 seconds
minute = 60 seconds
hour = 60 minutes = 3,600 seconds
day = 24 hours = 86,400 seconds
week = 7 days = 604,8000 seconds
month = 28 to 31 days
quarter = 3 months
year = 12 months = 365 days = 52 weeks + 1 day
leap year = 366 days = 52 weeks + 2 days
decade = 10 years
century = 100 years
millennium = 1,000 years

I don't believe it!

Air passengers crossing from Tonga to Samoa – a two-hour flight across the International Date Line – often arrive the day before they left!

Time leaps

☐ Most calendar years are 365 days long. In leap years, a day is added to the end of February to account for the extra quarter day in each solar year.

☑ Leap years happen in years divisible by four, except years ending in 00, which must be divisible by 400 to be a leap year.

☑ Earth's rotation is slowing down at a rate of about 0.6 seconds per year, so the solar day (the time it takes Earth to spin once) and the time on the most accurate atomic clocks gradually diverges.

☐ Since 1972, about every 18 months a leap second is added at the end of June or December to compensate for the slowdown.

Just a phase

01: Months are based on the phases of the Moon.

02: A phase is the time it takes for the Moon to orbit the Earth—about 29.5 days.

03: Calendar months are not very accurate and can vary between 28 and 31 days. So, in a year of 12 calendar months there are 12 and a bit lunar months.

RECORD BREAKERS

01: First demonstrated in February 2008, the world's **most accurate clock** uses strontium atoms and is accurate to one second in 200 million years.

02: The Colgate Clock in Jersey City, New Jersey, has a diameter of 50 ft (15.24 m) and is the **world's largest clock**.

03: The **tallest clock tower** is 787 ft (239.9 m) high and tops the NTT DoCoMo Yoyogi Building in Tokyo, Japan.

In numbers

0.01 second
a flash of lightning

0.1 second
blink of human eye

1 second
human heartbeat

15 seconds
space shuttle to travel 75 miles (120 km)

497 seconds
light reaching the Earth from the Sun

1,000 seconds
a snail to move 33 ft (10 m)

800 million seconds
a lifetime's sleep

2.5 billion seconds
human lifetime (80 years)

50,000–20,000 BCE
Pebbles and human fingers are the first tools for calculation. The Latin word *digit* means finger (or toe) as well as a number, and the Latin word for pebble is *calculus*, giving us the word "calculate"

20,000 BCE
The oldest-known objects used to represent numbers are bones with carved notches

c. 2400 BCE
The abacus—the first known calculator—is invented in Babylonia

c. 500–300 BCE
Ancient Indian writer Pingala describes the first binary (two digit code) numbering system

87 BCE
A mechanical computer used to predict the movement of stars is built. It is discovered in a shipwreck off the coast of the Greek island of Antikythera in 1901

724 CE
Chinese engineer Liang Ling-Can builds the first mechanical clock (driven by water) with parts that make a ticking sound. More than 1,300 years later, early computers and robots inherit the technology from the clock's gear and spring mechanism

820
In Baghdad, Muhammed idn Musa Al-Khwarizmi introduces the decimal numbering system and use of zero into Arabic mathematics

1492
Italian Leonardo da Vinci designs the first mechanical calculator and a humanoid robot (dressed in a suit of armor and programmed to sit up, wave its arms, and move its head)

1848
George Boole figures out how to write logical problems using algebra

1868
The modern QWERTY keyboard layout is designed by Christopher Latham Sholes, to avoid jamming keys when typing fast

1869
Using Boolean algebra, William Stanley Jevons designs the first practical machine that can solve a logical problem faster than someone without the machine!

1873
The first successful direct current electric motor is designed by Zenobe Theophille Gramme. Without it, there would be no hard disk drives or fans to keep PCs cool

1884–1892
Americans Dorr E. Felt and William S. Burroughs pioneer new adding machines called Comptometers. They are operated by pressing keys and have a printing device

1906
Lee De Forest develops a new electronic tube, the triode, which could be used as a switch—a key development in computing

1918
The German Enigma encryption machine can "scramble" a message by a complex system of substituting letters

1947
Physicist William Shockley and his team invent the transistor at Bell Laboratories in the US. Transistors miniaturize electronic circuits and help to make PCs in the future small, reliable, and affordable

1948
British engineer Andrew Donald Booth invents magnetic drum memory for computers

1949
Maurice Wilkes builds the EDSAC, the first practical stored-program computer, at Cambridge University in England. It contains 3,000 vacuum tubes and uses mercury delay lines for memory

1951
T. Raymond Thompson and John Simmons develop the first business computer, the Lyons Electronic Office (LEO)

▪ The UNIVAC I is the first business computer made in the US

1959
John Kilby and Robert Noyce figure out how to manufacture complete networks of components on to a single crystal of semiconductor material. Their invention, the integrated circuit, kick-starts the computer revolution

1961
Richard Mattessich develops computerized spreadsheets for use in accounting

1962
Steve Russell invents *SpaceWar!*—the first game intended for computer use

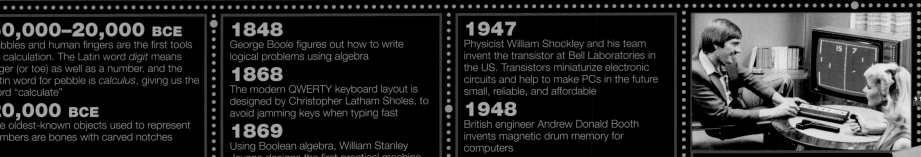

1972
Atari releases *Pong*, the first commercial video game, which sells 100,000 copies

1973
Robert M. Metcalfe at Xerox creates the Ethernet, a way of connecting computers in a local-area network (LAN)

▪ The minicomputer Xerox Alto is the first with GUI (Graphics User Interface), the desktop system that allows users to navigate using a mouse instead of typing in words

1975
Ed Roberts designs the first popular microcomputer, the Altair, named after a planet in *Star Trek*

1978
Micropro International launches WordStar, the first commercially successful word processing software

1980
Paul Allen and Bill Gates buy the rights to a simple operating system, QDOS. They use it to develop MS-DOS, which becomes the standard operating system in PCs

1614
Scotsman John Napier invents a system of moveable rods based on logarithms that could do addition

1679
German Gottfried Leibniz perfects the binary system

1642
Frenchman Blaise Pascal invents the "Pascaline," the first serious calculating machine, to help his father, a judge in the tax court

1801
Joseph-Marie Jacquard invents an automatic sewing loom controlled by punched cards. During its first demonstration in Lyon, France, the machine is destroyed by an angry mob

1834
Charles Babbage designs the Analytical Engine—the world's first computer, with punch card input devices, an arithmetic processor, and a memory to store numbers. He runs out of money before it is ever built

1843
Augusta Ada Lovelace (daughter of the poet Lord Byron) creates the first-ever computer program for Babbage's Analytical Engine

1937
Alan Turing develops the first software using binary

1938
German Konrad Zuse creates the first working binary digital computer, the Z1. On his Z2 and Z3 machines, he punches holes in old movie film to store his data

1939
John Vincent Atanasoff and Clifford Berry develop the ABC (Atanasoff-Berry Computer), the first computing machine to use electricity, vacuum tubes, binary numbers, and capacitors. It's the size of a desk, weighs 694 lb (315 kg), and contains half a mile of wire

1943
To counter the German Enigma machine, Alan Turing and engineer Tom Flowers develop the code-breaking machine Colossus, so-called because it filled an entire room

1945
John Presper Eckert and John W. Mauchly develop the ENIAC (Electronic Numerical Integrator and Computer), a monster machine with 18,000 vacuum tubes. It's the first to contain gates, buffers, and a high-speed storage-and-control device

1946
F. C. Williams develops the cathode-ray tube (CRT) storing device, forerunner to the Random-Access Memory (RAM) device

1963
Douglas Engelbart invents and patents the first computer mouse

1965
◼ The American Standard Code for Information Interchange (ASCII) is developed to standardize data exchange

Ted Nelson develops an idea for an interconnected network of documents with embedded links to each other that he calls "hypertext"

1967
David Noble at IBM creates the first floppy disk

1969
Seymour Cray develops the CDC 7600, the first supercomputer (a computer designed to receive and process vast amounts of data)

◼ The forerunner of the internet, the Advanced Research Projects Agency Network (ARPANET), is the first to connect researchers in universities in the United States

1970
Music-lover and inventor James T. Russell patents the first CD-ROM

1971
Researchers at the University of Hawaii create the wireless local-area network (LAN), using radio communications

◼ Computer engineer Ray Tomlinson sends the first email message between two machines

◼ James Fergason invents the first practical Liquid Crystal Display (LCD)

◼ Intel introduces the first microprocessor, the Intel 4004. The 4-bit silicon chip packs as much processing power as the first electronic computer—the ENIAC—into a space smaller than a thumbnail!

◼ The first truly pocket-sized electronic calculator, the LE-120A "HANDY," is launched by Busicom

1984
Jon Postel, Paul Mockapetris, and Craig Partridge pioneer the Domain Name System (DNS) used to access websites over the internet. Seven "top-level" domain names are introduced: edu, com, gov, mil, net, org, and int

◼ Apple introduces the Apple Macintosh, the first affordable computer that uses a mouse to navigate through drop-down menus, tabs, and icons

1986
The first PC virus, known as the Brain virus, is written in Pakistan

◼ Microsoft Windows and Excel (the first graphical spreadsheet software) are released

1989
Tim Berners-Lee develops a "hypertext" system, creating the modern internet

1992
Wolfenstein 3-D video game begins a revolution in PC gaming

2000
There are unfounded fears of a "Millennium Bug," causing computers to crash as they switch from 31/12/99 to 01/01/00

2003
Skype software allows people to make free international phone calls via their computers

2007
Increasing convergence of different technologies into single small gadgets as Apple's iPhone is released

2008
The world's first biodegradable computer, the Iameco, is produced in Ireland, built from waste products from the lumber and pulp industry

Where is the Internet?

The Internet is everywhere. It's a network linking millions of computers all over the world. With a computer, the right software, and a phone connection, anyone anywhere in the world can set up a website for anyone else to look at. There's no one in charge of the Internet, and since there's no limit to the number of computers that can be linked, there's no limit to the amount of information that can be held on it.

What's in a name?

ISP (Internet Service Provider)
The hub that connects a user to the Internet

HTTP (HyperText Transfer Protocol)
A request to retrieve a linked document on the Web

TCP/IP (Transmission Control Protocol/Internet Protocol) The standard method of communication that all Internet sites use

URL (Uniform Resource Locator)
A web address

WWW (World Wide Web)
All the interlinked pages that exist on the Internet

HTML (Hyper Text Markup Language)
The computer language websites are written in

untitled folder

Top ten Internet nations

US	211,108,086 users	
China	137,000,000 users	
Japan	86,300,000 users	
Germany	50,471,212 users	
India	40,000,000 users	
UK	37,600,000 users	
South Korea	34,120,000 users	
Brazil	32,130,000 users	
France	30,837,592 users	
Italy	30,763,848 users	

Four incredible Internet facts

01: The first message sent between computers was "lo." The sender was trying to write "login" but the system crashed before he finished typing.

02: New websites are added to the World Wide Web so rapidly that it is impossible for anyone to say how big it is.

03: The name "Google" is a play on the word "googol," which is the name for the number 1 followed by 100 zeros.

04: A wiki is a website that allows anyone to add to or change its content. The word "wiki" comes from a Hawaiian word for "quick."

In numbers

Rapid growth

year	number of Internet users
1982	**200**
1991	**600,000**
1995	**45,000,000**
1999	**150,000,000**
2008	**1,500,000,000**

untitled folder

hard drive

CD

untitled folder

untitled folder

untitled folder

How to: set up a search engine

01. Develop a "web spider"—a software program to browse the Internet.

02. Instruct the spider to begin its "web crawl" at popular websites, building an index of the words on the pages.

03. By following the links on the sites, the spider will quickly spread out across much of the web.

04. Build up an index of search words found by the spider and encode and store the data for users to access.

05. Develop search engine software—a program to sift through the millions of entries in your index and rank them in order of relevance.

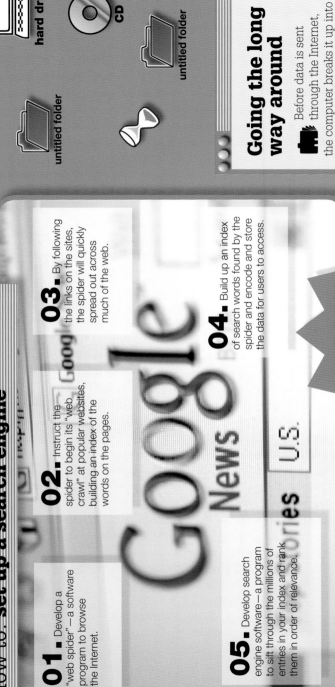

Google News U.S.

Name game

Top domain names (the letters after the dot at the end of a website address) work like international phone numbers, grouping websites.

.aero aviation industry
.biz business
.com commercial
.edu educational (US)
.gov government
.info general information
.int international organization
.mil US military
.net major service provider
.org nonprofit organization

untitled folder

Going the long way around

Before data is sent through the Internet, the computer breaks it up into small pieces called packets.

The packets are labeled with the address they are going to, then each packet travels separately to the destination by the best and quickest route available.

That means that part of your message may go via a computer in the next town, while another part goes via a location on the other side of the world!

When the packets reach their destination, they are sorted and joined up again.

RECORD BREAKER

The world's **biggest and most-used search engine**, Google has an index of millions of web pages and handles 250 million searches every day.

The company was set up in 1998 and today has around 20,000 employees.

I don't believe it!

It took 46 years after the invention of household electric power to wire 30 percent of American homes. Just seven years after the World Wide Web was created, 30 percent of American homes were connected to the Internet.

Blasts from the past

1969
Distant computers first communicate with each other when Arpanet is set up, linking computers at four US universities.

1971
The first email message is sent between computers.

1983
A new computer language called TCP/IP allows all computers on the network to communicate with each other. The network is called the Internet and governments and universities begin to use it

1991
The World Wide Web is created, giving people a simple way to navigate through the information on the Internet

2008
There are more than 100 million websites

Internet pioneer

British scientist Tim Berners-Lee invented a simple computer language (HTML) that allowed pages to be linked together and designed an addressing plan (URL) to locate each page. He then created the first web browser, to allow people to access his creation, the World Wide Web, making all the resources of the Internet available to everyone in the world.

Why did Archimedes shout "Eureka"?

The Ancient Greek scientist was trying to find a way of determining whether a crown was made of pure gold. While pondering the problem Archimedes climbed into his bathtub and saw the water level rise. He realized that he could compare the volume of gold in the crown with a lump of pure gold of the same weight by submerging them and comparing the rise in water level. He leapt out of his bath and cried "Eureka!" ("I have found it!")

Tell me more: **Nobel Prizes**

The Nobel Prizes are named after Alfred Nobel, who left almost all of the enormous fortune he had made from inventing and manufacturing dynamite to establish the awards. Each year, prizes are given for:

- ✿ **physics**
- chemistry
- **medicine or physiology**
- 🔪 **literature**
- economics
- 🕊 peace

How to: **be a scientist**

01. Find something you are interested in investigating. Ask yourself questions about your subject: "Why does this happen?" and "What is this made of?"

02. Think up a possible answer to your question based on what you already know about the subject. This idea is called a "hypothesis" — it's really just a kind of guess.

03. Scientists only consider things to be facts if they can be proved to be true, so you need to think up an experiment to test whether your hypothesis is true or not.

04. As you conduct the experiment, you need to observe everything that happens carefully and keep records. If your hypothesis is true, this data will be the proof.

Before the word **"scientist"** was invented in 1833, scientists were known as **natural philosophers.**

I don't believe it !

Albert Einstein never did a single experiment. All his ideas were worked out theoretically (with lots of very complicated equations).

Five ways to win a Nobel Prize

01: By mistake! Enrico Fermi received the 1938 Nobel Prize in Physics for discovering new radioactive elements, but it turned out that he had just found fragments of existing elements produced by nuclear fission.

02: Not for the theory of relativity. Albert Einstein's theory of relativity is a major scientific discovery, but he won his Nobel Prize in 1921 for proving that light exists in particles called photons.

03: Find the structure of DNA. James Watson, Francis Crick, and Maurice Wilkins won the 1962 Nobel Prize for Physiology when they discovered the double-helix shape of DNA.

04: Campaign for peace. Linus Pauling won the 1954 Nobel Prize for Chemistry, then followed this with the 1962 Nobel Peace Prize for working to end nuclear weapons testing.

05: Keep it in the family. Nobel Prize winners in the Curie family include Marie, her husband, Pierre, daughter Irène Joliot-Curie, and Irène's husband, Frédéric Joliot-Curie.

Ingenious but useless

The word *chindogu* (the Japanese for "weird tool") describes an invention that does actually work, but which no one would ever really use.

Duster slippers for cats—for helping with housework

Hayfever hat—a toilet-paper roll headpiece

Butter in a tube—like a stick of glue

Solar-powered flashlight (think about it...)

Noodle eater's hair guard—stops hair from trailing in the noodles

Timely designs

Renaissance artist Leonardo da Vinci kept notebooks crammed full of notes for new inventions. Many of these were way ahead of his time:

- helicopter
- tank
- solar-power generator
- scuba diving suit
- robot
- hang-glider

10 everyday inventions

date	invention	inventor	where
100	central heating	unknown	Rome
500s	toilet paper	unknown	China
1597	flushing toilet	John Harrington	England
1863	breakfast cereal	James Caleb Jackson	United States
1787	fridge	William Cullen	Scotland
1890	hairdryer	Alexandre F. Godefroy	France
1913	zipper	Gideon Sundback	United States
1928	sliced bread	Otto Rohwedder	United States
1943	ballpoint pen	Lázló Biró	Argentina
1956	velcro	Georges de Mestral	Switzerland

Five **accidental** inventions

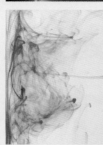

Ice-cream cones: An ice-cream stall at the 1904 World Fair in St. Louis, Missouri, ran out of dishes. The neighboring stall sold wafer-thin waffles and the stall holder came up with the idea of rolling them into a cone and topping with ice cream.

X-ray: While setting up a cathode ray generator in 1895, Wilhelm Roentgen noticed a faint fluorescent effect on a chemical coated screen in the room. He had discovered invisible X-rays, which pass through cardboard, wood, and paper, but not through bones.

Synthetic dye: In 1856, William Perkin was attempting to produce synthetic quinine to treat malaria but the experiment produced nothing but a purple mess. Perkin spotted an opportunity at once, and set up a factory to produce the first synthetic dye.

Microwave: A candy bar in Percy Spencer's pocket melted as he stood in the path of radiation from a radar-generating machine in 1945. He put corn kernels in the path of the beams, and they popped. He had discovered the principle behind the microwave oven.

Post-it® notes: In 1968, Spencer Silver was trying to find a new strong adhesive and came up with a glue that didn't even hold pieces of paper together firmly. In 1974, coworker Arthur Fry thought of a use for the nonsticky adhesive and the Post-it® note was born.

What is a **skyscraper?**

The term "skyscraper" was first used in the 1880s to describe a building with more than ten stories. Today, a building isn't considered to be a skyscraper unless it has at least 40 stories. Humans have constructed buildings for shelter for thousands of years and they come in all shapes and sizes.

Top 10 tallest buildings

01: **Burj Dubai** Dubai, United Arab Emirates, 2,559 ft (780 m)

02: **Taipei 101** Taipei, Taiwan, 1,670 ft (509 m)

03: **Petronas Towers** Kuala Lumpur, Malaysia, 1,483 ft (452 m)

04: **Sears Tower** Chicago, Illinois, 1,450 ft (442 m)

05: **Jin Mao Building** Shanghai, China, 1,380 ft (421 m)

06: **Two International Finance Center** Hong Kong, China, 1,362 ft (416 m)

07: **CITIC Plaza** Guangzhou, China, 1,283 ft (391 m)

08: **Shun Hing Square** Shenzhen, China, 1,260 ft (384 m)

09: **Empire State Building** New York City, 1,250 ft (381 m)

10: **Central Plaza** Hong Kong, China, 1,227 ft (374 m)

WHAT'S IN A NAME
"**Architect**" comes from the Greek term *arkhitekton*, meaning "master builder."

Building **high**

It wasn't until the first elevator was developed in 1857 that the first skyscrapers began to be built.

Modern skyscrapers have a central core made of reinforced steel containing elevators, staircases, and air ducts.

Steel and concrete floors extend from the core to a steel perimeter structure.

The outside is covered with a lightweight curtain wall of glass and metal.

Building types
- agricultural
- commercial
- residential
- educational
- leisure
- industrial
- government and social
- military
- religious
- transit ports

Dome sweet **dome**

Pantheon Rome, Italy 125 CE

Hagia Sofia Istanbul, Turkey 537

Dome of the Rock Jerusalem, Israel 691

The Duomo Florence, Italy 1502

St. Basil's Cathedral Moscow, Russia 1561

St. Peter's Basilica Vatican City 1593

Types of **building materials**

adobe

stone

wood

concrete

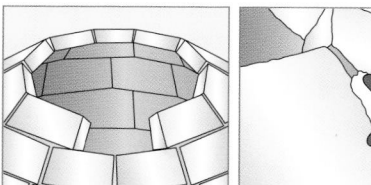

brick

glass and steel

Styles of architecture

- ⊙ Classical
- ⊙ Byzantine
- ⊙ Moorish
- ⊙ Gothic (pictured)
- ⊙ Georgian
- ⊙ Expressionist
- ⊙ Art Nouveau
- ⊙ Bauhaus
- ⊙ Modern
- ⊙ Art Deco
- ⊙ Deconstructivist
- ⊙ Postmodern

State homes

official residence	country	rooms
Palacio Real de Madrid	Spain (monarch)	2,800
Buckingham Palace	UK (monarch)	775
Abdeen Palace	Egypt (president)	500
Rashtrapati Bhavan	India (president)	340
White House (pictured)	US (president)	132
The Lodge	Australia (prime minister)	40
24 Sussex Drive	Canada (prime minister)	34

How to: **build an igloo**

01. Use a long-bladed snow-knife to cut blocks of compacted snow.

02. Lay a circle of blocks on a flat bed of snow.

03. Shave off the top of the blocks at a sloping angle to form the first part of a spiral.

04. Add blocks to the spiral, gradually placing them farther inward to form a dome shape.

05. Fill in the joints between the snow blocks with loose snow and leave a hole at the top for ventilation.

06. Build a narrow tunnel to lead into the igloo, and your shelter is finished!

Taj Mahal
Agra, India
1653

St. Paul's Cathedral
London, UK
1708

United States Capitol
Washington D.C.
1866

Louisiana Superdome
New Orleans, Louisiana
1975

Stockholm Globe
Stockholm, Sweden
1989

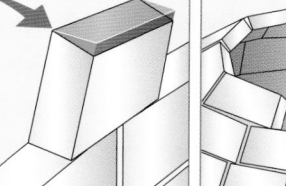
The O2
London, UK
2000

Eden Project
Cornwall, UK
2001

Where can you drive above the clouds?

Reaching 890 ft (270 m) above the Tarn River at its highest point, the deck of the Millau Viaduct in southern France is higher than any other road bridge in the world. It is counted among the planet's super structures—the most amazing feats of human design and engineering.

Types of bridge

Beam
The flat roadway rests on solid piers. Beam bridges are usually only used for short distances.

Cantilever
This type of beam bridge balances on a supporting pier embedded in the river.

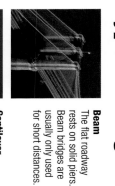

Suspension
The deck or roadway hangs from long steel cables attached to towers.

Cable-stayed
The deck is supported by steel cables connected to towers, but it also rests on piers.

Arch
A strong arch usually supports a flat roadway.

Bascule
Two sections are raised to allow traffic to pass underneath.

Pontoon
The bridge rests on floating hollow concrete blocks, anchored to the riverbed.

SKY HIGH
The Millau Viaduct's massive, curved roadway is 8,100 ft (2,460 m) long and 100 ft (32 m) wide. It is supported by seven concrete pylons, but appears to float delicately across the valley.

What's in a name?
The Latin word aqueduct means "a channel for carrying water." An aqueduct can be as simple as a canal or a tunnel, but the most spectacular aqueducts are huge arched bridges carrying the water over uneven terrain. The 161-ft- (49-m-) high, three-level Pont du Gard at Nîmes, France, was built by the Romans in the 1st century CE.

How to: go uphill in a boat

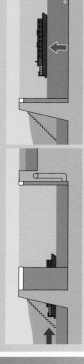

01. Open the lock gates. Move the boat into the lock and close the watertight gates behind it.

02. Open valves in the gate ahead, which allows water from the upper level into the lock.

03. When the water level inside the lock is the same as the higher level of the canal, open the gates in front.

04. Drive the boat through and make sure that you close the gate behind you.

05. To go downhill, pump water out of the lock once the gates are closed.

Or take the elevator!

The Falkirk Wheel in Scotland is a rotating boat elevator. It raises barges 79 ft (24 m) from one canal to another—the equivalent of an eight-story building.

Three canals that link seas

Suez Canal built 1869
Links Red Sea with Mediterranean Sea
108 miles (174 km) long

Kiel Canal built 1895
Links North Sea with Baltic Sea, Germany
61 m (99 km) long

Panama Canal built 1914
Links Atlantic Ocean and Caribbean Sea
with Pacific Ocean
50 miles (81 km) long

Swamp city

The city of Venice in Italy is built on 118 separate islands in a seawater lagoon. The swampy land was made habitable by digging drainage channels, which became the city's 150 canals. The islands are linked with 400 bridges. The foundations of Venice's massive brick and stone buildings rest on wooden piles buried in the damp ground.

WEIRD OR WHAT?

To protect Venice from rising sea levels, 79 **inflatable gates** are being installed in the seabed around the city. When **high tides** are predicted, the gates will inflate, blocking off the incoming water.

Super-structure landmarks

Great Wall of China
Beijing, China

Statue of Liberty
New York City

London Eye
London, UK

Stonehenge
Wiltshire, UK

Eiffel Tower
Paris, France

CN Tower
Toronto, Canada

Five artificial islands

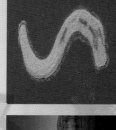

Kansai International Airport, Japan
Three mountains were excavated to provide landfill for this airport island, which has a terminal building and two runways.

Flevoland, Netherlands
This island was built on an inland sea between 1957 and 1968. It is the largest artificial island in the world and home to 370,000 people.

Uros Islets, Peru
There are 42 small islands on Lake Titicaca constructed from bundled dried reed by the Uros people hundreds of years ago.

Kamfers Dam, South Africa
This S-shaped island was built as a breeding ground for flamingos. An estimated 9,000 chicks were born on it in 2008.

Palm Islands, United Arab Emirates
These islands off the coast of Dubai are the largest artificial islands in the world and function as luxury vacation resorts.

Why go by bike?

The bicycle is the perfect form of transportation. It's a relatively simple machine that can be made and bought cheaply. Not much can go wrong with a bike, and if it does, it's usually easy and inexpensive to repair. Driven by human leg power, a bike gives off no pollution and keeps you in shape as you ride. What more do you want?

Cyclists in a long road race ride in a line one behind the other. This is called drafting and it reduces the effect of air resistance on the group, cutting energy use by up to 40 percent. Each rider takes a turn at the front, where the drag is greatest.

How to: ride a bike

01. Push your feet down on the pedals. This moves a set of levers called cranks.

sprocket

pedal

02. The cranks turn a chainwheel, the teeth of which fit into the links of a chain. The chain is also linked to the teeth of a sprocket on the back wheel.

chainwheel

chain

crank

Record breakers

In 2008, German Günter Mai created the world's **lightest bike**, weighing just 7 lb (3.1 kg).

The world's **longest bike** is 92 ft (28.1 m)—almost the length of a basketball court. It was built in 2002 at Delft University of Technology in the Netherlands.

The **first circumnavigation of the globe by bike** took place between 1884 and 1887, when American Thomas Stevens rode a penny-farthing around the world.

In 1995, Dutch cyclist Fred Rompelberg reached a **record speed** of 167 mph (268.831 kph), riding behind a dragster to reduce air resistance.

WEIRD OR WHAT?

To steer a bike you turn the handlebars to turn the front wheel, right? Think again! The handlebars are more to help you balance. To turn left, you turn the handlebars very slightly right and then tip your body to the left. This is called countersteering, and you do it automatically.

In the mid-1890s, so many people were coming up with improvements for the **design of the bicycle** that the US had **two patent offices**—one for bicycles and one for everything else!

Putting bikes to work

On the beat
Police bikes patrol the streets and can get almost anywhere quickly and quietly.

Special delivery
In busy cities, a bike courier can dodge the traffic to get an urgent package delivered.

Commuting
Office workers keep fit by cycling to work. If they need to take the train, they can just fold up the bike and take it with them.

Loaded
No job is too big or too small for a determined delivery bike.

Taxi!
A bicycle rickshaw, a human-powered taxi, is a cheap and pollution-free way to travel.

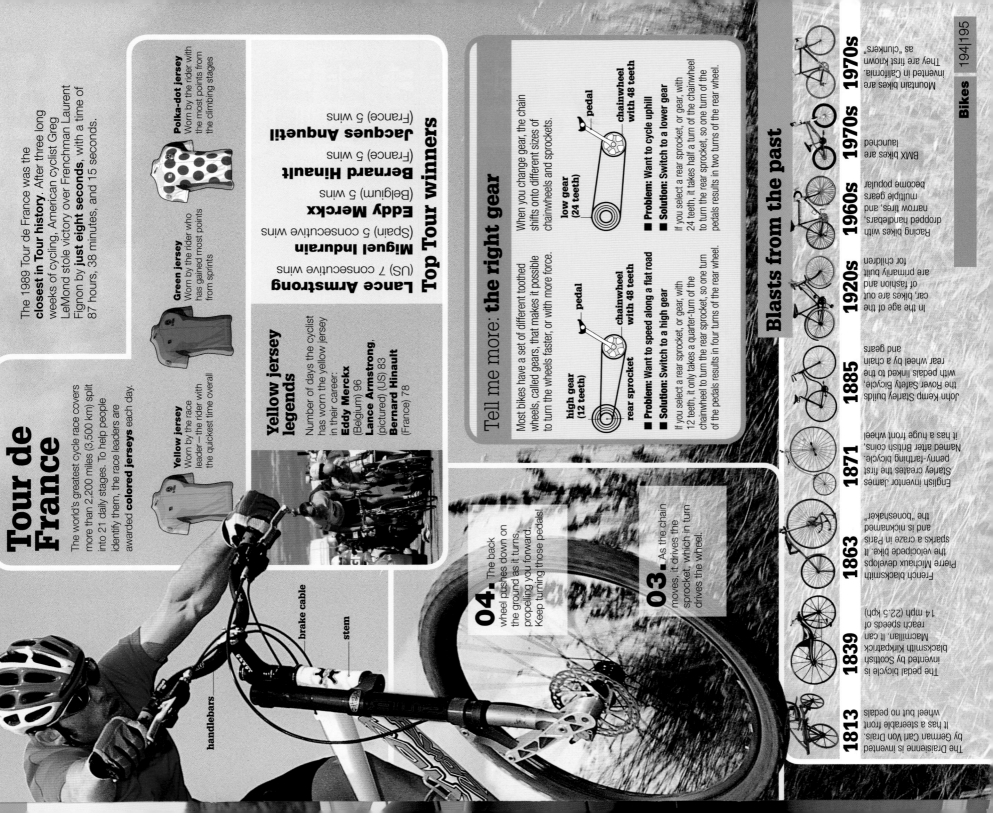

Tour de France

The world's greatest cycle race covers more than 2,200 miles (3,500 km) split into 21 daily stages. To help people identify them, the race leaders are awarded **colored jerseys** each day.

The 1989 Tour de France was the **closest in Tour history**. After three long weeks of cycling, American cyclist Greg LeMond stole victory over Frenchman Laurent Fignon by **just eight seconds**, with a time of 87 hours, 38 minutes, and 15 seconds.

Yellow jersey
Worn by the race leader—the rider with the quickest time overall

Green jersey
Worn by the rider who has gained most points from sprints

Polka-dot jersey
Worn by the rider with the most points from the climbing stages

handlebars

brake cable

stem

Yellow jersey legends

Number of days the cyclist has worn the yellow jersey in their career:
Eddy Merckx
(Belgium) 96
Lance Armstrong,
(pictured) (US) 83
Bernard Hinault
(France) 78

Top Tour winners

Lance Armstrong
(US) 7 consecutive wins

Miguel Induráin
(Spain) 5 consecutive wins

Eddy Merckx
(Belgium) 5 wins

Bernard Hinault
(France) 5 wins

Jacques Anquetil
(France) 5 wins

Tell me more: the right gear

Most bikes have a set of different toothed wheels, called gears, that makes it possible to turn the wheels faster, or with more force.

When you change gear, the chain shifts onto different sizes of chainwheels and sprockets.

high gear (12 teeth)
pedal
chainwheel with 48 teeth
rear sprocket

■ **Problem:** Want to speed along a flat road
■ **Solution:** Switch to a high gear

If you select a rear sprocket, or gear, with 12 teeth, it only takes a quarter-turn of the chainwheel to turn the rear sprocket, so one turn of the pedals results in four turns of the rear wheel.

low gear (24 teeth)
pedal
chainwheel with 48 teeth

■ **Problem:** Want to cycle uphill
■ **Solution:** Switch to a lower gear

If you select a rear sprocket, or gear, with 24 teeth, it takes half a turn of the chainwheel to turn the rear sprocket, so one turn of the pedals results in two turns of the rear wheel.

04. The back wheel pushes down on the ground as it turns, propelling you forward. Keep turning those pedals!

03. As the chain moves, it drives the sprocket, which in turn drives the wheel.

Blasts from the past

1813 The Draisienne is invented by German Carl von Drais. It has a steerable front wheel but no pedals

1839 The pedal bicycle is invented by Scottish blacksmith Kirkpatrick Macmillan. It can reach speeds of 14 mph (22.5 kph)

1863 French blacksmith Pierre Michaux develops the velocipede bike. It sparks a craze in Paris and is nicknamed the "boneshaker"

1871 English inventor James Starley creates the first penny-farthing bicycle. Named after British coins, it has a huge front wheel

1885 John Kemp Starley builds the Rover Safety Bicycle, with pedals linked to the rear wheel by a chain and gears

1920s In the age of the car, bikes are out of fashion and are primarily built for children

1960s Racing bikes with dropped handlebars, narrow tires, and multiple gears become popular

1970s BMX bikes are launched

1970s Mountain bikes are invented in California. They are first known as "clunkers"

Types of boat

canoe

rowboat

yacht

barge

speed boat

tug

junk

dhow

trawler

cruise liner

Mainsail: The boat's most important sail

Rigging: A system of ropes used to control the sails

Mast: Vertical pole support for sails

How do boats float?

Boats come in all shapes and sizes, from small canoes to giant supertankers. A boat pushes away a certain amount of the water beneath it. The water pushes back against the boat with an upward force, called buoyancy, which is equal to the weight of the displaced water. This upward force keeps the boat floating.

Size matters

⛵ Some tankers and container ships are so big that the **crew rides** around them on **bicycles**.

⛵ The world's biggest container ships can carry more than 14,500 truck-sized containers. Stacked end to end, one ship's containers would **tower over Mount Everest**.

⛵ The world's largest container ship, the *Emma Maersk*, is 1,302 ft (397 m) long. Its **anchor** is as **heavy as five African elephants**.

⛵ The largest oil tankers carry about **133,000,000 gallons (500,000,000 liters)** of crude oil.

⛵ The largest cruise ship, *Genesis of the Seas*, can carry **5,400 passengers**, has 16 decks, a tropical park in the center, and is about the same height as a 25-story building.

⛵ An aircraft carrier can carry **85 small fighter aircraft**.

Stern: Rear part of the vessel

WEIRD OR WHAT?

In 1992, several containers on a ship bound for the US fell overboard, spilling their contents. As a result, nearly **30,000 plastic bath toys** were left floating in the sea!

Around the world

In 1522, Portuguese explorer Ferdinand Magellan's crew completed the first **circumnavigation of the globe**. The journey took three years and 27 days. In 2005, French yachtsman Bruno Peyron sailed around the globe in just 50 days, 16 hours, and 20 minutes.

ferry

paddle steamer

oil tanker

container ship

Deck: The surface of the boat that people can stand on

Boom: Pole jutting out from the bottom of the mast to support the sail

Hull: The body of the boat

Bow: Front part of the vessel

Sailing boats cannot sail straight into an oncoming wind. To get around this you must use a zigzag maneuver called tacking.

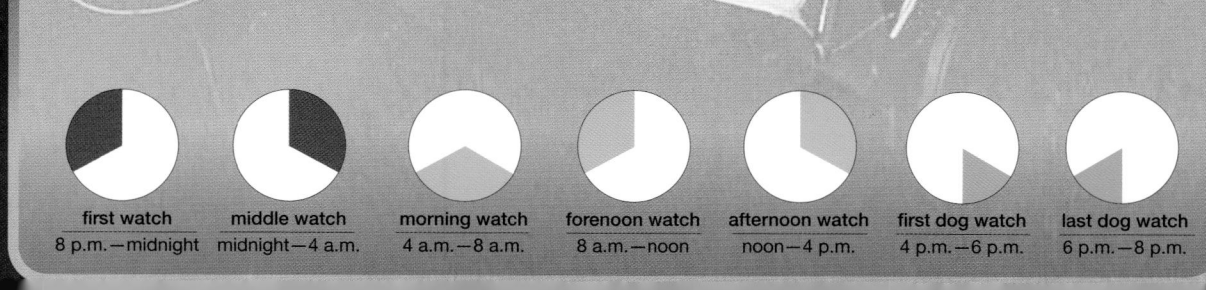

01. Make sure the sails are properly trimmed (set) for maximum speed.

02. Push the tiller (lever that turns the rudder) until the boat sails to the port side at an angle of between 35 and 45 degrees to the oncoming wind.

03. When your sail is flapping in the wind you are halfway through the maneuver.

04. The boom will move as you sail the boat to the starboard side, so remember to duck as it swings around.

05. The zigzag from port to starboard makes the sailing boat curve gently into the wind.

I don't believe it!

By hollowing out giant pumpkins and attaching motor engines, intrepid mariners can compete in pumpkin boat races. They are a bit squashed though!

Finding your way around on a boat

forward	at or near the bow
aft	at or near the stern
port	left-hand side
starboard	right-hand side

Sea time

first watch
8 p.m.—midnight

middle watch
midnight—4 a.m.

morning watch
4 a.m.—8 a.m.

forenoon watch
8 a.m.—noon

afternoon watch
noon—4 p.m.

first dog watch
4 p.m.—6 p.m.

last dog watch
6 p.m.—8 p.m.

How to: **sail into the wind**

Funicular
Tramlike vehicle that ascends or descends a steep slope

Subway
Train running through underground tunnels

Maglev (magnetic levitation)
Electromagnets create magnetic fields providing an air cushion for the train to ride friction free

Diesel
Powered by diesel-fueled internal combustion engine

Steam
Powered by steam generated by burning coal

Electric
Get their power from an overhead pickup or an electrically live third rail

Which is the fastest train?

A train is a series of cars pulled along a track by a locomotive engine. The top speed record-holder is a Japanese maglev (magnetic levitation) train, which reached 361 mph (581 kph) in 2003. When not setting records, trains provide an efficient means of transporting people and goods across land.

Tell me more: train anatomy

Wheels: Metal wheels ride on the rails

Pantograph: Picks up an electric current from overhead cables

Car connector: Flexible connections between cars allow train to make turns

Passenger car: Seating for commuters and baggage racks

WHAT'S IN A NAME?

British rail pioneer George Stephenson's engine Rocket was worthy of its name—it won an 1829 competition to find the **world's fastest locomotive**, reaching 35 mph (56 kph).

Blasts from the past

1803
British inventor Richard Trevithick builds the world's first steam railroad locomotive

1825
The first passenger train service is set up, running 26 miles (40 km) between Stockton and Darlington in the north of England pulled by a locomotive built by George Stephenson

1830
The first cities to be linked by railroad are Liverpool and Manchester in England. They are 40 miles (64 km) apart

1863
The first underground railroad opens in London. It runs 3.75 miles (6 km) between Paddington and Farringdon Street

Five amazing trains

01: Possibly the most famous train ever, the **Orient Express** was introduced in 1883, running between London, Paris, Vienna, Budapest, and Istanbul. Today the train only runs from Strasbourg to Vienna.

02: Introduced in 1939, the **Blue Train** runs along 1,000 miles (1,600 km) of rail track between Pretoria and Cape Town in South Africa. It is one of the most luxurious trains in the world. Its cars have gold-tinted windows and many of its compartments have full-sized bathtubs!

03: From 1902 to 1967, the **20th Century Limited** was an American express train running between New York City and Chicago. The train covered the 960-mile (1,550-km) journey in about 16 hours.

04: Since 1970, the **Indian Pacific** has covered the 2,704 miles (4,352 km) between Perth and Sydney, Australia, twice each week.

05: The **Flying Scotsman** has been running between London, England, and Edinburgh, Scotland, since 1862. The original journey took 10.5 hours, but today it takes about 4.5 hours.

In numbers

Longest rail networks

US	140,810 miles (226,612 km)	
Russia	54,157 miles (87,157 km)	
China	46,875 miles (75,438 km)	
India	39,284 miles (63,221 km)	
Germany	29,959 miles (48,215 km)	
Canada	29,868 miles (48,068 km)	
Australia	23,954 miles (38,550 km)	
Argentina	19,823 miles (31,902 km)	
France	18,250 miles (29,370 km)	
Brazil	18,203 miles (29,295 km)	

500 The number of cars on the world's longest freight train. It stretched for 4 miles (6.4 km) and ran on a track in Ohio in 1967

295 The number of stations on the Trans-Siberian railroad, which stretches 5,778 miles (9,300 km) from Moscow to Vladivostock

851,764 miles (1,370,782 km) The combined length of railroad track in the world

Subway systems

city	stations	passengers (per day)
New York	468	6.5 million
London	268	4.25 million
Seoul	266	5.9 million
Mexico	185	3.8 million
Moscow	177	6.8 million
Beijing	123	3.4 million

RECORD BREAKER

The world's deepest railroad is in the Seikan tunnel between the Japanese islands of Honshu and Hokkaido. It reaches 787 ft (240 m) below sea level in the middle.

Engineer's cab: Contains controls to power and steer train

365521

1869 A railroad crossing the United States is completed, cutting a six-month wagon journey to just seven days on a train

1879 The first electric railroad to supply power through the rails is a miniature locomotive demonstrated by German Ernst Werner von Siemens at an exhibition in Berlin

1912 Diesel locomotives are developed in Germany. Over the next two decades they replace steam trains

1964 The Japanese Shinkansen (bullet train) is introduced. These electric trains can reach speeds of 187 mph (300 kph)

1991 The first maglev train is installed in Birmingham, England. This short-distance, low-speed train shuttles people between the airport and the city railroad station

2003 The first high-speed maglev railroad opens in Shanghai, China, with speeds up to 311 mph (501 kph)

Who invented the helicopter?

Renaissance artist Leonardo da Vinci sketched an idea for a "helical air screw"—a craft that would spin in the air—in 1480. However, Frenchman Paul Cornu achieved the first successful helicopter flight in 1906. The craft lifted off the ground for 20 seconds.

RECORD BREAKER

The Westland Lynx holds the record as the **world's fastest helicopter**—a slightly modified version reached 249.09 mph (400.87 kph). At 131 ft 4 in (40.025 m) in length, the Mil Mi-26 is the **world's largest helicopter**. It is designed to carry up to 150 people or 44,000 lb (20,000 kg) of cargo.

What a helicopter can do that most planes can't

- ✈ take off and land vertically
- ✈ hover
- ✈ fly backward
- ✈ fly sideways

Tell me more: helicopter anatomy

Rotor blades: Provide lift and thrust. Tilting the blades allows the helicopter to change direction

Vertical fin: Protects the tail rotor

Horizontal fin: Helps stabilize the tail during flight

Tail boom: Hollow carbon fiber or aluminum tube that contains tail rotor mechanism

Tail rotor: Spins in an opposite direction to the main rotor to prevent a twisting force called torque, which makes the helicopter spin around

Cabin: Enclosed compartment where passengers are carried

G-HEMS

AMBULANCE

Air rescue

More than **3 million lives** have been saved by **rescue helicopters**. They can reach remote, inaccessible areas other vehicles can't.

VIPs on board

The US president travels in a Sikorsky VH-3D Sea King helicopter. When the president is on board, the helicopter's call sign is "Marine One."

Pope Benedict XVI has a pilot's license and flies the papal helicopter from the Vatican to his summer residence, Castel Gandolfo.

How to: fly a helicopter

01. Start the engine and ensure rotor blades are whirring at a flat pitch (with no angle).

02. Raise the collective control stick (a lever at your side) to increase the pitch (angle) of both blades. The blades force air downward and create an upward force, lifting the helicopter vertically.

03. To fly forward, backward, and to either side adjust the cyclic pitch (a control stick just in front of you) to vary the angles of the rotor blades. Move the stick to the left and the rotor tilts in that direction.

04. To control the pitch of the tail rotor (essential for straight flight), use the pedals on the cockpit floor.

Cockpit: Contains flight controls and pilot's seat

Landing wheels: Support the weight of the craft when it lands on the ground

---

Helicopter uses

- transportation
- search and rescue
- air ambulance
- aerial crane (to carry heavy loads to high or inaccessible places)
- aerial firefighting (carrying loads of water to dump on wilderness fires)
- law enforcement
- armed forces (used to attack ground-based targets with missiles)
- surveillance
- aerial photography
- traffic control

FAST FACTS

In a spin

Tandem rotor helicopters have two main sets of rotors and no tail rotor.

Coaxial rotor helicopters have two rotors mounted on the same mast.

Mass production

Russian-American Igor Sikorsky produced the first fully operational rotary-bladed helicopter in 1939. He founded a successful manufacturing company that still carries his name.

Robo-copter

The Yamaha RMAX helicopter is a UAV ("Unmanned Aerial Vehicle"). It can perform tasks that are too dangerous for a human pilot to undertake, such as filming a volcano erupting from close range.

Safe landing

If the engine **stop working**, the blades keep spinning so the air flows upward through them. This **rotate** the pivot the blades as it **automatically** the pilot to land safely. **Safe landing** a helicopter's blades can **rotate** upward so that flows autorotation. This enables the pilot to land safely.

There are **more than 45,000** military and civilian helicopters operating worldwide.

Why do planes fly above clouds?

Airplanes are powered, heavier-than-air aircraft with fixed wings. Most planes are flown above cloud level because there is not as much air resistance higher up in the atmosphere, so they use less fuel. There is also less turbulence above the clouds, meaning passengers don't get thrown around so much and there is less demand for air-sickness bags!

Types of **airplane**

VTOL
Vertical takeoff and landing jet used by the military

Jet aircraft
Powered by jet engines and used to transport passengers and cargo and as military craft

Supersonic plane
Military jets that can fly faster than the speed of sound

Propelled plane
Small planes powered by propellers that can take off from short runways

Light aircraft
Small planes used for leisure and short trips and powered by piston engines similar to small cars

Biplane
Small propeller-driven planes with double wings that are often used for aerobatic displays

Seaplane
Propeller-driven planes that can take off and land on water

What about me?
As an aircraft ascends, the change in pressure can cause your ears to hurt. Your body cannot cope with the sudden change in pressure, causing your ears to "pop" as they return to normal.

WEIRD OR WHAT?
At altitudes over 10,000 ft (3,000 m), **air pressure** is too low for people to absorb oxygen so air is pumped into the cabin. If the plane's door opened, the air would be sucked out along with anything loose in the cabin, the temperature would plummet, and people would quickly begin to suffer from **lack of oxygen.** Gulp!

I don't believe it!
Some Boeing 747s can carry 64,225 gallons (243,120 liters) of fuel—enough to fill the gas tanks of more than 5,000 small cars.

Rudder: Steers the plane

Wing: Generates the lift (upward force) to hold the plane in the air

Jet engine: Generates thrust to push the airplane forward

Elevator: Controls the plane's ascent and descent

A380

How to: fly an airplane

01. Taxi on to the runway and line up the plane. Apply full power. As you speed forward, the nose will begin to rise and the plane take off.

02. To pitch the plane up or down, raise or lower the elevator flaps on the tail wing.

03. To roll the plane, raise the ailerons on one wing and lower them on the other.

04. To make the plane yaw (swerve) to the left or right, turn the rudder.

05. To land, align the plane with the runway and lower the flaps. Just before touchdown, raise the nose so that the main wheels make contact with the ground first. Reduce power to idle and apply the brakes.

RECORD BREAKER
The **largest passenger aircraft** is the Airbus A380. It has a wingspan of 261¾ ft (79.8 m) and can carry 853 passengers.

Runways must be at least 8,000 ft (2,430 m) long to accommodate large jets. The world's **longest runway** is at Qamdo Bangda Airport, China. It stretches 18,045 ft (5,500 m).

Tell me more: anatomy of an airplane

Cockpit: Where the pilot sits to control the plane

Spoiler: Used during landing to slow the plane down

Aileron: Hinged part of wing used to bank (roll) the plane

Fuselage: Body of the plane

Flaps: Used at takeoff and landing to increase the amount of lift

CABIN CREW

The first female flight attendants had to be registered nurses.

The senior flight attendant on a jumbo jet is responsible for carrying top secret diplomatic mail from country to country. There is a special lockup to keep the documents safe.

The number of attendants on a flight is determined by the number of emergency exits on the plane.

RECORD BREAKER
The world's **fastest ground-launched aircraft** is the Lockheed SR-71A *Blackbird*, which achieved the record speed of 2,193 mph (3,529 kph) in July 1976.

PILOT CHECK LIST

To qualify as a pilot you must have good hearing and vision, pass a strict medical exam, and can't be color blind. Some airlines also have strict height and weight restrictions.

Pilots (and air traffic controllers) must be able to speak English—it is the international language for aviation.

Pilots have to be clean-shaven, since a beard could stop the oxygen mask from fitting tightly enough if the cabin pressure suddenly dropped.

Passenger jet pilots and copilots are never given the same inflight meal in case of food poisoning.

Places

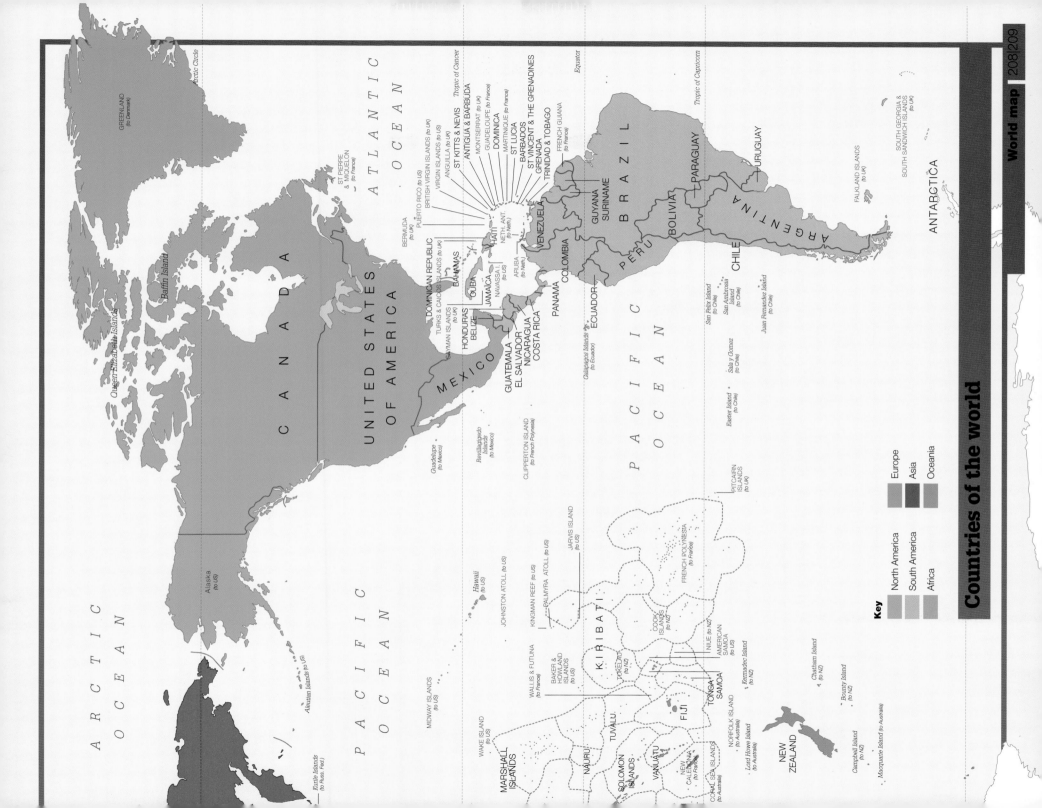

Countries of the world

Key

- North America
- South America
- Africa
- Europe
- Asia
- Oceania

What makes up North America?

This continent is home to three very large countries—Canada, the United States, and Mexico—and 20 smaller countries. It stretches all the way from the Arctic Circle to Central America (the narrow strip of land that joins South America) and includes Greenland and the long chain of Caribbean islands.

Canada's national emblem is the **maple leaf**—fair enough, since more than 85 percent of the world's supply of maple sugar comes from Canadian maple trees. Yummy on pancakes!

"Straight ahead" and "tout droit"

Canada has two official languages so road signs must be written in **English and French**. The first European settlers in Canada were French, followed by the British. In Québec, Canada's largest province, French is the only official language.

Tell me more: ancient origins

- Humans first arrived in North America about 20,000 years ago. They entered Alaska from Asia and spread throughout North America to become the ancestors of today's Native Americans.
- **There are about 3 million Native Americans living in the US and Canada.**
- The Native Americans of Mexico and Guatemala are descended from the ancient Aztec and Maya people, conquered by the Spanish 500 years ago.
- **Many Caribbean people are descendants of African slaves** forced to work on sugar plantations.

Five most populated countries in North America

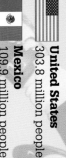

United States
303.8 million people

Mexico
109.9 million people

Canada
33.2 million people

Guatemala
13 million people

Cuba
11.4 million people

WEIRD OR WHAT?

Greenland belongs to Denmark. It is the second largest island in the world (after Australia), but only 56,000 people live there!

Most popular spectator sports

- **Football** (nearly half of American households watch the Super Bowl championship on TV)
- **Baseball**
- **Basketball**
- **NASCAR** (stock car auto racing)
- **Ice hockey** (it's a national obsession in Canada, where the modern game was invented)

How to: **elect a US president**

01. Every four years, choose two candidates—one from the Republican Party, one from the Democratic Party. Begin in January with the first state primaries—elections in which each of the 50 states vote to choose delegates to go to the party conventions.

02. There can be a lot of presidential hopefuls, so keep a running total of the primary results to see which candidate is winning the most pledges of support. Some states wait until June to hold their primaries and it may take some time to find a clear frontrunner.

03. Have lots of balloons and banners ready for the national conventions when the lucky candidates accept their nominations and announce vice presidential running mates.

04. Raise lots of money from backers for the final run to the White House. This is when the two presidential candidates confront each other in TV debates and rush backward and forward across the country shaking as many voters' hands as possible.

05. The presidential election always takes place on the first Tuesday in November. Stay glued to the TV as the results come in.

North America

FAST FACTS

Total land area
9,442,000 sq miles
(24,454,000 sq km)

Biggest country
Canada
3,848,655 sq miles
(9,970,610 sq km)

Smallest country
St. Kitts and Nevis
104 sq miles
(269 sq km)

Highest mountain
Mount McKinley, Alaska
20,322 ft (6,194 m)

Longest river
Mississippi/Missouri
3,740 miles (6,019 km)

Biggest lake
Lake Superior
US/Canada
31,820 sq miles
(82,414 sq km)

Most populated city
Mexico City
20,450,000 people

Tallest building
CN Tower, Toronto
1,815 ft (553 m)

Melting pot

Most Americans can trace their family roots back to other countries. The United States has opened its doors to immigrants from all over the world, making it an exciting mix of cultures and traditions. More than 28 million Americans speak Spanish as their first language.

Mexico City stands on the site of the **Aztec city** of **Tenochtitlan**, built in 1325 on an island in Lake Texcoco—that makes it 300 years older than New York City.

Blasts from the past

1000 Leif Eriksson, a Viking explorer, vists the coast of Canada

1492 Christopher Columbus lands on Hispaniola and Cuba

1519 The Spanish conquer Mexico and Central America

1620 Pilgrim Fathers found Plymouth colony, New England

1776 US declares independence from Britain

1821 Mexico gains independence from Spain

1865 US abolishes slavery

1867 Dominion of Canada created

1914 Panama Canal opens. It cuts across the country of Panama, linking the Pacific and Atlantic Oceans

1960s Caribbean islands win independence from Britain

Treasure ahoy!

Disney's three *Pirates of the Caribbean* movies grossed a record-breaking $2.79 billion—riches beyond the wildest dreams of Blackbeard, Sir Henry Morgan, Calico Jack Rackham, and the rest of the villainous pirates who once sailed the waters of the Caribbean in search of real treasure!

I don't believe it!

Guatemala's unit of currency, the quetzal, is named for a bird. With its brilliant golden-green feathers and long tail, the forest-dwelling quetzal was sacred to the Aztecs and Mayas.

Name that hurricane

The US National Hurricane Center has six lists of names to identify the hurricanes that batter the Caribbean islands and the Gulf of Mexico from July to November each year.

The lists are alphabetical and alternate male and female names.

If a hurricane causes heavy destruction, its name is retired.

In 2005, Hurricane Katrina flattened New Orleans. When the list of names from that year comes up again in 2011, Katia will replace Katrina. Other changes will be Don for Dennis, Rina for Rita, Sean for Stan, and Whitney for Wilma.

North America 210|211

Why do people in Brazil speak Portuguese?

Olá! In the 16th century, European nations conquered overseas lands to create empires. Portugal ruled Brazil, which is why Portuguese is spoken there today. Spain ruled the western half of South America from Venezuela to Argentina, bringing the Spanish language. More than 100 Native American languages are still spoken in the continent.

Tell me more: continent of extremes

- South America stretches from just north of the equator almost to Antarctica. At one end are tropical rain forests, at the other glaciers.

- **There are 12 countries, of which Brazil is by far the largest.**

- Chile and Ecuador are the only countries that do not border Brazil.

- **Bolivia and Paraguay are the only countries without access to the sea.**

- Suriname and Guyana are former Dutch and British colonies. French Guiana is an "overseas department" of France—that means it's part of France and the people are French citizens.

- **The island of Tierra del Fuego ("Land of Fire") at the southern tip of the continent is divided between Argentina and Chile. Ushaia, on the Argentine side, is the most southerly city in the world.**

The tango is more than a dance for Argentines. It's a way of life. As the saying goes, *"El tango no está en los pies. Está en el corazón."* ("Tango isn't in the feet. It's in the heart.")

Brazilian **Pelé** is the only soccer player to have played in **three World Cup winning teams**, the first in 1958. His career total of **1,281 goals**—77 for Brazil and 12 in World Cups—is still the highest ever achieved in the sport.

Under threat

- There are probably fewer than 100,000 native people living in the vast Amazon rain forest today.

- Experts believe as many as 50 or 60 tribes have never had contact with the outside world.

- Illegal forest clearance for logging and farming and pollution from oil drilling is threatening their existence.

Soccer crazy

South American countries have won the FIFA World Cup—soccer's premier event—nine of the 18 times it has been played since 1930:

Brazil (1958, 1962, 1970, 1994, 2002)

Argentina (1978, 1986)

Uruguay (1930, 1960)

Record **breakers**

The Andes is the world's **longest mountain range**, stretching 4,500 miles (7,200 km).

The world's **highest free-falling waterfall**, with a clear drop of 2,647 ft (807 m), is the Angel Falls in Canaimo National Park, Venezuela.

The world's **driest desert** is the Atacama (Peru/Chile). Some parts haven't seen a drop of rain since records began.

Bolivia's capital La Paz is 11,916 ft (3,682 m) above sea level, making it the world's **highest capital city**.

The **highest lake** is in the crater of the Licancábur volcano (Chile/Bolivia), 19,455 ft (5,930 m).

Weighing up to 200 lb (91 kg), the capybara, a native of the Amazon, is the world's **largest rodent**.

The Andean condor has the **largest wingspan of any living bird**—up to 10 ft (3 m).

WHAT'S IN A NAME?

Not many people can claim to have had an entire country named for them, but **Simón Bolívar**, the liberator of South America, can do just that. Bolivia was named in his honor in 1825.

Fries with everything!

Potatoes were first cultivated on the high plains of the Andes more than 2,000 years ago. From there they have conquered the globe.

Other South American foods: **chocolate, pineapples, peanuts, lima beans**

Top attractions

The Incan city of Machu Picchu, high in the Andes, is the most visited site in South America, with more than 400,000 tourists a year.

An international poll in 2007 named the famous statue of **Christ the Redeemer (shown here), which stands on a peak overlooking the Brazilian city of Rio de Janeiro, as one of the Seven New Wonders of the World.**

The spaceport of the European Space Agency is at Kouru in French Guiana. Its proximity to the equator makes it an ideal place for launching the *Ariane 5* launch vehicle, which places satellites in orbit above the Earth.

Five most populated countries in South America

Brazil		196.4 million people
Colombia		45 million people
Argentina		40.4 million people
Peru		29.1 million people
Venezuela		26.4 million people

Blasts from the past

1200s–1500s
Inca civilization flourishes in Peru region

1499
Italian explorer Amerigo di Vespucci explores northeast coast of Brazil

1531–1535
Spanish soldier Francisco Pizarro conquers the Inca Empire

1534
The first African slaves are landed in Brazil

1545
Spain grows rich after world's biggest silver mine is discovered at Potosi in the Andes

1565
The Portuguese found Rio de Janeiro

1816–1822
South America wins its independence from Spain and Portugal

1888
Brazil abolishes slavery

Where does Europe end?

That's a bit of a tricky one. Europe isn't a continent on its own but is attached to the western end of Asia. It is usually said to end at the Ural and Caucasus Mountains in Russia. Europe is the second smallest continent (only Australia is smaller). It occupies just 7 percent of the Earth's surface, but contains 25 percent of the world's population. There are 47 countries.

Big Ben, London, UK

Eiffel Tower, Paris, France

Your royal highness...

These European countries still have monarchies. In most, the monarch has no political powers, but is the official head of state.

- ♛ Belgium
- ♛ Denmark
- ♛ Liechtenstein
- ♛ Luxembourg
- ♛ Monaco
- ♛ Netherlands
- ♛ Norway
- ♛ Spain
- ♛ Sweden
- ♛ UK

WHAT'S IN A NAME?

The **Iron Curtain** was a widely used term for the political division of Europe during the Cold War (1948–1989). It was coined by British wartime prime minister Winston Churchill.

Cross countries

The Danube River flows through four capital cities—Vienna, Bratislava, Budapest, and Belgrade—on its journey from central Germany to the Black Sea.

Despite its name, you'll never run out of hot water in **Iceland**! This volcanically active island has many geysers and hot springs, including the Strokkur geyser, which spouts boiling water high into the sky.

Going up...

Membership of the European Union (EU)

The EU works for greater economic, political, and social cooperation between its member states.

6 in 1958
Belgium, France, West Germany, Italy, Luxembourg, Netherlands

9 in 1973
Denmark, Ireland, and UK join

10 in 1981
Greece joins

12 in 1986
Portugal and Spain join

15 in 1995
Austria, Finland, and Sweden join

25 in 2005
Cyprus, Czech Republic, Estonia, Hungary, Latvia, Lithuania, Malta, Poland, Slovakia, and Slovenia join

27 in 2007
Bulgaria and Romania join

Record breakers

▲ Mont Blanc, 15,771 ft (4,807 m), is the **highest peak in the Alps**. Europe's greatest mountain range and home to some of the world's top ski resorts.

● The **longest tunnel in Europe** is the Channel Tunnel linking England and France, which stretches 31 miles (50 km). The Gotthard Base Tunnel under the Alps (due for completion in 2012) will be 35 miles (57 km).

FAST FACTS

Europe

Total land area
3,956,000 sq miles (10,245,000 sq km)

Biggest country
(European) Russia
1,658,000 sq miles (4,294,400 sq km)

Smallest country
Vatican City
0.2 sq miles (0.4 sq km)

Highest mountain
Mount Elbrus, Russia
18,510 ft (5,642 m)

Longest river
Volga, Russia
2,299 miles (3,700 km)

Biggest lake
Lake Ladoga, Russia
6,834 sq miles (17,700 sq km)

Most populated city
Moscow, Russia
10,500,000 people

Tallest building
Naberezhnaya Tower, Moscow 881 ft (268 m)

Blasts from the past

1989 — Fall of Communism in Russia and Eastern Europe; end of the Cold War

1958 — Formation of European Union

1939–1945 — World War II

1917 — Communist revolution in Russia

1914–1918 — World War I

1789 — French Revolution

1595 — English playwright William Shakespeare writes *Romeo and Juliet*

1492 — Christopher Columbus crosses the Atlantic

1347 — Black Death plague devastates Europe, killing a third of the population

800 — Charlemagne crowned Holy Roman Emperor

455 — End of Roman Empire in western Europe

313 CE — Roman emperor Constantine allows Christianity throughout the Empire

63 BCE — Augustus becomes the first emperor of Ancient Rome

334 BCE — Macedonian leader Alexander the Great sets out to conquer Persians

776 BCE — First Olympic Games held in Ancient Greece

3000 BCE — Prehistoric stone monuments such as England's Stonehenge built

---

Europe's newest countries

After the Cold War ended, many regions declared independence and formed their own nations.

Belarus: Established 1991, was part of Soviet Russia

Estonia: Established 1991, was part of Soviet Russia

Latvia: Established 1991, was part of Soviet Russia

Lithuania: Established 1991, was part of Soviet Russia

Moldova: Established 1991, was part of Soviet Russia

Ukraine: Established 1991, was part of Soviet Russia

Croatia: Established 1991, was part of Yugoslavia

Serbia: Established 1991, was part of Yugoslavia

Slovenia: Established 1992, was part of Yugoslavia

Bosnia and Herzegovina: Established 1992, was part of Yugoslavia

Czech Republic: Established 1993, was part of Czechoslovakia

Slovakia: Established 1993, was part of Czechoslovakia

Macedonia: Established 1993, was part of Yugoslavia

Montenegro: Established 2006, was part of Yugoslavia

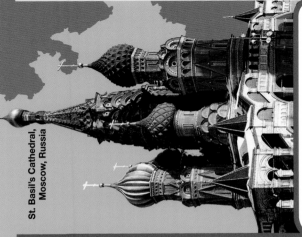

St. Basil's Cathedral, Moscow, Russia

Five most populated countries in Europe

Russia — 140.7 million people

Germany — 82.3 million people

France — 62.1 million people

UK — 60.9 million people

Italy — 58.1 million people

I don't believe it!

The town of Oulu in Finland hosts the annual Air Guitar World Championships. Competitors from all over the world pretend to play rock guitars, and scores are given for technical merit, stage presence, and "airness" (artistic interpretation).

How to: eat spaghetti like an Italian

01. Tie a large napkin around your neck and carefully lower your fork into the dish of steaming hot spaghetti in front of you. Pick up several strands between the tines (spikes) of the fork.

02. Raise the spaghetti-loaded fork a couple of inches above the dish to make sure the ends of the strands are clear of the mass of spaghetti. Twist your fork quickly to secure the strands.

03. Place the pointed end of your fork against the bottom of the dish and deftly turn the fork around and around until the spaghetti strands twist themselves into a roll.

04. Place the fork in your mouth and slide the spaghetti off. You'll probably find there are a few dangling ends of spaghetti left in midair. You can guide them into your mouth with your fork or simply suck them up—much greedier and more satisfying!

Leaning Tower of Pisa, Italy

Which is the largest continent?

Asia—it covers one-third of the total land area of the Earth. North to south it extends from the Arctic Circle to just south of the equator and at its widest point it measures 5,300 miles (8,500 km). Four billion people—three out of every five of the world's population—live in Asia.

Five most populated countries in Asia

China
1.3 billion people

India
1.1 billion people

Indonesia
237 million people

Pakistan
173 million people

Bangladesh
154 million people

Tell me more: sumo wrestling

- It is Japan's national sport.
- Professional sumo wrestlers live in "training stables" known as *heya* and eat a special high-protein diet to put on weight.
- The heaviest weight ever recorded for a sumo wrestler was 469 lb (212 kg)—no wonder they spend most of their time asleep when they're not fighting or eating!

Indonesia has about 13,000 islands, which makes it the **largest archipelago** (chain of islands) in the world. Fewer than 1,000 are inhabited, and 60 percent of the country's population live on one island—Java.

FAST FACTS

Asia

Total land area
17,179,000 sq miles
(44,493,000 sq km)

Biggest country
(Asiatic) Russia
4,934,385 sq miles
(12,780,000 sq km)

Smallest country
Maldives
120 sq miles (300 sq km)

Highest mountain
Mount Everest, Nepal/
China 29,050 ft (8,850 m)

Longest river
Yangtze, China
3,720 miles (5,980 km)

Biggest lake
Caspian Sea, Iran/
Russia/Turkmenistan/
Kazakhstan/Azerbaijan
143,240 sq miles
(371,000 sq km)

Most populated city
Tokyo, Japan
34,327,000 people

Tallest building
Burj Dubai, Dubai,
United Arab Emirates
2,559 ft (780 m)

Great Wall, China

The Great Wall of China

01: It is a myth that astronauts can see the wall from space.

02: It is a chain of fortified walls and towers about 4,000 miles (6,400 km) long.

03: Most of the wall standing today was built 500 years ago by the Ming emperors.

04: Parts of the wall were torn down and used as a quarry on the orders of communist leader Mao Zedong in the 1960s.

Aitaura, **Nepal**

Slick states

Five Middle Eastern countries possess some 70 percent of the world's oil reserves between them:
* **Saudi Arabia**
* **Iran**
* **Iraq**
* **United Arab Emirates**
* **Kuwait**

Sky high

Nine of the 10 highest mountains in the world are in the **Himalayas**, the gigantic mountain range that divides the Indian subcontinent from the rest of Asia.

WHAT'S IN A NAME?

In the past, the Maluku (Moluccas) islands in Indonesia were the world's only source of cloves and nutmegs. Europeans called the region the "Spice Islands."

Nara, **Japan**   Gojal, **Pakistan**

Holy land

Asia is the birthplace of six of the world's major religions:

Buddhism, Christianity, Islam, Judaism, Hinduism, Sikhism

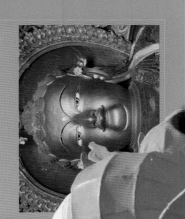

In numbers

Lake Baikal, Siberia, is the world's deepest lake

20%
Percentage of the world's entire supply of unfrozen freshwater stored in the lake

336
The number of rivers that drain into the lake (only one drains out)

500
The number of species of fish that live in the lake

1,304 miles
(2,100 km) The total length of coastline

5,662 cubic miles
(23,600 cubic km) The amount of water in the lake—enough to fill all the Great Lakes of North America

25 million years
The age of the lake—the oldest in the world

More than 50 percent of the world's silk comes from China and Japan.

The Chinese learned how to make silk 3,000 years ago but kept it a closely guarded secret for centuries. The Romans, who imported Chinese silk, thought it grew on trees!

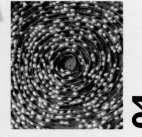

How to: **make silk**

01. You'll need a clean, warm environment, plenty of mulberry leaves, and lots of silkworm eggs. Silkworms are the caterpillars (larvae) of the white silkmoth, *Bombyx mori*.

02. The eggs will hatch in about a week. You will need to feed the larvae three times a day on chopped mulberry leaves—they're fussy eaters and won't touch anything else. They grow very fast.

03. After 25 days they are ready to spin cocoons. Each silkworm spins around 1 mile (1.6 km) of silk filaments from tiny openings in its head. The silk comes out as a liquid and hardens on contact with the air.

04. When the silkworm is completely enclosed in a cocoon, free the outside end of the filaments and start winding them onto a reel, twisting several filaments together to form yarn.

05. Each cocoon will produce approximately 12,000 ft (3,650 m) of yarn. After it has been carefully dried and graded, the raw silk yarn can be dyed various colors, ready for weaving into silk cloth.

Where can you find pyramids, palm trees, and penguins?

Africa. The Nile valley and delta in the north was home to the Ancient Egyptians, who constructed huge pyramids. At the southern end of Africa, the Cape of Good Hope is famous for its colonies of penguins. In the vast Sahara Desert, palm tree oases provide occasional shelter for travelers. Equatorial rain forests cover the center of Africa.

Africa

Total land area
11,696,000 sq miles
(30,293,000 sq km)

Biggest country
Sudan 966,749 sq miles
(2,504,530 sq km)

Smallest country
Seychelles 175 sq miles
(453 sq km)

Highest mountain
Kilimanjaro, Tanzania
19,340 ft (5,895 m)

Longest river
Nile 4,160 miles (6,695 km)

Biggest lake
Lake Victoria, Tanzania
26,827 sq miles (69,500 sq km)

Most populated city
Lagos, Nigeria 8,715,000 people

Tallest building
Carlton Tower, Johannesburg
(South Africa) 732 ft (223 m)

African hero
Nelson Mandela spent 27 years in prison for his part in leading the struggle against apartheid (segregation of blacks and whites) in South Africa. He was released in 1990 and four years later became South Africa's first black president.

Five most populated countries in Africa

Nigeria
146.2 million people

Ethiopia
82.5 million people

Egypt
81.7 million people

Democratic Republic of Congo
66.5 million people

South Africa
48.7 million people

Six of the ten **poorest countries in the world** are in Africa:

Malawi
Somalia
Comoros
Congo
Burundi
Tanzania

The **Sahel** is a belt of dry grassland that runs for 2,400 miles (3,862 km) along the southern edge of the Sahara from Senegal to Sudan and Eritrea. Droughts are frequent in this region, bringing devastating famine to millions of people.

Hot facts about the Sahara

01: The Sahara is HUGE—the whole of Australia could fit into it.

02. **Sahara is the Arabic word for "desert."**

03. Most of the Sahara is bare rock or gravel.

04. **Camels are not native to the Sahara. They were brought from Asia 2,000 years ago.**

05. About 4 billion gallons (15 billion liters) of water lies deep beneath the desert in underground pools called aquifers.

06. **Desert-living plants can sink their roots up to 80 ft (24 m) to find water.**

07. The highest recorded temperature was 136°F (57°C) in September 1922.

08. **Wind-blown dust from the Sahara ends up in the Caribbean.**

Blasts from the past

3000–300 BCE
Egyptian civilization flourishes in Nile Valley

814 BCE
Phoenicians found a trading city at Carthage (modern Tunis)

202 BCE
Romans destroy Carthage and colonize North Africa

350 CE
Ethiopia is converted to Christianity

700
Arab rule established in North Africa

1350
Kingdom of Great Zimbabwe at its height

1500
Portuguese found trading posts on the African coast

1871
Diamonds discovered at Kimberley, South Africa

1884
European race to colonize Africa begins

1960
First African states gain independence

Fossils show that **early humans** (*Homo sapiens*) were living in Africa about 150,000 years ago. They began to migrate out of Africa about 100,000 years ago and spread around the world by about 10,000 years ago.

RECORD BREAKER

The Great Mosque at D'jenne, Mali, is the **largest mud structure in the world**. Arab traders who crossed the Sahara from North Africa brought Islam to the region about 1,000 years ago.

What about me?

In 1960, Ethiopian Abebe Bikila ran the Olympic marathon barefoot and won the gold. East African athletes have dominated long-distance running events ever since.

I don't believe it!

The welwitschia plant grows only in the Namib Desert of southwest Africa. It lives for 2,000 years or more, and produces a single pair of leaves—they just keep growing... and growing.

Five top animal reserves

Name: Serengeti
Country: Tanzania
Key attraction: wildebeest migrations

Name: Masai Mara
Country: Kenya
Key attraction: big cats; lion, leopard, cheetah

Name: Kruger
Country: South Africa
Key attraction: buffalo, elephant, leopard, lion, rhino

Name: Luangwa
Country: Zambia
Key attraction: antelope, zebra, crocodile

Name: Selinda
Country: Botswana
Key attraction: elephant, lion

How big is Australia?

Australia covers 2,969,228 sq miles (7,692,300 sq km), making it the 6th largest country in the world and just slightly smaller than the United States. Depending on how you look at it, Australia is the smallest continent or the largest island in the world—and the least populated. It is located in the geographical region of Oceania, along with more than 25,000 islands. The islands are scattered across the enormous expanse of the South Pacific.

WHAT'S IN A NAME?

Aotearoa, the Māori name for New Zealand, means **"the long white cloud."** Legend has it that after many days' sailing, Polynesian explorers saw a cloud low on the horizon and decided to settle there.

Brush up on your strine
(Australian slang)

barbie barbecue
billabong watering hole
bluey redhead
dinkum real, genuine
g'day hello
joey baby kangaroo
moolah money
pommy someone from the UK
roo kangaroo
tucker food
ute utility vehicle, pickup truck
swagman itinerant worker

Tell me more: Easter Island

♦ Polynesian voyagers sailed 2,500 miles (4,000 km) across unknown seas from Tahiti to settle on Easter Island (Rapa Nui) 1,000 years ago.

♦ **They carved giant stone heads, called *moai*, which they erected around the island.**

♦ They felled the island's trees to use as rollers to transport the stone heads. This eroded the soil, causing food to become scarce. When Europeans arrived in 1722 (on Easter Day), there were few islanders left.

♦ **Today, the island belongs to Chile.**

Five famous New Zealanders

Russell Crowe
(b.1964)
Movie actor

Sir Edmund Hillary
(1919–2008)
Climber, conqueror of Everest, explorer

Peter Jackson
(b.1961)
Oscar-winning movie director

Bruce McLaren
(1937–1970)
Grand Prix racer, founder of McLaren cars

Ernest Rutherford
(1871–1937)
Atomic physicist, Nobel Prize winner

Blasts from the past

c. 40,000 years ago
The ancestors of today's Aborigines spread throughout Australia

6,000 years ago
Farming begins in New Guinea

500 BCE
Polynesian sailors begin to colonize the Pacific islands

1000 CE
Polynesians (Māori) settle New Zealand (Aotearoa)

1520–1521
Portuguese explorer Ferdinand Magellan is the first European to sail across the Pacific

1768–1771
English navigator Captain Cook proves that Australia is a separate continent

1788
British found the colony of New South Wales in Australia

1840
British lay claim to New Zealand

1908
Canberra becomes the capital of Australia

2000
Olympic Games held in Sydney

FAST FACTS

Oceania

Total land area
3,454,000 sq miles
(8,945,000 sq km)

Biggest country
Australia 2,969,228 sq miles
(7,692,300 sq km)

Smallest country
Nauru 8 sq miles (21 sq km)

Highest mountain
Mount Wilhelm, Papua New
Guinea 14,793 ft (4,509 m)

Longest river
Murray/Darling, Australia
2,310 miles (3,718 km)

Biggest lake
Lake Eyre, Australia
3,475 sq miles (9,000 sq km)

Most populated city
Sydney, Australia
4,297,100 people

Tallest building
Q1 Tower, Gold Coast,
Australia 1,059 ft (323 m)

Five things you may not know about Australia

01: It is compulsory to vote in Australian **political elections**.

02: The **Sydney Harbour Bridge** is known locally as "the coathanger."

03: 29 percent of **red back spider** bites come when people are putting on their shoes—the spiders hide in them.

04: The **largest cattle station** (farm) in Australia is the same size as the country of Belgium.

05: There are **58 million kangaroos**—more than twice the number of humans.

Five most populated countries in Oceania

Australia
21 million people

Papua New Guinea
5.9 million people

New Zealand
4.1 million people

Fiji
932,750 people

Solomon islands
581,300 people

Uluru
Called Ayers Rocks by
European settlers, Uluru is
a huge sandstone monolith
in the center of Australia.
It covers 1¼ sq miles
(3.3 sq km) and is 1 ft 2 in
(348 m) high. It is sacred
to Aboriginal people.

Q: WHAT DO YOU CALL A BOOMERANG THAT WON'T COME BACK?

A: A stick

How to: **throw a boomerang**

Australian Aborigines used boomerangs for hunting and sport. With a little practice you'll be able to get a boomerang to come back to you.

01. Grip one end of the boomerang as if you were holding a tennis racket. Make sure the curved side is toward you (it doesn't matter which end you grip).

boomerang

02. Face directly into the wind, and then turn about 45 degrees to the right. Fix your eye on a tree or building a little above the horizon. Aiming at that point, raise your arm back over your shoulder with your wrist bent backward.

wind

45°

03. Release the boomerang with a strong snap of the wrist. It should cartwheel forward, end over end. To catch it, hold one hand in the air, palm down, and the other below it, palm up. As the boomerang floats back toward you, slam your hands together.

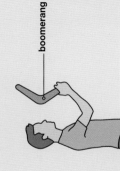

Who owns Antarctica?

No one—it doesn't have a government. The Antarctic Treaty, signed by 46 countries, requires that the continent is used only for peaceful scientific research. Antarctica is very dry, cold, and windy, and about 98 percent of its land surface is covered by ice. Very few plants grow there except mosses, lichens, and seaweed.

Tell me more: South Pole

✳ **The South Pole is the southernmost point on Earth.**

✳ It is located in the middle of a windswept icy plateau.

✳ **The ice at the South Pole is 9,000 ft (2,700 m) thick.**

✳ A plaque records the dates when Roald Amundsen and Robert Falcon Scott first reached it.

✳ **The Ceremonial South Pole, surrounded by the flags of Antarctic Treaty countries, is a short distance away.**

How to: survive the cold (if you are a penguin)

01. Grow densely packed, overlapping feathers. They will keep out the wind and make you waterproof. Downy feathers below the outer layer trap air and provide insulation during dives.

02. Your thick layer of fat (blubber) will provide extra insulation, but even so you need to stay active in water to generate body heat.

03. On land, the dark feathers on your back will absorb heat and help you warm up.

04. Tuck your flippers in close to your body—this will reduce heat loss. Shivering will also help.

05. If you are an Emperor penguin, rock back on your feet and rest your entire weight on your heels and tail so that only a tiny part of your body is touching the ice.

06. Huddle up to your neighbors. Male Emperor penguins crowd together in groups of up to 6,000 when the females go off feeding, leaving them to incubate the eggs.

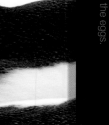

Winter blues
In winter, the area of frozen sea water, or **pack ice**, around Antarctica roughly **doubles in size** to 7.2 million sq miles (20 million sq km)—one and a half times the size of the US.

Creature comforts

Penguins are such good swimmers that early explorers mistook them for fish.

Four species of penguin breed in the Antarctic—Adélie, Chinstrap, Emperor, and Gentoo.

Many Antarctic fish have antifreeze in their blood to survive the cold waters.

Fears that dogs were passing on diseases to seals led to their being banned in 1994.

During the summer, a blue whale eats 4 million krill (small shrimplike creatures) a day.

Seven cool facts about the Antarctic ice sheet

01: It is the single largest mass of ice on Earth.

02: It contains about 60–70 percent of the fresh water on Earth.

03: Most of the ice sheet rests on land.

04: More than 70 lakes lie deep below the surface of the ice sheet.

05: Snow falling at the South Pole takes about 100,000 years to "flow" to the coast, where it drops off as part of an iceberg.

06: The Ross Ice Shelf is a large mass of floating ice, about the size of France, attached to Antarctica.

07: There are about 3 million icebergs in the Southern Ocean around Antarctica.

RECORD BREAKER

The **first baby to be born on Antarctica** was Emilio Marcos Palma in 1978. His parents were working on the Argentine Base Esperanza at the time.

Ice tours

✦ Around 37,000 tourists visit the waters of Antarctica every year, and numbers are growing.

✦ **There are fears that tourism may be putting the fragile Antarctic environment at risk.**

✦ Strict rules for disposing of wastes, including human waste, are enforced—organic matter can take decades to disappear. All recyclable and nonrecyclable waste must be separated and removed.

I don't believe it!

More than 500 million years ago, when Antarctica was part of the supercontinent of Gondwana, it lay almost on the equator.

Scientific research

❄ There are nearly 40 research stations in Antarctica.

❄ **The biggest research station is the US McMurdo Base on Ross Island (home to about 1,000 scientists in summer and 250 in winter).**

❄ Ice cores—long cylinders of ice drilled from the ice sheet—give information about the global climate going back tens of thousands of years.

❄ **Meteorites (lumps of rock or metal that crash to Earth from space) found buried in the ice sheet contain valuable clues about the solar system.**

Blasts from the past

1911 Norwegian party led by Roald Amundsen wins the race to be the first humans at the South Pole.

1912 British explorer Robert Falcon Scott and four others reach the South Pole a month after Amundsen. All die of extreme cold and starvation on the return journey.

1929 US Admiral Richard Byrd is first to fly over the South Pole.

1956 The US Navy lands a party by air to set up the Amundsen-Scott South Pole Station.

1958 Edmund Hillary and Vivien Fuchs meet at the South Pole during the Commonwealth Trans-Antarctic expedition.

1989 Arved Fuchs and Reinhold Messner are the first to reach the South Pole traveling on skis.

2007 Hannah McKeand sets the record for the fastest unsupported walk to the South Pole—690 miles (1,111 km) in 39 days.

How many **countries** are there in the **world?**

The United Nations (UN) recognizes 193 countries. They all have international land borders (though these are sometimes disputed) and an independent government. Countries usually have their own flag, official emblem, and national anthem. Size doesn't matter: the Vatican City, in Italy, the world's smallest country, is no bigger than a city block, and has a tiny population, too—about 1,000.

Top ten countries by population

China 1.3 billion people

India 1.1 billion people

United States 303 million people

Indonesia 237 million people

Brazil 187 million people

There are **58 dependencies or territories** in the world—countries or areas (most often islands) that are (usually) self-governing but come under the economic and military protection of another country. The largest is **Greenland**, which is **part of Denmark.**

How experts predict the top ten countries will look in 2050:

India 1.62 billion people
China 1.47 billion people
US 404 million people
Indonesia 338 million people
Nigeria 304 million people
Pakistan 268 million people
Brazil 207 million people
Bangladesh 205 million people
Russia 118 million people
Japan 101 million people

Largest countries

01: Russia
6,591,000 sq miles
(17,175,400 sq km)

02: Canada
3,848,655 sq miles
(9,970,610 sq km)

03: US
3,537,438 sq miles
(9,161,923 sq km)

04: China
3,705,406 sq miles
(9,596,960 sq km)

05: Brazil
3,285,618 sq miles
(8,511,965 sq km)

Smallest countries

01: Vatican
¼ sq miles (0.4 sq km)

02: Monaco
¾ sq miles (1.95 sq km)

03: Nauru
8 sq miles (21 sq km)

04: Tuvalu
10 sq miles (26 sq km)

05: San Marino
24 sq miles (61 sq km)

Land of two names

The people of Bhutan call their country Druk Yul, which means "Land of the Thunder Dragon." Bhutan is the name given to it by outsiders and is thought to come from a Sanskrit word meaning "high land."

Countries with the largest reserves of oil
(billions of barrels)

Saudi Arabia 265.3
Iraq 115
Kuwait 98.8
Iran 96.4
United Arab Emirates 62.8
Russia 54.3
Venezuela 47.6
China 30.6
Libya 30
Mexico 26.9

Right or left?

🏛 62 percent of countries drive on the right side of the road, 38 percent on the left.

🏛 At one time the US and Canada drove on the left.

🏛 Most of the countries that drive on the left are in Africa, Asia, Australia, and Oceania.

🏛 The majority are former British colonies, but Indonesia, Thailand, and Japan are not.

🏛 The UK, Ireland, Cyprus, and Malta are the only European countries to drive on the left. They are all islands.

🏛 Sweden was the last country in mainland Europe to drive on the left. It changed to the right on September 3, 1967. All cars were kept off the roads for five hours while the traffic signals were rearranged.

Of thee I sing: national anthems

🎵 Greece has the longest national anthem—158 verses. Luckily, they don't sing them all!

🎵 Uruguay's anthem takes five minutes to play.

The tune of the US anthem *The Star Spangled Banner* was originally a popular drinking song. The words refer to an incident in the War of 1812.

🎵 Japan can claim the world's oldest national anthem—the words are a poem written in the 9th century.

🎵 South Africa's anthem, *Nkosi sikelel' iAfrika,* has words in five languages—Xhosa, Zulu, Sesotho, English, and Afrikaans.

🎵 Spain's national anthem, *La Marcha,* doesn't have any words at all.

WHAT'S IN A NAME?

Libya's full name in Arabic is **Al Jamahiriya al-Arabiya al-Libya al-Shabiya al-Ishtirakiya,** the longest official name of any country in the world. Roughly translated, it means "Great Socialist People's Libyan Arab Republic of the Masses."

Seven countries that end in "stan"
("stan" means nation or land)

**Afghanistan
Kazakhstan
Kyrgyzstan
Pakistan
Tajikistan
Turkmenistan
Uzbekistan**

Pakistan
173 million people

Bangladesh
154 million people

Nigeria
146 million people

Russia
140 million people

Japan
129 million people

In numbers

12 countries in South America

14 countries in Australia and Oceania

23 countries in North America

44 countries in Asia

47 countries in Europe

53 countries in Africa

Ten countries that have changed their names:

new name	old name
Benin	Dahomey
Burkina Faso	Upper Volta
Democratic Republic of the Congo	Zaire
Ethiopia	Abyssinia
Ghana	Gold Coast
Moldova	Moldavia
Myanmar	Burma
Sri Lanka	Ceylon
Taiwan	Formosa
Thailand	Siam

Where in the **world?**

More than 20,000 people in **Japan** are over 100 years old.

The **US** has the biggest pet cat population in the world—76 million.

Switzerland recycles 52 percent of its waste—more than any other country.

India has the most universities in the world, with 8,507.

People in **Thailand** watch more TV than anyone else—an average of 22.4 hours a week.

The Netherlands has the best road safety record in the world.

How many people live in cities?

For the first time in history, more people live in cities than in rural areas, with 3 billion city dwellers. There are 22 megacities (with more than 10 million inhabitants) and upward of 300 cities with a population greater than 1 million.

Top 10 megacities

01: Tokyo, Japan
34 million people

02: Seoul, South Korea
23 million people

03: Mexico City, Mexico
22.4 million people

04: New York City, New York
21.9 million people

05: Mumbai, India
21.6 million people

06: Delhi, India
21.5 million people

07: Sao Paolo, Brazil
18.3 million people

08: Los Angeles, California
18 million people

09: Shanghai, China
17.5 million people

10: Osaka, Japan
16.7 million people

How the world's urban population has grown

1800
3 percent of people live in cities; 1 city has a population of more than 1 million

1900
9 percent of people live in cities; 13 cities have populations of more than 1 million

2000
50 percent of people live in cities; 330 cities have populations of more than 1 million

In 1900 only **four Asian cities** had populations of more than **1 million**; today, the number is 194, with the majority of them in China.

By 2015 there are predicted to be **253 cities in Asia** with more than **1 million** people, plus 65 in South and Central America, and 59 in Africa.

World's most polluted cities

Sumgayit Azerbaijan
Linfen China
Tianjing China
Sukinda India
Vapi India
La Oroya Peru
Dzershinsk Russia
Norilsk Russia
Chernobyl Ukraine
Kabwe Zambia

Do you know these capital cities?

1. Antananarivo
2. Bishkek
3. Bandar Seri Begawan
4. Dili
5. Nouakchott
6. Nuku'alofa
7. Ouagadougou
8. Port Moresby
9. Tbilisi
10. Tegucigalpa
11. Ulaanbaatar
12. Vaduz

(answers bottom right-hand page)

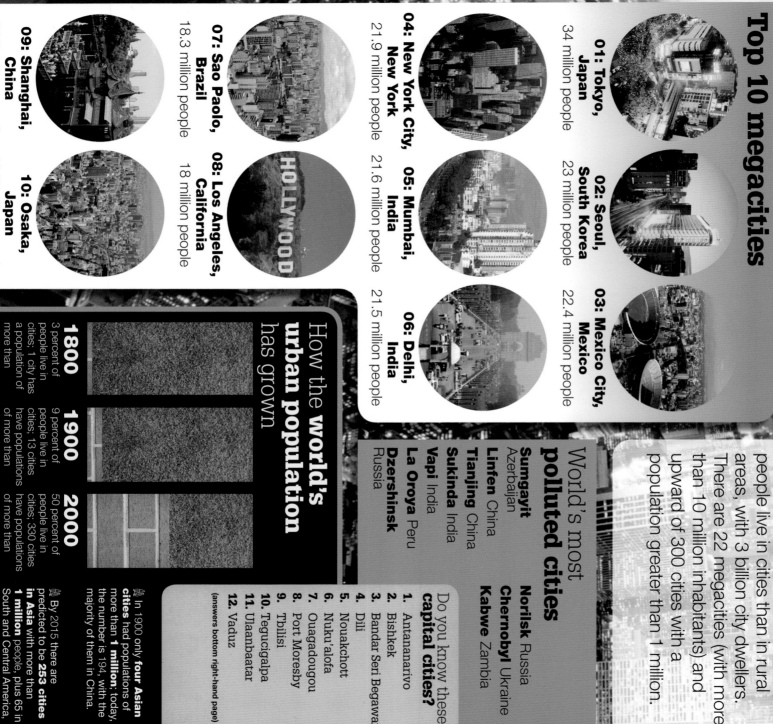

Cities with the most skyscrapers

Hong Kong China
New York City US
Tokyo Japan
Shanghai China
Chicago US
Bangkok Thailand
Guangzhou China
Chongqing China
Shenzhen China

WHAT'S IN A NAME?

According to an old Malay legend, a prince was shipwrecked and washed ashore on an island. He saw an animal he mistook for a lion and called the place **Singa pura** ("Lion city"). It's doubtful if the story is true, but today the national emblem of **Singapore is a lion.**

I don't believe it!

Nauru is the only country without a capital city; the reason is because the center of this tiny Pacific island is a phosphate mine. Its population of 13,000 lives on the narrow coastal strip fringing the shore.

Cities destroyed by major earthquakes

c.1400 BCE Ancient Troy and Armageddon (Megiddo)
1138 Aleppo, Syria
1755 Lisbon, Portugal
1906 San Francisco, California
1923 Tokyo, Japan
1960 Agadir, Morocco
1963 Skopje, Macedonia
1976 Guatemala City, Guatemala
1995 Kobe, Japan
2003 Bam, Iran

Blasts from the past

3,500 BCE First cities appear in Mesopotamia (Iraq)

1,600 BCE First cities in China

1 CE Rome's population reaches 450,000 people

500 Teotihuacan (Mexico) is the largest city in ancient America

800 Population of the city of Baghdad reaches 700,000

1800 London is world's first city to top a population of 1 million people

1950 New York is world's largest city, with a population of 12.4 million

1965 Tokyo is first city to top 20 million

1985 The average living space in the crowded city of Shanghai, China, is the size of a small car

High altitude cities

☐ Wenzhuan in Tibet, China, is the **highest city in the world**, with an altitude of 16,730 ft (5,100 m).

☐ La Paz, Bolivia, is the **highest capital city in the world** at 11,811 ft (3,600 m).

☐ **Highest city in Africa** is Dinsho, Ethiopia, at 10,522 ft (3,207 m).

☐ **Highest city in the US** is Alma, Colorado, at 10,355 ft (3,156 m).

☐ Andorra la Vella, Andorra, is **Europe's highest capital city** at 3,356 ft (1,023 m).

Think twice before moving to...

Istanbul, Turkey
Since it was founded (as Constantinople) in 330 CE, this city has been hit by 15 major earthquakes—the last was in 1999.

Naples, Italy
Some experts believe that Vesuvius, the volcano that buried Pompeii in 79 CE, will erupt again. Naples would be right in its path.

Mumbai, India
When it rains heavily in India's largest city, whole sections of the city flood since the drains cannot cope with the volume of water.

Shanghai, China
China's showplace city is sinking by ½ in (1.5 cm) a year due to the weight of skyscrapers built in the past decade.

Phoenix, Arizona
This city of 1 million people, built in the middle of the desert in Arizona, is in danger of running out of water.

ANSWERS: 1. Madagascar / 2. Kyrgyzstan / 3. Brunei / 4. East Timor / 5. Mauritania / 6. Tonga / 7. Burkina Faso / 8. Papua New Guinea / 9. Georgia / 10. Honduras / 11. Mongolia / 12. Liechtenstein

Which flag has flown the highest?

A national flag is the symbol of a country and an emblem of its people and history. The Stars and Stripes—the flag of the United States—star-trekked 238,855 miles (383,400 km) in July 1969 to the surface of the Moon, where it was planted by the Apollo 11 astronauts.

The stars and stripes of the US flag have special meaning. There are **13 stripes** for the original 13 states of the Union and **50 stars** for the number of states today. Alaska and Hawaii were the last to make their mark on the flag. Two stars were added in 1959, when they became states.

Under ice
In 2007 Russia planted its flag 14,000 ft (4,200 m) **below the North Pole.** Because the Arctic seabed is thought to be rich in oil and gas and the country was making a somewhat controversial claim to the ownership of these reserves.

How to: fold the US flag

The US flag is lowered at the end of each day. Then it is folded into the shape of a tricorner to symbolize the hats worn by soldiers in the Revolutionary War. As day becomes night, so the red and white stripes are folded into the dark blue section of stars.

01. Hold the flag waist-high between two people, so that its surface is parallel to the ground.

02. Fold the lower half of the stripe section lengthwise over the stars section. Fold again, with the stars section on the outside.

03. Make a triangular fold by bringing the striped corner of the folded edge to meet the open edge of the flag.

04. Turn the triangular end inward, parallel to the open edge, to form a second triangular fold.

06. ...until only a triangular blue section of stars is visible.

Birds that appear on flags

eagle Albania, Egypt, Mexico, Moldova, Montenegro, Kazakhstan, Serbia, Zambia

quetzal Guatemala

frigate bird Kiribati

crane Uganda

parrot Dominica

RECORD BREAKER

The **largest flag ever flown** was a US flag measuring 255 ft by 505 ft (78 m by 154 m) — more than big enough to cover an entire football field.

Flag rules

If you wash a Finnish flag, you must be sure to dry it indoors.

The flag of Chile can only be flown from a white pole.

The flag of Iceland should never be raised before seven o'clock in the morning.

The South African flag must never be used as a tablecloth.

I don't believe it!

The 27 stars in the blue globe at the center of the Brazilian flag depict the same pattern that was in the night sky above the city of Rio de Janeiro on November 15, 1889, the day Brazil became an independent republic.

Sun and stars

The flags of **Antigua and Barbuda**, **Kiribati**, and **Malawi** all feature a **rising Sun**.

The stars of the **Southern Cross** — the brightest constellation in the southern skies — appear on the flags of **Australia**, **Federated States of Micronesia**, **New Zealand**, **Papua New Guinea**, **Samoa**, and **Solomon Islands**.

There are **nine stars** on the **Tuvalu** flag, one for each of the country's islands.

Antigua and Barbuda

Australia

Samoa

Solomon Islands

Tuvalu

The study of flags is called **vexillology**, so a flag buff is known as a vexillologist. It can be a vexing hobby!

Flag nicknames

Auriverde ("gold and green") Brazil

Ay Yildiz ("Moon star") Turkey

Dannebrog ("Danish cloth") Denmark

Estrella Solitaria ("lone star") Chile, Cuba

Hinomaru ("circle of the Sun") Japan

Jalur Gemilang ("stripes of glory") Malaysia

Old Glory; Stars and Stripes United States of America

Tricolore ("tricolor") France

Union Jack United Kingdom

What about me?

Since ancient times, people have painted their faces to show tribal allegiance. At international sports events today, many people paint their faces with their national flag.

I don't believe it!

Want to see an array of the flags of many nations fluttering in one place? There are 192 national flags flying outside the United Nations headquarters in New York City.

Colorwise

There are **six colors** on the flag of **South Africa** — more than on any other national flag.

South Africa

Green, the symbolic color of Islam, features prominently on the flags of **Bangladesh**, **Libya**, **Mauritania**, **Pakistan**, **Saudi Arabia**, and **Turkmenistan**.

Bangladesh

Many African nations have flags with **green**, **yellow**, and **red**, symbolizing independence and unity.

Congo

Eight European nations have flags with **blue**, **white**, and **red** stripes. France is the only one on which the stripes are vertical.

France

Red appears on about **75 percent** of national flags.

Turkey

Libya is the only country to have a flag of a **single color**. It is a solid green rectangle.

Libya

05. Continue the triangular folding along the length of the flag...

bird of paradise Papua New Guinea

The flag of **Zimbabwe** has a statue of a **stone bird**.

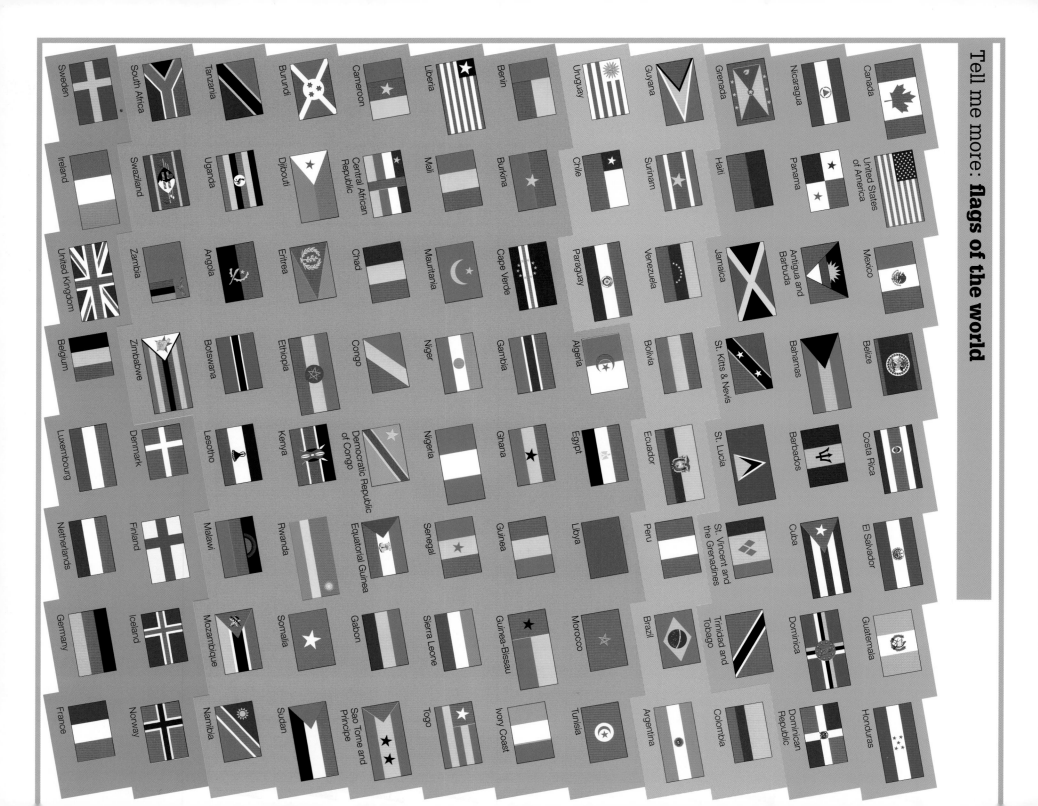

Tell me more: **flags of the world**

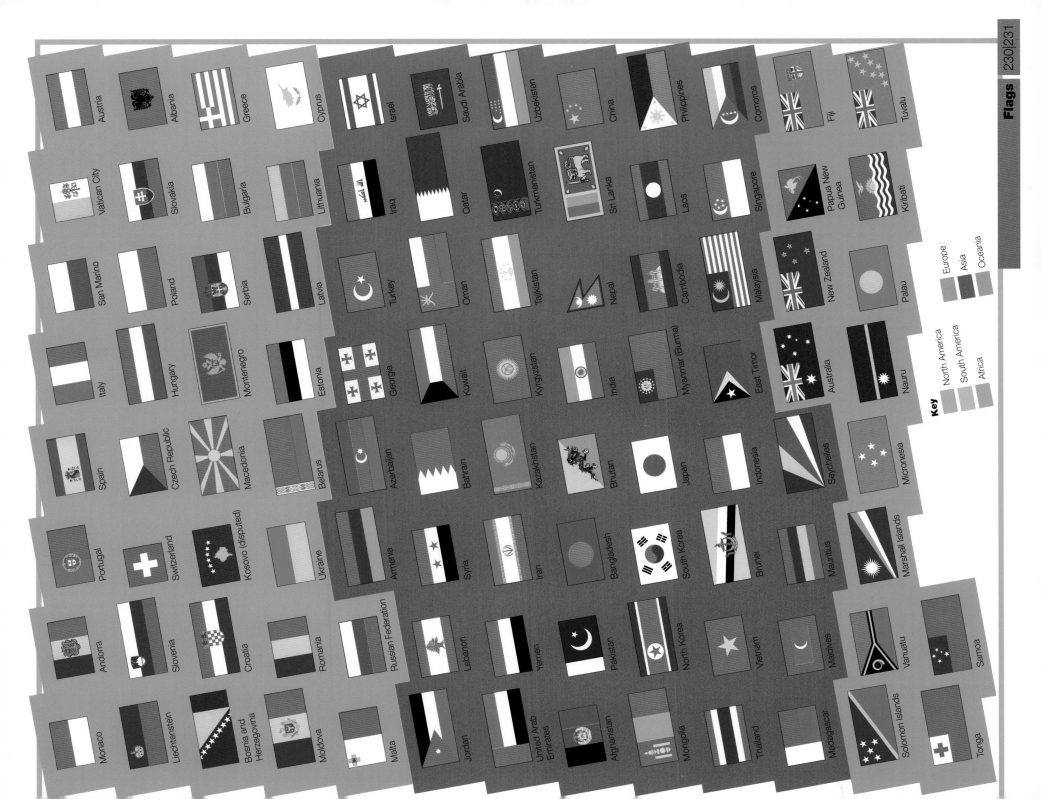

What do 900 million people do a year?

Take a vacation. Tourism is one of the biggest businesses in the world, generating at least 200 million jobs. It is vital for the economies of many countries. The downside is that tourism is a major contributor to climate change through the carbon emissions it creates. Sheer weight of tourist numbers threatens the survival of many of the Earth's most fragile ecosystems and ancient historical sites.

Top 10 most visited countries (2007)

01: France
81,900,000 visitors

02: Spain
59,200,000 visitors

03: United States
56,000,000 visitors

04: China
54,700,000 visitors

05: Italy
43,700,000 visitors

06: United Kingdom
30,700,000 visitors

07: Germany
24,400,000 visitors

08: Ukraine
23,100,000 visitors

09: Turkey
22,200,000 visitors

10: Mexico
21,400,000 visitors

Eiffel Tower, Paris, France

Six of the world's top dive sites

✈ **Yongala** Shipwreck dive off coast of Queensland, Australia

✈ **Blue Corner, Palau** Sharks and barracudas

✈ **Sharm el Sheikh, Egypt** Best reef diving in the Red Sea

✈ **Sipadan, Borneo** Matchless marine life, including turtles, barracudas, and sharks

✈ **Protea Banks, South Africa** Dramatic reef walls and coral gardens

✈ **Great Blue Hole, Belize** Exhilarating dive in the crystal clear waters of an underwater sinkhole

Have a blast!

What do Dennis Tito, Mark Shuttleworth, Gregory Olsen, Anousheh Ansari, and Charles Simonyi have in common? They are the first **space tourists**. They flew to and from the International Space Station on Soyuz spacecraft. Cost of a trip? Around $25 million.

I don't believe it!

On Mount Huashan in China, trekkers cling to a rusty iron chain while clambering along a 1-ft (30-cm) wide wooden plank above a 6,857 ft (2,090 m) cliff face without a safety barrier. The 24-hour hike attracts thousands of visitors, although it is said to claim 100 victims a year. That's extreme!

Extreme vacations

trekking

mountaineering

rapeling

Take a break (at a price!)

For **$1 million** you can enjoy a **seven-day** "once-in-a-lifetime" **stay** at the Emirates Palace Hotel, Abu Dhabi. For your money you get:

- accommodation in a 7,310 sq ft (680 sq m) suite
- a deep-sea fishing trip
- a sunset and desert island tour
- gifts including fine champagne, rare pearls, and a choice of the world's best sporting guns
- first-class travel from and to any international airport of your choice
- chauffeur-driven car at your disposal

Top 10 commandments of ecotourism

01 Respect the frailty of the Earth so that unique and beautiful places are left for future generations to enjoy.

02 Leave only your footprints behind. No graffiti, no litter!

03 Learn about the customs and cultures of the region you plan to visit.

04 Don't photograph people without asking them first.

05 Don't buy products made from endangered plants or animals.

06 Always follow marked trails. Never disturb animals, plants, and their habitats.

07 Support conservation programs and organizations.

08 Where possible, cycle or walk.

09 Use hotels and tour operators that conserve water and energy, recycle, and manage waste safely.

10 Encourage others to think environmentally.

Going green

Ecotourism is one of the fastest growing areas of tourism. It offers wilderness adventures in some of the most **remote parts of the world**, with top priority given to the protection of traditional **cultures** and the careful management of **wildlife**. Top destinations are:

* Alaska
* Galapagos Islands
* Serengeti, Tanzania
* Komodo Island, Indonesia
* rain forests of Madagascar
* Tasmanian wilderness

Blasts from the past

100s Romans tour monuments of Greece and Egypt

1200s Medieval pilgrims are the first mass tourists

1700s Rich young noblemen make the Grand Tour of Europe

1811 The word "tourist" is used for the first time

1830s Karl Baedeker publishes the first tourist guides for travelers in Germany; the guides soon cover whole of Europe

1841 Thomas Cook becomes the first travel agent when he organizes train excursions for workers in Britain

1860s Railroads bring growing numbers of tourists to the French Riviera

1900 First Michelin Guide published for drivers

1902 First packaged winter sports vacation

1950s Mass tourism takes off with cheaper air flights

In numbers

25 million
The number of international tourists in 1950

903 million
The number of international tourists in 2007

1.6 billion
The forecasted number of international tourists by 2020

1 trillion
The global income in US dollars generated by tourism in 2007

54%
The percentage of international tourists that visited Europe in 2007, making it the most popular continent for vacations

82.9 billion
The amount in US dollars spent by German tourists in 2007 – the global top-spenders

Some vacationers seek adventure. Here are some of the most popular thrill-seeking vacations:

snow boarding

surfing

rock climbing

zip lining

bungee jumping

white-water rafting

mountain biking

Society
and culture

✿ Buddhism

360 million followers

Place of origin: India, 2,500 years ago. Inspired by the teachings of the Buddha

✝ Christianity

2 billion followers

Place of origin: Palestine, 2,000 years ago Christians believe Jesus Christ to be the son of God

ॐ Hinduism

830 million followers

Place of origin: India, more than 3,000 years ago Embraces many gods and beliefs

☾⋆ Islam

1.25 billion followers

Place of origin: Arabia, 1,400 years ago Followers, called Muslims, obey the teachings of one God, Allah, as revealed to the Prophet Muhammad

✡ Judaism

14.5 million followers

Place of origin: Israel, 3,000 years ago Believe in one God, who appeared to Abraham and Moses and set out his laws

☬ Sikhism

24.3 million followers

Place of origin: India, 500 years ago Sikhs believe in one God, Sat Guru ("true teacher"), and the teachings of the 10 Gurus

---

World percentages

This bar chart shows the percentages of followers of the major world faiths. A further 12 percent of people follow other religions, while 12 percent of people are nonreligious.

Judaism	Sikhism	Buddhism	Hinduism	Islam	Christianity
0.23%	0.4%	5.8%	13.2%	21%	33.3%

Pilgrims in the Islamic holy city of Mecca

What is a religion?

A set of beliefs, shared by a group of people, that gives meaning to life and death is called a religion. Some religions are monotheistic—their followers believe there is only one god. Polytheistic religions have many gods.

Traditionally, **Muslims** are **called to their daily prayers** by a cry that goes out from the tower of a mosque. Today, however, many imams (prayer leaders) use **text messages** to summon the faithful instead.

The five Ks

As a sign they have dedicated themselves to their faith, Sikh men wear five "Ks."

01. Kirpan
A short ceremonial sword, kept in a sheath

02. Kara
A circular steel bracelet

03. Kachha
White undergarment

04. Kangha
A small wooden comb

05. Kesh
Punjabi for "uncut hair." Sikhs often wear turbans to keep their long hair neat

Hindu gods and their animals

Hindus believe that their gods and goddesses ride on a particular animal, known as a *vahana*. Here are just a few gods and their animals:

Varuna
The god of the sky and ocean, travels on Mukura—a sea monster

Indra
The god of storms and war, rides on Airaveta—a white elephant

Ganesh
The god of prosperity, Ganesh travels with a rat

Shiva
The creator and destroyer, sits on Nandi the bull

Lakshmi
Goddess of wealth and beauty, flies on an owl

Vishnu
The protector, flies with Garuda and is half-man, half-eagle

Brahma
The Hindu god of creation, rides on a white swan

Followers of the Indian Jain religion believe that every living thing has a soul. Some Jains sweep the ground as they walk, to avoid harming insects.

Shinto is the ancient religion of Japan. Followers worship many gods *(kam)* found in nature, such as waterfalls, rocks, and islands.

The number of Hindus who make the journey to the largest religious gathering in the world at Allahabad in India. During the 12-day Kumbh Mela festival, worshipers bathe in the sacred waters of the Ganges River

60 million

The number of sheep and cattle sacrificed by pilgrims in the world's largest slaughterhouse in Mecca during the week-long Haj festival

500,000

The number of Muslims who make the pilgrimage once in their life to the holy city of Mecca. All Muslims are expected to make the pilgrimage once in their life making the Haj—a pilgrimage to accommodate Muslims the Saudi Arabian government

44,000

The number of tents erected by touch the ground) bowing so low their heads Buddhist pilgrims take before kow-towing (kneeling and The number of steps some

3

A pilgrimage—a journey to worship at a holy place or shrine—is believed to bring special benefits to the traveler.

In numbers

Sacred books

Christianity: **Bible**
Hinduism: **Vedas**
Judaism: **Torah, Talmud**
Islam: **Qur'an, Hadith**
Buddhism: **Dharma**
Sikhism: **Adi Granth**

Patron saints

Saints are people who led holy lives and are revered by Christians.

saint	patron of
Andrew the Apostle	fishermen
Christopher	travelers
Apollonia	dentists
Hubert of Liege	mad dogs
Martin de Porres	hairdressers
Clare of Assisi	television
Drogo	the really ugly

A very holy city

Jerusalem, in Israel, is a holy city for three major religions.

For **Christians**, it is where Jesus, the son of God, died and came back to life.

Jews pray at the Western Wall, also called the Wailing Wall, which is all that remains of the Jewish people's ancient Second Temple in Jerusalem.

Muslims believe that the mosque of the Dome of the Rock marks the place where their prophet Muhammad was taken up into heaven.

One of the fastest-growing religions is **Baha'i**, founded in Iran in the 19th century. It seeks to unite all religions and has 7.5 million followers worldwide.

Places people go to **worship**

Buddhist temple
Relics (remains) of the Buddha, such as his robes, are often found in Buddhist temples.

Church
Christians meet together to worship in churches. Some churches have domes, others are topped with tall spires.

Hindu temple
Hindus worship images of their gods both in temples and in their homes.

Synagogue
The Jewish place of worship is called a synagogue. It is a place of prayer and study.

Mosque
Muslims pray in a mosque facing toward Mecca, the birthplace of Muhammad, in Saudi Arabia.

Gurdwara
A Sikh temple is called a Gurdwara, which means "gate to the guru." (A guru is a religious guide.)

What is a festival?

People get together at festivals to enjoy themselves. Many festivals have their origins in the agricultural past and mark the changing seasons, while others celebrate key events in the religious year. Festivals may be solemn or fun—or both—and often they are occasions for eating special foods or giving presents.

Tell me more: carnivals

■ **A carnival is a street party held in many Catholic countries in the days leading up to Lent (a traditional time of fasting), when people dance, wear masks, and parade in costumes.**

■ The Galo de Madrugada (Cockcrow Parade) in Recife, Brazil, is the biggest carnival parade in the world.

■ **Steel bands are an essential part of Trinidad's carnival celebrations.**

■ The word "carnival" may come from an Italian phrase *carne levare*, meaning "take away the meat."

■ **Revelers in the Italian city of Venice traditionally wear elaborate masks at the annual carnival.**

RECORD BREAKER

The **biggest festival in the world** is the Chinese New Year, celebrated in China and parts of Asia where there are large Chinese communities. People travel to be at home with their families, and the festivities last for several days, with dragon and lion dances, food, and fireworks.

I don't believe it!

In Sweden, people hold parties in August in honor of the crayfish, a lobsterlike crustacean that is fished at that time of year. They wear silly hats and sing songs about the crayfish!

Six Chinese New Year customs:

01 All debts must be paid before the start of the New Year.

02 The house must be thoroughly cleaned. During the festival, dust must not be swept out of the front door, since that takes away the family luck.

03 At midnight all the doors and windows are opened to let out the old year.

04 If you cry on New Year's Day, you will cry for an entire year.

05 If you wash your hair on New Year's Day you wash away good luck.

06 Red is a lucky color. Children and young people are given *lai see*—small amounts of money in red envelopes.

Eid

01: Eid al-Fitr marks the end of Ramadan, the Muslim month of fasting.

02: This festival is a three-day celebration with prayers and gifts.

03: Eid al-Adha (the big Eid, or festival of sacrifice) marks the end of the Haj (pilgrimage to Mecca).

04: A sheep, goat, or camel is slaughtered and the meat is shared with family and given to the poor.

FAST FACTS

Some things people do **at festivals**

Holi (Hindu)
Spray each other with brightly colored powders and water

Setsubun (Japan)
Throw handfuls of beans into dark corners shouting "Fortune in, devils out!"

Purim (Jewish)
Wear different types of fancy costume and eat cakes filled with poppyseeds

Easter (Christian)
Hunt around for hidden chocolate eggs and bunnies

Moon Festival (East Asia)
Carry lanterns and eat moon cakes under the Full Moon

Diwali (Hindu, Sikh, Jain)
Clean homes and light small oil lamps

Every year the Japanese weather bureau announces when the **cherry blossoms** are in bloom. Special parties (*hanami*) are held beneath the trees to view the flowers at their most beautiful.

Food with meaning

For Passover, Jewish people eat a symbolic ritual meal, the seder. The food they eat recalls the sufferings of the Jews during their exile and slavery in Egypt and their exodus (journey) to Israel.

Roasted egg: To remind Jews of temple sacrifices in Biblical times

Horseradish: Represents the bitterness of slavery

Lamb shank bone: A reminder of the lamb sacrificed on the first Passover

Apple and nut mix: Represents the mortar that held buildings together

Green vegetable: Represents new life

Parsley dipped in salt water: To remember the tears of the slaves

RECORD BREAKER

The **biggest food festival in the world** is Oktoberfest, held in Munich, Germany. More than 6 million people taste the famous beers and foods.

In numbers

Thanksgiving in the United States is held on the fourth Thursday in November. A turkey feast is central to the celebrations.

45 million
The number of turkeys consumed across the US at Thanksgiving

650 million lb
(295 million kg) The amount of cranberries used to make sauce

1.6 billion lb
(700 million kg) The number of sweet potatoes eaten

1 billion lb
(453 million kg) The amount of pumpkins consumed

Colors that light up New York City's Empire State Building on holidays:

Chinese New Year
St. Valentine's Day
St. Patrick's Day
Easter
Thanksgiving
Eid al-Fitr
Hanukkah
Christmas

Santa legends

Santa Claus (also known as Saint Nicholas, Father Christmas, or Kris Kringle) delivers gifts at Christmas.

Most people think of him as a fat, white-haired gentleman wearing a red suit with white cuffs and collar. He was first portrayed in this way in a 19th-century US cartoon.

Traditions in some countries have Santa living at the North Pole. Other people believe he lives in Lapland.

Dutch children believe that Sinterklaas comes just before the feast day of Saint Nicholas on December 6 and put their shoes out for him to fill with candy treats and little gifts if they have been good—if not, they get a small bag of salt!

What is money?

We exchange money for goods and services. In the past, people bartered (exchanged) goods of equal worth, but it's not very convenient to swap a chicken and two bags of corn for that DVD you want. That's why we use money—either cash (bills and coins), or a virtual payment using a debit or credit card.

In numbers

5
The number of sacks of grain it took to barter for a pig in Ancient Egypt

12
The number of sides on an Australian 50-cent piece (more than any other coin)

1 billion
The value in US dollars of the amount of Iraqi dinar currency that was stolen from the Central Bank of Iraq in Baghdad the day before the US bombings in 2001. $650 million was later found hidden in the walls of Saddam Hussein's palace

12 billion
The number of coins made by the US mint every year

56 billion
The net worth in US dollars of Microsoft founder Bill Gates—the richest man in the world

The Euro is used by 320 million Europeans in 20 countries.

What's in a name?

The word "salary" comes from the Latin word *sal*, meaning salt. Roman soldiers were paid a *salarium*—an allowance to buy salt.

WEIRD OR WHAT?

There was a time when British homeowners had to pay a window tax if they had more than a certain number of windows in their homes. To avoid paying, people simply bricked up some of their windows—no wonder they called it daylight robbery!

Plastic fantastic

Debit cards can be used to purchase goods. A simple swipe or input of numbers and money is debited directly from a bank account.

The first credit card (plastic card used to purchase goods and services on credit, to be paid off at a later date) was introduced in 1949 in New York City. Called the "Diners Club," it was accepted in restaurants.

There are more than 670 million credit cards in circulation in the United States.

Money around the world

A currency is the form of money used in a particular country. Here are some examples:

Symbol	Country	Currency	Subunit
$	US	Dollar	100 cents
£	UK	Pound	100 pence
L	Albania	Lek	100 qindarka
Tk	Bangladesh	Taka	100 paisa
元	China	Yuan	100 jiao
D	Gambia	Dalasi	100 butut
Rs	India	Rupee	100 paise
₪	Israel	Shekel	100 agorot
RM	Malaysia	Ringgit	100 sen
₮	Mongolia	Tugrik	100 mongos
zł	Poland	Zloty	100 groszy
руб	Russia	Ruble	100 kopecks
﷼	Saudia Arabia	Riyal	100 halalat
฿	Thailand	Baht	100 stang
ЛВ	Bulgaria	Leva	100 stotinki

RECORD BREAKERS

The **largest denomination banknote** ever issued was a bill for 100,000,000,000,000,000,000 pengo. It was issued by the Hungarian National Bank in 1946, when inflation was so high that prices were doubling every 15 hours.

RECORD BREAKERS

The world's first ATM

(Automated Teller Machine) was installed in London, England, in June 1967.

Funny money

Before money, a variety of things were used as payment instead:

metal amulets
tea
whales' teeth
iron nails
wampum
cowrie shells
cattle
tobacco leaves

How to: **play the stock market**

01. Select stock to buy. Companies issue stock (shares in the company) to raise money to enable them to grow.

02. Owning stock in a company means you own part of that company. Congratulations! Don't worry, you won't be expected to work at the company, but you will get a vote on important issues.

03. If the company makes a profit, you get a share of the money and the value of the stock goes up.

04. Decide whether to hold on to your stock or sell it. If the value of the stock rises, you can sell it to another investor for a profit. But if the value of the stock falls, you could end up losing money.

A **bear market** is when stock prices are falling.

A **bull market** is when stock prices are rising.

Key stock exchanges

country	city	index (shows the price of selected shares being traded)
Japan	Tokyo	Nikkei Average
US	New York	Dow-Jones
UK	London	FTSE-100
Germany	Frankfurt	DAX

Note worthy

Over the ages and around the world, famous faces have adorned banknotes (or bills) and coins. Many in this list are now out of

name of person	country issued	coin or note
George Washington, US president	United States	1 dollar
William Shakespeare, playwright	United Kingdom	20 pounds
Nelson Mandela, statesman	South Africa	5 rand
Napoleon Bonaparte, emperor	France	5 francs
Albert Einstein, scientist	Israel	5 lirot
Marie Curie, scientist	Poland	20,000 zloty
Galileo Galilei, scientist	Italy	2,000 lire
Karen Blixen, writer	Denmark	50 kroner
Mahatma Gandhi, political leader	India	5,10, 20, 50, 100 rupees

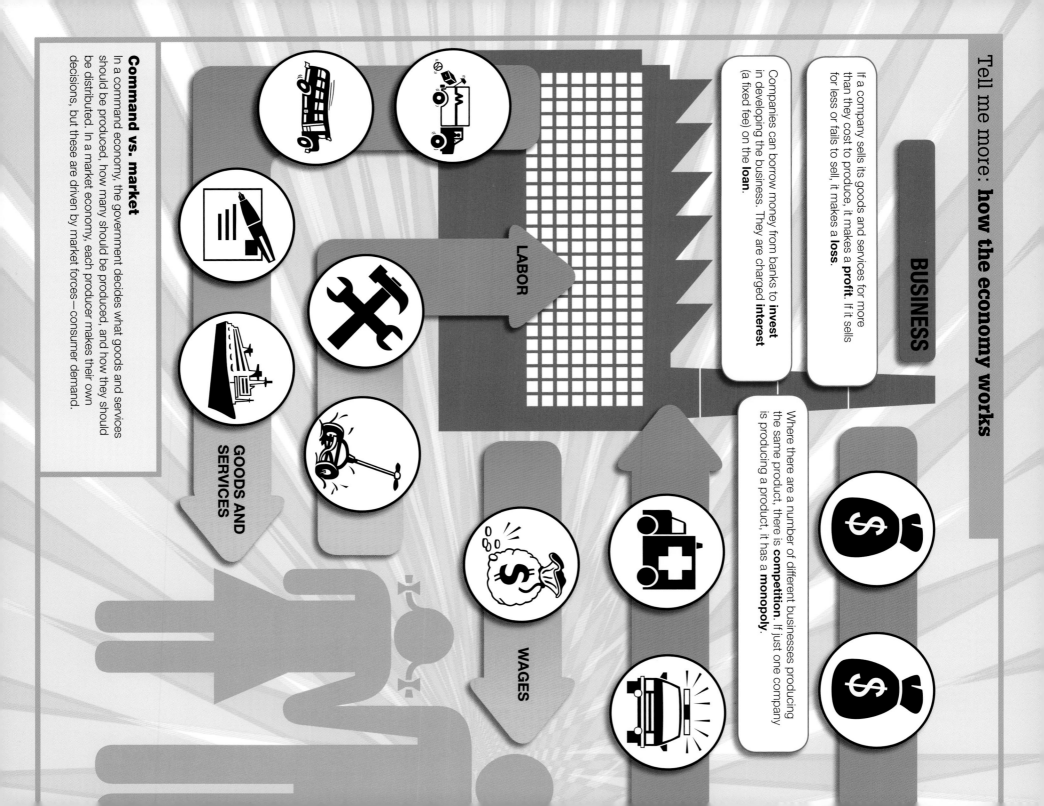

BUSINESS

If a company sells its goods and services for more than they cost to produce, it makes a **profit**. If it sells for less or fails to sell, it makes a **loss**.

Companies can borrow money from banks to **invest** in developing the business. They are charged **interest** (a fixed fee) on the **loan**.

Where there are a number of different businesses producing the same product, there is **competition**. If just one company is producing a product, it has a **monopoly**.

LABOR

GOODS AND SERVICES

WAGES

Command vs. market

In a command economy, the government decides what goods and services should be produced, how many should be produced, and how they should be distributed. In a market economy, each producer makes their own decisions, but these are driven by market forces—consumer demand.

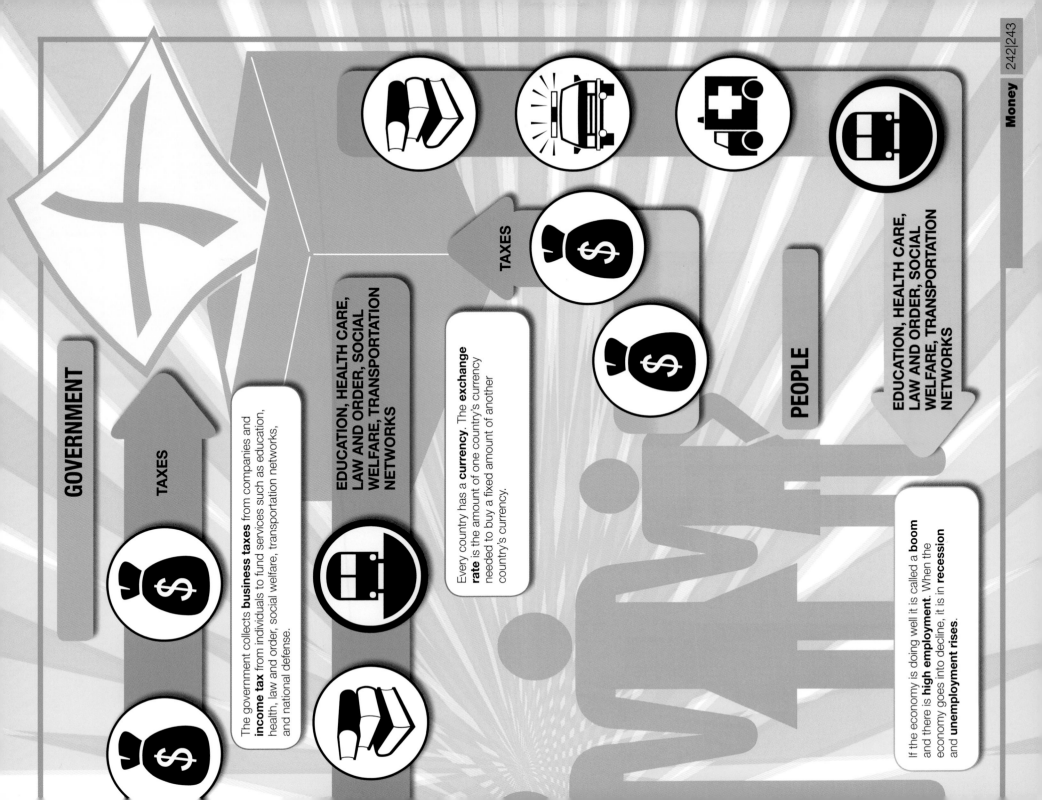

GOVERNMENT

TAXES

The government collects **business taxes** from companies and **income tax** from individuals to fund services such as education, health, law and order, social welfare, transportation networks, and national defense.

EDUCATION, HEALTH CARE, LAW AND ORDER, SOCIAL WELFARE, TRANSPORTATION NETWORKS

TAXES

Every country has a **currency**. The **exchange rate** is the amount of one country's currency needed to buy a fixed amount of another country's currency.

PEOPLE

EDUCATION, HEALTH CARE, LAW AND ORDER, SOCIAL WELFARE, TRANSPORTATION NETWORKS

If the economy is doing well it is called a **boom** and there is **high employment.** When the economy goes into decline, it is in **recession** and **unemployment rises.**

What is a law?

Laws are rules that spell out how people should behave in society. Throughout history, people have devised ways of settling disputes between neighbors and punishing wrongdoers. The earliest surviving set of laws was issued by Ur-Nammu, king of Sumer (modern Iraq), about 4,000 years ago.

I don't believe it!

In the UK, many lawyers and judges wear wigs made from white horsehair. This tradition dates back to the 17th century. The wigs are very expensive to make, so judges are paid a special wig allowance!

Blind justice

The Roman goddess Justitia (Justice) is still used as a symbol of law and order. Her statue can be seen on court buildings around the world. She wears a blindfold and carries a sword in her right hand and a pair of weighing scales in her left.

Sword: Represents punishment

Blindfold: Symbolizes how justice is impartial

10 fictional sleuths (who have also appeared on postage stamps)

Sherlock Holmes
(Arthur Conan Doyle)
Wears a deerstalker hat and lives on Baker Street

Hercule Poirot
(Agatha Christie)
Belgian detective with a distinctive moustache

Inspector Maigret
(Simenon)
French pipe smoker

Charlie Chan
(Earl Derr Biggars)
Chinese-American sleuth

Father Brown
(G. K. Chesterton)
Roman Catholic priest

Sam Spade
(Dashiell Hammett)
San Francisco's finest

Philip Marlowe
(Raymond Chandler)
Tough private eye with a penchant for poetry

Dick Tracy
(Chester Gould)
Fast-shooting comic-book hero

Miss Marple
(Agatha Christie)
Prim English spinster

Inspector Clouseau (Blake Edwards) Bumbling French policeman

Puzzling case

In 2008, a drugs trial in Australia was halted after members of the jury were found playing Sudoku to pass the time—the judge thought they were taking notes!

Crime categories

Against people: assault, battery, robbery, rape, kidnapping, manslaughter, murder

Against property: arson, theft, burglary, deception, vandalism

Against the state: tax evasion, espionage, treason

Against justice: obstruction of justice, bribery, perjury, malfeasance (wrongdoing by a public official)

Against international law: apartheid (racism), piracy, genocide, war crimes, slavery

WEIRD OR WHAT?

In medieval times, French villagers found a **pig guilty** of murdering a baby and hanged her. They **charged her six piglets** with being accessories, but let them off on grounds of youth and having a bad role model!

Most wanted

? The FBI (Federal Bureau of Investigation) posts photographs of the 10 most wanted fugitives in the US in public buildings and on the FBI website.

? Since 1950 more than **489 fugitives have been listed, eight of whom were women.**

? Occasionally, the FBI adds a "Number Eleven" if a criminal is regarded as extremely dangerous, but none of the other 10 can be removed until caught.

Who's who in the law

Lawmakers
Countries have their own laws, which often date back a long time. New laws and changes to existing ones are usually decided and voted on by a nation's government.

Cops
The police enforce the laws by patrolling the streets and investigating crime.

Legal eagles
Lawyers present the evidence in court cases and question witnesses. Some are hired to bring charges against the accused, while others argue the case for the defense.

Hammer time
Judges preside over court proceedings and rule on the law. They sit behind a high desk and sometimes bang it with a hammer. The judge interprets the law and decides the punishment.

Final verdict
In many countries, a jury (a group of ordinary citizens) listens to evidence and decides if the accused is guilty or not.

Global forces

■ **The United Nations (UN) Police** work in some of the most dangerous and unstable places around the world.

■ The UN's goal is to restore **peace and order** by rebuilding local police forces and promoting fair and humane laws for all citizens.

■ UN police officers are drawn from more than **90 countries** around the world.

■ Short for the International Criminal Police Organization, **INTERPOL** is an international crime-busting organization established in 1923 and based in Lyon, France.

■ INTERPOL has **186 member countries**, whose police forces share information to help bring fugitives to justice across national borders.

Four famous forces

01: **The Mounties (Royal Canadian Mounted Police)**
Canada's federal police force is famous for dashing red breeches and wide-brimmed hats. Their real motto is *"Maintiens le droit"* ("Uphold the law"), but the unofficial one is, "We always get our man."

02: **New York City Police Department (NYPD)**
The NYPD is the largest police force in the US, with more than 37,000 officers. It is nicknamed "New York's finest" and is portrayed in many television shows and movies.

03: **New Delhi Police** India's New Delhi Police force has nearly 58,000 officers. Its history stretches back to 1237, when a force was founded for the sultan of Delhi.

04: **Metropolitan Police** New Scotland Yard is the home of London's Metropolitan Police, founded by Sir Robert Peel in 1829.

Famous outlaws

💰 **Billy the Kid** was a 19th-century frontier gunman

💰 **Bonnie and Clyde** robbed their way across the United States in the early 1930s

💰 **Jesse James** was a legendary 19th-century Wild West bandit

💰 **Ned Kelly** was a 19th-century Australian bushranger and gang leader

💰 **Robin Hood** was the English folklore hero who robbed the rich to feed

Scales:
Show how justice weighs up opposing evidence

HOLY LAW
In the Muslim world, the law is called Sharia (meaning "way" or "path"), and it derives from the holy book of Islam, the Qur'an. Religious scholars can issue formal legal rulings called fatwas.

Most popular police dog breeds

German shepherd | Dutch shepherd | Belgian malinois | Labrador retriever | Springer spaniel | Bloodhound | Beagle

The usual police dog retirement age is seven years old.

Aboriginal languages of northern and western Australia

Amerindian languages of South American Andes

Siberian languages of northern Russia and China

Native American languages of Northwest Pacific (US and Canada)

Amerindian languages of Brazil, Paraguay, and Argentina

Native American languages of Southwestern US

Languages of **New Guinea and Melanesia**

Some endangered languages have only a single speaker left—when that person dies, the spoken language will vanish.

How many languages are there?

Give or take a few—6,912. Some languages are used by only a few people. Others, such as Mandarin Chinese and English, are spoken by millions. Many people speak two or more languages. They may use one language at home with family and friends, and another at work or school. Regional variations of a language are known as dialects.

Linguists (people who study languages) believe the **"click" languages** of southern Africa may descend from the earliest speech used by humans. Speakers **click their tongue** fast against the roof of the mouth to make different sounds.

Singapore condition breakers click easy
official click
million
two choice roots eccentric gesture
sprache agree beside
must
polite country
Britain Chinese
Portugal
lingua
speaking
verbalising
hello
laws
new
big
Germany suggest special simple
noun
learnt
create liberation
throughout
Spanish
books
langue
tongue apple convey derived
language
like
verbs
Dutch legal
According
Checking
English

Tell me more: a fine Romance

• The term "Romance language" sounds like the language of love, but is actually derived from Latin—spoken in much of western Europe during the Roman Empire. The main Romance languages are French, Portuguese, Italian, Romanian, and Spanish.

• English is not a Romance language. The Anglo-Saxons, who conquered Britain at the end of the Roman Empire, spoke a Germanic language that later became English. Other Germanic languages include Danish, Dutch, German, and Swedish.

• English also gained French-derived words after it came to be ruled by French-speaking kings following the Norman conquest.

English words with

Germanic roots (modern German equivalent)		French roots (modern French equivalent)	
apple	apfel	beef	boeuf
book	buch	castle	chateau
brother	bruder	law	loi
cow	kuh	parliament	parlement
daughter	tochter	soup	soupe
house	haus	tailor	tailleur

Top 10 languages in the world

01: **Chinese Mandarin**
1.12 billion speakers, mostly in China, Malaysia, Taiwan, and Singapore

02: **English**
510 million speakers, mostly in the US, UK, Australia, Canada, and New Zealand

03: **Hindi**
490 million speakers, mostly in India

04: **Spanish**
425 million speakers, mostly in South and Central America, the US, and Spain

05: **Arabic**
255 million speakers, mostly in the Middle East, Arabia, and northern Africa

06: **Russian**
254 million speakers, mostly in Russia and Central Asia

07: **Portuguese**
218 million speakers, mostly in Brazil, Portugal, and southern Africa

08: **Bengali**
215 million speakers, mostly in Bangladesh and northern India

09: **Malay/Indonesian**
175 million speakers, mostly in Indonesia, Malaysia, and Singapore

10: **French**
130 million speakers, mostly in France, Canada, western and central Africa

Record breakers

☺ The Pacific island of Papua New Guinea has **more languages** than any other country—832 languages for a population of only 3.9 million.

☺ South Africa has the **most official languages**—11. An official language has legal status within a country, which means it is used for government business and in the law courts. Many countries have several official languages.

☺ Khmer, the official language of Cambodia, has the **largest alphabet**, with 74 letters.

English language
English is an official language in 48 countries, although, funnily enough, not in the UK and the US, where it is the first language but does not have legal status!

20 ways of saying "I love you"

Ami tomay bhalo bashi (Bengali)
Bon sro lanh oon (Cambodian)
Jeg elsker dig (Danish)
Ik hou van jou (Dutch)
Je t'aime (French)
Hoon tane pyar karoo choon (Gujarati)
Ich liebe dich (German)
Kimi o ai shiteru (Japanese)
Mahal kita (Tagalog)
Mina rakastan sinua (Finnish)
Muhje tumse mohabbat hai (Urdu)
Rwy'n dy garu di (Welsh)
S'agapo (Greek)
Szeretlek (Hungarian)
Taim l'ngra leat (Irish)
Te quiero (Spanish)
Ti amo (Italian)
Tora dust midaram (Farsi)
Wo le ni (Chinese)
Ya vas liubliu (Russian)

Invented languages

Esperanto — Polish linguist **Ludwig Lazarus Zamenhof** came up with Esperanto in 1887. Supposed to be a universal language, it never really took off.

Elvish — *Lord of the Rings* author **JRR Tolkien** invented Elvish languages for his mythological creation of Middle Earth.

Klingon — Linguist **Marc Okrand** devised Klingon for the *Star Trek* television series. Klingon even has its own dictionary!

SUPERCALIFRAGILISTEXPIALIDOCIOUS

(invented for the movie *Mary Poppins*) is one of the longest words in the English dictionary, checking in at a whopping 34 letters!

Donaudampfschiffahrtselektrizitätenhauptbetriebswerkbauunterbeamtengesellschaft

is a record-breaker from Germany at 79 letters! Don't ask for details, but it has something to do with the management of a steamship company on the Danube River.

Why are books important?

They feed our imagination, amuse and inform us, and introduce us to new ways of understanding the world. Most of human knowledge is recorded in books.

Tell me more: printing in the past

The Chinese invented printing. The world's oldest printed book is a copy of the *Diamond Sutra*—one of Buddhism's most sacred texts—which was printed in China in 868 BCE.

Printing didn't take off in China, though, because the Chinese script has thousands of different characters.

Johann Gutenberg of Germany came up with the idea of the "printing press" in about 1450.

The printing press could produce books quickly and in multiple copies—a technological breakthrough that has been compared to the invention of the internet.

The first book printed was the Bible.

What is an ISBN?

An International Standard Book Number—a 13-digit number that is printed at the front of every book to show where it was published. In this book, you'll find the ISBN on page two.

Record breaker

The oldest book in the world dates from 2,500 years ago. It is six pages of gold, hinged together at the top and written in ancient Etruscan—a language no one can read today.

The most expensive book ever sold at auction is the *Codex Leicester*—the manuscript (handwritten) notebooks of Renaissance genius Leonardo da Vinci. It was bought by Microsoft founder Bill Gates for $30.8 million in 1994.

A copy of James Audubon's *Birds of America* sold for $8.8 million in 2000, making it the world's most expensive printed book.

Do books have a future?

Some people have suggested that the **internet** threatens the long-term survival of books, since more and more works can be **downloaded**. But books still have many **advantages**: they are more **easily read** than a screen, are good to handle, and can be taken almost* **anywhere**—don't write them off yet.

* until someone invents waterproof books!

10 great children's authors

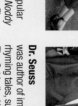

Enid Blyton wrote many popular series such as *Noddy* and the *Famous Five*.

Dr. Seuss was author of imaginative rhyming tales, such as *The Cat in the Hat*.

J. K. Rowling wrote the immensely popular *Harry Potter* magical adventures.

R. L. Stine has thrilled many with his horror stories, such as the *Goosebumps* series.

C. S. Lewis authored the fantasy novels that made up *The Chronicles of Narnia*.

J. R. R. Tolkein wrote *The Hobbit*, followed by the *Lord of the Rings* sequel.

Beatrix Potter wrote 23 small books about animal characters, such as Peter Rabbit.

These authors sold more than 100 million copies of their books.

ISBN 978-0-7566-5195-4

9 780756 651954

Best sellers

The best-selling book of all time is the Bible, followed by the collected works of Chinese communist leader Mao Zedong.

The world's best-selling novel is thought to be Charles Dickens's *Tale of Two Cities.*

The best-selling book in French is *Le Petit Prince* (The Little Prince) by Antoine de Saint-Exupéry.

The best-selling practical book is *Scouting for Boys* by Robert Baden-Powell, founder of the international scout movement.

In numbers

32 million
The number of books in the library

530 miles
(853 km) The total length of all the bookshelves in the library

The Library of Congress in Washington, D.C., is the largest library in the world.

470
The number of books in the library

2.7 million
How many different languages the books are written in

13 million
The total number of recordings stored in the library

4.5 million
The number of photographs in the library

61 million
The number of manuscripts in the library
How many maps there are

The Nobel Prize for Literature, founded in 1901, is given for outstanding work in the field of literature in any language. Moody French philosopher Jean-Paul Sartre is the only person known to have declined it.

WEIRD OR WHAT?

With nanotechnology (engineering on a molecular scale) you can create books smaller than a grain of salt. A book called *Teeny Ted from Turnip Town*, made in 2007 at Simon Fraser University, Canada, measures 0.0027 x 0.0004 in (0.07 x 0.1 mm). The only way to read it is with an electron microscope at 8,000 times magnification.

Potter Power

The *Harry Potter* series has sold 400 million copies and been translated into 65 languages.

Harry Potter and the Deathly Hallows, the seventh and last book of the series, sold 11 million copies in 24 hours—an all-time record.

J. K. Rowling penned the final words of the series in Room 652 of the Balmoral Hotel, Edinburgh.

An original copy (where only 500 were printed) of *Harry Potter and the Philosopher's Stone* sold for $40,355.

18,400 tons of paper (16,700 metric tons) were used for the first printing of *Harry Potter and the Deathly Hallows*.

J. K. Rowling dreamed up the names of the Hogwarts houses while flying and scribbled them on the back of an airplane air-sickness bag.

The initials "J. K." stand for Joanne Kathleen.

Fact or fiction

Books come in two types:

fact books that tell you about real things, like this one

fiction books, which are made up stories or novels

Comic capers

Manga are highly popular **Japanese comic books**, or graphic novels.

Manga is a huge business in Japan— worth about **$4.4 billion** a year.

Manga is not just for sci-fi and fantasy geeks—you'll see businessmen, schoolchildren, and housewives reading manga books on all kinds of subjects, from **sports** and **historical fiction** to **romance** and **cooking**.

Animated game and **movie versions** of manga stories have boosted their popularity around the world.

Comic books in France and Belgium are known as **Bandes Dessinées** (BDs).

Richard Scarry wrote and illustrated many books, such as *Best Word Book Ever.*

Roald Dahl became a best-seller with novels like *Charlie and the Chocolate Factory.*

Roger Hargreaves created the *Mr. Men* and *Little Miss* books, carried on by his son (pictured).

Who wrote the first play?

People have been going to the theater to watch plays (stories performed by actors) for thousands of years. The Ancient Greeks were the first to write these plays down. They performed "tragedies," in which characters come to a sticky end, and "comedies," in which characters make audiences laugh.

Five famous theaters

01 : Amazon Theater, Manaus, Brazil This grand Italian opera house has an unusual location—in the middle of the Brazilian rain forest.

02: Epidauros Theater, Epidauros, Greece A stunning ancient theater where you can see classical Greek tragedies performed today.

03: Sydney Opera House, Sydney, Australia An iconic Australian landmark on Sydney Harbour that opened in 1973.

04: Ford's Theater, Washington, D.C. President Abraham Lincoln was fatally shot here during a performance of *Our American Cousin* in 1865.

05: Globe Theatre, London, UK This replica open-air Elizabethan theater is built on the site of the original Globe Theatre where Shakespeare's plays were first performed.

Speak up!

The Ancient Greeks built open-air theaters consisting of rows of stone seats rising one above the other. They were designed so that sound would travel, allowing people sitting at the top to hear every word spoken by the actors on the circular stage. There were no microphones in those days!

How to : stage a play

01. Select a play to perform and hold auditions to cast the right person for each role.

02. Ensure the cast learns the lines of the script and hold plenty of rehearsals.

03. Appoint people to create the costumes and build the stage scenery.

04. Publicize the play to make sure you get a big audience to come and watch.

Theater forms

Plays
are stage performances in which actors act out stories

Operas
are plays in which the actors sing all the words

Ballets
are plays where the story is told through music and graceful dance techniques

Musicals
are popular shows packed with singing and dancing

Noh
is an old form of Japanese theater in which actors retell traditional stories

Kabuki
is another form of Japanese theater; it is performed only by men

RECORD BREAKER

The Mousetrap, a play by murder-mystery writer Agatha Christie has been showing in London since 1952—more than 55 years!

Theater don'ts

✗ **Never say the word "Macbeth."** Actors believe saying it will bring bad luck. Instead, they always call William Shakespeare's play "the Scottish play."

✗ **Never accept flowers before a performance.** Receiving flowers before a play begins is regarded as a bad omen. Don't worry afterward though—it is a lucky sign to be given flowers after the performance.

✗ **Never wish a fellow actor good luck.** Instead, tell them to "break a leg," although nobody is quite sure why.

10 longest-running Broadway shows

01: *The Phantom of the Opera* January 1988–present

02: *Cats* October 1982–September 2000

03: *Les Misérables* March 1987–May 2003

04: *A Chorus Line* July 1975–April 1990

05: *Oh Calcutta!* September 1976–August 1989

06: *Beauty and the Beast* September 1976–August 1989

07: *Chicago* September 1976–August 1989

08: *Rent* April 1996–September 2008

09: *The Lion King* November 1997–present

10: *Miss Saigon* April 1991–January 2001

I don't believe it!

In silent plays, called mimes, actors tell the stories using only facial expressions and movements of the hands and body. The French mime artist Marcel Marceau made audiences believe he was trapped in a room or taming a lion without saying a word.

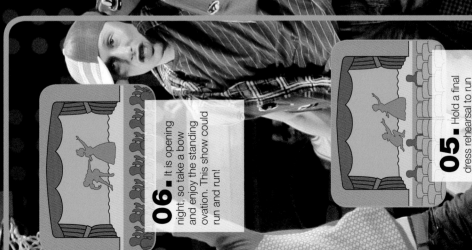

06. It is opening night, so take a bow and enjoy the standing ovation. This show could run and run!

05. Hold a final dress rehearsal to run through the script and perfect the performance.

Worldwide Will

William Shakespeare (1564–1616) was an English poet and playwright. Considered by many to be the greatest playwright of all time, his poems and plays have been translated into many languages and are popular all over the world. He was a master of both tragedies and comedies.

Famous Shakespearean tragedies
Romeo and Juliet
Hamlet
Othello
King Lear
Macbeth

Famous Shakespearean comedies
A Midsummer Night's Dream
The Merchant of Venice
The Merry Wives of Windsor
As You Like It
Twelfth Night

How do we spend free time?

People have found ways of relaxing and enjoying leisure time since history began. Some of the games we still play today have ancient origins, but the media and technology boom of the 20th century brought a rush of new entertainments and pastimes, with the spread of popular newspapers, movies, recorded music, radio, television, and computer games.

Ancient games

Mancala
The oldest game in the world, played with stones or shells placed in a series of holes.

Go
A 5,000-year-old Chinese strategy game with black and white playing pieces called "stones."

Senet
A board game enjoyed by the Egyptian pharaohs (kings). Tutankhamun was buried with senet boards.

Knucklebones
Popular in Greece and Rome; players toss bones in the air and catch them on the backs of their hands.

Chess
A popular board game that originated in India about 2,000 years ago.

INTERNET BOOM

The Internet is huge and still growing. It would take about 300 years to index all the current webpages.

SQUARE EYES

People in the US watch 250 billion hours of television a year, and two out of three households own three or more television sets.

Blasts from the past

713 BCE
First newspaper printed in China

1605
First newspaper printed in Europe

1880
First photograph in a newspaper

1895
Lumière brothers stage the first commercial screening of a film

1920
First commercial radio station goes on air in Pittsburgh

1936
BBC launches television service in the UK

1951
Color television in the US

1954
First transistor radio

1958
Hollywood Walk of Fame opens, studded with stars bearing the names of celebrities

1990
World Wide Web is launched

1994
First online newspapers

1994
First Internet café opens

2001
First podcast

- Early computer games ran on university computers. The first was *SpaceWar*! (1962).
- Atari developed home video games in the 1970s. The first, *Pong*, sold 150,000 copies.
- *Pokémon Red*, *Blue*, and *Green* is the highest selling computer game (20 million copies), followed by *Super Mario Bros 3* (18 million).
- Nintendo's console Wii is the fastest selling console of all time.

FAST FACTS

Radio first

The human voice was first heard on the radio on December 24, 1906. Canadian radio pioneer Reginald Fessenden sang *Oh, Holy Night* during a Christmas broadcast to radio operators at sea in the Atlantic.

WHAT'S IN A NAME?

The Academy of Motion Picture Arts and Sciences held its first award ceremony, the **Oscars**, in 1928. Librarian Margaret Herrick gave the Academy Awards their famous nickname—she said the statue for the winners reminded her of her Uncle Oscar!

TELEVISION RECORD BREAKERS

- *Meet the Press*, a news show, has appeared weekly on US television since 1947.
- The longest-running soap opera is *Guiding Light*, shown on US television since 1952. It began originally as a radio serial in 1937, making it more than 70 years old.
- The oldest sports show is *Hockey Night in Canada*, running since 1952.
- The UK's *Blue Peter* is the longest running children's show, begining in 1958.

Top 10 countries with the most moviegoers

01:	India	3,591,000,000
02:	US	1,402,700,000
03:	France	175,700,000
04:	Mexico	165,000,000
05:	UK	164,700,000
06:	Japan	160,500,000
07:	South Korea	143,000,000
08:	China	138,000,000
09:	Germany	127,300,000
10:	Spain	126,000,000

Gem of a gadget

Russian-Canadian millionaire Alex Schnaider owns the world's most expensive MP3 player. Made of 18 carat gold adorned with diamonds, it was a bargain, at $20,000!

Heavyweight read

The Sunday edition of the *New York Times* for September 14, 1987, contained 1,612 pages and weighed 12 lb (5.4 kg)!

NEWSPAPER INVENTOR

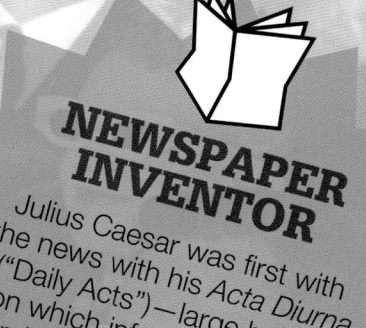

Julius Caesar was first with the news with his *Acta Diurna* ("Daily Acts")—large boards on which information about military victories, coming events, or major trials were displayed in Rome.

Best-selling newspapers, by country

Yomuiri Shimbun
Japan: 14 million

Das Bild
Germany: 3.8 million

Canako Xiaoxi
China: 2.6 million

The Sun
UK: 2.4 million

Chosun Ilbo
South Korea: 2.3 million

USA Today
US: 2.3 million

Dainik Jagran
India: 1.9 million

Liberty Times
Taiwan: 1.3 million

Thai Rath
Thailand: 1.2 million

Al-Ahram
Egypt: 900,000

What is art?

Art is paintings, sculptures, and a whole lot more. Artists today work with all kinds of media and materials—video clips, computer graphics, piles of bricks, driftwood, old car parts. Art is what the artist says it is. The goal is to make the viewer think and reflect on life and... well... art.

I don't! believe it!

It weighs 200 tons, is the height of four double-decker buses, and is almost as wide as a jumbo jet. *The Angel of the North*, a giant steel sculpture by Anthony Gormley stands beside a busy road in northeast England. It is 65 ft (20 m) high and has a wingspan of 175 ft (54 m).

Wall art

You think graffiti art was invented recently? Think again. It's one of the oldest art forms. The Italian word *graffiti* means "scratched," and the first graffiti artists were busy chipping patterns on rocks and pebbles 30,000 years ago. In the 1970s, graffiti got its modern meaning of spray-painted tags on urban buildings.

Some weird and wacky ideas

- Smear your body with honey and fish oil and wait for the swarms of flies (Zhang Huan)
- Put cans of your poop on show (Piero Manzoni)
- Cut a cow and calf in half (Damien Hirst)
- Exhibit your unmade bed and filthy underwear (Tracy Emin)
- Use dried elephant dung in your paintings (Chris Ofili)
- Freeze nine pints of your blood and use it to make a life-size cast of your head (Mark Quinn)

WEIRD OR WHAT?

Vincent van Gogh felt so badly about threatening fellow artist Paul Gauguin with a razor that he cut off part of his own ear. Then he painted a portrait of himself with a bandage around his head.

10 women artists

Until very recently art has been a man's world. These women artists did make it to the top.

- **Artemisia Gentileschi** Italian painter of the 1600s. Specialized in large pictures of heroic women

- **Elisabeth Louise Vigée-Lebrun** French portrait painter; she painted Queen Marie Antoinette, who later lost her head (no connection, apparently)

- **Rosa Bonheur** French 19th-century artist known for her animal sculptures and paintings; she liked to dress as a man

- **Berthe Morisot** French Impressionist. The artist Eduard Manet, her brother-in-law, painted a famous portrait of her looking very gloomy

- **Mary Cassatt** American 19th-century artist admired for her sensitive studies of women and children

- **Grandma Moses** Won fame for her folksy paintings of life down on the American farm when she was 80. It's never too late!

- **Georgia O'Keeffe** Pioneering figure in American 20th-century art noted for her paintings of flowers and buildings

- **Käthe Kollwitz** German artist and sculptor haunted by the death and suffering of World War I

- **Barbara Hepworth** English sculptor of abstract works in wood, stone, and metal. She died in a fire in her studio

- **Frida Kahlo** Mexican artist known for her stormy life and for brilliantly colored paintings

Self portrait by Elisabeth Louise Vigée-Lebrun

What was Pop Art?

A 1960s movement that turned everyday objects like soup cans and comic strips into cultural icons. Many of its images came from the world of entertainment—like the famous print of Marilyn Monroe by Andy Warhol.

It's a wrap

Avant-garde artists Christo and his wife Jeanne-Claude like to think big. Among their favorite large-scale projects is wrapping huge structures in fabric. In the past they have covered the Reichstag parliament building in Berlin, Germany (pictured), and Pont Neuf bridge in Paris, France.

Flat out

Contrary to popular belief **Michelangelo** did not paint the magnificent ceiling of the **Sistine Chapel** lying flat on his back—he crouched on a platform jutting out from the walls. The work took him four painful years.

So you want to be an art buff

Impressionism
Began in Paris during the 1860s, with artists painting glimpses of outdoor scenes

Post-impressionism
20th-century developments in French art

Cubism
Abstract paintings with squares and cubes

Fauvism
Artistic preference for strong, bright colors

Expressionism
Exploring feelings and emotions in paintings

Dadaism
Antiwar artists expressing their outrage

Constructivism
Using everyday items in abstract art

Surrealism
Exploring the mind by creating fantasy art

Postmodernism
Giving up on all previous "isms" and experimenting with new types of art

Great art robberies

💲 Most casual art theft
In 1911, a thief took Leonardo da Vinci's *Mona Lisa* off the wall of the Louvre in Paris, France, tucked it under his coat and strolled out. It was missing for two years.

💲 Biggest art haul
Thirteen artworks worth a total of $500 million were snatched from the Isabella Stewart Gardner Museum, Boston, in 1990. They are still missing.

💲 Most prolific art thief
In 2005, French waiter Stéphane Breitwieser admitted to stealing 239 artworks, said to be worth a total of $1.4 billion, over a 10-year period.

💲 Most stolen painting
Dutch painter Rembrandt's *Portrait of Jacob de Gheyn*, a picture of a man wearing a ruff, has been snatched four times. It has turned up in a taxi, in the luggage rack of a train, under a bench in a graveyard, and on the back of a bicycle.

💲 Most exciting recovery
Edvard Munch's masterpiece *The Scream*, seized from the National Gallery in Oslo during Norway's Winter Olympics in 1994, was recovered in a potato cellar three months later after a dramatic sting operation.

How do musicians know what notes to play?

When composing a piece of music, the composer writes down all the notes that each of the instruments will play—this is known as the score. The way the notes are written down indicates how high or low, fast or slow they should be played. Special instructions in Italian give the players more information.

Musical instructions

adagio
slow, restful
allegro
lively, fast
andante
at a moderate pace
appassionato
with passion
crescendo
getting louder
forte
loud
legato
smoothly
maestoso
majestic
piano
soft
presto
very fast
prestissimo
very, very fast
rallentando
slowing down
scherzando
humorously
strepitoso
noisy, boisterous

How to: sing like a superstar

01. Before you even start singing it is important to relax and stand with your feet shoulder-width apart.

02. Breathing correctly is crucial. Learn to inhale from the belly up. When you exhale, let the air come out rather than forcing it—imagine there is a candle in front of you and you are trying not to blow it out.

In the past, people made drums, rattles, and whistles out of **wood, seeds, and animal hide**. Simple flutes have been found that are between 22,000 and 35,000 years old. They were made by boring a series of holes into a **hollow animal bone** and blowing down it.

Beyond the grave

These dead musicians are still raking it in...

Elvis Presley
Died 1977
$49 million
(earnings in 2007)

John Lennon
Died 1980
$44 million
(earnings in 2007)

George Harrison
Died 2001
$22 million
(earnings in 2007)

Tupac Shakur
Died 1996
$9 million
(earnings in 2007)

James Brown
Died 2006
$5 million
(earnings in 2007)

Top ten best-selling albums ever

01: *Thriller*
Michael Jackson 1982
65 million Pop/R&B

02: *Back in Black*
AC/DC 1980
42 million Rock

03: *The Bodyguard*
Whitney Houston 1992
42 million Pop/R&B

04: *Greatest Hits*
Eagles 1976
41 million Rock

05: *Saturday Night Fever*
Bee Gees/various 1977
40 million Disco

06: *Dark Side of the Moon*
Pink Floyd 1973
40 million Rock

07: *Bat Out of Hell*
Meat Loaf 1977
37 million Rock

08: *Come on Over*
Shania Twain 1997
36 million Country

09: *Sgt. Pepper's Lonely Hearts Club Band* Beatles 1967
32 million Rock/Pop

10: *Falling into You*
Celine Dion 1996
32 million Pop

In numbers

88
The number of keys on a piano (36 black and 52 white)

1982
The year compact discs were introduced

$164,930
The amount a Led Zeppelin fan paid for two tickets for the group's 2007 reunion concert in London

$3.5 million
The sum paid at a Christie's auction in 2006 for a rare 300-year-old violin made by Stradivarius

1.7 billion
Digital music downloads in 2007

Bum notes

● The worst singer ever must be Florence Jenkins Foster, who gave recitals to fashionable audiences in New York City in the 1930s despite her inability to hold a note. She claimed she could reach top F (that's really high) after being involved in an accident in a taxicab. You can hear her murdering Mozart on YouTube.

● William Hung was a contestant on the television program *American Idol*. His audition was noteworthy for all the wrong reasons, but it did land him an album deal.

World music

shaman's rattle *Native American*

sitar *Indian*

mbira *Southern African*

bagpipes *Scottish*

didgeridoo *Aboriginal Australian*

Types of music

■ classical
■ country
■ jazz
■ hip hop
■ latin
■ rap
■ reggae
■ R&B
■ rock
■ blues
■ pop
■ soul
■ world
■ folk
■ opera
■ disco
■ metal
■ punk
■ reggae
■ ska
■ dance and techno

03. Once you have chosen a song you love (or something you have written), try to sing by making the sound resonate from your cheeks and the roof of your mouth.

WHAT'S IN A NAME?

As Slow as Possible is the appropriate name of a piece of music written by American composer John Cage. The performance, which is being played on a church organ in Germany, started in 2001 and is due to finish in 2639!

04. Practice makes perfect. Do this by standing in front of a mirror and try not to laugh at the faces you find yourself making as you sing. Soon you will be performing in front of thousands of adoring fans.

Weird or what?

■ The **thermin** is an electronic musical instrument that is **played without even touching it.** To play, you must move your hands around various antennas to control the pitch and volume. The instrument generates an eerie sound, which makes it perfect for use in thriller movie soundtracks.

Bob Marley
Died 1981
$4 million
(earnings in 2007)

timpani

01

piccolo

violin

02

xylophone

06

flute

tubular bells

01 At the heart of the orchestra, the **string family** makes up the largest part. Played with a bow or by "plucking," they usually lead the way through a musical piece.

02 Comprising anything that makes a noise when struck, the **percussion family** is known as the "kitchen department" and includes both tuned instruments, like the xylophone, and untuned instruments, such as cymbals.

03 With many of its instruments originally made from wood, the **woodwind family** today is a clan of plastic, silver, and gold versions. They mostly make their sound when the player blows against a reed (thin piece of wood) in the mouthpiece.

04 The instruments of the **brass family**, such as the trumpet and trombone, produce a distinctive sound made by the vibration of the players' lips as they blow into their instruments.

05 **Keyboards** include the piano and its relatives, as well as the electronic synthesizer, which can make a variety of weird and wonderful sounds. It stands apart from the rest of the orchestra in producing sounds digitally rather than acoustically.

06 Standing on a raised platform waving a baton to keep time, the **conductor** directs the orchestra through the musical piece. All members of the orchestra must be able to see the conductor for guidance and prompts.

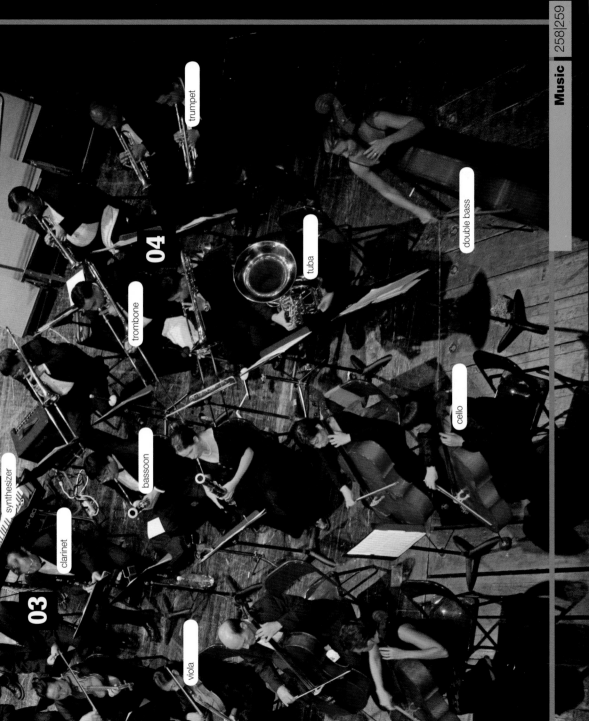

piano

drums

french horn

oboe

synthesizer

clarinet

viola

bassoon

cello

trombone

tuba

trumpet

double bass

05

03

04

Ways to be a good sport

Grr... it's easy to fly off the handle when playing a game. A tricky opponent, a disappointing performance, or a suspicion of cheating can all add fuel to the fire. Show what a good sport you are with these top tips.

01 Learn the rules of the game so you know what's right and what's wrong.

02 Listen to your coach so you can improve your game.

03 Shake hands with your opponents and the referee before and after the game.

04 Be prepared to sit out a game so a teammate can have a turn, even if you are the star player.

05 Don't show off. Just play your best and people will notice you.

06 Don't cheat or blame your teammates when decisions are not going your way.

07 Keep a clear head. Congratulate your teammates and opponents on their performance, regardless of the outcome.

Top 10 most popular sports worldwide

The most popular sports could mean most watched, most played, or most revenue-generating. This list considers all three factors, with soccer topping the charts for all of them.

01: Soccer
02: Cricket
03: Tennis
04: Hockey
05: Baseball
06: Basketball
07: Volleyball
08: Table tennis
09: Rugby
10: Golf

What game do 250 million people play?

Soccer. From streets to stadiums, the beautiful game is played all over the world. It's a sport that everyone understands—kick a ball, score a goal. Whether it's hit, struck, passed, or caught, a ball is at the heart of many of the most popular sports. Even those that don't involve a ball still revolve around fixed rules and physical effort. Ready to play?

Tribal traditions

Many rugby teams from the Southern Hemisphere don war paint and perform traditional dances to prepare themselves and intimidate their opponents before big international matches.

Sporting superstars

Pelé
Scoring 77 goals for his country (a national record), the legendary Brazilian is regarded as soccer's perfect player.

Michael Jordan
The US basketball star had an incredible scoring rate and defensive record during the 1980s and 1990s.

Babe Ruth
Playing for 20 years from 1914, Babe Ruth is the most celebrated baseball player in US history.

Jonah Lomu
In 1994, New Zealand rugby player Jonah Lomu became the youngest player for the All Blacks, at age 19.

How to: serve an ace

01. Stand sideways behind the baseline and throw the tennis ball up above you.

04. Push up with your legs and roll your right shoulder forward to hit the ball.

Bizarre sports terms

SILLY
A fielder who stands very close to the batter in cricket

DRIBBLING
Running with a soccer ball under close control. In basketball, the term is used to describe the motion of bouncing the ball

SPIKE
When a beach volleyball player jumps above the net to smash the ball hard at the ground

LOVE
A zero-point score in a tennis game

BIRDIE, EAGLE, DOUBLE EAGLE
These golfing terms refer to the par (standard number of golf strokes) for each hole. "Birdie" means a score of one stroke under par, "eagle" means a score of two strokes under par, and "double eagle" is a rare three strokes under par

Sound idea
In 2008, the first blind tennis tournament was held in the UK. A bell inside the tennis ball helps the players keep track of it during rallies, while tactile lines around the court assist them in finding their way.

I don't believe it!
The only sport to be played on the Moon is golf. In 1971, *Apollo 14*'s US astronaut Alan Shepard landed on the lunar surface and struck two golf balls. He described the balls as going for "miles and miles and miles!"

02. Raise your racket and start to swing.

03. While bending the knees, drop the racket behind your back.

05. Snap your wrist down and smash your racket against the ball, generating as much speed as possible.

06. Watch the ball fly past your helpless opponent and enjoy your first ace (unreturnable serve)!

In numbers

0.3
The time, in seconds, that it takes a volleyball to travel from one baseline of the court to the other when served by a top player at a speed of 121 mph (194 kph)

1
The total number of paying spectators at the Olympic croquet final in 1900, the first and last time the sport was played at the Games

8
The number of left-handed tennis players to have won a Wimbledon singles title

152
The highest margin in an international rugby match, when Argentina beat Paraguay 152–0 in 2002

173
The number of hits during one 60-second table tennis rally between two female players in 1973

155 mph
(259 kph) The fastest recorded tennis serve, delivered by Andy Roddick at the UK's Stella Artois Championships in 2004

501
The highest ever individual score in a cricket match, made by Brian Lara for Warwickshire (UK) in 1994

2,666
The number of strokes in a single squash rally, recorded in the UK in 1994

199,854
How many spectators watched the 1950 World Cup game between Brazil and Uruguay, the highest official attendance at a soccer match

5 million
Soccer officials worldwide

20 million
Netball players worldwide

1 billion
The average global audience for soccer's World Cup final

Cathy Freeman
Australian sprinter Cathy Freeman won gold in the 400 m race at the Olympic and Commonwealth Games, and World Championships.

Martina Navratilova
Czech-born Martina Navratilova won 59 tennis titles (18 singles, 31 doubles, and 10 mixed doubles).

Ellen MacArthur
This British yachtswoman broke the world record for fastest solo circumnavigation of the globe in 2005.

Jack Nicklaus
Known as "Golden bear," this US golfer won a record-breaking 18 titles in a career spanning 25 years.

Odd origins

Tennis
French monks first played tennis in about the 11th century. The name "tennis" means "take this" in French, which the monks would shout as they served the ball.

Table tennis
This sport began in Victorian England, when dinner guests turned their tables into mini tennis courts and used their champagne corks as balls.

Croquet
During the 14th century, French peasants used wooden mallets to whack a wooden ball through hoops of bent branches.

Basketball
This game was first played using peach baskets on poles for hoops. If a team scored, the referee climbed a ladder to get the ball.

How to: **win the decathlon**

The decathlon consists of 10 track and field events. It is held over two days and the winner is the athlete with the highest total points across all 10 events. Decathlon contests are open to male athletes. Female athletes compete in the heptathlon, which has seven different sports: 100 meters hurdles, high jump, shot put, 200 meters, long jump, javelin, and 800 meters. Ready, set, go!

Decathlon events
- ☺ 100 meters
- ☺ long jump
- ☺ shot put
- ☺ high jump
- ☺ 400 meters
- ☺ 110 meters hurdles
- ☺ discus
- ☺ pole vault
- ☺ javelin
- ☺ 1,500 meters

Event 6: 110 meter hurdles

01. Sprint toward the first hurdle. As you approach, raise the knee on your leading leg.

02. As you jump, the knee on the leading leg should be in line with the center of your body and the trailing leg kept low to minimize the height of the leap so your speed is not affected.

03. Pull your trailing leg down as quickly as possible when your heel crosses the hurdle.

04. On landing, the trailing leg should go straight into the running stride.

Event 1: 100 meters sprint

01. Wear an aerodynamic body suit and very light shoes.

02. Position yourself on the starting blocks. Crouch on one knee with your feet on the pedals of the blocks.

03. With your hands slightly more than shoulder-width apart, place your fingers on the track.

04. At the command of "set," push your feet back firmly against the pedals of the blocks.

05. Raise your hips higher than your shoulders.

06. On the starter's gun, explode out of the blocks. Pump your arms, keep your eyes on the track, and run as fast as you can until you cross the finish line.

Event 7: discus

01. Grip the discus with the tips of your fingers and your palm resting on top, and extend your throwing arm behind you. Rotate your torso to set a throwing rhythm.

02. Spin around one and a half times from the back of the circle to the front, shifting your body weight from foot to foot.

03. Release the discus at shoulder level. As it spins into the distance, continue to turn your body to avoid overstepping the boundary.

Event 2: long jump

01. Run as fast as you can down the approach runway.

02. When you reach the takeoff board (a white strip in the runway), jump!

03. Move your legs and arms in a rapid cycling motion to maintain an upright body position.

04. Land feetfirst in the sand pit, leaning forward to prevent losing distance by falling backward into the pit.

Event 8: pole vault

01. Grasp the pole at one end and hold it aloft. Run up to the crossbar and lower the pole as you approach.

02. Plant the pole in the box in front of the crossbar. The pole will bend as you lever yourself over the crossbar.

03. As you descend, push the pole away so it does not knock down the crossbar.

180

Event 3: shot put

01. Stand in the throwing circle. Face away from the direction of the throw (the white board marks at the front of the throwing circle), tuck the shot (a heavy metal ball) between your neck and shoulders, and crouch.

02. Shift your weight from right to left side and then spin on the ball of the left foot. Your left arm should come forward and point in the direction you want to throw.

03. Keeping your left side braced, release the shot. Aim to throw it farther than any of your competitors.

04. The crossbar height is raised after every round and the winner is the competitor who clears the highest crossbar.

Event 4: high jump

01. Make a curved run up to the high jump and launch yourself upward. Twist your legs, hips, and shoulders as you ascend.

02. As you reach the horizontal bar, arch your body backward and propel yourself over the bar headfirst.

03. As your body crosses the bar, flex your hips to bring your legs up and over.

04. Land shoulder first on the cushioned landing area.

Event 9: javelin

01. Hold the javelin over your shoulder and, as you near the throwing line as you run down the track, cross your legs in preparation for the ultimate throw.

02. Untwist your legs as you reach the throwing line and pull your throwing arm backward.

03. Thrust the throwing arm forward and release the javelin. The person who throws the javelin the farthest is the winner.

Event 5: 400 meters

01. Take up your position on the starting block, following the top tips recommended in the 100 meters sprint.

02. At the sound of the starter's gun, start running, and be sure to stay in your lane for the entire race.

03. This distance is exactly one lap on a standard running track, so pace yourself and build up to your fantastically fast finish!

Event 10: 1,500 meters

01. Start running. After the first curve, leave your lane and move toward the inside lane so you can compete for pole position with the other competitors.

02. Stay behind the front runner for as long as possible—they take the full brunt of wind resistance.

03. When you are ready, make a break for the finish line and start accelerating.

Who was the first Olympic champion?

The first Olympic Games were held in Greece in 776 BCE. There was only one event—a sprint of about 600 feet (200 meters) in which the competitors ran naked! The winning runner was a male cook named Koroibos. The prize for athletes back then, along with great fame, was a wreath of olive leaves and a statue of them placed at Olympia. The modern Olympic Games take place every four years with (fully dressed) competitors from all around the world.

The Olympic gold medals are actually sterling silver, covered with a very thin coat of gold.

SINCE 1928, OLYMPIC MEDALS HAVE FEATURED THE SAME DESIGN ON THE FRONT.

- ribbon
- Olympic rings
- Colosseum of ancient Athens
- Greek goddess

XXIX OLYMPIAD BEIJING 2008

WHAT'S IN A NAME?

Gymnasium comes from the Greek word *gymnos*, which means "**school for naked exercise**." The original Olympians did just this, whipping their clothes off to strut their stuff in a range of challenges and competitions.

FAST FACTS

On your mark

01: An **electronic gun** sound generator is used to start races. When the trigger is pulled, a signal is passed to the **sound generator**, which produces a sound and transmits it by cable to a loudspeaker in the back of each competitor's starting block.

02: Electronic starting blocks can distinguish between an athlete's unintentional movement and a **false start**.

03: At the finish line, athletes can be timed to within a thousandth of a second using a **split-video photo-finish system**. An image of the athletes is shown on monitors for judges to study. They can move a cursor over each athlete and read the time from a scale.

In numbers

0
The number of female competitors at the first modern Olympic Games

4
How many years between each Olympics

5
The number of rings on the Olympic logo. They represent the five competing continents—counting North and South America as one continent, and not counting Antarctica as there are no events for penguins—yet

10
The age of the youngest Olympic competitor—Greek gymnast Dimitrios Loundras who competed in Athens in 1896

72
The age of the oldest Olympic medal winner—Swedish shooter Oscar Swahn won silver in 1920

205
How many nations are eligible to qualify

3.5 billion
The global television audience of the Olympics, the world's largest broadcast event, made up of people from 220 countries

Olympic greats

Lucius An ancient stone records the achievements of this Roman athlete who competed "in all the athletic festivals in a manner worthy of victory."

Jesse Owens At the 1936 Olympics, this US athlete won gold in four events and his long jump world record was held for more than 25 years.

Tanni Grey-Thompson One of the greatest Olympic paralympians, this UK athlete competed in a wheelchair, winning 16 medals, including 11 golds.

Nadia Comaneci In 1976, this 14-year-old Romanian became the first Olympic gymnast to score a perfect 10.0.

Steve Redgrave This British rower picked up five golds in the 1980s, 1990s, and 2000, with all his medals won as part of a team.

Raisa Smetanina In the 1980s, this Russian skier became the first woman in history to win ten winter Olympic medals.

Michael Phelps This US swimmer has won 14 golds, more than any Olympian in history. He holds the record for most golds from a single Olympics, winning eight gold at the Beijing Games in 2008.

Good sports?

Olympic sports come and go. These weird and wonderful events were once part of the games, but have since bitten the dust.

- tug-of-war ▪ croquet ▪ chariot racing ▪ running ▪ wearing armor ▪ jumping ▪ holding weights

Winter sports include:

- alpine skiing ▪ bobsleding
- cross-country skiing ▪ curling
- figure skating ▪ freestyle skiing
- ice skating ▪ luge ▪ short-track
- speed skating ▪ ski jumping
- snowboarding
- tobogganing

Summer sports include:

- archery ▪ badminton ▪
baseball ▪ basketball ▪
boxing ▪ canoeing ▪ cycling ▪
decathlon ▪ diving ▪ fencing ▪
gymnastics ▪ handball ▪ hockey
▪ horseback riding ▪ judo ▪ modern
pentathlon ▪ rowing ▪ sailing ▪
shooting ▪ soccer ▪ softball ▪
swimming ▪ tennis ▪ table
tennis ▪ track and field ▪
triathlon ▪ volleyball ▪
water polo

No horseplay

There was no entry for the neighing nags hoping to compete in Australia's Olympics in 1956. Due to quarantine laws, all events involving horses had to be held 9,600 miles (15,500 km) away in Sweden.

Cold conditions, poor publicity, and a lack of international backing resulted in a disastrous Olympics in Athens in 1896. Not only did some athletes pay their travel expenses themselves, but some contestants were tourists who just happened to be on vacation in Greece!

Climate and conditions

Snow shortage

There was **not enough snow** at Innsbruck for the winter Olympic Games in 1964. Instead, the Austrian army **moved 20,000 ice bricks** for the bobsleigh and luge runs, and 130,000 ft³ (40,000 m³) of snow to the ski slopes.

High altitude

When the summer Olympic Games were held in Mexico City in 1968, it proved a challenge for the competitors. At **7,200 ft (2,200 m) above sea level**, the location gave many athletes **breathing difficulties**, as they struggled to adapt to air with **30 percent less oxygen** than normal.

Extreme weather

Warm sunshine at the winter Olympics in the Swiss town of St. Moritz resulted in the **cancellation of** a skating contest in 1928. This was followed by **18 hours of torrential rain**, with all events postponed.

Record breakers

The US has won in excess of 2,400 **summer Olympic medals**, more than any other country.

The country to win the **most winter Olympic medals** is Norway, with almost 300.

Australia, France, Greece, Switzerland, and the UK are the only five **countries to compete in all the modern Olympic Games**, since they began in 1896.

Cycling, fencing, gymnastics, swimming, and track and field are the only **five sports to feature at every modern summer Olympic Games**.

How to: **manage the Olympic flame**

01. Angle a special mirror toward the Sun to light the wick of the torch.

02. Stay in shape because running is the most common way to transport the famous flame between Olympia, Greece, and the Olympic site of the host city.

03. If you're not up to the run, take your pick from these other popular methods of torch transportation: boats, aircraft, horses, canoes, or camels.

04. Keep the flame burning overnight in special cauldrons along the route.

05. It's the home straight now. On arrival at the host stadium, enjoy a lap of honor before lighting the cauldron of cauldrons with the Olympic flame.

History

When did the pharaohs rule?

The great Ancient Egyptian civilization arose more than 5,000 years ago among farmers living on the banks of the River Nile. It lasted for 3,000 years—longer than any other civilization on Earth. What is really remarkable is that throughout this long history, the way of life and the art and sculpture of Ancient Egypt remained largely unchanged.

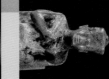

Khufu
Ordered the construction of the Great Pyramid

Hatshepsut
Powerful queen who ruled Egypt for 20 years and even wore the pharaoh's ritual false beard

Akhenaten
Banished the traditional gods and set up his own religion

Tutankhamun
In 1922, the tomb of this boy-pharaoh was found with all its magnificent burial goods intact

Rameses II
Reigned over Egypt for 67 years and built more monuments and statues than any other pharaoh

Cleopatra VII
One of the most famous women in history, she killed herself when Egypt fell to the Romans

FAST FACTS

Pharaohs

01: The king of Egypt was called the "pharaoh," a word that originally meant "great house," or "palace," but came to describe the man who lived there.

02: He was thought to be a living god and wore a ritual false beard as a symbol of royalty.

03: He also wore a red crown and a white crown symbolizing the union of Upper Egypt (the river valley) with Lower Egypt (the Nile delta).

THE WRITE STUFF
The Egyptians used a form of writing called hieroglyphs, made up of about 700 different picture signs.

Nile River
» Flood water used to irrigate farmland
» Was a highway for transporting goods
» Provided fish for food

In numbers

The Great Pyramid is the largest stone structure on Earth.

2.5 tons
The average weight of each block used in the construction of the Great Pyramid

20
How many years it took to build

480 ft
(146 m) The height from ground to capstone

755 ft
(230 m) The length of each of the four sides

500 miles
(800 km) The distance blocks were transported from the quarry to the pyramid site

4,000
The number of workers involved in building it

2,300,000
The total number of blocks used in its construction

6,500,000 tons
The total weight of the pyramid

RECORD BREAKER

The pharaoh Pepy II reigned for 94 years—the **longest reign** in all of recorded history. He was only six when he came to the throne in 2278 BCE and died in 2184 BCE, at the ripe old age of 100.

Egyptian gods

Ra
The Sun god, who also represented kingship

Amun
Creator god, associated with fertility

Mut
Wife of Amun and goddess of war

How to: make a mummy

01. Wash the body as soon as possible after death.

02. Take out the brain. It is useless, so you can yank it out through the nostrils using a hook and throw it away.

03. Remove the internal organs and place them inside special containers called canopic jars. Leave the heart as it contains the soul.

04. Fill the body cavity with a salty mineral called natron to absorb moisture. Cover the body with more natron and leave it to dry for 40 days.

05. Rub the skin with oils, stuff sawdust inside the body to give it shape, and put balls of linen into the eye sockets.

06. Wrap the body in linen bandages, placing amulets (magic charms) between layers to protect the mummy on its journey to the afterlife.

Tell me more: kingdoms and dynasties

Early Dynastic Period
c. 3100–2686 BCE
1st and 2nd dynasties

Old Kingdom
c. 2686–2181 BCE
3rd–6th dynasties

First Intermediate Period
c. 2181–2055 BCE
7th–11th dynasties

Middle Kingdom
c. 2055–1650 BCE
11th–14th dynasties

Second Intermediate Period
c. 1650–1550 BCE
15th–17th dynasties

New Kingdom
c. 1550–1069 BCE
18th–20th dynasties

Third Intermediate Period
c. 1069–715 BCE
21st–25th dynasties

Late Period
c. 715–332 BCE
26th–30th dynasties; Persian kings

Ptolemaic Period
333–30 BCE
Macedonian and Ptolemaic dynasties

Royal burials

The pyramids were built as tombs for the pharaohs during the period known as the Old Kingdom, more than 4,500 years ago.

I don't believe it!

Egyptian noblewomen at court tied scented cones of animal fat to the tops of their wigs to make themselves smell nice as the perfumed fat melted. Both men and women wore colored eye makeup.

WHAT'S IN A NAME?

The Egyptians knew their country as **Kemet**, which means "the Black Land," from the rich dark soil of the Nile valley. They called the surrounding desert "the Red Land" — *Deshret*.

The Egyptians worshiped around 2,000 different gods and goddesses.

Anubis
Jackal-headed god of the dead and mummification

Sobek
Crocodile god and ruler of the Nile

Osiris
God of the dead and the afterlife

Isis
Wife of Osiris and goddess of nature and fertility

Horus
Falcon-headed god of the sky, light, and life

Seth
God of deserts, storms, chaos, and evil

Thoth
God of wisdom and writing

Who were the Ancient Greeks?

Ancient Greece was not a single country—the Greeks lived in separate city-states all around the Aegean Sea and often fought violently with each other. They were united by the Greek language and writing, by shared myths and legends about the gods, and by a common enemy, the Persians.

Athenian politics

- The Athenians introduced a new form of government called democracy ("rule of the people"). **All male citizens over 18 could speak and vote in the assembly, where laws were made.**
- They also made up the juries that heard legal cases.
- Once a year Athenians voted to banish an unpopular citizen from the city.

Blasts from the past

2000–1450 BCE
Minoan civilization flourishes on Crete

1450–1100 BCE
Mycenaean civilization rises and falls on mainland Greece

800–600 BCE
Greeks found colonies in Ionia and Sicily and around the Black Sea

776 BCE
First games held at Olympia

c. 750 BCE
Homer composes the *Iliad* and the *Odyssey*

508 BCE
Start of Athenian democracy

490 BCE
Battle of Marathon—Athenians defeat a Persian invasion

480–479 BCE
Sparta and Athens combine forces to prevent a second Persian invasion

450 BCE
Parthenon temple is built in Athens

441–404 BCE
War between the city-states ends in Spartan victory

371 BCE
Defeat of Sparta by Thebes

338 BCE
Philip of Macedon makes himself effective ruler of the Greek city-states

334–300 BCE
Philip's son Alexander the Great conquers Persia

Places in the Greek world

Mount Olympus: Legendary home of the Greek gods

Delphi: Site of a famous oracle (wise counsel) that the Greeks consulted about the future

Athens: Most powerful of the city-states; birthplace of Greek democracy

Olympia: Where the Olympic Games were held

Sparta: Warrior city/state in southern Greece

Greek gods and goddesses

Aphrodite
Goddess of love

Apollo
God of the Sun, healing, and medicine

Artemis
Goddess of the Moon and hunting

Asclepius
God of medicine and healing

Athena
Goddess of wisdom and war

Demeter
Goddess of grain and the harvest

Five famous Greeks

Archimedes
Mathematician and inventor. He developed a device for pumping water, which is known as the Archimedes screw

Aristotle
Philosopher who studied the natural world, one of the most influential figures in the history of learning and science

Hippocrates
Physician who believed there was a rational explanation for illnesses and made careful notes of symptoms

Homer
Every Greek knew this poet's most famous works, the *Iliad* and the *Odyssey*, which told the story of the Trojan War

Socrates
Philosopher who was interested in how people should behave. He was condemned to death by drinking a deadly poison

I don't believe it!

According to a famous legend, the playwright Aeschylus was killed when an eagle dropped a tortoise on his head. Seems that the bird mistook the old fellow's shining bald pate for a handy rock to crack open the shell!

Spartan living

Sparta, Athens' main rival for power in Greece, was a military state. From age seven, boys lived in army barracks. Spartan girls were also trained in gymnastics and athletics. The goal was to make them healthy mothers of future soldiers.

The Greek god Pan was half-man and half-goat.

He played a set of reed pipes—the "panpipes." When humans saw him they were overcome by a terrible fear—from which we get our word "panic."

Good sports

- The Olympic Games was the greatest of four athletic festivals that attracted competitors from all over the Greek world.
- **Events included running, chariot racing, horse races, boxing, wrestling, discus, and javelin.**
- Athletes were naked.
- **They competed for a prize of an olive crown.**
- Wars stopped to allow people to travel to and from the games.

Alexander the Great

01: Alexander became king of Macedon when he was only 19.

02: He led a great invasion force of Greeks and Macedonians against the Persians.

03: He made himself master of an empire that stretched from Egypt as far as Afghanistan and northwest India.

04: He founded more than 70 towns, naming 13 of them after himself.

05: He died suddenly at the age of 32.

FAST FACTS

Greek architecture

Doric columns
Thick and the capitals (top stones) were undecorated

Ionic columns
More elegant—the capitals were decorated with two scrolls (volutes)

Corinthian capitals
Elaborately carved with acanthus leaves

Zeus
King of the gods, master of the sky

Poseidon
God of the sea and earthquakes

Hermes
Messenger of the gods

Hera
Wife of Zeus, protector of women

Hades (Pluto)
god of the underworld

Dionysius
God of wine, drama, and fertility

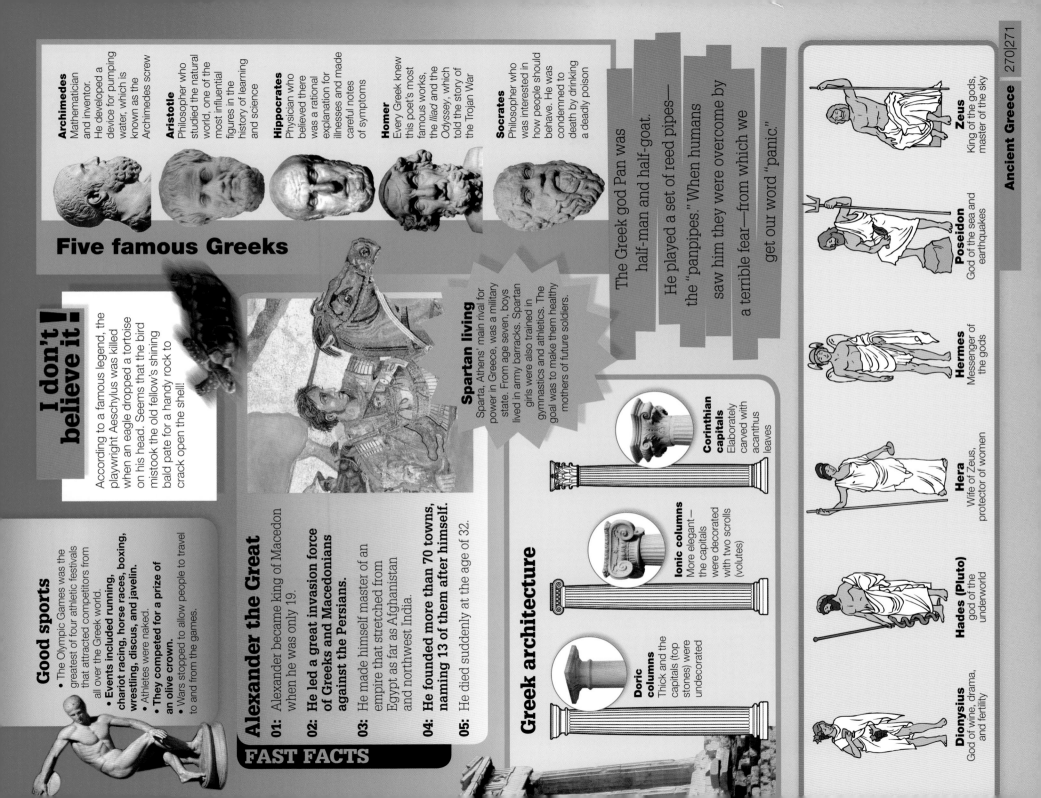

How large was the Roman Empire?

At its fullest extent, in the 2nd century CE, it stretched 2,500 miles (4,000 km) from Spain in the west to the Caspian Sea in the east, and from Britain in the north to Egypt in the south. Of course, this didn't happen overnight—in fact, it took more than 700 years for Rome to grow from a small village into a superpower.

Types of gladiator

Gladiators were trained in the art of killing for the entertainment of the Roman crowds in the Colosseum. They mostly fought armed combats with swords (gladii), but some specialized in other weapons and tactics.

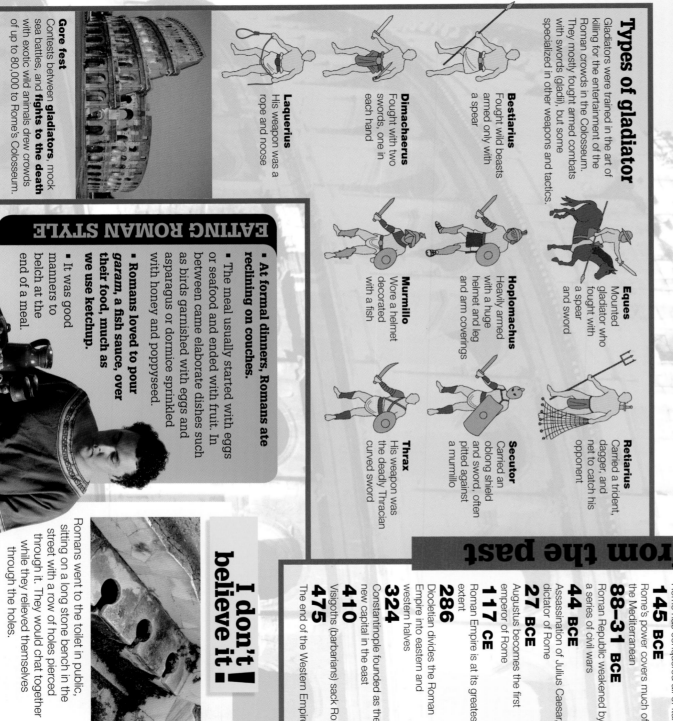

Laquerius
His weapon was a rope and noose

Dimachaerus
Fought with two swords, one in each hand

Bestiarius
Fought wild beasts armed only with a spear

Eques
Mounted gladiator who fought with a spear and sword

Murmillo
Wore a helmet decorated with a fish

Hoplomachus
Heavily armed with a huge helmet and leg and arm coverings

Retiarius
Carried a trident, dagger, and net to catch his opponent

Thrax
His weapon was the deadly Thracian curved sword

Secutor
Carried an oblong shield and sword, often pitted against a murmillo

Gore fest
Contests between gladiators, mock sea battles, and **fights to the death** with exotic wild animals drew crowds of up to 80,000 to Rome's Colosseum.

EATING ROMAN STYLE

- **At formal dinners, Romans ate reclining on couches.**
- The meal usually started with eggs or seafood and ended with fruit. In between came elaborate dishes such as birds garnished with eggs and asparagus or dormice sprinkled with honey and poppyseed.
- **Romans loved to pour *garam*, a fish sauce, over their food, much as we use ketchup.**
- It was good manners to belch at the end of a meal.

I don't believe it!
Romans went to the toilet in public, sitting on a long stone bench in the street with a row of holes pierced through it. They would chat together while they relieved themselves through the holes.

Blasts from the past

753 BCE
Traditional date of the foundation of Rome

509 BCE
Romans drive out their kings and found a republic

272 BCE
Rome has conquered all of Italy

145 BCE
Rome's power covers much of the Mediterranean

88–31 BCE
Roman Republic weakened by a series of civil wars

44 BCE
Assassination of Julius Caesar, dictator of Rome

27 BCE
Augustus becomes the first emperor of Rome

117 CE
Roman Empire is at its greatest extent

286
Diocletian divides the Roman Empire into eastern and western halves

324
Constantinople founded as the new capital in the east

410
Visigoths (barbarians) sack Rome

475
The end of the Western Empire

5,000 animals were killed in a single afternoon in the **games** held to celebrate the opening of the **Colosseum** in 80 CE.

How to: put on a toga

01. Drape one end of the toga over your left shoulder so that it falls all the way down at the front to your left foot.

02. Holding the rest of the toga about midway along its length, take it under your right arm at waist level.

03. Lift it loosely across the front of your body and throw the remaining length of cloth over your left shoulder.

04. Arrange the folds of cloth neatly and pull the left end up to hang elegantly over your left forearm.

Warning! Better not to attempt toga dressing unless you have a house slave to help you!

Roman army

Legionary
Ordinary footsoldier. Legionaries were Roman citizens and joined up for 20 to 25 years. They were armed with a shield, sword, and dagger

Contubernium
Unit of eight legionaries led by a decanus

Century
Unit of 10 contubernia (80 men)

Centurion
Commanded a century

Cohort
Usually made up of six centuries (480 men)

Legion
Made up of 10 cohorts (about 5,000 men)

Legate
Commanding officer of a legion

Signifer
Carried the legion's silver eagle standard into battle

Cornicen
Trumpeter who blew a horn to signal each command during a battle

Cavalry soldier
Fought on horseback with spears and javelins. The cavalry were usually noncitizen soldiers, often foreign recruits

The Romans built **aqueducts** to carry water into their cities. One of Rome's aqueducts brought water from 43 miles (70 km) away.

Five terrible emperors

Tiberius 14–37 CE
Gloomy and paranoid, he spied on his enemies. Eventually retired to the island of Capri, where he is said to have thrown his victims off a cliff.

Caligula 37–41 CE
Tiberius's grandson, famous for his cruelty and probably insane. He tried to have his horse elected to the senate

Nero 54–68 CE
A hated monster who murdered his own mother and believed himself to be a great musician, even though he was awful.

Commodus 180–192 CE
Addicted to gladiatorial combat and even performed in the arena himself (the other gladiators had blunted swords)

Elagabalus 218–222 CE
Loved dressing up and behaving outrageously. At one party he showered so many roses on his guests that many of them suffocated

The Romans invented **concrete** by mixing rubble with lime (burned chalk) and volcanic ash.

Five strong emperors

Augustus 27 BCE –14 CE
Ended the chaos of civil war (and the Republic) by making himself emperor. Created a lasting system of strong, efficient government

Hadrian 117–138 CE
Traveled throughout the Empire and strengthened its frontiers. He built Hadrian's Wall in Britain as a barrier against the Picts

Marcus Aurelius 161–180 CE
Philosophically minded emperor who wrote a famous book of meditations. Biggest mistake was to make Commodus his heir (see above)

Diocletian 284–305 CE
General who reorganized the army and split the Empire in two to make it easier to govern, then astonished everyone by retiring to the seaside

Constantine I 307–337 CE
The first Christian emperor who founded the city of Constantinople (modern-day Istanbul) as a second capital

How old is China?

Chinese history traditionally begins with the Shang Dynasty, nearly 4,000 years ago, but Chinese civilization goes back much further, to around 9,000 years ago, when farming started on the Yellow River in northern China. The Shang Dynasty was the first in a line of imperial dynasties that lasted until 1911.

Tell me more: Chinese dynasties

商 **Shang Dynasty**
c. 1766–1122 BCE

西周 **Zhou Dynasty**
1122–221 BCE

春秋 **Springs and Falls Period**
770–480 BCE

戰國 **Warring States period**
480–221 BCE

秦 **Qin Dynasty**
221–206 BCE

西漢 **Han Dynasty**
206 BCE–220 CE

三國 **Three Kingdoms**
220–581

隋 **Sui Dynasty**
581–618

唐 **Tang Dynasty**
618–907

五代十國 **Five Dynasties and Ten Kingdoms**
907–960

南宋 **Song Dynasty**
960–1279

元 **Yuan (Mongol) Dynasty**
1279–1368

明 **Ming Dynasty**
1368–1644

清 **Qing Dynasty**
1644–1911

How to: make paper

01. Take lots of old rags, the inner bark of a mulberry tree, and pieces of bamboo.

02. Leave to soak in water and pound thoroughly with a wooden mallet to break up all the fibers.

03. Pour the mixture through a coarsely woven cloth and let the water drain through it, leaving the fibers behind on the cloth.

Testing times
The Chinese invented the world's **first written exams** to select candidates to become state officials. The tests lasted up to 72 hours and when a candidate had finished, an official recopied their answers so that their handwriting would not be recognized.

Legend has it that a Han court official, Ts'ai Lun, invented paper in 104 CE. This is how he did it.

Boning up
The Shang kings used oracle bones to ask the gods questions, such as "Will this war turn out well?" The question was written on an ox bone or a tortoise shell, which was heated until cracks appeared. The shape of the cracks would reveal the answer.

Chinese inventions

1100 BCE silk

500 BCE cross bow

100 BCE iron plow

Blasts from the past

c. 1600 BCE
First use of pictographic writing in China

c. 600 BCE
Iron is first used in China

551–479 BCE
Life of Confucius, philosopher and teacher

221 BCE
China is united under Qin Shi Huang, the First Emperor

100 BCE
Han emperors expand China's frontiers westward and open up the Silk Road, the overland trade route to the Mediterranean

610 CE
The Grand Canal, built to carry trade between north and south China, is completed; it runs for 1,100 miles (1,770 km)

1000 CE
Science and technology flourish under the Song Dynasty

1275
Venetian explorer Marco Polo arrives at the court of Kublai Khan, Mongol emperor of China

1368
A peasant leader, Zhu Yuanzhang, overthrows the Mongols and becomes the first Ming emperor

1644
Manchu (Mongolian) warriors seize Beijing and establish the Qing Dynasty (until 1911)

Five facts about the First Emperor

- When Ying Zheng became king of Qin, China was divided into seven warring states. He conquered them all and declared himself Qin Shi Huang (the First Emperor) of China, in 221 BCE.

- **He determined to make China a single state. Everyone had to obey the same laws, adopt the same writing style, and use the same coins, weights, and measures.**

- He ordered the construction of an earthen barrier stretching more than 1,000 miles (1,600 km) to keep out invasions—the beginning of the Great Wall of China.

- **Qin Shi Huang feared one thing only—death—and is supposed to have traveled to the islands of Japan in search of a magic elixir to give him eternal life.**

- It took 700,000 men 36 years to build his massive tomb. It is 165 ft (60 m) high and is said to contain a replica of his capital city.

Buried army

Buried near the tomb of Qin Shi Huang is the Terra-cotta Army—7,000 clay soldiers, 600 horses, and more than 100 wooden war chariots to protect the emperor in the afterlife.

All at sea

In 1405, Chinese admiral **Zheng He** led an expedition to spread Chinese trade and military power around the Indian Ocean. His fleet consisted of more than 200 ships, with a crew of up to 28,000.

The Forbidden City

FAST FACTS

01: Built as the imperial palace for the Ming emperors in Beijing

02: Construction took 15 years and employed more than 1 million workmen

03: The world's largest palace complex, it covers an area of 183 acres (75 hectares) and is surrounded by a wall 32 ft (10 m) high and a moat 20 ft (6 m) deep

04: Contains 980 buildings and 9,000 rooms

05: Was the residence of 24 emperors—14 from the Ming Dynasty and 10 from the Qing

04. Spread the fibrous mixture out in a thin layer and smooth well.

05. Leave to dry in the sun. When dry, remove the paper and write on it using brush and ink.

200 CE woodblock printing

500 paddlewheel ship

600 porcelain

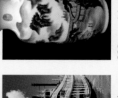

600 fireworks and gunpowder

950 navigational compass

Dates are approximate. Many Chinese inventions predated similar European inventions by several hundred years.

Who were the ancient Americans?

The Maya and Aztecs of Central America and the Incas of Peru developed remarkable cultures that were swept away by Spanish invaders in the 1500s. They were the final witnesses to the long history of human civilization in ancient America.

Lines in the desert

01: Two thousand years ago, the Nazca civilization in Peru created mysterious designs in the desert.

02: They consist of a series of lines, some up to 1,000 ft (300 m) long.

03: The designs can only be seen from the air.

04: Some depict animals—for example, a hummingbird, monkey, condor, or spider. Others are abstract geometrical shapes.

05: No one knows what the lines mean. Some historians believe they formed part of an astronomical calendar and were connected in some way with irrigation.

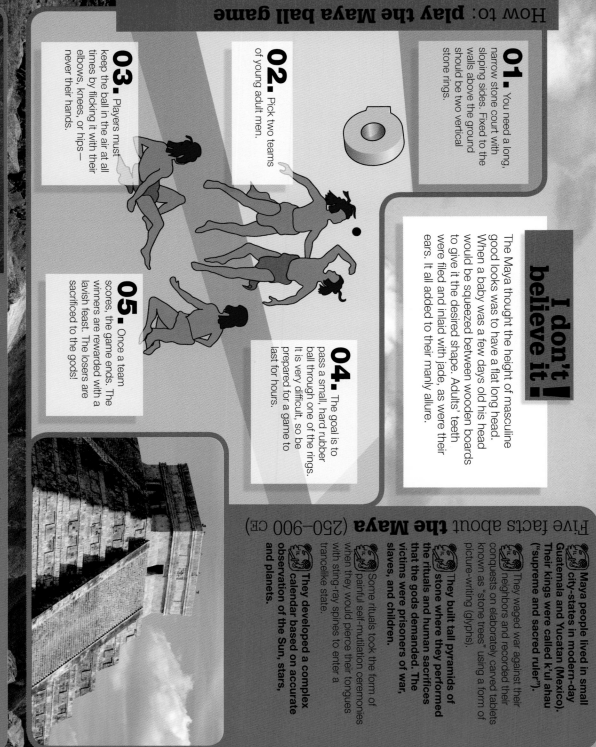

How to: play the Maya ball game

01. You need a long, narrow stone court with sloping sides. Fixed to the walls above the ground should be two vertical stone rings.

02. Pick two teams of young adult men.

03. Players must keep the ball in the air at all times by flicking it with their elbows, knees, or hips—never their hands.

04. The goal is to pass a small, hard rubber ball through one of the rings. It is very difficult, so be prepared for a game to last for hours.

05. Once a team scores, the game ends. The winners are rewarded with a lavish feast. The losers are sacrificed to the gods!

I don't believe it!

The Maya thought the height of masculine good looks was to have a flat long head. When a baby was a few days old his head would be squeezed between wooden boards to give it the desired shape. Adults' teeth were filed and inlaid with jade, as were their ears. It all added to their manly allure.

Five facts about the Maya (250–900 CE)

1. Maya people lived in small city-states in modern-day Guatemala and Yucatán (Mexico). Their kings were called k'ul ahau ("supreme and sacred ruler").

2. They waged war against their neighbors and recorded their conquests on elaborately carved tablets known as "stone trees" using a form of picture-writing (glyphs).

3. They built tall pyramids of stone where they performed the rituals and human sacrifices that the gods demanded. The victims were prisoners of war, slaves, and children.

4. Some rituals took the form of painful self-mutilation ceremonies when they would pierce their tongues with sting-ray spines to enter a trancelike state.

5. They developed a complex calendar based on accurate observation of the Sun, stars, and planets.

Aztec gods

There were more than 100 gods in the Aztec religion.

Chalchiuhtlicue
Goddess of lakes and streams

Cihuacoatl
Goddess of fertility and childbirth

Coatlicue
Goddess of life and death

Quetzalcoatl
Feathered serpent, god of the wind

Tlaloc
God of rain who makes things grow

Xipe Totec
God of springtime and agriculture

Xochiquetzal
Goddess of sensual love, pleasure, and art

Choc-tastic!

- ❖ The Aztecs drank a bitter spicy drink called *chocolatl* made from the beans of the cocoa tree.

- ❖ Cocoa was first cultivated by the Maya in the rain forests of Central America.

- ❖ The beans were used as a form of currency—10 could buy a rabbit, 100 a slave.

- ❖ The Aztecs believed chocolate had been brought to Earth by the god Quetzalcoatl.

- ❖ Aztec king Montezuma II is said to have served Spanish invader Cortés with chocolate in a golden goblet.

- ❖ Cortés took cocoa beans back with him to Spain. The Spanish kept the source of chocolate a closely guarded secret.

Five facts about the **Incas** (1200–1532 CE)

- ◎ The Inca Empire extended for 3,000 miles (4,800 km) along the Andes from Ecuador to central Chile.

- ◎ The Incas loved gold, which they called "the sweat of the Sun." They called silver "the tears of the Moon."

- ◎ The Incas built more than 25,000 miles (40,000 km) of roads to carry goods, armies, and messages quickly around the Empire.

- ◎ Although they made wheeled toys for children to play with, they did not have wheeled carts—instead they carried goods on surefooted llamas and alpacas over the steep mountain roads.

- ◎ Records were kept on *quipu*—knotted strings of different colors attached to a main cord. The color of the string and the number of knots along it indicated the nature and quantity of goods and supplies.

Lost city
Perched on a mountain ridge, the Inca city of **Machu Picchu** was so well hidden the Spanish never discovered it when they conquered Peru. Around 400,000 tourists visit the city every year.

Five facts about the **Aztecs** (1300–1519 CE)

- 🜲 The Aztecs were the last people to dominate Mexico before the arrival of the Spanish.

- 🜲 They waged continual war to capture prisoners to sacrifice to the gods and to demand tribute from neighboring states.

- 🜲 Soldiers were rewarded with elaborate costumes to show how many prisoners they had captured.

- 🜲 The last Aztec ruler was Montezuma II. He believed a rumor that the Spanish commander Hernán Cortés was the god Quetzalcoatl in human form and invited him to his palace.

- 🜲 Bad mistake—the Spaniards took Montezuma prisoner and conquered his empire.

Who were the Vikings?

The Vikings were sailors who came from Norway, Sweden, and Denmark. They began raiding places on the coasts of England, Ireland, and France just before 800 CE and later settled there as farmers and traders. Some Vikings voyaged across the Atlantic to Iceland, Greenland, and North America. Others traveled down the great rivers of Russia to the Black Sea.

Tell me more: Viking dress

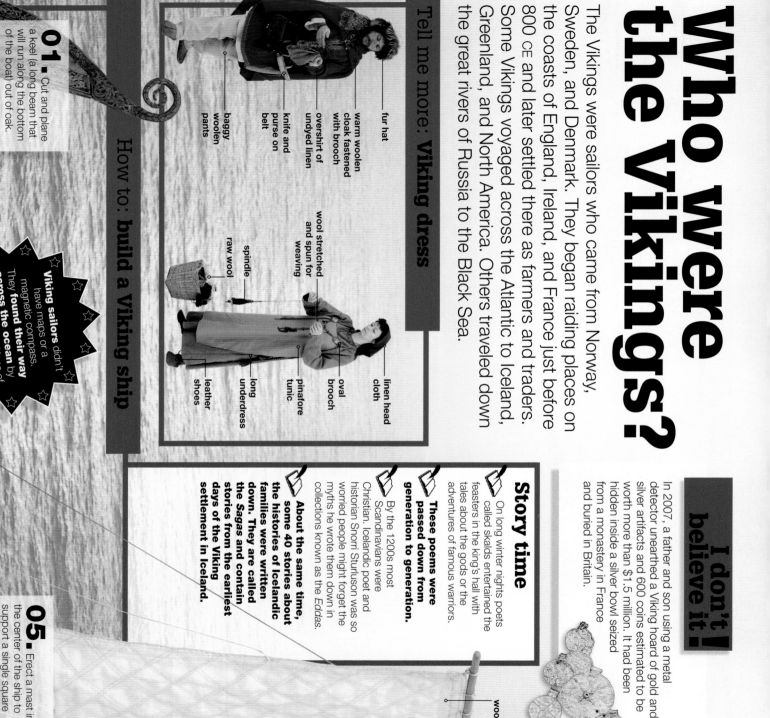

- fur hat
- warm woolen cloak fastened with brooch
- overshirt of undyed linen
- knife and purse on belt
- baggy woolen pants

- linen head cloth
- wool stretched and spun for weaving
- oval brooch
- pinafore tunic
- raw wool
- spindle
- long underdress
- leather shoes

How to: build a Viking ship

01. Cut and plane a keel (a long beam that will run along the bottom of the boat) out of oak.

02. Construct the sides of the ship using overlapping strakes (side timbers) for strength.

03. Make sure you caulk (waterproof) the gaps between the strakes with a mixture of tar and animal hair.

04. Add holes for the oars (oarports) along both sides so that the ship can be steered when there is no wind.

05. Erect a mast in the center of the ship to support a single square sail made of wool. This should be lowered at night and can be used as a tent in bad weather.

steering oar

oarport

woolen sail

Viking sailors didn't have maps or a magnetic compass. They **found their way across the ocean** by observing the positions of the **Sun and stars** and the direction of the **wind**.

Story time

On long winter nights poets called skalds entertained the feasters in the king's hall with tales about the gods or the adventures of famous warriors.

By the 1200s most Scandinavians were Christian. Icelandic poet and historian Snorri Sturluson was so worried people might forget the myths he wrote them down in collections known as the *Eddas*.

About the same time, some 40 stories about the histories of Icelandic families were written down. They are called the *Sagas* and contain stories from the earliest days of the Viking settlement in Iceland.

These poems were passed down from generation to generation.

Norse gods

Odin
The god of war was said to gather up the warriors who had fallen in battle and carry them back to his hall, Valhalla.

Thor
Armed with his hammer Mjollir, Thor, the god of thunder defended Asgard (where the gods lived) against giants and dragons.

Loki
Thor's companion, Loki was a mischievous and sometimes nasty creature who made lots of trouble for the other gods.

Freyr
The god of fertility and controller of sunshine and rain, Freyr was responsible for making Viking crops grow.

Freyia
The twin of Freyr, Freyia was the goddess of love. She could turn herself into a bird by putting on a magic falcon skin.

Raiding season

"Dire portents... immense whirlwinds and flashes of lightning, and fiery dragons flying in the air." That's how one monk described the first Viking attack on the monastery of Lindisfarne, northeast England, which came out of the blue on June 8, 793.

The Viking war fleets came every summer, raiding all around the coasts of England, Scotland, and Ireland before returning home with their booty.

They were soon raiding along the coast of France and far inland along its rivers. Paris was attacked and burned several times.

The Viking raiders attacked mercilessly with their long, double-edged swords and battle axes. They wore conical iron helmets, but no horns—that's a 19th-century myth.

They picked on monasteries because they were undefended and contained precious objects.

Blasts from the past

790s
Viking raids start in western Europe

841
Viking settlement founded at Dublin, Ireland

856–857
Vikings sail up the Seine to sack Paris for the first time

860s
Swedish Vikings found Novgorod and Kiev in Rus (Russia and Ukraine)

870
Farmers from Norway found a settlement on Iceland

886
Eastern England comes under Danish rule (Danelaw)

900
Vikings raid along Mediterranean coast

911
Viking chief Rollo granted land in France (Normandy)

941
Rus Vikings attack Constantinople (Istanbul)

986
Erik the Red founds settlement on Greenland

1000
Leif Erikson explores coast of Newfoundland

Go west!

Erik the Red was exiled from Iceland in 982 for murder. Three years later he was back with tales of a land he called Greenland. He set off with about 1,000 volunteers to start a new colony, which flourished for 300 years.

In 1000, Leif Erikson sailed from Greenland and landed at a place he called Vinland. Historians believe it was Newfoundland, making him the first European to reach the Americas.

WHAT'S IN A NAME?

Most chroniclers called the Vikings *Norsemen* or *Northmen* because they came from the north. The name "Viking" may originate from the Scandinavian word *vik*, meaning a creek or inlet.

Writing in runes

Vikings wrote in runes—letters that were specially designed for incising into wood and stone.

They carved runic inscriptions on memorial stones and decorated them with fantastic designs of writhing dragons and serpents.

Halfdan, a Viking warrior who traveled to Constantinople (Istanbul), scratched his name on a marble slab in the church of Hagia Sofia—you can still see it there today.

The runic alphabet, or futhark, takes its name from the first six characters—fehu (f), unuz (u), thurisaz (th), ansuz (a), raido (r), kanaz (k).

ᚠ fehu (f)

ᚢ unuz (u)

ᚦ thurisaz (th)

ᚨ ansuz (a)

ᚱ raido (r)

ᚲ kanaz (k)

---

06. Attach a steering oar to the right or "steering board" side of the ship—the origin of the term "starboard."

07. Decorate the post at each end of the ship. On fighting ships, a carved dragonhead is often fitted to the front post.

mast

When were medieval times?

The period after the Dark Ages (the time that followed the collapse of the Roman Empire in Europe) is called the medieval era (also known as the Middle Ages). Trade and learning revived. The population rose and people became richer. Kings held power by granting their nobles landed estates to live on.

Blasts from the past

800
The Pope crowns Charlemagne king of the Franks (France), Holy Roman Emperor

1066
William the Conqueror, Duke of Normandy, conquers England

1088
The first European university founded in Bologna, Italy

1095
Pope Urban II calls for a crusade to the Holy Land

1140
The abbey of St. Denis, near Paris, is built in the new Gothic style

1298
Marco Polo publishes his account of his travels in Asia

1326
Cannons are used for the first time in European warfare

1337
The start of the Hundred Years' War between France and England (ends 1453)

1347–1351
Black Death (plague) devastates Europe

1431
Joan of Arc is burned at the stake

Power pyramid

A medieval king agreed to protect his nobles, while the nobles swore to come to his aid when asked. The nobles in turn rewarded their followers with smaller grants of land. This system, which began in France, is known as **feudalism**.

The Crusades

- The Crusades were a series of wars fought between Christians and Muslims for control of the Holy Land (Palestine).

- The word "crusade" comes from the French croix ("cross"). European crusader knights wore a red cross on their tunics.

- Crusaders believed they would go straight to heaven if they died fighting on crusade.

- The knights of the First Crusade (1095–1099) captured the city of Jerusalem.

- In 1187 Saladin, a Muslim leader, recaptured Jerusalem. Little by little the crusaders were driven out of the Holy Land.

I don't believe it!

Medieval peasants ate more healthily than we do (no sugar, lots of vegetables). Their main food was bread, but they burned off the calories working at least 12 hours a day.

How to: become a knight

01. Be born the son of a nobleman. At age eight you'll be sent to be a page in another nobleman's castle. You'll be taught how to handle a sword and spear.

02. At age 15 or 16 you'll be made the squire to a knight. Look after him at all times—dress him, prepare his meals, and take care of his horse and armor.

03. So long as you've performed your duties well, when you're 20 or so you'll be made ("dubbed") a knight in a special ceremony.

04. The night before, put on a white tunic and red robe and spend all night praying solemnly in the castle chapel. The chaplain will bless your sword and place it on the altar. Next morning confess your faults to him.

05. You'll be led outside to kneel in front of your lord, who will tap you lightly on each shoulder with his sword. You've been made a knight! Let the feasting begin!

06. A shortcut way to becoming a knight is to perform some brave deed in combat—best of all, save your lord's life. Then he'll take his sword and dub you Sir Lancelot (or whatever) on the field of battle.

A knight was expected to obey the code of chivalry. He promised to:

- **protect the poor and weak, especially women**
- **obey his lord and show courage, honesty, loyalty, and strength**
- **defend the Church and go on crusade**

In numbers

The Black Death was a deadly outbreak of bubonic plague that raged through Asia and Europe, spread by fleas and rats.

4 years
The time it took to spread through Europe (1348–1351)

5–8 days
Average length of illness

50%
Chance of dying

25–50 million
The number of victims in Europe (30–60 percent of population)

75 million
The number of victims in Asia

Boom towns

🏰 Towns were on the up as trade and commerce boomed.

🏰 Towns grew rich through the right to hold weekly or seasonal fairs.

🏰 Thanks to the cloth trade, northern Italy and Flanders (in modern-day Belgium) had the richest towns in Europe.

🏰 Skilled craftsmen and merchants formed guilds—associations to look after their interests.

🏰 Insurance and banking were invented at this time.

WHAT'S IN A NAME?

Medieval comes from two Latin words *medium* ("middle") and *aevum* ("age"). It's the filling in the sandwich between the age of the Romans and the modern world.

WEIRD OR WHAT?

One "cure" for the Black Death was to drink a glass of urine twice a day. Placing a live hen next to the black swellings on the patient's body was also believed to help draw the pestilence out.

Gothic architecture

Cathedrals and churches soared upward as medieval masons (builders) discovered the pointed Gothic arch.

Spire: Tall and thin, it pointed upward to heaven

Rounded arch: Romanesque style (Norman in England), used throughout Europe until 1100s

Pointed arch: Springing from the top of narrow columns, pointed Gothic arches allowed masons to build much taller structures. The style spread rapidly in Europe after 1150

Flying buttress: Stone arch on the outside of the building that supported the high walls

Stained glass window: Windows became larger and were filled with colored stained glass

Gargoyles: Stone water spouts in the shape of strange creatures were built along the gutters

Monks and monasteries

✝ Only Church people could read and write, so abbots (heads of monasteries) were powerful men who advised the king and sat on his council.

✝ Landowners gave monasteries grants of land so that the monks would pray for their souls. Some monasteries grew very rich, since the monks were highly efficient farmers.

✝ Monks spent hours copying religious books by hand and decorating them with gold and colored pictures—these are known as illuminated manuscripts.

✝ Women who followed a religious life were called nuns. They lived in convents.

✝ The monks had to pray seven times a day (they also attended mass, the main service of the Church, every day).

Daily prayers:

sunrise — matins ("morning prayer")
6 a.m. — prime ("first hour")
9 a.m. — terce ("third hour")
noon — sext ("sixth hour")
noon — none ("ninth hour")
3 p.m. — vespers ("evening prayer")
sunset — compline ("night prayer")
9 p.m.

How to: **joust**

Jousting started as a way for knights to test their horsemanship and weapons' skills in preparation for war. Over the centuries it developed into a popular tournament event, attracting hundreds of spectators and offering big money prizes. It was the ultimate extreme sport!

01. Have your squire dress you in your armor and prepare your horse.

02. Mount your horse, sitting hard in the saddle with your feet in the stirrups.

03. Take hold of your lance in your right hand. Keep it upright.

You will need:

Suit of armor

For the very best protection, you should wear a full suit of plate armor. Special jousting armor is available; it has heavier protection on the side facing the opponent.

Helmet

Make sure the eyes are well protected. In 1559, a splinter of lance entered through the visor of King Henry II of France and pierced his brain. He died nine days later.

Horse

The most popular horses are chargers (bred for agility) or destriers (heavy war horses). You will need to dress it in an ornamental covering and protect its head with armor.

04. When the herald signals, ride straight ahead with the tilt barrier to your left. Make sure your lance is still upright.

05. As you near your opponent, lower your lance at an angle across the tilt barrier (fence).

06. Aim for your opponent's torso, clinging tightly to your horse as you strike.

07. Repeat until either you or your opponent falls out of the saddle.

Lance
This should be made of solid oak and decorated with your coat of arms (family symbol).

Tilt barrier
Before tilt barriers were introduced in the 15th century, jousts were a lot more dangerous. The barrier protects the horses and ensures lances are pointed at a safer angle.

Herald
Heralds keep score and act as masters of ceremony by announcing the contests and reading out the rules of the tournament.

Opponent
The knight challenging you in the joust should also be wearing armor, be mounted on a horse, and be carrying a lance.

Who were the Ottomans?

A Turkish dynasty of sultans who ruled one of the most powerful Muslim states in modern history. At its height, the Ottoman Empire stretched from Hungary to Egypt and from Algeria to Iraq, putting fear into the hearts of the European powers. Over time it became weaker, but managed to survive from 1301 until 1922.

WHAT'S IN A NAME?

When the Ottomans took over the city of **Constantinople** they would hear the Greek inhabitants say they were going "eis tin polis" ("to the city"). This became shortened in Turkish to **Istanbul**—and the name stuck ever since.

A **cannon** used by the Ottomans at the siege of Constantinople was the **largest the world had seen**—its bronze barrel was 28 ft (8.5 m) long and 8 in (20 cm) thick. It could fire a ball weighing 1,200 lb (544 kg) more than 1 mile (1.6 km). A special carriage drawn by 30 oxen and 700 men was needed to drag it into place.

Five Ottoman sultans

Murad I
(ruled 1359–1389)
Made inroads into Europe across the Dardanelles and established a capital at Edirne (the former Byzantine city of Adrianople). He was killed after the battle of Kosovo.

Bayezid I "the thunderbolt"
(ruled 1389–1403)
Conquered Bulgaria, Serbia, and Macedonia but was defeated and imprisoned by Tamurlane, a fearsome Mongol warlord.

Mehmed II "the conqueror"
(ruled 1451–1481)
Ended the Byzantine Empire by capturing Constantinople in 1453, which he made his capital.

Selim I "the grim"
(ruled 1512–1520)
After getting rid of his father and killing off all his brothers and nephews, he extended Ottoman rule to Syria, Palestine, Saudi Arabia, and Egypt.

Suleyman I "the magnificent"
(ruled 1521–1566)
The Ottoman Empire reached its largest extent during his 46-year reign.

Top title

Suleyman I called himself: "Slave of God, powerful with the power of God, deputy of God on Earth, obeying the commands of the Qur'an and enforcing them throughout the world, master of all lands, the shadow of God over all nations, Sultan of Sultans in all the lands of Persians and Arabs, the propagator of Sultanic laws, the tenth Sultan of the Ottoman Khans, Sultan, son of Sultan, Suleyman Khan."

A pretty magnificent name!

FAST FACTS

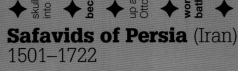

A soldier's life

01: Janissaries were the Ottoman Sultan's crack infantry corps.

02: Their name is made up of two Turkish words—*yeni* (new) *çeri* (soldier).

03: Recruits were drawn from the *devshirme*—the annual tribute of Christian boys sent as slaves to Constantinople and made to convert to Islam.

04: The janissaries were loyal only to the sultan. They lived in barracks and were forbidden to marry.

Battlefront reports

- The Battle of Kosovo (1389) ended Serbian independence for 500 years and is still bitterly remembered.

- **When a Venetian army laid siege to Athens, Greece, in 1687, the Ottomans used the ancient Parthenon as an ammunitions store. It blew up, destroying much of the temple.**

- Mustafa Kemal (pictured) served as an Ottoman division commander at the World War I Battle of Gallipoli (1915). He became the first president of the Turkish Republic (1923), taking the name of Atatürk ("Father of the Turks").

Under siege!

↗ Constantinople stood on a triangle of land with water on two sides. The city wall on the land side, built in the 5th century ce, was 12 miles (20 km) long.

↗ The siege lasted 57 days, from April 6 to May 29, 1453.

↗ The defenders had 7,000 men and 26 ships, and the Ottomans an estimated 100,000 men and 126 ships.

↗ The fall of the city brought to an end the 1,000-year-old history of the Greek Byzantine Empire, the successor to the Eastern Roman Empire.

↗ Constantine XI, the last Byzantine emperor, died defending Constantinople in the final Turkish assault on the city walls. His body was never found.

↗ Hagia Sophia ("Holy Wisdom"), the great domed church built by the Emperor Justinian 900 years earlier, was turned into a mosque. Today it is a museum.

Mughals of India
1501–1857

✦ Babar (ruled 1501–1531) was the founder of the Mughal dynasty. He invaded northern India in 1526.

✦ His grandson Akbar (ruled 1556–1605) **expanded the Empire. A wise Muslim ruler, he showed tolerance to his Hindu subjects.**

✦ Jahangir (ruled 1605–1627) invited Persian artists, writers, and architects to his court.

✦ Jahan (ruled 1627–1666) built the Taj Mahal (pictured) as a memorial to his wife.

✦ Aurangzeb (ruled 1658–1707), the last of the great Mughal conquerors, was a mean-spirited emperor who lost the trust of his people.

Modern states (or parts of them) that belonged to the Ottoman Empire

✤ Albania	✤ Israel
✤ Algeria	✤ Jordan
✤ Armenia	✤ Libya
✤ Azerbaijan	✤ Macedonia
✤ Bosnia-	✤ Montenegro
Herzegovina	✤ Romania
✤ Bulgaria	✤ Russia
✤ Croatia	✤ Saudi Arabia
✤ Cyprus	✤ Serbia
✤ Egypt	✤ Syria
✤ Georgia	✤ Tunisia
✤ Greece	✤ Turkey
✤ Hungary	✤ Ukraine
✤ Iraq	✤ West Bank

Ottoman terms

divan council (literally, a low couch)

firman imperial decree

gazi warrior dedicated to fighting for Islam

harem private family quarters of palace

janissary the sultan's infantry guard

kiosk pavilion

pasha high official

Sublime Porte ("High Gate") the sultan's government

sultan Muslim ruler

sultana wife or daughter of a sultan

vizier royal minister

Safavids of Persia (Iran)
1501–1722

✦ 14-year-old Ismail I declared himself shah (king) of Persia. He had the skull of a defeated Uzbek leader made into a drinking cup.

✦ **The Safavids were followers of the Shia branch of Islam, which became the state religion.**

✦ The greatest Safavid ruler was Abbas I (ruled 1587–1629). He built up an army and seized Baghdad from the Ottomans in 1623.

✦ **Abbas's capital at Isfahan was one of the glories of the Muslim world. It had 162 mosques, 272 public baths, and 48 madrasas (schools).**

✦ In 1722, Afghan invaders captured Isfahan and killed the last shah.

What was the **Renaissance?**

The word Renaissance means "rebirth." It's the name historians give to a cultural movement that started in northern Italy in the 1400s and spread throughout Europe in the course of the next 150 years.

Techniques of Renaissance painting

Perspective: Giving an illusion of distance

lifelike figures

bright colors

Sfumato: Blurring or softening of sharp outlines to give a 3-D effect

Chiaroscuro: Strong contrast of light and dark

Leonardo da Vinci: Renaissance man of genius (1452–1519)

01: At age 14 he entered the workshop of Andrea Verrocchio, a leading sculptor, painter, and goldsmith in Florence.

02: He once wrote to the Duke of Milan offering to work for him as an engineer designing forts, bridges, weapons, and canals—but almost forgot to say he could paint as well. He got the job.

03: It took him four years to paint the *Mona Lisa*. No one knows who she is or why she is smiling. She hasn't any eyebrows—women shaved them off at that time.

04: He was passionately interested in how everything works, from the human body to the movement of water, and filled notebook after notebook with his ideas.

05: His designs for ingenious machines included an armored car, machine gun, helicopter, and underwater diving suit.

Renaissance

01: Wealthy trading and banking cities like Florence, Milan, Urbino, and Venice became hotspots of artistic activity.

02: Artists developed new styles of painting, sculpture, and architecture based on the ideals of the Ancient Greeks and Romans.

03: Scholars began to study Greek and Latin manuscripts. This sparked new interest in philosophy and science.

04: Growing criticism of the corruption of the Church led to a lasting split in Christianity (the Reformation).

Five Renaissance artists

Sandro Botticelli
Painted women with long flowing tresses like his *Birth of Venus*, which shows the goddess appearing from the sea on a large shell.

Albrecht Dürer
Greatest German artist of the Renaissance era. Some of his woodcuts, like *Knight, Death, and the Devil*, are pretty spooky.

Michelangelo Buonarroti
Sculptor, painter, and architect who is always called by his first name. His masterpiece is the ceiling of the Sistine Chapel in the Vatican.

Raphael (Raffaello Sanzio)
His greatest works are in Rome, including the frescoes he painted for the Pope's apartments in the Vatican.

Titian (Tiziano Vecellio)
Venetian painter who painted kings and popes and lived to a ripe old age before falling victim to the plague.

Advice for kids

One of Erasmus's best-selling books was *A Handbook on Good Manners for Children*. Among the gems of advice he doled out are these:

✔ **Always put your hand in front of your mouth when you yawn.**

✘ Don't lick your greasy fingers at table or wipe them on your coat—use the table cloth.

✘ **Don't rock your chair backward and forward—people will think you are farting.**

✘ Don't look for boogers in your hanky after blowing your nose.

✘ **Don't lend your filthy hanky to a friend.**

The Reformation in five easy steps

01: German priest Martin Luther composes a list of 95 complaints against the Church (1517).

02: The Pope throws Luther out of the Church and he is hauled before an imperial court at Worms (1521). He refuses to back down and is outlawed by Emperor Charles V.

03: He goes into hiding. Germany is torn apart by conflict and revolt. Support for his reforms (demands that the Church mend its ways) spreads through northern Europe.

04: A number of German princes refuse to give in to pressure from the emperor to reject the reformers. They are called Protestants.

05: The Peace of Augsburg (1555) gives individual German princes the right to decide what faith (Protestant or Roman Catholic) their subjects should follow.

How to: print a book on Gutenberg's press

About 1450, a German craftsman, Johann Gutenberg, invented a printing press using moveable type. Gutenberg's first printed book was the Bible. It took him about a year to print all 180 copies—about the same time it would have taken a copyist to produce a single handwritten copy.

01. Create your moveable type (raised metal shapes for each letter of the alphabet). Carve the shape of the letter, back to front, onto a metal punch. Hammer this into a copper sheet to make your mold. Fill the mold with hot metal, and when it cools, you have your metal type.

02. Arrange the pieces of type to make up the words and sentences of the text you want to print line by line in a wooden frame known as a form. When the form is full, ink the letters well with an oil-based ink and place a sheet of paper on top.

03. Place the form on a table and lower a wooden screw so that it presses a board down onto the paper.

04. Raise the screw, remove the paper, and put in another sheet. Repeat until you have printed all the copies you need.

Blasts from the past

1434
The Medici family of bankers become unofficial rulers of Florence

1455
First printed book in Europe

1492
Fall of Granada, last Muslim kingdom in Spain

1498
Leonardo da Vinci paints *The Last Supper* in Milan

1504
Michelangelo's giant nude statue of *David* goes on show in Florence

1509
Humanist scholar Erasmus publishes *The Praise of Folly*, his most famous essay

1513
Niccolò Machiavelli writes *The Prince*, a handbook for Renaissance rulers

1534
King Henry VIII declares himself Supreme Head of the Church in England

1543
Nicolaus Copernicus publishes a book proving the Earth revolves around the Sun

---

WHAT'S IN A NAME?

The **Sistine Chapel** in the Vatican is named for Pope Sixtus IV, the pope responsible for building it. There have been five popes called Sixtus. If there had been one more he would have been called Pope Sixtus the Sixth!

Movers and shakers

Nicolaus Copernicus
This Polish astronomer argued that the Earth moves around the Sun, rather than the other way around, contrary to the Church's teachings.

Niccolò Machiavelli
Italian statesman and writer whose name has become a byword for political cunning and intrigue.

Desiderius Erasmus
Foremost Humanist scholar (the Humanists found their inspiration in the works of Plato and other Greek and Roman writers). Erasmus's writings were best-sellers, thanks to the new technology of printing.

What started the Age of Discovery?

The desire of European merchants to control the trade in luxury goods from Asia—silk, cotton, and spices—combined with technological advances in shipbuilding and navigation led to a wave of long-distance voyages of exploration that redrew the map of the globe between the 15th and 18th centuries.

The sought-after spices

ginger

black pepper

cinnamon

cloves

nutmeg

Wrong way!

In 1492, self-taught navigator **Christopher Columbus** attempted to reach the Spice Islands in the east by **sailing west**. His three ships—the *Santa Maria*, *Pinta*, and *Niña*—reached the Bahamas and Columbus mistook the Americas for Asia.

What's in a name?

When Ferdinand Magellan finally made his way safely through the towering waves around Cape Horn on November 28, 1520, he was so relieved to see calm, tranquil water ahead, he called it *Mar Pacifico*—the **Pacific Ocean**. He had no idea how wide the ocean was though. He wouldn't see land again for more than three months, reaching Guam on March 6, 1521.

Blasts from the past

1487–1488
Portuguese navigator Bartolomeu Dias sails down the west coast of Africa and rounds the Cape of Good Hope to enter the Indian Ocean

1492
Christopher Columbus sails west from Spain to discover America

1497
Italian-born John Cabot (Giovanni Caboto) sails from Bristol to Nova Scotia

1497–1498
Vasco da Gama makes the first return voyage from Portugal to India

1499
Amerigo de Vespucci explores the coast of South America

1500
Pedral Alvarez Cabral discovers Brazil while sailing to India

1509–1510
Lopez de Sequeiro is the first European to reach Malacca (the Spice Islands)

1516
Portuguese explorer Rafael Perestrello reaches China

How to: make ship's biscuit

01. Mix together four parts of flour with one part of water. Add salt.

02. Roll out the dough and score with a knife to make squares, or cut into rounds. Bake in an oven until rock hard.

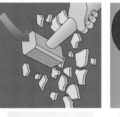

03. To eat, bash into crumbs with a handy implement or soak in broth until mushy enough to swallow.

04. Watch out for weevils (tiny black insects)!

What to pack for a sea voyage

- Maps and charts based on discoveries of earlier explorers
- Compass—essential for knowing in which direction you are traveling
- Cross-staff—to figure out latitude (how far you are from the equator) by measuring the height above the horizon of the North Star (at night) or Sun (at noon). Only works when the skies are clear
- Lots and lots of rope
- Spare canvas for sails
- Water—as much as possible, stored in barrels below decks as ballast to keep the ship stable
- Ship's biscuit—also known as hard tack
- Pickled or dried meat, dried beans, hard cheese, salted fish
- Goods to trade with, such as beads and trinkets
- Guns—to keep hostile natives and pirates at bay

maps and charts

compass

cross-staff

rope

Killer at sea!

A lack of fresh fruit and vegetables led on long voyages to **scurvy**, many a sailor to fall victim. It made gums bleed and teeth fall out and victims got weaker and weaker until they died. The British Navy made sailors drink lots of lime juice—that's how they came to be nicknamed "limeys."

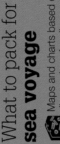

I don't believe it!

In 1494 the Atlantic was divided between Spain and Portugal by papal decree (a ruling from the Pope). All new land found west of an imaginary north-south line running down the middle (i.e., the Americas) would belong to Spain and all land east of it (i.e., the route to India and beyond) to Portugal. No one knew quite where the line lay, which allowed Portugal to claim Brazil in 1500.

Explorers who came to a bad end

- Bartolomeu Dias died in a storm off the Cape of Good Hope in 1500
- **Ferdinand Magellan was killed in a fight in the Philippines in 1521**
- Giovanni de Varrazano was killed and eaten in Guadeloupe in 1528
- **Henry Hudson was cast adrift by his mutinous crew in 1611 and never seen again**
- Sir Francis Drake died of scurvy on a West Indies raiding expedition against the Spanish in 1596
- **Captain James Cook was murdered by angry islanders in Hawaii in 1779**
- Sir John Franklin's ship became trapped in thick ice while looking for the Northwest Passage through the Arctic to the Pacific in 1847. He and 105 others died of starvation

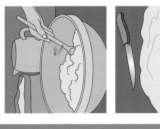

Sir John Franklin's ship trapped in Arctic ice

Timeline

1519–1522 Ferdinand Magellan leads the first round-the-world voyage but dies in the Philippines. Sebastian del Cano completes the voyage

1524 Giovanni da Varrazano sails the length of the Atlantic coast of North America

1535–1536 Frenchman Jacques Cartier explores the St. Lawrence River of Canada

1606 Dutch explorer Willem Janz explores the coast of Northern Australia

1642–1644 Dutchman Abel Janszoon Tasman reaches Van Diemen's Land (Tasmania) and New Zealand

1767–1768 Louis-Antoine de Bougainville explores the islands of the South Pacific for France

1768–1771 James Cook explores New Zealand and the eastern coast of Australia on the first of three great voyages of discovery in the Pacific

Why did kings become so powerful in Europe?

Before the 1500s, nobles were always plotting revolts against kings. Over time, kings raised the money to pay for full-time armies, putting an end to civil wars. Kings started to believe they had a divine right to rule and that no one could tell them what to do.

Happy families?

The key to power in the 16th century was to marry well. Here's how some royals were related:

Emperor Charles V was the **nephew** of Catherine of Aragon, the first **wife** of Henry VIII of England.

Charles V's **son** Philip II of Spain **married** Queen Mary I of England, who was Catherine and Henry's **daughter**. When Mary died he proposed to her **half-sister**, Elizabeth I, but she turned him down flat.

Mary, Queen of Scots was Henry VIII's **great-niece** and a **cousin** of Elizabeth I. She was the **widow** of King Francis II of France, who was the **brother** of Elizabeth of Valois, who became Philip II's next **wife**. Another **sister** of Francis II, Margaret of Valois, was **married** (for a time) to Henry IV of France.

Who said that?
(supposedly)

01. "I speak Spanish to God, Italian to women, French to men, and German to my horse."

02. "You have sent me a Flanders mare!"

03. "I have the heart and stomach of a king, and of a king of England, too."

04. "Paris is well worth a mass."

05. "*L'Etat, c'est moi.*" ("I am the state.")

(answers far left)

In numbers

The palace of Versailles, France, is vast.

26 acres
(11 hectares) of roof

67
staircases

357
mirrors in Hall of Mirrors

1,650 ft
(500 m) frontage

2,000 acres
(800 hectares) of grounds

700
rooms

1,250
fireplaces

1,400
fountains

2,153
windows

551,220 sq ft
(51,210 sq m) of floors

Versailles court etiquette

- Only the king or queen (or visiting monarch) could sit on an armchair.
- **The king's brother or children might sit on a chair with a back and no arms.**
- Duchesses were allowed to sit on a *tabouret*, a padded, drum-shaped stool.
- **Everyone else had to stand.**

- Courtiers had to scratch on the king's door with their little finger and then wait for permission to enter—they were not allowed to knock.
- **Around 100 nobles were on hand every day to attend to the king's ritual *levée* (rising) and *couchée* (going to bed). They would quarrel for the privilege of holding his shirt or fetching his chamber pot.**

THE SUN KING

King Louis XIV (main picture) of France (1643–1715) insisted all his nobles lived at his vast palace at **Versailles** so they couldn't plot against him. Life revolved around him, gaining him the nickname "*le roi soleil*" ("the Sun king").

The six wives of Henry VIII

**King of England
(1509–1547)**

divorced
Catherine of Aragon

divorced
Anne of Cleves

beheaded
Anne Boleyn

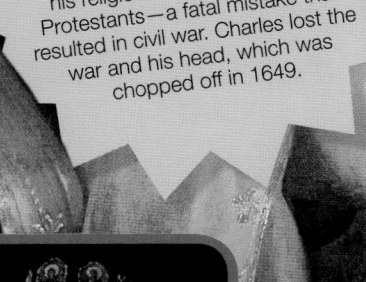

beheaded
Catherine Howard

died
Jane Seymour

survived
Catherine Parr

For the chop

Kings might insist on their divine right to rule, but their subjects did not always agree—as **King Charles I** of England found out the hard way. He thought he could govern without parliament and tried to impose his religious views on hardline Protestants—a fatal mistake that resulted in civil war. Charles lost the war and his head, which was chopped off in 1649.

Terrible czar

🖒 Ivan the Terrible (1530–1584) was the first grand prince of Russia to crown himself czar.

👎 His nickname in Russian, "*Grozny,*" more accurately translates as "awesome."

🖒 He started off terribly well, introducing new laws, updating the army, and more than tripling the size of his kingdom.

👎 But then it all went terribly wrong—he used his army to terrorize his subjects and had thousands executed.

👎 His rages got worse and worse until one day he killed his son, Ivan, in a terrible fit of anger. He felt really terrible about it afterward and never forgave himself.

Europe's royal households

Bourbon:
France (1589–1792),
Spain (1700–1931,
restored 1975)

Braganza:
Portugal (1640–1910)

Habsburg:
Austria (1282–1918),
Spain (1516–1700),
Portugal (1598–1640)

Hanover:
Great Britain (1714–1901)

Hohenzollern:
Brandenburg-Prussia
(1415–1918);
emperors of Germany
(1871–1918)

Orange-Nassau:
Netherlands (1815–)

Romanov:
Russia (1613–1917)

Savoy:
Sardinia and Piedmont
(1720–1861),
Italy (1861–1946)

**Saxe-Coburg/
Windsor:**
Great Britain (1901–)

Stewart/Stuart:
Scotland (1327–1601)
England and
Scotland (1603–1714)

Tudor:
England (1485–1603)

Valois:
France (1328–1589)

What is a colony?

A settlement set up by a group of people in a new country, with close ties to the country from where they came. Between 1500 and 1900 the European powers founded colonies all around the world, from America to Africa, Asia and the Pacific. Countries with large numbers of overseas colonies are called empires. Spain was the first European power to create an overseas empire in the 1500s, but by 1900 Britain had the largest empire.

Four facts about the British Empire

01: The Empire reached its greatest extent during the reign of Queen Victoria (1837–1901).

02: It covered one-fifth of the Earth's surface and contained one-quarter of its population.

03: The colonies supplied Britain with raw materials—sugar, cotton, tea, bananas, rubber, palm oil—and provided important markets for British goods.

04: The British developed courts of law, hospitals, schools, and railroads, but they did so with little regard to the traditions, religions, and languages of the people they governed.

Tell me more: 19th-century European empires

Belgium: Congo

Britain: Australia, Canada, New Zealand, South Africa, Gibraltar, India and Burma (Myanmar), Sri Lanka, Egypt and Sudan, west and southeast Africa, Malaya and Singapore, Fiji and other Pacific islands, British Guiana (Honduras), West Indies (Jamaica, Trinidad, and other islands)

France: Algeria, Morocco, French Central Africa, French West Africa, Madagascar, Indochina (Vietnam, Cambodia, and Laos), French Polynesia (Tahiti), French Guiana

Germany: Cameroon, German East Africa (Tanzania), German Southwest Africa (Namibia)

Italy: Libya, Eritrea, Somalia

Netherlands: Dutch East Indies (Indonesia), Dutch Antilles (Aruba), Suriname

Portugal: Angola, Mozambique

Spain: Philippines, Puerto Rica, Cuba

Foreign invasion

Colonization was tough on native peoples—their lands were stolen from them, and they were wiped out by diseases such as smallpox, measles, and mumps, since they had no natural immunity to them. Resistance was useless, since the foreigners had guns.

Jewel in the crown

The so-called "Jewel in the Crown" of the British Empire was India. Queen Victoria became Empress of India in 1877, but she never went there. India was ruled by a viceroy representing the British crown until the country won independence in 1947.

One lump or two...

■ Portuguese navigators discover **Madeira** and the **Canary Islands** in the Atlantic. They colonize the islands and begin growing **sugarcane** there.

■ By 1550 they have established large **sugar plantations** in **Brazil** and are importing **African slaves** as labor.

■ Sugar cultivation spreads to the **Caribbean islands**, which are now mostly owned by the Dutch, French, and British.

■ As all the **local people have been wiped out** by disease and war, thousands of **slaves are imported from Africa** to work on the sugarcane plantations.

The original 13 colonies:

Name: **New Hampshire**
Year founded: **1623**
Nickname: **Granite State**

Name: **Massachusetts**
Year founded: **1620**
Nickname: **Bay State**

Name: **Rhode Island**
Year founded: **1636**
Nickname: **Ocean State**

Name: **Connecticut**
Year founded: **1635**
Nickname: **Nutmeg State**

Name: **New York**
Year founded: **1664**
Nickname: **Empire State**

Name: **New Jersey**
Year founded: **1664**
Nickname: **Garden State**

Name: **Pennsylvania**
Year founded: **1682**
Nickname: **Keystone State**

Name: **Maryland**
Year founded: **1634**
Nickname: **Old Line State**

Name: **Delaware**
Year founded: **1638**
Nickname: **First State**

Name: **Virginia**
Year founded: **1607**
Nickname: **Old Dominion**

Name: **North Carolina**
Year founded: **1653**
Nickname: **Tar Heel State**

Name: **South Carolina**
Year founded: **1663**
Nickname: **Palmetto State**

Name: **Georgia**
Year founded: **1732**
Nickname: **Peach State**

Colonial America

■ Many early settlers were Puritans (Protestants) who came to avoid religious persecution in England. They created the patchwork of small farms and rural communities that makes up the landscape of New England (the northeastern states of the US) today.

Thanksgiving Day, celebrated on the fourth Thursday of November, is said to date from 1621, when the settlers of New Plymouth celebrated their first harvest.

■ Life was hard for the Jamestown settlers in Virginia until they hit on the idea of growing tobacco and exporting it to England—put that in your pipe and smoke it!

■ American beaver furs became all the rage for fashionable hats in Europe. French traders traveled far into the interior to obtain pelts (furs) from Native American trappers.

In numbers

Colonization of the Americas had a terrible consequence. Between 1500 and the early 1880s millions of Africans were forcibly transported across the Atlantic Ocean to work as slaves for European plantation owners.

2,000
The average number of Africans transported each year in the 1550s

10,000
The average number of Africans transported each year in the 1650s

100,000
The average number of Africans transported each year in the 1750s

12 million
The total number of African slaves transported to work on plantations

...in your tea?

◗ **Portuguese traders** in China bring **tea** back to Europe.

◗ The **British** begin growing **opium** in India to **sell to China** in exchange for tea. They also introduce **tea plantations** to **India** and **Sri Lanka**.

◗ The British put a tax on **tea** in their North American colonies. The **Americans don't like it** and dump a cargo of tea in Boston Harbor—no wonder they develop a taste for coffee!

I don't believe it!

In 1667 the Dutch agreed to a swap with the English—their settlement of New Amsterdam on Manhattan Island for the tiny island of Run in the Spice Islands and Suriname, a swampy area of forest on the coast of South America. The English renamed the settlement New York—and got themselves a chunk of prime real estate!

Countdown to independence

1776
The 13 American colonies rebel against British rule

1810–1823
South America is liberated from Spanish rule

1922
Ireland (previously British) becomes a Free State

1946
Philippines gain independence from the United States

1947
India and Pakistan gain their independence

1949
Indonesia wins its independence from the Netherlands

1957–1975
Former colonies around the world gain independence

1990
Namibia is the last country in Africa to gain independence (from South Africa)

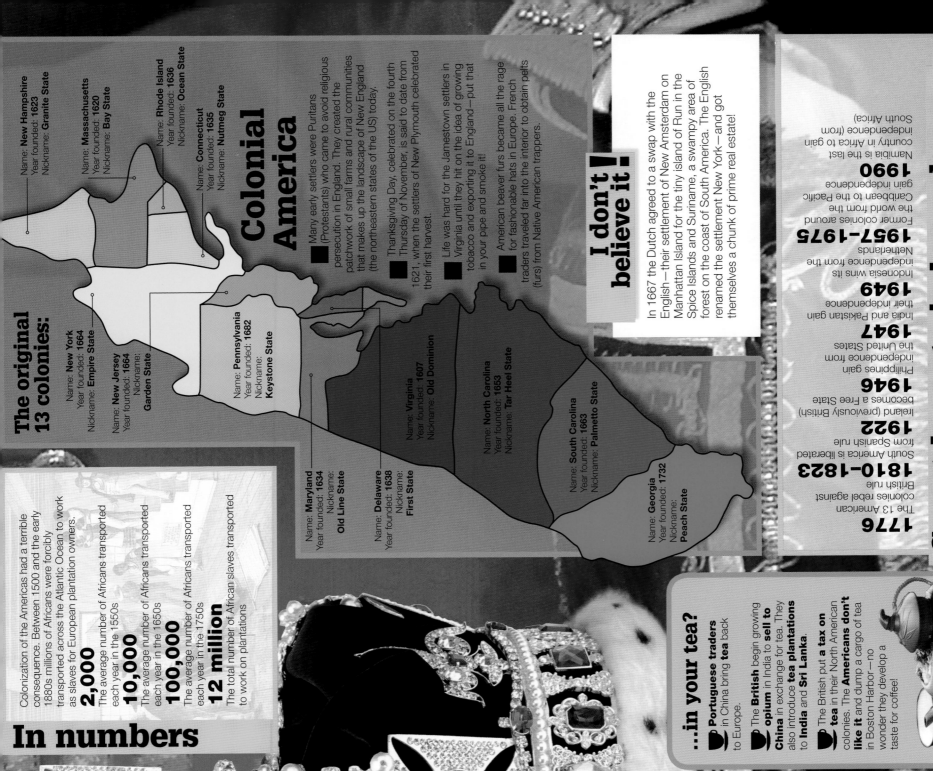

What are revolutions?

Periods of rapid or dramatic change when the world is turned upside down. Political revolutions take place when people become so fed up or unhappy with their rulers they overthrow them and set up a new government. The outcome is often bloody and violent—this happened in France in 1789 and in Russia in 1917.

Tell me more: political revolutions

✪ Revolutionary War (1775–1783)
13 colonies throw off British rule to become the United States of America

✪ French Revolution (1789–1793)
Antiroyalist uprising leads to the setting up of a republic; the king loses his head

✪ Year of Revolutions (1848)
Revolutions break out across Europe

✪ Chinese Revolution (1911)
Popular uprising topples Qing Dynasty

✪ Russian Revolution (1917)
The czar (king) is forced to abdicate (resign) and a Bolshevik (communist) government seizes power

✪ Cuban Revolution (1959)
Fidel Castro overthrows a right-wing dictatorship and sets up a communist state in Cuba

✪ Cultural Revolution (1966–1976)
Mao Zedong launches a terror campaign to eradicate the "enemies of socialism" in China

✪ Khmer Rouge (1975)
Communist guerrillas seize power in Cambodia. Their hardline regime causes the deaths of more than 3 million people

✪ Iranian Revolution (1979)
The shah (king) is overthrown and an Islamic republic set up in Iran (Persia)

✪ Velvet Revolution (1989)
Peaceful protests topple Czechoslovakia's communist regime as communist rule collapses in Eastern Europe and Soviet Union

Cuban revolutionary Che Guevara

How to: have a revolution in France

01. Have the king and queen lead a life of luxury in the palace of Versailles while the rest of France starves.

02. Get the king to call a meeting of the Estates General (parliament) so he can raise taxes. This will cause the Third Estate, who represent commoners, to storm out and set up a rival assembly.

03. Start a rumor that the king is sending his army to close down the assembly. Rioters in Paris will storm the Bastille, a royal fortress, in protest and release all seven prisoners inside. It's July 14, 1789, and the French Revolution begins!

04. Have bands of revolutionary citizens (the sans-culottes or "people without breeches") roam the streets demanding an end to aristocratic power under the slogan "Liberty, Equality, Fraternity!"

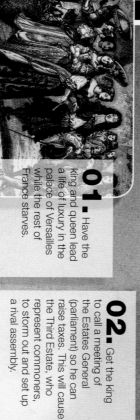

Five revolutionary leaders

George Washington
(1732–1799) After winning the war against British rule, this Virginia farmer was elected the first president of the United States.

Maximilien de Robespierre *(1758–1794)* Unleashed a wave of terror against French aristocrats and political opponents before losing his head on the guillotine.

Vladimir Lenin
(1870–1924) Led the Russian Bolsheviks to power in October 1917 and became the first leader of Soviet (communist) Russia.

Leon Trotsky
(1879–1940) Key figure in the Bolshevik revolution who fell out with Stalin (Lenin's successor) and ended up with an ice pick in his head.

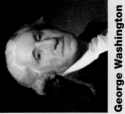

Mao Zedong
(1893–1976) Chinese communist leader who masterminded the creation of the People's Republic of China in 1949.

Scientific Revolution (c. 1550–1800)

Laid the foundations of modern science. Starting with the discovery that the planets move around the Sun, and not the other way around as the medieval Church had taught, scientific advances revolutionized the way people thought about the world.

Agricultural Revolution (1700–1850)

Brought sweeping changes to the countryside. Fewer people were needed to work on the land thanks to more efficient ways of farming.

I don't believe it!

Russian revolutionary leader Lenin's body has been on public display in a marble mausoleum (tomb) in Moscow's Red Square since his death in 1924. The mausoleum is closed every 18 months so his corpse can be treated with special embalming fluids and his clothes changed.

FAST FACTS

Industrial Revolution

01: New machines are invented in Britain to speed up the spinning of wool and cotton. At first, they are powered by waterwheels, but later steam engines are developed.

02: Iron becomes cheaper and stronger as iron-making techniques improve.

03: Thanks to changes in farming, fewer people are needed to grow food, forcing them to leave the countryside to find work in mills and factories. Industrial towns grow rapidly.

04: Canals are dug to carry coal from the mines and to transport finished goods.

05: Within 50 years railroads replace the canals. The first public railroad opens in 1825.

06: In the United States, the first coast-to-coast railroad is completed in 1869, opening the way to rapid industrial expansion. Mass-production techniques are developed to drive down costs.

Information Revolution (1980s onward)

Computer technology and the microchip have revolutionized our world. The Internet is reinventing the way we do business and politics, study, and access entertainment.

Industrial Revolution (1760–1900)

A period of rapid social and economic change when people left the countryside to live in towns and work in factories.

WHAT'S IN A NAME?

The **guillotine**—bloody symbol of the French Revolution—takes its name from anatomy professor Dr. Joseph Guillotin, a professor of anatomy who championed its use as a speedy, clean, and humane method of **execution**. The **razor-sharp blade**, falling from a great height, separated the victim's head from the body in less than a second, much quicker than hanging or beheading with an ax.

05. When the king tries to flee the country, arrest him and put him on trial for plotting to betray France. Send him to the guillotine, along with his hated wife.

06. Now that France is a republic, it is time for the revolutionary leaders to turn on each other in a frenzy of political feuding. Paris is awash with blood as thousands of people lose their heads on the guillotine.

Which century has seen the most wars?

During the 20th century a war was being fought somewhere on the planet every year and there were at least 165 major conflicts. About 40 million soldiers died, nearly 75 percent of them in the two World Wars. Millions of civilians also lost their lives in the conflicts.

10 major 20th-century wars

01 : World War I
(1914–1918)

02: Russian
Civil War (1918–1921)

03: Chinese
Civil War (1927–1949)

04: Spanish
Civil War (1936–1939)

05: World War II
(1939–1945)

06: Arab-Israeli
Wars (1948–1973)

07: Korean War
(1950–1953)

08: Vietnam War
(1964–1973)

09: Iran–Iraq War
(1980–1988)

10: Gulf War
(1991)

RECORD BREAKER

The **shortest war** on record lasted just 38 minutes. It was fought between Britain and Zanzibar, an island off the east coast of Africa, in 1896.

Blasts from the past

For 40 years superpower rivalry between the US and the USSR (communist Russia) brought the world close to conflict. During this Cold War, the superpowers amassed enough nuclear weapons to destroy the planet.

1945–1948
The USSR takes control of Eastern Europe, imposing communist regimes

1949
China becomes a communist Republic and forms a pact with the USSR

1950
Communist North Korea invades South Korea and is pushed back by a US-led force

1952–1953
A nuclear arms race begins

1956
Soviet troops put down an uprising in Hungary

1961
The Berlin Wall is built, sealing off communist East Berlin from West Berlin

1964
US enters war against communist North Vietnam

1970
The US and USSR begin talks to reduce nuclear weapons

1979
USSR invades Afghanistan

1985
Mikhail Gorbachev becomes the leader of the USSR and introduces reforms

1988–1991
Communist rule collapses in Eastern Europe and USSR

Danger! More than 110 million APLs (Anti Personnel Landmines) litter war-torn countries of the world. These **deadly devices** kill or maim thousands of people a year.

10 famous **military leaders**

Alexander the Great
Macedonian empire-builder who never lost a battle

Hannibal
Led his men (and several war elephants) across the Alps and beat the Romans

Julius Caesar
Conquered Gaul (France) and made himself master of Rome

Saladin
Organized Muslim resistance to the Crusaders

Genghis Khan
Mongol warlord who ruled an empire from the Black Sea to the Pacific

Napoleon
Took on all the armies of Europe and beat them—until he faced...

Duke of Wellington
British general who defeated Napoleon at the Battle of Waterloo

Robert E. Lee
Successful Confederate (Southern states) general in the Civil War

Erwin Rommel
Led the World War II German army in North Africa, but later fell out with Hitler

Georgi Zhukov
Most successful Soviet general of World War II

Guess how long it lasted?

? Hundred Years' War
(1337–1453)* Fought (with interruptions) between England and France

? Thirty Years' War
(1618–1648) Bitter struggle between Catholics and Protestants fought mostly in Germany

? Seven Years' War
(1756–1763) European conflict that spilled over to become the first global war

? Seven Weeks' War (1866)
Prussia made a smash-and-grab raid on Austria, aided by Italy

? Six Day War (1967) The time it took Israel to defeat Egypt and Syria and occupy the West Bank

? Hundred Hours' War (1969)
Fought between Honduras and El Salvador after rioting broke out at a soccer match

*good call—it was actually 116 years!

War stories

🐾 In medieval sieges it was very common to hurl dead plague victims over the wall at your enemy—an early form of germ warfare.

🐾 The first use of chemical weapons came in World War I, when the Germans released mustard gas (a yellow oily liquid that attacks the lungs) into the Allied trenches.

🐾 German and British troops fighting in the trenches called a temporary truce on Christmas Day 1914 to play a game of soccer.

🐾 The Soviet army trained dogs to crawl under tanks with explosive devices strapped to their backs in World War II. The explosives were then triggered, destroying the tanks—and the dogs.

I don't believe it !

The Thirty Years' War started when some Protestants chucked two Catholic envoys out of a castle window in Prague onto a heap of poop. It caused quite a stink!

US President George W. Bush declared a "**War on Terror**" after Al-Qaeda Islamic terrorists flew two airliners into the Twin Towers of the World Trade Center in New York City on September 11, 2001, killing nearly 3,000. It led to military action in Afghanistan and Iraq.

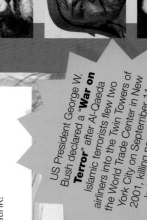

Feeling hungry? Try these food wars

Potato War (1778)
This conflict got its strange name because both sides (Prussia and Austria) spent more time combing the countryside for food supplies than fighting.

War of the Oranges
(1801) This war is named after a present of oranges sent to the queen of Spain by her lover after he'd invaded Portugal on Napoleon's orders. Sweet!

Pastry War (1838)
Some Mexican soldiers wrecked a shop belonging to a French pastry cook. The Mexican government refused to compensate him, so a French army invaded.

Cod War (1975)
This was a clash between the United Kingdom and Iceland over fishing rights in the North Atlantic. There was not much actual fighting, but a lot of net cutting!

Tell me more: 20th century

1900s

↓ **1903:** The Wright brothers achieve the first powered flight at Kitty Hawk, North Carolina

↑ **1902:** The teddy bear becomes a popular toy. It is named after US President Theodore (Teddy) Roosevelt

↓ **1906:** Finland is the first European country to give women the vote

↓ **1908:** Henry Ford launches the Model-T Ford, the world's first mass-produced car

1910s

↓ **1912:** SS *Titanic* hits an iceberg and sinks on its maiden voyage

↓ **1914:** World War I begins (ends 1918)

↑ **1917:** Russian Revolution

↓ **1918:** Spanish flu epidemic kills millions of people worldwide

↑ **1916:** Easter Rising against British rule in Ireland

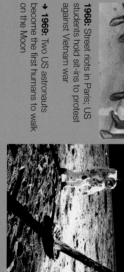

1920s

↑ **1923:** Charleston dance becomes all the rage

NEW YORK CITY WOMEN HAVE NO VOTE AT ALL

1950s

↓ **1951:** Colour TV introduced in the United States

↓ **1955:** African-American woman Rosa Parks refuses to give up her seat on bus to a white person, triggering the start of the civil rights movement in the US

↓ **1953:** DNA is discovered by scientists at Cambridge University, England

↑ **1956:** Ghana is the first former British colony in Africa to gain independence

↑ **1959:** The Barbie doll is launched (wearing a black and white zebra striped swimsuit)

1960s

↓ **1968:** Street riots in Paris; US students hold sit-ins to protest against Vietnam war

↓ **1969:** Two US astronauts become the first humans to walk on the Moon

↑ **1964:** The Beatles take the United States by storm

↓ **1961:** The Berlin Wall (separating communist East from the West) is built

↑ **1967:** First heart transplant

↑ **1963:** US President John F. Kennedy is assassinated

1970s

↓ **1979:** Islamic Revolution brings regime change in Iran

↓ **1978:** The first test tube baby born

↑ **1972:** Pocket calculators are introduced

1940s

1940: The first McDonald's restaurant opens in San Bernardino, California

↑ **1941:** Japanese bomb the US naval base at Pearl Harbor, Hawaii. The United States enters World War II

↓ **1942:** Soft (two-ply) toilet paper goes on sale for the first time

→ **1945:** US drops atomic bombs on the Japanese cities of Hiroshima and Nagasaki

↑ **1948:** State of Israel founded

→ **1949:** Communists win the civil war in China

1990s

→ **1990:** Nelson Mandela is released from prison after 27 years. He is elected president of South Africa four years later

← **1991:** Communist rule in Russia comes to an end

↓ **1992:** War breaks out in Balkans as Yugoslavia falls apart

→ **1994:** Genocide in African state of Rwanda

↑ **1996:** Dolly the sheep is the first cloned animal

→ **1997:** J. K. Rowling publishes the first Harry Potter novel

1930s

→ **1931:** The Empire State Building opens in New York City

→ **1933:** Adolf Hitler becomes Chancellor of Germany and passes the first anti-Jewish laws

↓ **1934:** Start of Stalin's "Great Terror" in Russia. Millions die in labor camps

→ **1935:** Nylon invented

↓ **1936:** African-American athlete Jesse Owens wins four gold medals at the Berlin Olympics. Hitler walks out

→ **1939:** Hitler invades Poland. Start of World War II (ends 1945)

1980s

→ **1980:** The World Health Organization declares that smallpox has been eradicated

↓ **1982:** Michael Jackson's *Thriller* becomes the best-selling album ever

→ **1984:** AIDS virus is discovered

↑ **1986:** The world's worst nuclear disaster occurs at Chernobyl, Ukraine

→ **1989:** Cold War comes to an end as communism collapses

↓ **1920:** Women win the right to vote in the United States

→ **1922:** Archeologists discover Tutankhamun's tomb in Egypt

1926: First pictures transmitted by television

↑ **1927:** First talking movie, *The Jazz Singer*

↓ **1928:** Alexander Fleming discovers penicillin

↑ **1973:** The United States pulls out of the war in Vietnam

↓ **1975:** Pol Pot becomes the communist dictator of Cambodia and kills millions

Index

Credits

DK would like to thank:
Steven Carton, Jenny Finch, and Fran Jones for additional editorial work, Stefan Podhorodecki for additional photography, and Lee Ritches for additional design. Peter Pawsey for creative technical support, Nick Deakin of www.spaceboosters.co.uk and Carole Stott for mission patches, Charlotte Webb for proofreading, Jackie Brind for preparing the index.

The publisher would like to thank the following for their kind permission to reproduce their photographs:

Key: a-above; b-below/bottom; c-center; f-far; l-left; r-right; t-top

1 Corbis: Andrew Brookes (ftr/light bulb); Jason Horowitz / Zefa (ftr/ganesh); Images.com (tl/heart); Fred Prouser / Reuters (cra/tutankhamun). Getty Images: Philippe Body / Hemis (bc/pyramids); Photographer's Choice RR / Steve McAlister (cb/brain); 3 Corbis: Andrew Brookes (ftr/light bulb); Jason Horowitz / Zefa (ftr/ganesh); Images.com (tl/heart); Fred Prouser / Reuters (cra/tutankhamun). Getty Images: Philippe Body / Hemis (bc/pyramids); Photographer's Choice RR / Steve McAlister (cb/brain); 4 Corbis: Andrew Brookes (ftr/light bulb); Images.com (tl/heart). 5 Corbis: Jason Horowitz / Zefa (ftr/ganesh); Images.com (tr/heart). 6-7 Getty Images: Stocktrek Images (br). 10 ESA: (cl), NASA / AURA / NSF: (cra) (cr) (c) (fbr); NOAO / AURA / NSF: (cra) (cr) (c) (fbr). 11 2MASS: J. Carpenter, T. H. Jarrett, & R. Hurt (cl). Galaxy Picture Library: NASA/JPL-Caltech (t). Science Photo Library: Magrath Photography (cr). 12 Anglo Australian Observatory: Royal Observatory, Edinburgh/David Malin (bl). NASA: (bc) (br); HST (l) (cl). 12-13 NASA: HST. 13 Galaxy Picture Library: DSS1 (tr); Gordan Garradd (tl); Gordon Garradd (tc). NASA: HST (ftl) (cr) (cd); JPL-Caltech/K. Su (University of Arizona) (ftr); SST/IRAS (fbr); X-ray: NASA/CXC/PSU/S.Park & D.Burrows:, Optical: NASA/STScI/CfA/P.Challis et al. 14 NASA: SOHO (c) (cb). Science Photo Library: Lawrence Berkeley, National Laboratory (b). 15 Science Photo Library: Pekka Parviainen (tl); Eckhard Slawik (c). 16 NASA: (bl). Science Photo Library: John Sanford (c). 17 Corbis: Roger Ressmeyer (br). NASA: (l). 18 Corbis: NASA/Roger Ressmeyer (t). 18-19 Corbis: NASA/Roger Ressmeyer (t). 19 Corbis: Araldo de Luca (bl). NASA: JPL (c). 20 Corbis: Araldo de Luca (bl); miranda (fcrb/photos). NASA: JPL (c). 21 Galaxy Picture Library: Robin Scagell (background). 22 Galaxy Picture Library: Robin Scagell (c). 22-23 NASA: JPL. 23 Galaxy Picture Library: Robin Scagell (c). 24-25 Alamy Images: Ian McKinnell (c). 25 Corbis: The Gallery Collection (bc). NASA: JPL (tr). 26 Corbis: Roger Ressmeyer (crb). 26-27 NASA: HST (t). akg-images: (tr/Archimedes); Alamy Images: Wiskerke (tl). ESA: (c). 27 Corbis: NASA: HST (cb); JPL-Caltech/STScI (crb). 28 NASA: JHUAPL/CIW (tr); JPL (t). 28-29 NASA: ESA/Johns Hopkins University. 29 NASA: JPL/Cornell University/Maas Digital (br). 31 NASA: Bettmann (tr). 33 DK Images: (tr). 34 Corbis: (tl). European Southern Observatory: H. Zodet (cra). NASA: (br). 34-35 NASA. 35 Corbis: NASA TV/epa (bl); NASA KSC (bc); NASA: KSC (bc). 36 Getty Images: The Image Bank / Matthew

Alamy Images: David R. Frazier Photolibrary, Inc. (tc/new orleans); Johan Furusjö (tr/stockholm); Jon Arnold Images Ltd. (ftr/cornwall). DK Images: Bethany Dawn (fclb); Jamie Marshall (bl); Rough Guides (c). Getty Images: Gallo Images / Travel Ink (tr/london); Brendan Hoffman (tl/washington). **190** Corbis: Keith Hunter / Arcaid (tr). DK Images: Lindsey Stock (fcrb/London Eye). Getty Images: Walter Bibikow (crb/aqueduct); Dennis Flaherty (br/bascule); Tim Hawley (cl/San Francisco bridge); Hiroyuki Matsumoto (tl/flat roadway); Hiroakai Otsubo (fbl); Kim Steele (clb/arched bridge); Travel Ink (clb/cable-stayed bridge); Hiroyuki Yamaguchi / Sebun Photo (cla). **190–191** Corbis: Jean-Pierre Lescourret (c). **191** Mark D. Anderson: (br/Kamfers Dam). Corbis: Kevin Schafer (bc/Uros Islets). Getty Images: AFP (fbl); Adam Jones (cra); Preston Schlebusch (fbr); Spaceimaging.com (ca). **192** Getty Images: (c); AFP (clb); Ian Cumming (crb); John William Banagan (bl). **192–193** Getty Images: Scott E. Barbour (c/highway). **193** Getty Images: Stocktrek Images (bl). **194** Alamy Images: Geoff Waugh (clb/folding bike). Corbis: Claro Cortes IV (bl/plastic containers); Robert Harding World Imagery (bl/rickshaw); Xinhua photo / Zhou Hua (cla/police bikes). **195** Corbis: Hulton-Deutsch Collection (bl/1839 bike); Jean-Yves Ruszniewski (cla/Lance Armstrong). DK Images: Clive Streeter / courtesy of the Science Museum, London (bl/1863 bike) (bc/1885 bike). Science & Society Picture Library: Science Museum (bc/1920s bike). **196** Alamy Images: Paul Cox (cb); Photo Network (cra). DK Images: Simon Clay / courtesy of the National Motor Museum, Beaulieu (tl/Benz car). **196–197** Bugatti Automobiles S.A.S.: (c). **197** Alamy Images: izmostock (ftr); Annette Price / H2O Photography (cr/Gibbs Aquada). DK Images: Dave King / courtesy of the National Motor Museum, Beaulieu (tc/pneumatic tyre). Getty Images: Jeff T. Green (cra/Tango car). Rinspeed Inc.: (br/Rinspeed Squba). **198** Anglo Australian Observatory: Noah Addis / The Star-Ledger (bc/barge). DK Images: Tina Chambers / courtesy of the National Maritime Museum (fbr/cruise liner) (bc/junk) (br/dhow); James Stevenson & Tina Chambers / courtesy of the Exeter Maritime Museum / The National Maritime Museum, London (fbl/canoe); James Stevenson & Tina Chambers / courtesy of the National Maritime Museum, London (br/trawler). **198–199** Corbis: Jack Atley / Reuters (c). **199** DK Images: Tina Chambers / courtesy of the National Maritime Museum (bc/container ship); David Peart (fbl/ferry); James Stevenson & Tina Chambers / courtesy of the National Maritime Museum, London (bl/oil tanker). Solent News & Photo Agency, Southampton: Zachary Culpin (cb/pumpkin boat). **200** Getty Images: Tim Sloan (bc). **200–201** DK Images: Rowan Greenwood (c). **201** Alamy Images: Alistair Scott (cb). Corbis: David Bathgate (c); Ashley Cooper (tr). Bruce Wood: (bl). **202** Alamy Images: Stan Kujawa (fclb/Underground train); Liu Xiaoyang (fclb/Maglev). Corbis: Rudy Sulgan (fbl). DK Images: Mike Dunning (ftl). Getty Images: Hulton Archive (fbr/underground railway). Science & Society Picture Library: NRM / Pictorial Collection (bc/Stevenson's locomotive); National Railway Museum (bl/Trevithick's locomotive); Science Museum (bc/Liverpool & Manchester Railway). **202–203** Alamy Images: Alvey & Towers Picture Library (c); Bobbo's Pix (c/background). **203** Alamy Images: China Images (fbr/maglev railway); Colin Underhill (br/Birmingham maglev). Corbis: Wolfgang Kaehler (tr). Getty Images: Keystone (br/bullet train); MPI / Andrew Joseph Russell (fbl/USA rail completion). Milepost 92 1/2: railphotolibrary.com (bc). **204** Corbis: Wally McNamee (fcl). **204–205** Corbis: Fridmar Damm /zefa (c/clouds); Reuters (cb). **206–207** Getty Images: Scott Robin Barbour (c). **207** Getty Images: ChinaFotoPress (fcrb); Digital Vision (bl); Mark Segal (cr); James Strachan (br); Stephen Studd (clb); Gordon Wiltsie / National Geographic (fcra). **210** Corbis: Roy Dabner / epa (c). DK Images: Gunter Marx / courtesy of Stanly Park, Totem Park, Vancouver (cl). **211** Corbis: Kelly Owen / NOAA (cl); Peter Turnley (tr). **212** Alamy Images: Sue Cunningham Photographic (cb). Corbis: Stephane Reix (fbr). **212–213** Alamy Images: Jim Zuckerman (c). **213** Alamy Images: Krys Bailey (fcra/Atacama Desert); Tom Brakefield (fcrb/capybara); Martin Harvey (ftr); Tom Till (fcra). Corbis: Richard Cummins (cra); Betrand Gardel (fcrb); Buddy Mays (fbr); Alison Wright (fcr). **214** Corbis: Jonathan Blair (cl); Svenja-Foto / zefa (c/River Danube). Getty Images: Uyen Le (ca). **215** Corbis: Seppo Sirkka / epa (bc). **216** Corbis: Creasource (cb). **216–217** Alamy Images: John Arnold Images Ltd. (c). **217** Corbis: Stephanie Colasanti (br); Redlink / Li Shao Bai (ftr); Mark Remissa / epa (fbr/spinning silk); Sygma / Dung Vo Trung (fbl); WildCountry (ca). DK Images: Jamie Marshall (tl/Gojal). **218** Corbis: David Turnley (bl). Getty Images: Daryl Balfour (clb); Jack Dykinga (br). **218–219** Corbis: Bruno Fert (c). **219** Alamy Images: JTB Photo Communications, Inc. (ca). Corbis: Michel Gounot / Godong (tr). Getty Images: Central Press (cb). **220** Corbis: Morton Beebe (cb/Sir Edmund Hillary); Bettmann (fcrb/Sir Ernest Rutherford); Lucas Jackson / Reuters (clb/Russell Crowe); Lucy Nicholson / Reuters (cb/Peter Jackson); Schlegelmilch (crb/Bruce McLaren). DK Images: Rowan Greenwood (fcl). **220–221** Corbis: zefa / Larry Williams (c). **222** Getty Images: Daisy Gilardini (crb). **223** Corbis: Ralph A. Clevenger (tc); Robert Harding World Imagery (ftr); Rick Price (tr); Denis Scott (ftl); Paul Souders (tl); Wolfgang Kaehler (c). Getty Images: NASA (bl); Time Life Pictures / NASA (br). **224** Alamy Images: Nicholas Eveleigh (br). **225** Corbis: Fly Fernandez / zefa (cb/laptop); Nicj Hawkes / Ecoscene (bl); Karen Kasmauski (tr); Paul W. Liebhardt (cb/watching tv); Andy Rain / epa (clb); Benjamin Rondel (tl); Christian Schallert (bc). **226** Alamy Images: F1online digitale Bildagentur GmbH (ftr/Shenzhen); ImageState (fclb). Corbis: Fly Fernandez / zefa (cl/Mumbai); Danny Lehman (ca/Mexico City); Christine Schneider / zefa (fcla); TongRo Image Stock / Brand X (cla/Seoul); Tsukioka Youichi / amanaimages (bl/Osaka). DK Images: Demetrio Carrasco / Rough Guides (clb/Hollywood sign). **226–227** Corbis: Hiroyuki Matsumoto / amanaimages (c/background). **227** Alamy Images: Mathias Beinling (tr/Guangzhou skyscraper); Matt Lim (tr/Chongqing skyscraper); Marek Zuk (br/Phoenix). Corbis: Ralf-Finn Hestoft (tc/Chicago skyscraper); Attila Kisbenedek / epa (fbl); Vishal Olwe / epa (bc/Mumbai); Qilai Shen / epa (bc/Shanghai); Tony Waltham / Robert Harding World Imagery (cla); Nik Wheeler (tc) (c). **228** Alamy Images: Richard Levine (c) (bc/Kiribati flag) (bl/Guatemala flag) (fbl/Eagle flag button) (fbr/Dominica flag); tompiodesign.com (bl/Uganda flag). **228–229** Alamy Images: Stuwdamdorp (c). **229** Alamy Images: Sylvia Cordaiy Photo Library Ltd. (tl) (fbl/Papu New Guinea flag); tompiodesign.com (bl/Zimbabwe flag). Photolibrary: Marcel Jolibois (br). **232** Alamy Images: imagebroker (tr). Getty Images: Aaron Black (br/mountaineering); Ian Cumming (bc/trekking); Alex Misiewicz (c); Richard Price (fbr). **232–233** Alamy Images: Robert Harding Picture Library Ltd. (c/beach scene). **233** Corbis: Guido Cozzi (bc/zip lining); Sean Davey (br/surfing); Kennan Ward (clb). DK Images: Rowan Greenwood (cra). Getty Images: Aaron Black (bc/rock climbing); Steve Bly (bl/rafting); John Kelly (fbl); Darryl Leniuk (fbr); Anne-marie Weber (bc/bungee jumping). **234** Getty Images: Ed Kash / National Geographic (tc). **234–235** Corbis: Bruno Morandi / Hemis (c). **235** Getty Images: Domino (tc); Larry Gilpin (cra); Jose Luis Paleaz (tr); Spencer Platt (br); VIsions of America / Joe Sohm (cr). **236** Corbis: Kazuyoshi Nomachi (tr). Getty Images: Reinhard Hunger (cr/white undergarment). **237** Corbis: Richard Bickel (cla/Buddhist temple); Jason Horowitz (tc/Ganesh); Ivan Vdovin (cl/church). **238** Alamy Images: SCPhotos (tl). **238–239** Getty Images: Ary Diesendruck (c/background). **239** Alamy Images: View Stock (cl/Moon festival). Corbis: Bob Krist (cla/Diwali); Frédéric Soltan (bl/Holi). Getty Images: Mehdi Fedouach / AFP (clb/Purim); Mitch Hrdicka (tr); Dennis Mosner (clb/Easter); Yoshikazu Tsuno / AFP (clb/Setsubun). **240–241** Photolibrary: John Lawrence (c). **241** Alamy Images: David Preutz (ca). DK Images: Kate Warren / Museum of Mankind / British Museum (tc/bead belt). Getty Images: Hulton Archive (fbl/Karen Blixen). **245** Corbis: Creasource (crb). Getty Images: Douglas C. Pizac / Pool (crb/lawyer); Michael Kelly (crb/jury). **246** iStockphoto.com: Kronick (cl). **247** akg-images: (cra/Zamenhof); New Line Productions / Album (cra/Lord of the Rings). Alamy Images: Pictorial Press Ltd. (fbr). iStockphoto.com: Kronick (tc). The Kobal Collection: Paramount (tr) (bl/Dr Zeus) (br/JRR Tolkein). **248** Corbis: Bettmann (bc/CS Lewis); Hulton-Deutsch Collection (fbl); Reuters (bc/JK Rowling). Getty Images: Time & Life Pictures (fbr/Beatrice Potter). Rex Features: Marty Hause (bc/RL Stone). **248–249** Alamy Images: Porky Pies Photography (c/background books). **249** Bloomsbury Publishing Plc: J.K. Rowling / Harry Potter and the Philosopher's Stpne / Bloomsbury (cr). Corbis: Hulton-Deutsch Collection (bl); Andanson James / Sygma (fbl); Kelly-Mooney Photography (tc). DK Images: Clive Streeter (clb/manga). Nobel Foundation: (cr/Nobel Prize). TopFoto.co.uk: PA (bc/Adam Hargreaves). **250** Corbis: Hubert Stadler (bl). **250–251** Rex Features: Alastair Muir (c). **251** Alamy Images: North Wind Picture Archives (bc). Corbis: Eriko Sugita / Reuters (br). Lebrecht Music and Arts: Dee Conway (cb/ballet); Tristram Kenton (cra/Opera). Photolibrary: Steve Vidler (crb/Noh). Photostage: Donald Cooper (tr/play). Rex Features: Alastair Muir (cr/musical). **252** akg-images: Bildarchiv Steffens (cla/knucklebones). Corbis: James Leynse (cb); Lawrence Manning (cl/Go). DK Images: Geoff Dann / Royal Pavilion Museum and Art Galleries, Brighton (cl/Mancala); Peter Hayman / The British Museum (cla/Senet). **252–253** Getty Images: Time & Life Pictures (c/background). **253** Corbis: Bettmann (bl). trekstor.de: (c). **254** Corbis: Summerfield Press (tr). Getty Images: Dave Etheridge-Barnes (bl). **255** Alamy Images: Picture Contact (bc). Getty Images: AFP (cr); Wolfgang Kumm / AFP (br). **256** Alamy Images: Pictorial Press (bl). Corbis: Bureau L.A. Collection (br). Getty Images: Scott Barbour (fbr); Kevin Mazur (bc); Michael Ochs Archives (fbl). **256–257** Alamy Images: Content Mine International. **257** Corbis: Lyn Goldsmith (bl); Nancy Kaszerman (cb). Rex Features: Skyline Features (tr). **258–259** Getty Images: Alvis Upitis. **260** Alamy Images: The London Art Archive (tr). Corbis: Matthew Ashton / AMA (bl); Jon Hrusa (br); William Sallaz / Duomo (tc/Michael Jordan). Getty Images: Stu Forster (ftr); Popperfoto (tc). **261** Corbis: Tony Roberts (tc/Jack Nicklaus); Jon Simon (tl). Getty Images: Hamish Blair (ftl); Marcel Mochet (tc/Ellen MacArthur). **264** Corbis: Adrian Bradshaw / epa (cl). **264–265** Corbis: Gero Breloer (c). **265** Corbis: Tom Fox / Dallas Morning News (tl); Elizabeth Kreutz (tr); Wally McNamee (tc); STR / EPA (bc). **266–267** Getty Images: Taxi / Keren Su. **267** Getty Images: The Bridgeman Art Library / Amadeo Preziosi (tr); De Agostini Picture Library / DEA Picture Library (ftl); Gallo Images / Travel Ink (cla); Kenneth Garrett / National Geographic (cr); Photographer's Choice / Hugh Sitton (fcrb); Photographer's Choice RF / Guy Vanderelst (fcra). **268** akg-images: (fclb/cleopatra); Andrea Jemolo (ftl/khufu). Corbis: Gianni Dagli Orti (fcl/ramses); Fred Prouser / Reuters (fcl/tutankhamun). DK Images: The British Museum (fcla/hatshepsut) (fbr/amon). iStockphoto.com: magaliB (br/ra). **268–269** Photolibrary: Age Fotostock / P Narayan (bc/isis) (bl/osiris) (br/horus) (br/seth) (fbl/sobek). **269** iStockphoto.com: magaliB (fbl/anubis). **270** DK Images: Michelle Grant / Rough Guides (c). iStockphoto.com: Mlenny (cb). **271** Alamy Images: Roger Cracknell 05 (crb/Socrates); The London Art Archive (cra/Aristotle) (cr/Homer); The Print Collector (cra/Hippocrates). Corbis: Gianni Dagli Orti (tl); Araldo de Luca (c). DK Images: Jerry Young (tc/turtle). iStockphoto.com: fajean (clb/Column illustrations) (cb/Corinthian column top); PhotographerOlympus (clb/Ionic column top); skm2000 (fclb/Doric column top). **272** Alamy Images: The Print Collector (br) (fcr/Elagabalus). **273** akg-images: (br/Diocletion); Electa (cr/Commodus). Alamy Images: Interfoto Pressebildagentur (cl/Caligula); Louvre, Paris / Peter Willi (fbr/Constantine I). The Bridgeman Art Library: Louvre, Paris / Index (bc/Marcus Aurelius); Naples, Museo Archeologico Nazionale (c/Nero). DK Images: The British Museum / Alan Hills and Barbara Winter (fcl/Tiberius). **274** Alamy Images: andrewwheeler.com (bc/silk); Robert Harding Picture Library Ltd. (crb); Arni Katz (fbr). Corbis: Asian Art & Archaeology, Inc. (bl); Lester V. Bergman (br). Getty Images: China Photos (clb) (ca); dk (br/cross bow). **274–275** Corbis: Wolfgang Kaehler (cl). **275** Alamy Images: GFC Collection (bc/Porcelain); Interfoto Pressebildagentur (cr); Ian McKinnell (bc/fireworks); Natural Visions (clb). Corbis: Richard Cummins (bl); Louis Laurent Grandadam (cb); Chris Hellier (fbr); Danny Lehman (crb); Richard Swiecki (tl). Getty Images: China Photos (cla); Alfred Eisenstaedt (fbl). **276** Getty Images: Alejandro Balaguer (bl). iStockphoto.com: KeithBinns (crb). **276–277** Corbis: Beneluх / zefa (ca/sky). Getty Images: Wide Group (cb). **277** Alamy Images: aerialarchives.com (cl); The Anthony Blake Photo Library (cr); Peter Horree (tr/Tlaloc); The London Art Archive (ftl); Photofrenetic (tl/Coatlicue). The Bridgeman Art Library: AISA / Museo de Arqueologia Mexico City, Mexico (tr/Xipe Totec); Bildarchiv Steffens Henri Stierlin (tc/Quetzalcoatl). Corbis: Werner Forman (ftr/Xochiquetzal). **278** The Bridgeman Art Library: Giraudon / Viking Ship Museum, Oslo (tr). iStockphoto.com: bubaone (cr/book icons). **278–279** Alamy Images: Horizon International Images Limited (c/calm sea). Corbis: Jon Sparks (bc/waves). DK Images: Tina Chambers / courtesy of the National Maritime Museum (bc/viking boat). **279** The Bridgeman Art Library: Archives Charmet / Private Collection (bl). Corbis: Werner Forman (tl). DK Images: Peter Anderson / courtesy of the Statens Historiska Museum, Stockholm (tr/Freyr). iStockphoto.com: Pshenichka (cb/runes); zmajdoo (cr/longboat drawing). Werner Forman Archive: (cr); Arhus Kunstmuseum, Denmark (tc); National Museum, Copenhagen (ftr); Statens Historiska Museum, Stockholm (ftl). **280** Getty Images: The Bridgeman Art Library (bc). **282** DK Images: Wallace Collection / Geoff Dann (bc). **282–283** Alamy Images: imagebroker. **283** DK Images: Wallace Collection / Geoff Dann (fbl). **284** akg-images: Erich Lessing (cl/Bayezid I) (bl/Suleyman I); Dagli Orti (A) /Museo Correr Venice (clb/Selim I). The Art Archive: Dagli Orti (A) / Turkish & Islamic Art Museum, Istanbul (cla/Murad I). The Bridgeman Art Library: Stapleton Collection (clb/Mehmed II). DK Images: Mike Dunning / courtesy of the Capitoline Museums, Rome (cr). **284–285** DK Images: Christopher & Sally Gable (c). **285** Corbis: Kazuyoshi Nomachi (tl). DK Images: Barnabas Kindersley (br). **286** Alamy Images: Interfoto Pressebildagentur (tl). The Bridgeman Art Library: The Weston Park Foundation, UK (br). Corbis: Bettmann (cb/Michelangelo); Alexandre Evariste Fragonard (cra); The Gallery Collection (cb/Albrecht Dürer); Michael Nicholson (bc) (cb/Raphael); Summerfield Press (cb). **287** The Bridgeman Art Library: Private Collection / Philip Mould Ltd. London (c/Erasmus); The Stapleton Collection / Private Collection (cb). **288** Alamy Images: Mikael Utterstrom (c). The Bridgeman Art Library: Royal Geographical Society, London (clb). DK Images: Jerry Young (cla/nutmeg). **288–289** The Bridgeman Art Library: British Library, London (background map). **289** Alamy Images: Mary Evans Picture Library (bl). DK Images: James Stevenson / National Maritime Museum, London (br/cross-staff). **290** DK Images: Max Alexander / courtesy of l'Etablissement Public du Musee et du Domaine National de Versailles. Reunion des Musees Nationaux / Art Resource, NY. (cla). Getty Images: The Bridgeman Art Library (br). **290–291** Getty Images: The Bridgeman Art Library (c) (cb/Anne of Cleves) (crb/Catherine Parr). **291** Getty Images: The Bridgeman Art Library (fbr) (bc) (bl) (c) (crb). **292** National Portrait Gallery, London: (bl). **292–293** Getty Images: C Squared Studios (c/crown); Toby Melville / AFP (background). **293** Corbis: Leonard de Selva (tl). **294** Corbis: Stefano Bianchetti (c). DK Images: Jamie Marshall (cl). **294–295** Corbis: Alfredo Dagli Orti (bc). **295** Corbis: Hulton-Deutsch Collection (tr/Trotsky). Getty Images: Arthur S. Aubry (cla/cog); Grant Faint (cr); Saul Gravy (bc). **296** Corbis: Bettmann (tl). **296–297** Chris Stowers: Panos (c). **297** Alamy Images: Interfoto Pressebildagentur (cra/Saladin); North Wind Picture Archives (cra/Hannibal). Corbis: Bettmann (crb/Rommel) (br) (cra/Caesar); Araldo de Luca (tr/Alexander the Great). Getty Images: Ira Block (cr); Hippolyte Delaroche / The Bridgeman Art Library (cr/Napoleon); Alexander Gardner / Hulton Archive (cb/Robert E. Lee); Marie-Victoire Jaquotot / The Bridgeman Art Library (crb/Wellington). **298** Corbis: (br/Moon landings) (ca/Spanish flu) (ca/WWI) (cb/Berlin Wall) (cla/woman voting) (crb/heart transplant) (crb/Kennedy motorcade) (fbl/Rosa Parks) (fbr/baby) (fcra/Flemming) (fcrb/Pol Pot) (ftr/US Women votes) (tl/Wright brothers); Bettmann (fcra/Charleston) (ftl); FrEdEric Neema / Sygma (bl/Barbie); Swim Ink 2, LLC (ca/Russian poster); Underwood & Underwood (tc/SS Titanic). DK Images: Dave King / courtesy of the Science Museum, London (fclb) (bc/The Beatles) (cra/Easter Rising). Getty Images: (bl/Ghana); Thomas Northcut (clb/DNA). Science & Society Picture Library: Science Museum (fcrb/calculator). **298–299** Corbis: The Gallery Collection (tc/Tutankhamun). **299** Bloomsbury Publishing Plc: J.K. Rowling / Harry Potter and the Philosopher's Stpne / Bloomsbury (fbr). Corbis: (ca) (cla/Jesse Owens) (cra/Israel founded) (fcla/The Jazz Singer) (fclb/Vietnam War) (fcra/Chinese truck) (fcra/Hiroshima); Bettmann (tc/Empire State Building); CDC / PHIL (clb/smallpox); Igor Kostin / Sygma (cb/Chernobyl); Colin McPherson / epa (br/sheep); Reuters (fcrb/besieged Sarajevo); Christine Spengler (fbl) (br/Rwanda); David Turnley (crb/fallen statue); Peter Turnley (bc/Berlin Wall); Paul Velasco (fcrb/Nelson Mandela). DK Images: Andy Crawford / courtesy of the Museum of the Revolution, Moscow (ca/Stalin); courtesy Glasgow Museum (ftl/early tv). Getty Images: (tl/Hitler); Time & Life Pictures (ftr/Pearl Harbor). Science Photo Library: Eye of Science (bl/virus). **300** Corbis: Images.com (fcla/heart); Fred Prouser / Reuters (ftl/tutankhamun). Getty Images: Photographer's Choice RR / Steve McAlister (tl/brain). **301** Corbis: Andrew Brookes (tc/light bulb). **302** Corbis: Jason Horowitz / Zefa (fclb/ganesh); Images.com (fcla/heart); Fred Prouser / Reuters (ftl/tutankhamun). Getty Images: Philippe Body / Hemis (ftl); Photographer's Choice RR / Steve McAlister (tl/brain). **303** Corbis: Andrew Brookes (tc/light bulb). **304** Corbis: Jason Horowitz / Zefa (fclb/ganesh); Images.com (fcla/heart); Fred Prouser / Reuters (ftl/tutankhamun). Getty Images: Philippe Body / Hemis (ftl/pyramids); Photographer's Choice RR / Steve McAlister (tl/brain)